THE ARDEN S

THIRD SERIES
General Editors: Richard Proudfoot, Ann Thompson
and David Scott Kastan

LOVE'S
LABOUR'S
LOST

The Arden Shakespeare

*Second Series

LOVE'S LABOUR'S LOST

Edited by
H. R. WOUDHUYSEN

The Arden website is at
http://www.ardenshakespeare.com

The general editors of the Arden Shakespeare have been
W. J. Craig and R. H. Case (first series 1899-1944)
Una Ellis-Fermor, Harold F. Brooks, Harold Jenkins and
Brian Morris (second series 1946-82)

Present general editors (third series)
Richard Proudfoot, Ann Thompson and David Scott Kastan

This edition *Love's Labour's Lost* by H. R. Woudhuysen
first published 1998 by Thomas Nelson and Sons Ltd

Published by the Arden Shakespeare
Reprinted 2001

Arden Shakespeare is an imprint of Thomson Learning

Thomson Learning
Berkshire House
168-173 High Holborn
London WC1V 7AA

Printed in Singapore

British Library Cataloguing in Publication Data
A catalogue record for this book is available from the British Library
Library of Congress Cataloguing in Publication Data
A catalogue record has been requested

ISBN 1-903436-19-2 (hardback)
NPN 9 8 7 6 5 4 3 2
ISBN 1-904271-10-3 (paperback)
NPN 9 8 7 6 5 4 3 2 1

The Editor

H. R. Woudhuysen is Professor of English at University College London. His publications include *Samuel Johnson on Shakespeare* (1989), *The Penguin Book of Renaissance Verse* (ed., 1992) and *Sir Philip Sidney and the Circulation of Manuscripts, 1558-1640* (1996).

CONTENTS

Contents

LIST OF
ILLUSTRATIONS

GENERAL EDITORS' PREFACE

The Arden Shakespeare is now nearly one hundred years old. The earliest volume in the first series, Edward Dowden's *Hamlet*, was published in 1899. Since then the Arden Shakespeare has become internationally recognized and respected. It is now widely acknowledged as the pre-eminent Shakespeare series, valued by scholars, students, actors and 'the great variety of readers' alike for its readable and reliable texts, its full annotation and its richly informative introductions.

We have aimed in the third Arden edition to maintain the quality and general character of its predecessors, preserving the commitment to presenting the play as it has been shaped in history. While each individual volume will necessarily have its own emphasis in the light of the unique possibilities and problems posed by the play, the series as a whole, like the earlier Ardens, insists upon the highest standards of scholarship and upon attractive and accessible presentation.

Newly edited from the original quarto and folio editions, the texts are presented in fully modernized form, with a textual apparatus that records all substantial divergences from those early printings. The notes and introductions focus on the conditions and possibilities of meaning that editors, critics and performers (on stage and screen) have discovered in the play. While building upon the rich history of scholarly and theatrical activity that has long shaped our understanding of the texts of Shakespeare's plays, this third series of the Arden Shakespeare is made necessary and possible by a new generation's encounter with Shakespeare, engaging with the plays and their complex relation to the culture in which they were – and continue to be – produced.

THE TEXT

On each page of the play itself, readers will find a passage of text followed by commentary and, finally, textual notes. Act and scene divisions (seldom present in the early editions and often the product of eighteenth-century or later scholarship) have been retained for ease of reference, but have been given less prominence than in the previous series. Editorial indications of location of the action have been removed to the textual notes or commentary.

In the text itself, unfamiliar typographic conventions have been avoided in order to minimize obstacles to the reader. Elided forms in the early texts are spelt out in full in verse lines wherever they indicate a usual late twentieth-century pronunciation that requires no special indication and wherever they occur in prose (except when they indicate non-standard pronunciation). In verse speeches, marks of elision are retained where they are necessary guides to the scansion and pronunciation of the line. Final -ed in past tense and participial forms of verbs is always printed as -ed without accent, never as -'d, but wherever the required pronunciation diverges from modern usage a note in the commentary draws attention to the fact. Where the final -ed should be given syllabic value contrary to modern usage, e.g.

> Doth Silvia know that I am banished?
> (*TGV* 3.1.221)

the note will take the form

> 221 **banished** banishèd

Conventional lineation of divided verse lines shared by two or more speakers has been reconsidered and sometimes rearranged. Except for the familiar *Exit* and *Exeunt*, Latin forms in stage directions and speech prefixes have been translated into English and the original Latin forms recorded in the textual notes.

COMMENTARY AND TEXTUAL NOTES

Notes in the commentary, for which a major source will be the *Oxford English Dictionary*, offer glossarial and other explication of verbal difficulties; they may also include discussion of points of theatrical interpretation and, in relevant cases, substantial extracts from Shakespeare's source material. Editors will not usually offer glossarial notes for words adequately defined in the latest edition of *The Concise Oxford Dictionary* or *Merriam-Webster's Collegiate Dictionary*, but in cases of doubt they will include notes. Attention, however, will be drawn to places where more than one likely interpretation can be proposed and to significant verbal and syntactic complexity. Notes preceded by * involve editorial emendations or readings in which the rival textual claims of competing early editions (Quarto and Folio) are in dispute.

Headnotes to acts or scenes discuss, where appropriate, questions of scene location, Shakespeare's handling of his source materials, and major difficulties of staging. The list of roles (so headed to emphasize the play's status as a text for performance) is also considered in commentary notes. These may include comment on plausible patterns of casting with the resources of an Elizabethan or Jacobean acting company, and also on any variation in the description of roles in their speech prefixes in the early editions.

The textual notes are designed to let readers know when the edited text diverges from the early edition(s) on which it is based. Wherever this happens the note will record the rejected reading of the early edition(s), in original spelling, and the source of the reading adopted in this edition. Other forms from the early edition(s) recorded in these notes will include some spellings of particular interest or significance and original forms of translated stage directions. Where two early editions are involved, for instance with *Othello*, the notes will also record all important differences between them. The textual notes take a form that has been in use since the nineteenth century. This comprises, first: line reference, reading adopted in the text and closing square bracket; then: abbreviated reference, in italic, to the earliest edition to adopt the accepted reading, italic semicolon and noteworthy alternative reading(s), each with abbreviated italic reference to its source.

Conventions used in these textual notes include the following. The solidus / is used, in notes quoting verse or discussing verse lining, to indicate line endings. Distinctive spellings of the basic text (Q or F) follow the square bracket without indication of source and are enclosed in italic brackets. Names enclosed in italic brackets indicate originators of conjectural emendations when these did not originate in an edition of the text, or when this edition records a conjecture not accepted into its text. Stage directions (SDs) are referred to by the number of the line within or immediately after which they are placed. Line numbers with a decimal point relate to entry SDs and to SDs more than one line long, with the number after the point indicating the line within the SD: e.g. 78.4 refers to the fourth line of the SD following line 78. Lines of SDs at the start of a scene are numbered 0.1, 0.2, etc. Where only a line number and SD precede the square bracket, e.g. 128 SD], the note relates to the whole of a SD within or immediately following the line. Speech prefixes (SPs) follow similar conventions, 203 SP] referring to the speaker's name for line 203. Where a SP reference takes the form e.g. 38 + SP, it relates to all subsequent speeches assigned to that speaker in the scene in question.

Where, as with *King Henry V*, one of the early editions is a so-called 'bad quarto' (that is, a text either heavily adapted, or reconstructed from memory, or both), the divergences from the present edition are too great to be recorded in full in the notes. In these cases the editions will include a reduced photographic facsimile of the 'bad quarto' in an appendix.

INTRODUCTION

Both the introduction and the commentary are designed to present the plays as texts for performance, and make appropriate reference to stage, film and television versions, as well as introducing the reader to the range of critical approaches to the plays. They discuss the history of the reception of the texts within the theatre and scholarship and beyond, investigating the interdependency of the literary text and the surrounding 'cultural text' both at the time of the original production of Shakespeare's works and during their long and rich afterlife.

PREFACE AND ACKNOWLEDGEMENTS

In addition to personal debts, I owe a great deal to those who have worked on *Love's Labour's Lost* in the past. I have relied heavily on the editorial labours of H. C. Hart, John Dover Wilson, R. W. David, John Kerrigan and G. R. Hibbard; Paul Werstine's textual studies of the play, as well as his more general writings on biblio-graphical matters, have made me think about these subjects again; William C. Carroll's critical book and Miriam Gilbert's account of the play in performance have been invaluable. I have borrowed much material from all of these and have constantly benefited from their work even where I have disagreed with them. Likewise I have profited greatly from the comments and suggestions of two of the General Editors of the series, Richard Proudfoot and Ann Thompson, and have (often silently) incorporated their many ideas and necessary corrections, for which I am deeply grateful. No author is a hero to his copy-editor, but Linden Stafford's care, tact and patience have been truly heroic. My publisher, Jessica Hodge, has been patient and more than helpful. I am glad to acknowledge financial assistance from my Department which helped with the cost of the plates.

Rosemary Ashton, Katherine Duncan-Jones and René Weis were kind enough to read and comment on an earlier version of the Introduction; René Weis also generously scrutinized my account of the play's text. They all made valuable and encouraging contributions to my work, as did John Pitcher with whom I have discussed the play on many occasions. Another long-standing debt I should like to acknowledge is to Harry Quinn, with whom I first read the play. If he had lived to see it, I hope that David

Fleeman would have approved of at least some parts of this edition. I am also grateful to Peter Bayley, Tom Craik, Elsie Duncan-Jones, Lorna Flint, Giorgio Melchiori, Patricia Parker, Margarita Stocker and Brian Vickers for showing me published and unpublished material about the play. I am indebted to Robin Harcourt Williams who, at short notice, graciously helped me to examine copyright material at Hatfield House; it is quoted with the permission of the Marquess of Salisbury. Helen Hackett helped me at several different points; Gillian Robson very kindly advised me about art historical matters; and Christopher Wintle pointed me in useful directions in relation to the play's musical associations. Lastly (but not leastly) Edward Woudhuysen pointed out an important rhyme in the play to me. Without my wife's help and support I would not have begun or finished this edition. For the errors, half-truths and evasions which remain, I alone am responsible.

Finally, Keith Walker encouraged me to keep on working on the play and with characteristic generosity lent me his own richly annotated copy of it. What is mine in this edition I dedicate – 'Welcome, pure wit' – to him.

I have introduced one practice in the commentary which needs some explanation. In seeking to indicate the richness of Shakespeare's linguistic playfulness and innovation in *Love's Labour's Lost*, I have signalled all first citations from the play in the *Oxford English Dictionary* by a single asterisk; usages in the play which ante-date the *OED*'s first citation are marked with two asterisks. I have abandoned the *OED*'s date of 1588 for the play and placed it in about 1594. It should be stressed that the *OED*'s examples of first citations, and my ante-datings of them, can only be very approximate and are intended merely to give an idea of the play's verbal freshness.

In the textual notes 'QF' means that the Quarto and the Folio share the same reading: unless otherwise indicated, variant spelling and punctuation forms cited are those of Q only in places where F is in substantial agreement. However, all variant forms of SPs are given for both Q and F. Functional indentation has been imposed on rhyming lines and poems, but this has not been recorded in the collations. Nor do they usually record the hyphens which have been supplied by editors for the many compound adjectives in the play, such as '*high-born*' (1.1.170), '*snow-white*' (1.1.236), '*curious-knotted*' (1.1.239), '*low-spirited*' (1.1.240), '*small-knowing*' (1.1.242) and so on. Finally, the collations do not record uncontroversial expansions of SDs to include the names of characters.

H. R. Woudhuysen
London

INTRODUCTION

'If we were to part with any of the author's comedies,' Hazlitt
wrote of *Love's Labour's Lost*, 'it should be this' (Furness, 357), yet
Johnson said that 'there are scattered through the whole many
sparks of genius; nor is there any play that has more evident marks
of the hand of Shakespeare' (*Johnson on Shakespeare*, 182). *Love's
Labour's Lost* can be seen as characteristic of early Shakespearean
comedy and it can be a great success in the theatre, but it remains
a distinctly odd and difficult play. Its audience might well wonder
why Shakespeare plunges it into a world populated by a king and a
princess, by lords and ladies, but also by fantastic and strange figures whose language is at times almost impossible to understand.
Is the play really about these people or has it some hidden meaning
which can be recovered only if the right key to it is found? In this
Introduction I try to answer these questions by looking at some
aspects of the Renaissance humanist culture that lies behind the
play and in particular at Shakespeare's interest in the works of the
courtier poet Sir Philip Sidney. An examination of the two writers'
attention to endings leads into a discussion of the play's concern
with words and things and with the world of the court. I then turn
to the style and structure of the comedy, its date, the sources
Shakespeare may have drawn on when he was writing it and the
contexts out of which it grew. Finally, I discuss its early history (as
far as it is known) and subsequent reactions and responses to it
inside and outside the theatre. The aim of this edition is to supply
the reader with sufficient material to find the 'evident marks' of
Shakespeare's hand and to make one of his cleverest and funniest
plays as accessible as possible.

1

SIDNEY

Among the many volumes which a visitor to London bookshops in 1598 would have found were two new ones on sale: one was a slim quarto of a play, *Love's Labour's Lost*, the other was a bulkier folio containing a substantial collection of the writings of Sir Philip Sidney, issued under the general title of *The Countess of Pembroke's Arcadia. Now the third time published, with sundry new additions of the author.* Here the reader would find a hybrid version of the *Arcadia*, in which the ending of the *Old Arcadia* was grafted on to the three books of the *New Arcadia* which was all that Sidney had written of it before his death in 1586. To these were added reprintings of Sidney's sonnet sequence *Astrophil and Stella* (first published in 1591) and of his critical work *A Defence of Poetry* (first published in 1595) and two new pieces, the collection of poems called *Certain Sonnets* and an untitled entertainment for Queen Elizabeth which has come to be known as *The Lady of May*. Set beside this wealth of new and relatively familiar material *Love's Labour's Lost* may seem a slight piece, but it contains great riches of its own, riches which are bound up with Shakespeare's appreciation of Sidney's achievement as an imaginative writer. Both volumes constitute storehouses of Renaissance humanist concerns.

Samuel Johnson was the first to see there might be a link between Sidney's work and Shakespeare's play, when he commented that he had

> considered the character of Holofernes as borrowed from the Rhombus of Sir Philip Sidney who, in a kind of pastoral entertainment exhibited to Queen Elizabeth, has introduced a schoolmaster so called, speaking 'a leash of languages at once' and puzzling himself and his auditors with a jargon like that of Holofernes in the present play.
>
> (*Johnson on Shakespeare*, 181)

The entertainment was *The Lady of May*, and Rombus' and Holofernes' language may both owe something to Thomas Wilson's *Art of Rhetoric*, in which he denounces the use of 'inkhorn' terms, that is newfangled jargon, by printing a ridiculous letter from a Lincolnshire man seeking a benefice. Rombus and Holofernes delight in using Latin phrases in their speeches and, both being pedants, may also owe something to Rabelais's *Gargantua and Pantagruel* (1.14 and 19), in which Thubal Holofernes is made Gargantua's tutor and the book's hero endures a harangue richly larded with Latin phrases by Master Janotus de Bragmardo, as well as to the stock types of the *commedia dell'arte*. The existence of these possible common sources for the two characters makes any argument that Shakespeare was influenced by Sidney's pastoral piece no more than a possibility – furthermore, since *The Lady of May* was not printed until 1598, unless he had access to a manuscript version, how could Shakespeare have seen it?

There are, however, other links between the two comic pedants: Holofernes and Rombus both belong to the type of 'self-wise-seeming schoolmaster' which Sidney described in his *A Defence of Poetry*. The relevant passage was cited in a valuable article by Richard Proudfoot:

> For what is it to make folks gape at a wretched beggar and a beggarly clown; or, against law of hospitality, to jest at strangers, because they speak not English so well as we do? What do we learn, since it is certain
>
> > Nil habet infelix paupertas durius in se,
> > Quam quod ridiculos homines facit?
>
> But rather, a busy loving courtier; a heartless threatening Thraso; a self-wise-seeming schoolmaster; an awry-transformed traveller. These, if we saw walk in stage names, which we play naturally, therein were delightful laughter, and teaching delightfulness.
>
> (Sidney, *DP*, 116)[1]

1 I have changed the edition's emendation, which added an 'and' between 'courtier' and 'a heartless threatening', by separating them with a semicolon. The quotation from Juvenal can be translated as 'Poverty contains no sharper misery than that it makes men ridiculous'. Proudfoot, 17, cites the passage: the connection between it and the play was made as early as 1863: see Furness, 343.

Sidney's indictment of playwrights who make 'sinful' things ridiculous and 'miserable' ones scorned bears a striking relationship to Shakespeare's play. If Costard is not 'a wretched beggar', there is something in him of the 'beggarly clown' – clown in the sense of a rustic character. Armado's eccentric English and his being a traveller are combined in the play in which he appears as a Thrasonical braggart, a descendant of the boastful soldier Thraso in Terence's play *Eunuchus*; he is also a melancholy lover reminiscent of Sidney's *personae* Philisides and Astrophil. The 'self-wise-seeming schoolmaster' is a peculiarly apt description for Holofernes. Boyet, the King and his lords could each be characterized by the formula of 'a busy loving courtier'.

A page or so before the discussion of delight and laughter Sidney had been condemning mixed dramatic genres and insisting on the need to maintain decorum. He refers to Euripides' *Hecuba* as a model for keeping to the unities, but declares he will not labour the point: 'the dullest wit may conceive it'. He then immediately condemns plays which are 'neither right tragedies, nor right comedies, mingling kings and clowns'. He disapproves of the way they 'thrust in the clown by head and shoulders to play a part in majestical matters with neither decency nor discretion' (Sidney, *DP*, 114). It is hard to read this without being reminded of the later part of the play's first scene. The King has been discussing his proposed royal academy with his courtiers when suddenly one of 'the dullest wits' in Shakespeare, a constable called Dull, comes on to the stage. He has a prisoner, Costard, a clown, whose conversation certainly has neither 'decency nor discretion'. Costard's wit thrusts him into the centre of the scene and his name perfectly suggests, at the least, a head, for which 'costard' was a slang term.[1]

In addition to these two sections, Shakespeare's play and

---

1 Sidney's complaint evidently became something of a joke in its own right: in *The Pilgrimage to Parnassus*, 1599, Dromo enters '*drawing a clowne in with a rope*' and explains, 'Clownes haue bene thrust into playes by head & shoulders, euer since Kempe could make a scruey face' (Leishman, 129: 661.1, 664–7); the association with Kemp is interesting in the light of the possibility that he played Costard.

Sidney's critical essay share a number of other parallels. In the first passage Sidney's theme is the mixture of delight and laughter in comedy. One example he gives of this is that of 'Hercules, painted with his great beard and furious countenance, in a woman's attire, spinning at Omphale's commandment' (Sidney, *DP*, 115). This ridiculous emblem was a popular one in the Renaissance, a convenient figure for the ease with which love can transform and overthrow its victims. This is well demonstrated within the play, in which Hercules is consistently associated with the power of love.[1] Armado hopefully believes that 'Cupid's butt-shaft is too hard for Hercules' club' (1.2.168–9) and Berowne mocks his love-lorn companions when he compares their behaviour to seeing 'great Hercules whipping a gig' (4.3.164). Hercules appears in person when the diminutive Moth represents him in the show of the Nine Worthies: Moth's small size, but his great power as Hercules, neatly associate him with 'This Signor Junior, giant dwarf, Dan Cupid' (3.1.175). Although Shakespeare does not allude directly to Hercules' captivity by the Amazonian queen Omphale, he does have the madness of Ajax' killing sheep (4.3.6–7) which Sidney (wrongly) says Sophocles presents on stage (Sidney, *DP*, 86). The two share Aesop's fable of the ass in lion's skin (5.2.618–19; Sidney, *DP*, 108) and Sidney glances (Sidney, *DP*, 104) at the suitability of the story of Judith's killing Holofernes as a subject for painting. One possible direct verbal link between the two works may relate to a joke Sidney tells about a man 'that once told my father that the wind was at north-west and by south, because he would be sure to name winds enough' (Sidney, *DP*, 117), which may be picked up in Armado's description of '*that obscene and most preposterous event*', Costard's courting of Jaquenetta, as taking place '*north-north-east and by east from the west corner of thy curious-knotted garden*' (1.1.235, 238–9).

---

1 See Carroll, appendix B, and Jeff Shulman, 'At the crossroads of myth: the hermeneutics of Hercules from Ovid to Shakespeare', *English Literary History*, 50 (1983), 83–105. Roslyn Lander Knutson, *The Repertory of Shakespeare's Company, 1594–1613* (Fayetteville, Ark., 1991), 82–3, discusses the fact that the sign of the Globe Theatre may have consisted of Hercules carrying the world on his shoulders; cf. *Ham* 2.2.361–2.

These and other elements suggest some sort of relationship between the play and Sidney's *Defence*, but they may just as well come out of a common Renaissance literary culture. Yet the discussions of comic types and of the clown and the beggar seem to go beyond this. It is almost as if Shakespeare were replying to Sidney's theoretical work and showing that indecorous juxtapositions and satirical characters can be funny, can be made to work on the stage. *Love's Labour's Lost* is Shakespeare's first extended and focused treatment in a comedy of life at court: perhaps it is fitting that its presiding spirit, as I shall seek to argue, is Sir Philip Sidney, who, in his life and even more after his death, came to represent the figure of a perfect courtier. This is not to suggest that the play is in some sense 'about' Sidney and his friends – it is not an allegory of them or a satire on them – but it draws on a range of Sidney's writings and develops some of the literary and artistic problems which exercised him. Its 'mere style of narration', as Coleridge (1.96) observed, 'seems imitated with its defects and its beauties from Sir Philip Sidney'. By 1593 Shakespeare could have read in print all of Sidney's works apart from *A Defence of Poetry* and *The Lady of May*; although there is no firm evidence that he did so, it is possible he saw these in manuscript.[1] Shakespeare is showing he has mastered Sidney's writings, and that he can overgo them: he can turn the stuff out of which Sidney's life and art were made, or at least appeared to be made, into drama. No doubt some of the play's oddity and difficulty – the very obscurity which has turned it into such a happy hunting-ground for conspiracy theorists – can be put down to a courtly playfulness, a Sidneian sense of the delightful comedy of life. Although the dedications to *Venus and Adonis* and *The Rape of Lucrece* suggest he could have come into contact with the court through the Earl of Southampton, Shakespeare did not need to be part of it to write about its life. But, in addition to its comic playfulness and exuberant wit, *Love's Labour's Lost* also has an

---

1 See H. R. Woudhuysen, *Sir Philip Sidney and the Circulation of Manuscripts, 1558–1640* (Oxford, 1996).

intellectual toughness and resilience which may derive from a more critical and determined reading of Sidney's works.

PLOT

In its bare form the plot of *Love's Labour's Lost* is easily told. A would-be humanist monarch, Ferdinand, King of Navarre, persuades three of his lords, Berowne, Longaville and Dumaine, to give their oaths to renounce seeing women while they study and fast for three years. No sooner have they sworn to cut themselves off from the world than the Princess of France arrives on an embassy to recover money owed to her father. She is accompanied by a lord, Boyet, and three ladies, Rosaline, Maria and Katherine. The King falls in love with the Princess and amid poems, disguises and merriment the lords and ladies pair off: once the lords discover that each is in love, Berowne justifies the breaking of their vows. A messenger, Marcadé, arrives and tells of the Princess's father's death; before they leave in haste, the ladies impose year-long tasks on the lords, promising (more or less) after that period to return to marry them. Interwoven with this courtly plot are the concerns of a group of less exalted characters. A witty rustic, Costard, is the rival in love of a fantastic Spanish knight and traveller, Don Adriano de Armado, both seeking the hand of a dairymaid, Jaquenetta. A pedantic schoolmaster, Holofernes, and his friend, a dim and servile curate, Sir Nathaniel, are joined at the end of the play by Costard, Armado and his boy, Moth, in putting on a show of the Nine Worthies to entertain the courtiers. *Love's Labour's Lost* concludes with the songs of Ver and Hiems (Spring and Winter).

The plot is at once complicated in parts, involving letters which have gone astray and mistaken identities, and extremely simple. In G. R. Hibbard's words, 'It has less story interest than any other play that Shakespeare ever wrote' (Oxf[1], 71). The reason for the Princess's arrival at court is as soon and as easily forgotten as the King's convenient absent-mindedness – 'For well you know here comes in embassy / The French King's daughter' (1.1.132–3) – that she was coming in the first place. The complex negotiations, not easy to grasp at first, relating to Navarre's debt to France (2.1.128–65) are delayed pending the arrival of a packet of acquittances due to be delivered the next day. The business is not referred to again until the end of the last act when the Princess casually mentions her 'great suit so easily obtained' (5.2.733). The play does not advance its story through plot or narrative so much as through a series of encounters and conversations: conflicting attitudes, opposed ideas and values, provide it with its motive force. It seems to steer towards an ending in which the courtly couples will marry, but this comic resolution is avoided and only the eloquent Armado ends up with his love, the tongue-tied Jaquenetta, for whom he promises to 'hold the plough' during three years (5.2.871–2). She is pregnant, 'the child brags in her belly already' as Costard puts it (5.2.672–3), but its paternity (despite the association of 'brags' with the braggart Armado) is finally elusive.[1] The ending provides a conclusion in which nothing is concluded.

Such a literary device was not altogether new. The most obvious analogy for the play's open ending is Chaucer's *The Parliament of Fowls*. At the end of the poem, the formel eagle asks Nature for a respite from her suitors 'unto this yer be don' and then she wants her 'choys al fre' (*Riv*, 647, 649). The tercelet eagles are dismissed by Nature, who tells them:

> 'Beth of good herte, and serveth alle thre.
> A yer is nat so longe to endure,
> And ech of yow peyne him in his degre
> For to do wel, for, God wot, quyt is she
> Fro yow this yer; what after so befalle,
> This entremes is dressed for yow alle.'
>
> (*Riv*, 660–5: an 'entremes' is literally something
> served between the courses at a banquet)

---

1 The matter is debated in Dorothea Kehler, 'Jaquenetta's baby's father: recovering paternity in *Love's Labor's Lost*', *Renaissance Papers 1990*, 45–54.

The situation of the lovers at the end of the two works is different: in Chaucer's poem the suitors will serve a year while the lady makes up her mind, but in Shakespeare's play the matches have been proposed and await their consummation (Thompson, 85). Even so, both works delay their resolution, and the play's audience may well feel that at the end of the romance period of a year and a day (a period which also figures in 'The Wife of Bath's Tale') not all the couples will get together again – perhaps none will. The fickle and silly men who took their oaths at the beginning of the play and broke them with such ease will again fail to keep to the terms of the new injunctions laid upon them by their more intelligent and sensible ladies. Where Chaucer ends his poem with the wonderfully moving hymn to St Valentine, Shakespeare concludes his play with matchingly paradoxical poems of Ver and Hiems.

The effect of the play's postponed courtships, its lack of resolution, anticipates Shakespeare's concern in the problem plays with the audience's desire for the sense of an ending. The imposed formulaic conclusions of *All's Well That Ends Well* and *Measure for Measure* are over-resolved, they are too neat to satisfy, while *Troilus and Cressida* leaves the audience wanting to know what will happen next. The contrast with Chaucer's version of that story is telling: in Shakespeare Cressida's lover is left unhappy and alive, but Chaucer's is killed and laughs at the world of woe he so recently inhabited. His contempt for it and for love is matched by the Chaucerian narrator, who goes on to reject the very human love he has spent five books describing and making so real. Shakespeare's play is open-ended, Chaucer's poem closed, but in a way which may well puzzle and frustrate an audience in search of meaning and resolution. *Love's Labour's Lost* shares this playful concern with endings. In the simple sense of wanting to know what will happen next, the audience is left unsatisfied; but they may also have a feeling that the lack of finality is much more like life than the neatly tailored conclusions of most works of art. Its very irresolution challenges our desire not just for happy endings but for fiction to work its powerful charm over us.

In this respect, Shakespeare's choice of language at the play's pivotal moment is telling:

MARCADÉ
I am sorry, madam, for the news I bring
Is heavy in my tongue. The King, your father –
PRINCESS
Dead, for my life!
MARCADÉ   Even so; my tale is told.
(5.2.713–15)

The messenger's choice of word, 'tale', is curious: it is both a piece of information or a statement of fact and a very short story which he begins and the Princess completes for him. The tale's power is paramount and brings to mind the other passage on the same subject in the play. Rosaline describes Berowne's speech, which

Delivers in such apt and gracious words
That aged ears play truant at his tales
And younger hearings are quite ravished,
So sweet and voluble is his discourse.
(2.1.73–6)

Fiction's enchanting and seductive effect on young and old – characteristically it is the old, not the expected young, who play truant – is itself reminiscent of Sidney's classic description of what the poet does: 'with a tale forsooth he cometh unto you, with a tale which holdeth children from play, and old men from the chimney corner' (Sidney, *DP*, 92). Despite the echo, Shakespeare did not need to have this passage in mind when he was thinking about the way audiences expect to get a 'proper' story when they go to a play, one which fulfils its premises. On the whole they want tales either of the chivalric romance kind which Armado will tell to entertain the court (1.1.169–71) or of the tragic love kind such as the story of Katherine's sister who died for love (5.2.14–17). Marcadé's tale is told and yet still there is no resolution.

The overall effect of the play's lack of resolution is reminiscent of Sidney's own interest in tales and their endings. In the *Old Arcadia*, written between 1577 and 1580 and whose ending Shakespeare could have read in the hybrid edition of 1593, Sidney experimented with the over-resolved conclusion. The Duke of Arcadia, Basilius, turns out not to have been murdered; he is reconciled to his wife, Gynecia, and the princes and princesses can pair off to marry: Basilius' extreme foolishness, the guilty grief of Gynecia, Pyrocles' successful seduction of Philoclea, his subsequent attempt at suicide and Musidorus' attempted rape of Pamela are all cheerfully passed over and the story ends happily ever after. By contrast, *Astrophil and Stella*, dating from 1581, has an ending which is unashamedly open. In the penultimate sonnet 107, the lovelorn Astrophil asks to be relieved from his servitude to Stella; 'dismisse from thee my wit', he says, concluding:

> O let not fooles in me thy workes reprove,
> And scorning say, 'See what it is to love'.[1]

But in the last sonnet, 108, he is no freer from her attractions than he was at the beginning of the sequence:

> So strangely (alas) thy works in me prevaile,
> That in my woes for thee thou art my joy,
> And in my joyes for thee my only annoy.

The story of *Astrophil and Stella* is one of erotic obsession without resolution. All of Astrophil's efforts to win Stella fail and the sequence's narrative is one of – in Astrophil's own words – 'lost labour' (*AS*, 64.6). Like Shakespeare's Troilus, Astrophil is left damaged by an experience which does not have a satisfactory story-book ending. In sonnet 45 Astrophil meditates on Stella's crying over 'a fable, which did show / Of Lovers never knowne'.

---

1 All quotations are from *The Poems of Sir Philip Sidney*, ed. William A. Ringler, Jr (Oxford, 1962).

He concludes the poem by saying:

> Then thinke my deare, that you in me do reed
> Of Lover's ruine some sad Tragedie:
> I am not I, pitie the tale of me.

Unaffected by the circumstances of Astrophil's life, Stella is moved to tears by art. Astrophil tells his tale of adulterous love in his songs and sonnets, but it does not end in the desired way, and the artificiality of the sequence is set off by the painful naturalism of its ending.

If Shakespeare began writing his sonnets when the theatres were closed in the early 1590s, Sidney's recently published sequence of 108 sonnets may have supplied him with a model: Shakespeare's grouping of what are now sonnets numbered 18 to 126 form a similar sequence of 108 sonnets with an additional non-sonnet envoy.[1] It was not just a shared interest in larger formal matters that Shakespeare found in *Astrophil and Stella*. There are several other links between the sonnet sequence and the play. The first of the King's and his lords' poems – Berowne's 'If love make me forsworn' (4.2.105–18), a sonnet in alexandrines, or twelve-syllable lines – is written in the metre of the first (and other sonnets) in Sidney's sequence.[2] The King's poem, 'So sweet a kiss the golden sun gives not' (4.3.23–38), contains the same complex metaphors of tears and glasses with references to a coach that are also found in *Astrophil and Stella*, 105.[3] Dumaine's short trochaic lyric, 'On a day – alack the day!' (4.3.98–117), is reminiscent in tone and setting of the eighth song in Sidney's sequence. Both take place in the open air in May and meditate on the wind's freedom to kiss whom it wants (see especially *AS*, viii.57–60) and both have the effect of exposing their speakers to

1 Katherine Duncan-Jones, 'Was the 1609 *Shakes-speares Sonnets* really unauthorized?', *RES*, NS, 34 (1983), 151–71, at 165–7.
2 See also *AS*, 6, 8, 76–7, 102; Shakespeare's rhyme-scheme in the sonnet is one Sidney only uses in his ten-syllable sonnets.
3 J. M. Purcell, 'Sonnet CV of *Astrophel and Stella* and *Love's Labours Lost*', *PQ*, 10 (1931), 399.

a certain amount of comic ridicule. Once again, it is hard not to feel that Shakespeare is paying some sort of homage to the poet and showing he can surpass him. In general, the sonnet sequence and the play explore a similar series of ideas about day and night, light and dark, eyes and seeing, the sun and moon, the stars and planets. More particularly, Stella's eyes are black (*AS*, 7, 9, 91), as are Rosaline's eyes and hair. Although amber-coloured hair was common in Italian poetry, it may be more than a convention that Dumaine's Katherine has it (4.3.84), and so has Stella (*AS*, 91) and, for that matter, Philoclea in the *Arcadia* (*OA*, 303.17). Where Berowne accuses his fellows of being 'pick-purses in love' (4.3.205), Astrophil vehemently asserts, 'I am no pick-purse of another's wit' (*AS*, 74).

Perhaps the most compelling link between the two works was first pointed out by Frances Yates. In sonnet 2:

> when Sidney finally succumbs to Stella's complete domination over him he calls himself a 'slave-borne Muscovite'. At the moment when Navarre and his men finally put themselves in the power of the ladies they come disguised as 'frozen Muscovits', to pay their respects and worship like 'savages' [5.2.202] before them.
>
> (Yates, 133–4)

There are links between the King's entry, accompanied by Blackamoors (5.2.157.1), and the Gray's Inn revels of 1594–5 (for which see below, pp. 63–4), but the reference in Sidney's sonnet to the paradoxical belief that Russians preferred slavery to freedom – 'I call it praise to suffer Tyrannie' – may explain why the lords come on as Muscovites, to show they are slaves in love to the ladies. Describing how he fell gradually in love, Astrophil tells how 'At length to *Love's* decrees, I forc'd, agreed', which brings to mind the decrees against love to which the lords agree in the play's first scene (1.1.117, 145). 'Now', Astrophil continues, 'even that foot-step of lost libertie / Is gone': the steps the disguised Muscovite lords have taken are dwelt on at some length in the play

(5.2.184–97). Sidney returns to the theme of love and liberty in sonnet 47.

Attention has rightly focused on the Muscovites here, but the Blackamoors who accompany them with music deserve a moment's consideration too. Again, there is a parallel with the Gray's Inn entertainments, but there is also a possible link with Sidney which may be suggestive. In the *New Arcadia* the first time the maiden Queen Helen of Corinth is introduced she enters in a coach 'drawn with four milk-white horses furnished all in black, with a blackamoor boy upon every horse – they all apparelled in white, the coach itself very richly furnished in black and white' (*NA*, 58). In Sidney's romance the blackamoors do not have any music, but Helen's coach plays on the contrast between black and white in much the same way that Shakespeare opposes the hot climate from which the Blackamoors come to the cold of Russia. Of course, Shakespeare did not need to borrow the Blackamoors from Sidney – they had featured in earlier shows and were to become more common – but, if he did, then they may lead elsewhere. For Queen Helen in the *Arcadia* is in love with the complex and difficult character Amphialus. He, cruelly, loves Philoclea, and the orphaned Helen's self-appointed mission is 'only to follow him who proclaimeth hate against me' (*NA*, 65). After the wounded Amphialus has tried to kill himself, Helen turns up at his castle to 'carry away Amphialus with her to the excellentest surgeon then known, whom she had in her country, but so old as not able to travel – but had given her sovereign anointments to preserve his body withal, till he might be brought unto him' (*NA*, 443). She is advised to apply her 'excellent medicines', leaves 'some surgeons of her own to dress the body' and is allowed to carry it away with her in her litter (*NA*, 445).

All this is remote from the plot of *Love's Labour's Lost*, but it bears some similarity to that of *All's Well That Ends Well*. Many circumstances are admittedly different, but in *All's Well* the virginal and orphaned Helena – the lover of 'a bright particular star' and herself a sonneteer (1.1.86, 3.4.4–17) – is the heir to her father's 'prescriptions / Of rare and prov'd effects' (1.3.221–2) with which she manages to cure the King of France's illness, claim Bertram as her husband and set out in pursuit of him. In adapting his immediate source in Boccaccio, Shakespeare did not need to do much to change '*Beltramo Counte of Rossiglione*' to Bertram, Count of Roussillon; similarly, his mother survives as the Countess and '*Gerardo of Narbona*' emerges as Gerard de Narbon.[1] But Shakespeare chose to change the name of Boccaccio's heroine from 'Giletta' to Helena, perhaps for its association with Sidney's man-hunting, orphaned, virginal and medically skilled heroine: Shakespeare also gave the name to one of the heroines of *A Midsummer Night's Dream*. If there are possible links between Sidney's romance, *Love's Labour's Lost* and *All's Well*, there are also links between the two plays. Many are purely verbal – they both have a lot to say about winning and being won – but some of the echoes go beyond the immediate context. For example, in *Love's Labour's Lost* the logical formula of 'when ... then', dwelt on in the concluding songs and mentioned elsewhere (3.1.161–2, 5.2.817–18), is frustrated and inverted in the King's first speech (1.1.3–4). In *All's Well*, where it forms the central riddling pivot of Bertram's letter to Helena ('When thou canst get the ring upon my finger . . . then call me husband; but in such a "then" I write a "never"'' (3.2.57–60)), it is unexpectedly fulfilled. It is also worth noticing that Shakespeare includes a pair of French lords, the brothers Dumaine, in the Florentine army, and that the gulled Parolles takes some of his French companions as 'Muskos' or Muscovites (4.1.69). Lafew could, arguably, be a later and older version of Boyet, Lavatch is kin to Costard, but several other circumstances are particularly arresting. I have already mentioned one of these, the plays' employment of different sorts of endings for differ-

---

1 Quotations from William Painter's translation are taken from *All's Well That Ends Well*, ed. G. K. Hunter, Arden Shakespeare (1967), 145.

ent, but equally unsettling, dramatic and narrative effects. In one play Moth is Armado's follower; in the other, Parolles – a braggart like Armado – is Bertram's. Their French-sounding names can be closely related: one is the singular written word, the other represents plural spoken language. In both plays there are sick kings: Helena cures the King of France, but the Princess's father, 'decrepit, sick and bedrid' (1.1.136), dies. Finally, the initial setting of *All's Well*, taken from Boccaccio, is in Roussillon, the most eastern part of France next to the Spanish border. The court of the King of Navarre is geographically close on the south-west border with Spain – hence the presence of the Spanish knight Armado.

In these respects it is tempting to suggest that *Love's Labour's Lost* and *All's Well* are closely related, sharing Sidney's powerful influence, a common concern with endings, adjacent settings and some connected characters. Despite their differences of tone and structure, it is even more tempting to associate *All's Well* with the lost play *Love's Labour's Won* (for which, see below, pp. 78–81). However, this would require either a radical redating of *All's Well* from as late as 1604–5 or a theory of wholesale revision and rewriting to account for its existence in some form by 1598, the year in which *Love's Labour's Won* is first heard of. If there is no necessary link between *All's Well* and the lost play, there may be one between it and *Love's Labour's Lost*, as if Shakespeare wanted to return to the subject and answer the earlier play's account of courtly behaviour and of love: he is intent on going from a consideration of the power of the word (Moth) to a meditation on the power of words (Parolles).

WORDS AND THINGS

At the beginning of *Love's Labour's Lost* the King and his three lords sign a document setting out statutes in a schedule; by doing so they give their oaths to agree to its conditions, that they will study for three years, not seeing any women, fasting and sleeping little during that time. Berowne argues strongly against the laws and decrees, on the grounds that this is not the right way to study and to gain true knowledge, but in the end he too swears to them. The contract between the King and the three lords is not abandoned until the end of 4.3 when they all agree to turn their attentions fully on the Princess and her three ladies. The play works around a series of puns about swearing to something, forswearing something – that is giving it up – and being forsworn or breaking one's oath, perjuring oneself. In the end, the men are dismissed to their different tasks by the ladies because, as the Princess rightly points out to the King, 'Your oath I will not trust' (5.2.788), and Katherine tells Dumaine not to swear again 'lest ye be forsworn again' (5.2.820).

The initial oath, reminiscent of Faustus' contract with Mephistopheles or of Olivia's seven-year seclusion to mourn her brother in *Twelfth Night* or of the different bonds in *The Merchant of Venice*, sets up what should be a closed system of submission and obedience. But even before Berowne has signed he reminds the King that the French King's daughter has come to negotiate with him, so that the part of the oath excluding women from the court will have to be dispensed with immediately or at least for the time being, since 'She must lie here on mere necessity' (1.1.146). The details of the contract between France and Navarre which brings the Princess and her ladies to the King's court are discussed by the two sides in 2.1. Before she hands over a paper for the King to read, the Princess points out how wrong Navarre is to have sworn an oath against 'housekeeping. / 'Tis deadly sin to keep that oath, my lord, / And sin to break it' (2.1.104–6). The paper is the French King's view of how much money Navarre still owes him after the wars: Navarre is outraged by the claim and evidently feels a contract or agreement between the two has been flagrantly broken. Without further documents, the issue cannot be resolved and it is postponed until their arrival next day. Thus at the beginning of the play the King is given a lesson twice over in what it means to break your word and in the uncertainty of deferral – he is as fickle as Proteus in *The Two Gentlemen of Verona*, of whom Julia so wrongly says, 'His words are bonds' (2.7.75).

In a short but useful article Ralph Berry sketched out the different attitudes to language of the four main groups of characters in the play.[1] The King and his followers devalue language either by making words mean what they want them to mean or by using them to argue either side of a case. The Princess and her followers do quite the reverse, believing that words have meaning and consequences. For Costard, Dull and Moth words are symbols of things, they are real, while for the fantastics – Armado, Holofernes and Nathaniel – words are things in themselves and their relationship to reality is tenuous. The play's comedy and its more serious concerns come out of the clash of these different attitudes to language among those who are broadly realists and those whose grasp of reality is less firm. These descriptions are convincing, and without reducing the play to a schematic form can be taken further. Language is a system of signs and there is no natural relationship between the thing and the word which represents it. This is fine so long as people do not abuse language, but if they do, if they deceive themselves and others by what Hobbes called 'the inconstancy of the signification of their words', then they undermine its contractual basis and so society as a whole (Hobbes, 14–15). At the beginning of the play the King and his companions break their oaths and what they say throughout it has no real force; or, as Diana says to Bertram in *All's Well*, 'your oaths / Are words and poor conditions, but unseal'd' (4.2.29–30). The lesson of the earlier comedy is that those who use language as though words are open-ended in their meanings are rewarded with an ending in which the fate of their loves is indeterminate.

The play combines these two themes in its dramatic investigation of the contractual nature of language: words and things, the signifier and the signified, do not have a natural but an

---

1   Ralph Berry, 'The words of Mercury', *SS*, 22 (1969), 69–77; cf. Carroll, esp. 12–29.

arbitrarily imposed, purely socialized relationship. In their search for fixity and permanence, the male characters act as though language – and not just spoken language but symbolic representations of it – is not a closed system of absolute values, but an open one, in which words can be clipped, bent or melted down like coins to become something other than they are. Of course, the play enters into Elizabethan debates about language and its pronunciation, modernizers against traditionalists, neologizers against conservatives, and so on: it satirizes the ways in which people speak, how they pronounce words, but it also raises more fundamental questions about the nature of the spoken and the written. In the end, as I shall argue, Shakespeare wants to suggest that people who spurn closed systems of meaning in life, language and art will ultimately be disappointed: they will discover that there is one finally closed system they cannot avoid and that is death. The very open-endedness of the play's long last scene suggests the inevitability of death, the only conclusion in which anything is concluded.

One aspect of the play's concern with language and how to do things with words is its extraordinary wealth of puns and of obscene jokes. Characters regularly play with the ambiguity of language on their own or together and behind the most innocuous remark a sexual or scatalogical innuendo can lie. This is part of the banter of the courtly and the 'common' people, the rough trade, as it were, between and among the high and the low, but it is also a way of enacting both the copiousness of language and its slipperiness. Those who do not surrender absolutely to its ambiguity have various means by which they try to avoid ambiguity. One way is by the use of enumeration and repetition.[1] When Berowne exclaims, 'O, what a scene of foolery have I seen, / Of sighs, of groans, of sorrow and of teen!' (4.3.160–1), or when Nathaniel explains that Dictynna is 'A title to Phoebe, to Luna, to the moon' (4.2.39), it is as if, by using three or four terms

---

1   See Jörg Hasler, 'Enumeration in *Love's Labour's Lost*', *ES*, 50 (1969), 176–85.

when one should suffice, they are trying to tie down meaning which is otherwise elusive. Repetition and variation contribute to the play's patterning, but they also seek to define the language it uses, to prevent or offset the punning ambiguity from which much of its humour and brilliance arise.

The play contains an extended series of jokes about letters (of the kind people write to each other) and about the letters of the alphabet, in other words about *epistolae* and *litterae*. In addition to the letters which accompany the favours sent to the ladies in 5.2 (6–9, 38, 49–52, 54), there are four epistles in the play. Dull brings on the first just over halfway through 1.1: it is from Armado to the King and reveals that Costard has been consorting with Jaquenetta – whose very name rhymes well with 'letter'. The second letter takes the form of the French King's written final demand for payment from Navarre in 2.1. A little after the middle of the next scene (3.1.127) Armado gives Costard a letter he has written to Jaquenetta, but in no time at all (3.1.164) Berowne gives him another addressed to Rosaline. Inevitably, in a play of social and other confusions, Costard gives the wrong letter to the wrong person (4.1.55) and the inquisitive Princess makes Boyet read Armado's letter out. In the next scene Jaquenetta asks Nathaniel (4.2.88–90) to read out her letter from Armado: it turns out to be Berowne's verses to Rosaline. Jaquenetta brings it on stage again in 4.3 and Berowne, who recognizes the embarrassment it will cause him, tears it up (4.3.195 SD, 196), like Julia in *The Two Gentlemen of Verona* (1.2). Six out of the play's nine scenes therefore have the four letters in them, in each playing a more or less central part. *King Lear* likewise places a heavy reliance on letters whose postal histories are confused and slightly confusing; but in the tragedy the letters are a means to an end, whereas in the comedy they are an end in themselves. Shakespeare wants to keep what is written and the business of writing itself to the fore. Letters are like the oaths to which the lords subscribe their names (1.1.19, 23): they are signed and carry a 'superscript' (4.2.130), but they are also intended to be contractual documents between people – hence the comedy of misdirected letters – and essentially closed systems of communication. Letters or oaths, like words, are no more (or less) than signs: giving his letter to Costard, Armado calls it 'this significant' (3.1.127). 'Sign' and 'signature' come from the same Latin root *signum*, a mark – and the play abounds in different kinds of signs whose interpretation is by no means fixed or certain.

The written documents – 'letters full of love' (5.2.771) – are composed of letters, of marks on the page, which go to make up whole words. Moth and Holofernes have a hornbook lesson in the letters of the alphabet, including the vowels: 'a, b, spelt backward' becomes the bleating of a sheep, and 'o, u' turns into 'Oh, ewe' or 'Oh, you' (5.1.44–53). But the individual letters can also stand on their own. When Katherine says that Rosaline is as 'Fair as a text B in a copy-book' (Fig. 1), she replies by regretting that her friend's face is 'so full of O's' (5.2.42–5). The B is relatively straightforward but the O's, which the Princess implies are smallpox scars ('A pox of that jest' (46)), could be almost anything: they are ciphers – which is how Moth insults his master (1.2.55) – noughts whose meaning is yet to be determined. By its very nature an O can signify all sorts of things (the earth, the stars, the theatre and so on) and tends to be a signifier in search of something signified. In the context of the play's witty punning it is easy to associate the O with a vagina and so to join it with Holofernes' desire to 'affect the letter' in his poem, which alliterates on P for pricket and perhaps penis (4.2.54–61 and cf. Ellis, 59 and his appendix II).

Here, then, the letter O represents an open system of thought and interpretation. The play is also full of other signs and signifiers which court but often elude fixed signification. In the play's second scene Armado asks Moth 'what sign is it when a man of great spirit grows melancholy', to which the page replies, 'A great sign, sir, that he will look sad' (1.2.1–3). Armado is primarily asking 'What is melancholy a sign of, what does it mean?'

1 'Fair as a text B in a copy-book'; a page from John de Beau Chesne and John Baildon, *A booke containing divers sortes of hands* (1602)

He may expect to be told it is a sign that means he is in love. A further interpretation is possible, however, which is suggested by the astrological connection between melancholy and Saturn: Armado may be asking about the star sign which is dominating him. Moth's deflating reply argues that signs mean what they are: if you are melancholy, you will be sad. The signs of the zodiac turn up again at the end of the play when the Princess sentences the King to stay in his hermitage 'until the twelve celestial signs / Have brought about the annual reckoning' (5.2.791–2). Her use of the symbols to measure actual time is characteristic: for her the 'reckoning' (the word is carefully chosen) of the signs is fixed and the passing of time, under the aegis of death, is absolute.

Earlier in the long last scene there has been more about signs. Berowne grasps the trick the ladies have played on the lords through their disguises in the Muscovite episode:

> The ladies did change favours and then we,
> Following the signs, wooed but the sign of she.
>
> (5.2.468–9)

This lays bare the superficial understanding the men have of the nature of their beloved, for it shows how they are deceived by outward signs which can be so easily misinterpreted: when signs can be interchanged in this way, their signification becomes open-ended. The favours which the ladies exchanged (5.2.130–6) perform their task perfectly. The ladies see that these outward signs are interchangeable, yet here the men want them to have fixed meanings, for that is how they think when they see the ladies for the first time: Longaville's Maria is 'she in the white' and Berowne's Rosaline the one 'in the cap' (2.1.196, 208). The point of this is to indicate that the King and his lords believe that what people wear constructs their identity and acts, in accordance with Elizabethan sumptuary law, as a sign for their rank or status. The symbolism of the lords' Muscovite disguise and Rosaline's 'statute-caps' (5.2.281) belongs to this category, as do Berowne's wearing of Cupid's 'colours' (3.1.183), Armado's lack of shirt, his wearing of wool rather than linen and Moth's allegation that the Spanish knight keeps 'a dishclout of Jaquenetta's . . . next his heart for a favour' (5.2.705–10). His very state of mind is expressed through his hat and his doublet (3.1.15–17): these clothes and how he wears them spell out the conventional signs of the melancholy lover. Berowne's renunciation of affected speech and behaviour is more telling still: 'Taffeta phrases, silken terms precise, / Three-piled hyperboles' will, he promises, be replaced by 'russet yeas and honest kersey noes' (5.2.406–13). His choice of different kinds of material for his imagery reveals the play's constant engagement with language as a system of signs and with signs as a system of language for which clothes and disguises, or language and rhetoric, supply parallel systems. Of course, while denouncing it in favour of plain country speech, Berowne only shows his strong and continuing attachment to rich courtly language: the denunciation forms a self-contained sonnet.

There are many other signs and signifiers present within the play, for example Berowne's 'Lord's tokens', which are both the marks of the plague and also, for the Princess, the favours which were given to her and to her ladies (5.2.423–4), or the long sequence of objects to which Holofernes as Judas is compared: a cittern-head, the head of a bodkin, a death's face in a ring, an old Roman coin, the pommel of Caesar's sword, a carved face on a flask and a cap brooch (5.2.604–13; Fig. 2). The connection between signs and words is powerfully insisted on and made explicit at such moments as when the Princess reports that the King's letter was so closely written that 'he was fain to seal on Cupid's name' (5.2.9). The seal is the sender's personal sign, closely related to the King's heart, which Boyet tells his mistress is 'like an agate with your print impressed' (2.1.235). Signs and words come together again in one of the play's best known and most controversial passages (4.3.243–52). Berowne defends Rosaline's darkness by arguing that if she is like ebony then it is a 'word divine'. He then asks 'who can give an oath', calling for

2   Early Tudor cap brooch, showing Judith with the head of Holofernes

a book to swear on that 'No face is fair that is not full so black'. This recapitulates the play's insistence on the word as signifier and on the nature of oaths, but what follows is even more to the point when the King exclaims:

> O paradox! Black is the badge of hell,
>   The hue of dungeons and the school of night;
> And beauty's crest becomes the heavens well.

Much critical attention has focused on the nature of the 'school of night' and perhaps not enough notice has been paid to the significance of the badge and of the crest. The imagery is clearly based on heraldry – in itself a complicated and important system of signs – but the exchange also suggests that language cannot express the thing itself, only an image of it: words are approximate counters, convenient signs whose meaning is socially constructed. In a play which is so much concerned with beauty and its nature, the inability of language to represent and describe that beauty at first hand leads to its constant references to eyes, faces, fairness, seeing, sweetness and so on, as well as to its concern with the artifice of surface appearances, with glossing, painting and varnishing (1.2.43, 2.1.14, 47, 4.1.16, 4.3.240, 5.2.885).

Berowne returns to the King's badge at the end of the play and makes the connection between words and signs quite explicit. After Marcadé has told his tale the King restates his love for the Princess in the most involved and complex language ('The extreme parts of time extremely forms' (5.2.734–45)) which she does not understand. Berowne then steps in to try to explain:

> Honest plain words best pierce the ear of grief;
> And by these badges understand the King.
>
> (5.2.747–8)

The plain words he is about to speak are signs, symbols, emblems, badges representing what the King has said: words are not the things which they represent themselves, but images used to identify them. The same is true for names and titles. In the play's first scene, while the King and his followers are debating about signing the articles of oath, Berowne argues against book learning by saying that people who 'give a name to every fixed star' get no greater benefit from them than those who do not know their names (1.1.88–91; cf. Holofernes and Nathaniel's discussion of titles to the moon at 4.2.36–9). In other words, names are no more intrinsic to the stars than titles, which do not necessarily belong to people and places – like the French King's title to Aquitaine (2.1.145).

The play's concern with numbers might suggest we are on stronger ground with arithmetic than with slippery words: 'the use of words in registring our thoughts', Hobbes wrote, 'is in nothing so evident as in Numbring' (Hobbes, 16). But this is clearly not always the case, for in the mouths or minds of some of the play's characters numbers too are regularly shown to be arbitrary in their signification. On the other hand their reality is insisted on by their being beyond the wit of some of the people in the play to calculate. *Love's Labour's Lost* dwells on the question of how much things amount to, both in the sense of how much they add up to and to what they are equivalent in value or significance. In the play there are frequent references to numbers which are often exaggeratedly large or mere handfuls: people either seem unable to sort out sums amounting to no more than three or four or they think with an abandoned sense of hyperbole in thousands. Berowne states that the lords will break their oaths 'Three thousand times within this three years' space' (1.1.148); he compares Rosaline to 'twenty thousand fairs' (5.2.37); Dumaine sends Katherine 'Some thousand verses' (5.2.50); and Cupid has been 'five thousand year a boy' (5.2.11).

The simple reality of numbers in relation to words is represented by how hard sums are. Armado, who is 'ill at reckoning' (1.2.40), cannot work out what three times one is, and the joke is returned to in conversation with Moth (3.1.35–45). Costard tells Berowne off for getting three times three wrong: 'it were pity you should get your living by reckoning, sir' (5.2.495–6). Earlier in the play the exchange between Armado and Moth about 'The fox, the ape and the humble-bee' (3.1.82–95) is a counting rhyme – 'I will add the l'envoy' – meant to teach Armado what three plus one comes to. Another counting game seems to be alluded to with the Princess's enumeration of 'Honey, and milk, and sugar', which Berowne caps with 'Metheglin, wort and malmsey' (5.2.231, 233). Costard believes that 'In manner and form following' constitutes 'all those three' (1.1.202–3). Moth is not certain about how many of the humours (four, three, two or one) determined Delilah's complexion (1.2.77–8). Part of the comedy of the show of the Worthies lies in the characters' attempts to represent nine characters with five actors. Holofernes offers to play three of them himself, becoming, as Moth points out (he can do the sum), a 'Thrice-worthy gentleman' (5.1.135).

The most elaborate joke about numbers comes in Holofernes' poem on the death of the deer (4.2.56–61). The pricket is turned into a sore by being wounded when shot at; the yelling of the hounds turns it into a sorrel and, since 'l' in roman numerals is fifty, Holofernes is able to make fifty sores out of one sorrel and can double this: 'Of one sore I an hundred make by adding but one more "l".' This is indeed, as Nathaniel calls it, a rare talent, and the point of it is that numbers can be as arbitrary or symbolic as words and are open to being played with in just the same way: 'And how easy it is', Moth says (1.2.51–3), 'to put "years" to the word "three", and study three years in two words.' His point is that using words in this way is not the same as doing the studying itself.

The courtiers are as fascinated by numbers and by playing with their true value as the minor characters. One particularly telling moment comes when the Princess replies to the King's complex speech, 'The extreme parts of time extremely forms' (5.2.734), just after she has heard of her father's death, by replying 'I understand you not. My griefs are double' (5.2.746). She may mean this only metaphorically, but a literal interpretation suggests her extreme distress at her father's death and her lover's obtuseness. A similar and related moment of doubt comes when Berowne talks about the power of love to double power (4.3.305). Yet what is double is also deceptive, as when Longaville tells the masked Katherine that she has 'a double tongue within your mask' (5.2.245). Doubling also enters into the sum that is in dispute between France and Navarre: the hundred thousand crowns are mentioned four times in the course of the King's speech (2.1.128–52) and they are but half of the principal sum involved. Three is also a number associated with the courtiers: the King has three companions (1.1.15); they are to study, avoid women and fast for three years and sleep for only three hours

28

each night (1.1.16, 24, 35, 42, 129); Costard is sentenced by the King to fast three days a week (1.2.123); the three lords fall in love with three ladies (3.1.190); Katherine wishes Dumaine the three elements of 'A beard, fair health and honesty; / With threefold love' (5.2.812–13).

Distances can also be taken literally – '*no woman shall come within a mile of my court*' (1.1.119–20) – or metaphorically, as when Maria protests that Longaville's letter is 'too long by half a mile' (5.2.54). When the lords appear as Muscovites claiming they have 'measured many miles' to dance with the Princess (5.2.184), Rosaline challenges them to work out how many inches there are in one mile. They are evasive and say that they 'measure them by weary steps', but Rosaline refuses to be put off by this inexactitude and tries to pin them down more precisely by demanding, 'How many weary steps, / Of many weary miles . . . Are numbered in . . . one mile?', and again the lords will not or cannot do the sum relating to a journey they have not made. If the calculations are truthful, the lords, like the fantastics, are also interested in doing their sums and capable of them. When Berowne reveals that, like his three companions, he is in love and is about to 'tell' them more, Dumaine reckons that 'Now the number is even', to which Berowne helpfully responds, 'True, true, we are four' (4.3.207) – the exchange looks back to Armado's difficulties with adding one to three in 3.1.

Numbers should allow for the fixed computation of distance and time, but both of these can be changed or misreckoned by error or manipulation. The three years of the lords' studies can be contracted to two words, and the year and a day of the lords' separation from their ladies is both a precise legal formulation and a romance length of time signifying for ever. Dull's riddle, 'What was a month old at Cain's birth, that's not five weeks old as yet?' (4.2.35), shows how numbers, language and time can be duplicitous. When Berowne subscribes to the oath, agreeing to 'bide the penance of each three years' day' (1.1.115), he means he will endure every day in the three years, but it is possible to understand him as also saying that the three years will seem like a day. The feeling is strengthened when Longaville concludes the discussion among the lords by saying that Costard will be their entertainment, 'And so to study three years is but short' (1.1.178). For the King and his lords numbers are no more fixed and solid than what they say and what they write. Numbers are themselves words and more specifically the stuff of poetry, which is made out of metrical numbers and feet.

That formidable literary critic Holofernes dismisses Berowne's poem, saying, 'Here are only numbers ratified' (4.2.121). In the next scene Longaville, dissatisfied with his poem, announces, 'These numbers will I tear and write in prose' (4.3.54), and Berowne argues that the ladies' eyes alone could have inspired his companions to 'Such fiery numbers' (4.3.296). However, the business of poetry as numbers is not as simple as it looks at first sight. For, essentially, poetry is not truthful. It may be metrically correct, but in what it says it lies: Rosaline says that in the verse she has received from Berowne 'The numbers' are 'true, and, were the numbering too, / I were the fairest goddess on the ground' (5.2.35–6). The ladies further insist on the untruthfulness of poetry: for Katherine, who has been sent 'Some thousand verses of a faithful lover', they constitute 'A huge translation of hypocrisy' (5.2.50–1). Verse, made up of words and numbers, is as arbitrary and socialized in its meaning as its constituent parts. In the same way the play puns on the two senses of telling, as in telling a story or a lie and as in counting. The dancing horse can 'tell' by stamping its hoofs (1.2.53) and Armado offers to 'tell you a thing' after Holofernes and Moth have been joking about one man playing three parts in the show of the Worthies (5.1.136). When Rosaline challenges the Muscovites to calculate how far they have come, she says, 'the Princess bids you tell' how many inches there are in a mile (5.2.192). The King's poem elaborates on these senses by combining the idea of telling with the falsity of poetry. 'No thought can think,' it concludes, 'nor tongue of mortal tell' how far the

Princess excels other women (4.3.38): the distance cannot be counted but is implied by the poem's own hyperbole.

The particular association of telling is with coins. Armado's and Jaquenetta's exchange about telling wonders, 'With that face?' (1.2.133–4), hints at this, but the matter is more clearly spelled out by the Princess to Boyet in the next scene. She says she is 'less proud to hear you tell my worth / Than you much willing to be counted wise / In spending your wit in the praise of mine' (2.1.17–19). Telling and counting go together here and spending suggests money: the point is that, once again, the falsity of Boyet's language is being described here, for he is inflating language. On the other hand, the Forester is tipped by the Princess 'for telling true' (4.1.18). The 100,000 crowns the Princess has come to claim provide half of the plot's initial impetus and the play is piled high with references to coins. First of all, they have signs on them: 'I love not to be crossed,' Armado tells Moth, who replies, by referring to the devices on coins, that he is lying, since 'crosses love not him' (1.2.32–4). At the end of the play Longaville insults Holofernes by saying that he looks like 'The face of an old Roman coin, scarce seen' (5.2.607–8). In a contrary way, tokens, the signs of the plague, are like coins (5.2.423). Coins are also words, in the sense that 'remuneration' can be the Latin for three farthings and hence 'a fairer name than French crown' (3.1.133–8). 'Remuneration', which can also be expressed as 'halfpenny-farthing' (144), is, however, not as good as 'guerdon', which is the word, according to Costard, for a shilling (165–6). The connection between words and coins was a Renaissance commonplace: 'His purse is empty already:' Horatio says of Osric, 'all 's golden words are spent' (*Hamlet*, 5.2.130–1). However, the association is brought out with particular power in the King's description of Armado as someone who has 'a mint of phrases in his brain' (1.1.163), followed by Berowne's calling him 'A man of fire-new words' (1.1.176). In the hot fire of the mint, new words and phrases are coined.

The mint's iterative work supplies a potent image for the copiousness, the inexhaustibility, of language – new words can always be coined and new ideas created – but it also warns against inflation, which devalues coins and language, rendering words worthless. 'This fellow pecks up wit as pigeons peas' (5.2.315), Berowne says of Boyet, and the play describes and enacts the inventive richness of language: money itself may be scarce but clever talk is not and witty language is there for the taking. Costard is so pleased by Moth's jokes that he gives him his 'remuneration', calling him 'thou halfpenny purse of wit, thou pigeon-egg of discretion' (5.1.67–8). Costard's praise of the diminutive page is not the only reference to purses in the play and contrasts strongly with Berowne's description of the King and his followers as 'pick-purses in love' (4.3.205). They are trying to get love by theft, as if it were a coin that could be pocketed, and their behaviour here is not significantly different from their belief at the beginning of the play that knowledge or wisdom can be acquired in the same way by book learning alone. The King and his lords pursue love in exactly the same imma-ture and exhibitionist fashion that they had at first pursued learning. Frances Yates describes the superficiality of their approach in terms which should be familiar:

> a man must be large enough to absorb and digest his learning, to make it one with himself, to experience it as something which applies to life as he knows it. Those who fail to do this become pedants, persons who, like Holofernes and Armado, think of learning as something external to themselves, a coin or a counter passed from hand to hand to make a glorious show.
>
> (Yates, 197)

The ease with which the King and his friends are deceived by the signs of the Princess and her ladies shows they make the same mistakes about love as they do about learning. The mistake antic-ipates Hobbes's warning about words and false learning: 'For words are wise mens counters, they do but reckon by them: but they are the mony of fooles, that value them by the authority of an *Aristotle*, a *Cicero*, or a *Thomas*, or any other Doctor whatsoever, if but a man' (Hobbes, 18). The inevitability of the inadequacy of their conversion from learning to love is laid deep within Berowne's specious arguments that women's eyes will become their 'books', 'arts' and 'academes' (4.3.326).

At the end of *All's Well* the Widow produces Helena before the astonished King. He asks, 'Is't real that I see?', to which Helena replies, 'No, my good lord, / 'Tis but the shadow of a wife you see, / The name, and not the thing' (5.3.306–8). The chief lesson of *Love's Labour's Lost* is that, as with stories in which we always want a definite end, so with love and life we want conclusions in which something is concluded. If we see and use language as an open-ended system of signs in which meaning is forever changeable, if we swear to oaths which we know we cannot keep, if our words are not our bonds, if 'Vows are but breath, and breath a vapour is' (4.3.65), then that closure, that 'world-without-end bargain' of which the Princess so fittingly speaks (5.2.783), will constantly elude us. We shall have plenty of names, plenty of words, plenty of fun, but never the thing itself – until death comes. This may make life unsatisfactory for the King and his followers, but not for the audience: the play's open-endedness is aesthetically satisfying and like life.

THE COURT

Shakespeare's choice of setting for the play places the life of the court under scrutiny: no doubt his view of it is partly based in reality, but much of it perhaps represents his idea of what courts and courtiers were like. If it was, as the title-page to the first quarto claims, played at court, it would be interesting to know what the Queen's courtiers made of Shakespeare's depiction of their French cousins. Again, it is tempting to see some relationship between Navarre and Sidney's *Arcadia*, with its story of a ruler who seeks to avoid death by withdrawing his family from the world and going to live in a lodge in the country. Behind both works lurks the Latin motto *Et in Arcadia ego*. Among the playful courtships, the clever jokes and the games, death has a part: its messenger in the play is Marcadé and his name can be taken to suggest the marring of Arcadia. The play's courtly language, its witty style and evident use of patterns and patterning all point to its realization of court life and conduct in which codes of honour and shame are maintained through occupations which range from one extreme of repartee through gambling to duelling. Embedded in the comedy lies a view that what is playful need not necessarily be unimportant or lacking in seriousness or, as Walter Pater put it in his essay on the comedy, 'Play is often that about which people are most serious' – a view Sidney would have found congenial and one which is deeply felt throughout Renaissance culture.[1]

Pater's suggestive essay singles out Berowne for particular attention, arguing he 'is never quite in touch, never quite on a perfect level of understanding, with the other persons of the play', and that in him 'we see, perhaps, a reflex of Shakspere himself'.[2] At first sight Pater's judgement is mildly surprising – how can Berowne be marked off from the other characters when so much of the play revolves around him? – but it is also acute. He makes 'up the mess' (4.3.203) with his friends, but he stands slightly aloof from them: he was the man who did not want to sign but, like the Fool in *King Lear* or Enobarbus in *Antony and Cleopatra*, followed but for form (*Lear*, 2.4.79). A modern audience might feel Berowne is the ideal courtier, an accomplished lover, a witty scholar and an amusing friend whose fashionable behaviour seems to come straight out of the works of Italian humanist courtesy writers like Baldassare Castiglione, Stefano

---

1 Walter Pater, *Appreciations* (1889), 170: the essay dates from 1878. On play, more generally, see e.g. Montrose.
2 Pater, *Appreciations*, 175. For the play's possible autobiographical element – so attractive also to those who believe it is a political or literary satire – see, for example, Coleridge, 1.92, 97, and A. D. Nuttall, *Why Does Tragedy Give Pleasure?* (Oxford, 1996), 86–7, and cf. the choice of 'honey-tongued' as an epithet for Boyet, 5.2.334n.

Guazzo and Giovanni della Casa. Yet this does not accord with
his own sense of himself. Rather, he sees in his antagonist Boyet
what appears to be the perfect pattern of a courtier:

> This gallant pins the wenches on his sleeve.
> Had he been Adam, he had tempted Eve.
> 'A can carve too, and lisp. Why, this is he
> That kissed his hand away in courtesy.
> This is the ape of form, Monsieur the Nice,
> That when he plays at tables chides the dice
> In honourable terms. Nay, he can sing
> A mean most meanly; and in ushering
> Mend him who can. The ladies call him sweet.
> The stairs, as he treads on them, kiss his feet.
> This is the flower that smiles on everyone,
> To show his teeth as white as whale's bone;
> And consciences that will not die in debt
> Pay him the due of 'honey-tongued Boyet'.
>
> (5.2.321–34)

The passage is characteristic of the comedy in several ways. It presents a fair sample of the play's attention to rhymes and proverbs;
it is paradoxical; it is witty and bitter at the same time; it mixes the
high and the low, painting the exalted life of the courtier but insid-
iously undermining it with a string of sexual innuendoes.

Berowne's use of rhyme in this passage – it is worth noticing
that he avoids it in his longest speech, 4.3.285–339 – shows some
of Shakespeare's witty handling of the device. In particular, the
sweet/feet rhyme makes the point about the ladies' devotion to him
twice over and the *debt/Boyet* rhyme refers back to Holofernes'
unhappiness about the pronunciation of 'debt' as 'det' (5.1.20–1).
The proverbs start with one on its own, 'To pin on one's sleeve',
but then come three at a time at its end: 'To laugh to show one's
teeth', 'As white as whale's bone' and 'I will not die in your debt'.
Berowne reverses the biblical story, so that it is not Eve who
tempted Adam, but paradoxically Adam who would have tempted

Eve. Boyet is such an accomplished courtier that he has worn his hand out by kissing it so much, but he is also a social climber, 'the ape of form', an animal who merely follows what is fashionable without thinking about it. Nevertheless, women flock to him, thinking he and his talk are sweet: he carves, he lisps, he is an usher and with his white teeth smiles on everyone (like James Carker in Dickens's *Dombey and Son*). Berowne is also sexually jealous of his conquests; the women he has 'chalked up' are pinned on his sleeve; and even when he treads on the stairs the very stairs kiss his feet – his wanderings around houses result in seduction. Boyet is not only sexually active himself, he is 'an old love-monger' (2.1.253), with a suggestion that he is a pander or pimp. He is 'honey-tongued' – the characteristic compound also has interesting associations with Shakespeare himself – suggesting both his rhetorical skill and his erotic powers.

Berowne pictures Boyet as a successful creature of the court where courtesy and sex thrive together. When they are not paying extravagant compliments or getting into bed with each other, the courtiers pass the time by playing games. Even at the backgammon board Boyet scolds the dice for the throw he needs, but he does so politely, without swearing too strongly – even so, Hamlet's 'As false as dicers' oaths' (3.4.45) comes to mind. Backgammon is only one of many games in the play: there are references to card games like Post and Pair (5.2.67), to dice games such as hazard (1.2.46) and novum (5.2.540), and mentions of treys (5.2.232) and of cogging (5.2.235). If you do not play, you sit out the game (1.1.110), but more active pastimes may appeal, such as bowling (4.1.137, 4.2.109, 5.2.577–8), archery (4.1.107–37) – to which hitting the target, being 'quick and home' (5.1.55–6), may be related – bandy or tennis (5.2.29), bear-baiting (5.2.625–6), the cheating game of fast and loose (1.2.151, 3.1.100) and the more domestic sports of flap-dragon (5.1.41), whipping a top (4.3.164, 5.1.61–2), push-pin (4.3.166) and hide-and-seek or blindman's bluff (4.3.75). In addition to all of these there is dancing, which is a pastime (2.1.114–15,

3.1.7–8, 4.3.353, 5.1.144–5, 5.2.122, 145, 185ff., 209ff., 400),
and, of course, watching and taking part in masques and entertainments. So pervasive is the use of disguise in the play that
only Boyet, Dull and Jaquenetta do not go in for it (Booth, 148).

The court entertains itself with these sports: gambling and
games show that the courtiers are wealthy and do not have to
work or take part in business. But the games also hint at how
boring court life must have been – there was nothing much else
to do, so that 'courtship, pleasant jest and courtesy' (5.2.774) are
essential to passing the time. The play presents these games as
the very stuff of court life: Moth flatters and insults his master,
calling him 'a gentleman and a gamester', to which Armado
responds that they are 'both the varnish of a complete man'
(1.2.42–4) – the stress on surface quality is telling, but a
'gamester' is also a male prostitute. These formal games fill the
time and divert the courtiers from what they really want to play.
'Away', Holofernes says to Nathaniel at the end of 4.2, 'the gentles are at their game and we will to our recreation'. The gentles'
other game is love, for the 'court' is both where the play's action
takes place and what the lords and ladies do there. The play
itself, in describing these courtly pastimes, is also meant to
entertain the court.

When the Princess settles on the plan to confuse the
Muscovite wooers by changing favours, she announces:

> There's no such sport as sport by sport o'erthrown,
> To make theirs ours and ours none but our own.
> So shall we stay, mocking intended game,
> And they, well mocked, depart away with shame.
>
> (5.2.153–6)

After the encounter the King apologizes for the ladies' poor reception, but the Princess responds that on the contrary they 'have had
pastimes here and pleasant game' (5.2.360). It has all been to a certain extent a game, played on both sides but with different rules,
and the resolution defers a conclusive result. It may not 'end like

37

an old play' (5.2.862), but its action has been playful. This aspect
of its concern with court life is set deep in the play's language
when Boyet refers to the King in front of the Princess as
'Matchless Navarre' (2.1.7): he is without equal, without a mate,
but he also has no 'match' in the sense of being without what we
might call a 'fixture' – there's nobody to play against him.

The court is the scene for matches and matchmaking, for
games for money and for games of love. Those games can also be
spoken of using different types of language, relating to fighting,
hunting and wit. The male courtiers, especially, present love
through the imagery of warfare, which allows for some obvious
sexual innuendoes:

> Advance your standards and upon them, lords!
> Pell-mell, down with them! But be first advised
> In conflict that you get the sun of them.
>
> (4.3.341–3)

The men believe that love will transform them into military
heroes, just as Armado allows himself to be consoled with the
examples of the heroic lovers Hercules and Samson (1.2.64–71).
But as their stories reveal – Hercules captured by the Amazon
Omphale, Samson betrayed by Delilah – in the war between the
sexes the women will win and, far from looking heroic, the men
will simply appear foolish and behave badly. Shakespeare's other
metaphor for love in the play is another game – in fact it is game
itself. The play is set in a park (1.1.205) with a lodge (1.2.129),
and with a scene based around hunting in 4.1 it suggests an obvious analogy – one made more explicitly and violently in *Titus
Andronicus* – between the predatory natures of hunters and of
lovers: puns on dear/deer, heart/hart and suitor/shooter play a
part in this. Hunting deer was a particularly apt occupation for a
princess, since in England the right to sell deer was the
monarch's alone and, as events at Kenilworth in 1575 and at
Cowdray in 1591 showed, Queen Elizabeth enjoyed this sort of
sport (Fig. 3). The King, who begins the play by referring to the

3 Queen Elizabeth 1 on a stag-hunt; plate from George Turberville, *The noble arte of venerie or hunting* (1575)

fame 'that all hunt after in their lives', which he will achieve through study and learning, is said to be 'hunting the deer' by the beginning of 4.3, but by the end of the scene has turned to hunting the Princess. Conversely, she herself admits (4.1.29) that she hunts for fame, 'more for praise', than to kill.

Yet all this courtly behaviour is belied by the lords' treatment of the ladies and of the actors in the pageant of the Worthies: in their combined mocking cruelty, Berowne and Boyet become friends (5.2.545). The high-minded but flawed ideals of their academy degenerate into the baiting of the Worthies in their show. As their chief victim, Holofernes protests during it 'This is not generous, not gentle, not humble' (5.2.623). The male courtiers may be gently born, but they do not behave gently: even when they devise their horrible penalty for women who come near to their academe, Berowne points out it is 'A dangerous law against gentility' (1.1.127). Their language and pastimes are courtly but they are merely so on the surface, without depth. On the other hand, it is noticeable that, after some initial astonishment at the show (5.2.522, 524), the Princess (who is the only one of the ladies to speak during it) makes comments which are all kindly or encouraging (5.2.553, 563, 581, 625–6, 662). The play's concern with discussing and demonstrating wit looks forward to the sharp verbal skirmishes between Beatrice and Benedick. But instead of using their tongues to lash each other, the Princess instructs her ladies: 'This civil war of wits were much better used / On Navarre and his bookmen' (2.1.225–6). There are more uses of the word 'wit' and its derivatives in *Love's Labour's Lost* than in any other of Shakespeare's works. Costard is greeted by Berowne (who should know) as 'pure wit' (5.2.484), and he also calls his rival Boyet 'wit's pedlar' (5.2.317), having just said that he 'pecks up wit as pigeons peas' (315): so that when he 'utters it again' (316) he is presumably excreting or regurgitating it.

In this way the wit which dominates the play not only expresses its courtly values and its engagement with Sidney's worlds, but subverts them.[1] It is so full of sexual puns and jokes both because wit is at a premium at the court and because it is a displacement activity for real sexual relations: as Rosalie Colie put it (45), 'wordplay approaches ever more nearly the procreative powers of life'. The play also has much to say directly and

---

1 The following discussion is indebted to Patricia Parker's brilliant article 'Preposterous reversals: *Love's Labor's Lost*' (Parker, 435–82).

indirectly about the body and its functions. The concern with sexual parts (sublimated, as Parker has argued (437, 442, 466–7), into feet, shoes and eyes) is matched by an interest in the scatalogical, in purging and the excremental. The ability to talk 'greasily' (4.1.136) and to understand greasy talk is distributed democratically throughout the characters. The courtly and academic decorum which an audience might expect is overthrown by the coarse, the obscene and the simply popular. The lofty manner in which characters speak, drawing on the languages and methods of law, grammar, logic and rhetoric, is subverted by their earthy subjects: 'high-born words' often end up being about low matters (1.1.170, 189–90). The play is full of such paradoxical mismatches between what is said and how it is said, but also, at a more literal level, it is rich in what Parker calls 'verbal reversals and rhetorical turns' (445). The play's much-quoted 'great feast of languages' (5.1.35–6) – the plural, eliminated in Carroll's valuable book on the play, is worth noting – is not an ordered and disciplined meal but a wild and carnivalesque spread, perhaps related to the 'wakes and wassails, meetings, markets, fairs' (5.2.318) where Boyet sells his wit. The world of the play is far removed from the atmosphere of erotic romance which Sidney projects in his works even when his heroes' chivalric language disguises their naked lust.

This linguistic mixing of the 'high' and the 'low' is only one of a number of such reversals and inversions in the play. In it order and sequence are overturned, 'then' does not implicitly follow on from 'when', things are back to front and what should regularly follow does not: the ending is just one of a number of such non sequiturs. The play begins with the King's unnatural decision to withdraw with his three courtiers from the world. In doing this he is doing something fundamentally wrong, failing to fulfil his obligations to society. He is like Basilius in the *Arcadia* when he decides to retire to a solitary lodge away from the world, or with his schedule and three lords he is like King Lear with his map and three daughters, only one of whom (like Berowne) can begin to tell the truth (Kerrigan, 15). Navarre's initial act of folly in abrogating his kingship is compounded by oath-taking and, as the Princess pointedly remarks, ''Tis deadly sin to keep that oath, my lord, / And sin to break it' (2.1.105–6). Yet it is the play's unnatural reversals which allow the women to overcome the men, when they refuse to conform to their inferior roles and marry them. In the low or popular language of the play, Jack does not get Jill (5.2.863), the courtly lords and ladies do not pair off as an audience might expect them to do at the end of a comedy. Hercules is overcome by Omphale and Judith cuts off Holofernes' head.

As always in Shakespearean comedy the women are cleverer and wittier than the men. That great exemplar of wit, ' "honey-tongued" Boyet', has to admit that 'The tongues of mocking wenches are as keen / As is the razor's edge invisible' (5.2.256–7): his imagery inverts the punishment of losing her tongue proposed for any woman who comes within a mile of the court (1.1.122–3). The women are not just more verbally adroit than the men, they are constant. The men are fickle, not just in their sexual relations or their ability to keep to their vows, but also in their grasp of the idea that words have a true value which must be maintained. The women weigh and value their words, recognizing that they must not be viewed as open-ended in their signification if life is to go on. It has to be remembered that the Princess and her party have come to Navarre not to find husbands or to 'fleet the time carelessly, as they did in the golden world' (*As You Like It*, 1.1.118–19), but to negotiate a complicated political and economic settlement. In the ladies, the lords have met their intellectual and moral superiors, who constantly return the ill-chosen words of the men to them and with interest:

> KING   Fair Princess, welcome to the court of Navarre.
> PRINCESS   'Fair' I give you back again, and 'welcome'
>   I have not yet. The roof of this court is too high to
>   be yours, and welcome to the wide fields too base to
>   be mine.
>
>   (2.1.90–4)

Furthermore, as the expected romantic relations between the sexes are reversed, in a similar way the class relations between Armado and Jaquenetta are inverted: the travelling knight – who ends up behind the plough (5.2.871) – is in love for the first time and with a dairymaid, a situation that is parallel to King Cophetua's love for the beggar-maid (1.2.104–5, 4.1.65–79) or to Touchstone's involvement with Audrey. And as Armado is in love with Jaquenetta, so Berowne is drawn to the conventionally unattractive Rosaline.

What he says about her reveals something about his view of the sexual world of the court. She is 'one that will do the deed / Though Argus were her eunuch and her guard' (3.1.193–4). On the whole, the male courtiers' separation of words from their meanings enables them to indulge in what might be called safe sexual banter. Yet Berowne's language here is not witty and evasive, but blunt and to the point. Furthermore, he is alone and, although he may be indulging in the sort of misogyny which lies behind some of what the male courtiers say, his view of Rosaline is shared by Boyet, who in the next scene tells Rosaline that, if she marries, 'Hang me by the neck if horns that year miscarry' (4.1.111). To male eyes Rosaline will have sex on any occasion that she can and, by implication, with anyone. She is therefore close to what Moth alleges Jaquenetta is when he tells Armado that his love is 'perhaps a hackney' (3.1.30). The courtiers may varnish their amatory games with jokes and sexual puns, but their physical appetites are seen as no different from those of the other members of the 'commonwealth' (4.1.41). Johnson famously said, 'there are many passages mean, childish and vulgar' in the play, 'and some which ought not to have been exhibited, as we are told they were, to a maiden queen' (*Johnson on Shakespeare*, 182). With the notable exception of the Princess, who never herself contributes to the obscene and sexual exchanges but understands them, what is particularly evident in the play is the way that court life is depicted as being so at ease with the power of carnal appetite.

As well as the play's concern with the low, its deliberate inversion of courtly values, it also juxtaposes the youthful would-be seriousness of Navarre's court, its being 'Still and contemplative in living art' (1.1.14), with the presence of death. The academe seeks to evade the disgrace of death, to blunt time's sharp scythe by conferring immortality on the lords: death is inevitable but its effects can be mitigated by fame and memory, which will record their deeds on their tombs, much as Armado is meant to entertain the lords with tales of knights 'lost in the world's debate' (1.1.171). So strongly present in the play's opening speech (1.1.1–14), the reality of death can be represented by Marcadé's dramatic entrance towards the end of 5.2 in the middle of the show of the Worthies. They themselves, as acted by Armado and his friends, are an object lesson in what happens to the great and famous after death: they may be immortalized, but they are also the butt of the humour. Holofernes as Judas Maccabaeus is transformed by the rude lords into Judas Iscariot, and when Holofernes asks, 'What mean you, sir?', Boyet obliges by saying, 'To make Judas hang himself' (5.2.597–8). There are important references in the play to punishment – grossly disproportionate penalties of public shame for men talking to women and of losing their tongues for women coming within a mile of the court (1.1.122–3, 129–30); fasting for Costard (1.1.284–5); whipping for Armado (5.2.676) – but there is more in it about hanging. Anticipating the jokes about Judas, Costard says that they will 'turn' the show of the Worthies 'finely off' (5.2.507), as if they were turning someone off the ladder on the gallows: Armado as Hector is to be hanged for killing Pompey (5.2.677–8). Hanging plays a part in the men's oaths and exclamations (4.1.111, 4.3.8) and the Princess thinks that the shamed Muscovites will 'hang themselves tonight' (5.2.270). When Longaville joins the King in being revealed as a lover, Berowne says that he makes up 'the triumviry, the corner-cap of society, / The shape of Love's Tyburn, that hangs up simplicity' (4.3.50–1), and, following the same strain, Katherine, who lost her sister for love, calls Cupid 'a shrewd unhappy gallows too' (5.2.12). Hanging is a most uncourtly means of execution and, like the references in the play to the plague, represents a deliberate determination to show that Navarre is not as removed from the 'real' world as it seems.

The tale Marcadé tells when he interrupts the show of the Worthies is soon told and the play put on to entertain the courtiers is abandoned. The King's elaborate courtly language still cannot persuade the Princess to stay, nor can Berowne's equally sophisticated but plainer words. To the King's appeal, 'Now, at the latest minute of the hour, / Grant us your loves', the Princess replies that it is 'A time, methinks, too short / To make a world-without-end bargain in' (5.2.781–3). The lovers and the play have both run out of time and resolution is deferred. At the end of the play, rather than the expected and desired marriages of comedy, death puts all in doubt. Instead, the matches are postponed for a year and a day: the King is sentenced to a truly ascetic life in a hermitage and the all-too-eloquent Berowne is instructed by Rosaline to 'Visit the speechless sick and still converse / With groaning wretches' (5.2.839–40) – the sick perhaps are meant to remind the audience of the Princess's 'decrepit, sick and bedrid father' (1.1.136). The circularity of the play's action, its open-endedness, its failure to resolve itself, are inherent in its concern with the passing of the year, the 'annual reckoning' of 'the twelve celestial signs' (5.2.791–2). The year and the day are 'too long for a play' (5.2.866), but can nevertheless be represented by 'the dialogue that the two learned men have compiled, in praise of the owl and the cuckoo' (5.2.873–5).

  Armado's description raises the question of praise in the play: there is more about praise in *Love's Labour's Lost* than in any of Shakespeare's other plays (cf. Carroll, 88–96). It is especially reminiscent of the paradoxical praise of the worthless object of which Moth's praise of the eel (1.2.26) is another example. The subject of praise is bound up with the play's questioning of the nature of language – what happens to words, it asks, when they are extravagantly lavished on objects which do not precisely deserve them? Although like Berowne they may deny it (4.3.180–3), when they are in love, the male courtiers are great praisers, inflating language to support their courtship. The women are more concerned that praise should only be given where it is due: 'my beauty,' the Princess tells Boyet, 'though but mean, / Needs not the painted flourish of your praise' (2.1.13–14). The praise of the owl and the cuckoo therefore takes the audience back to the play's central concern with the value of words and to its playful handling of the paradoxical and of the unexpected reversal.

The apparent resolution of the play through song owes something again to Chaucer's *The Parliament of Fowls*, and the debate between Ver and Hiems can be related to the seasonal concerns of Thomas Nashe's play, *Summer's Last Will and Testament*, of 1592. Yet Shakespeare's two poems are quite distinctive. Ver's song celebrates the pleasures of spring with a pastoral vision of shepherds, maidens, flowers and birds, in which early in the morning the country wakes up again and new life is promised. All is not well, however, for in this landscape there is the cuckoo 'on every tree'; its cry 'Mocks married men' and acts as a 'word of fear, / Unpleasing to a married ear' (5.2.895–6, 898–9). Hiems's song reminds the audience of how cold and hard winter is in England, but with its logs in the hall, the simmering pot and apples in the bowl, even with the parson in church, its setting is domestic and at least partly inside: it has people – Tom, Dick, Marian and Joan – with names. Furthermore, the 'nightly' song of the owl has 'A merry note' (5.2.905, 907). One is set outside, the other inside; one is light, the other is dark. Yet spring is full of fear, winter of merriness. Men's fear of the cuckoo is, of course, the fear of cuckoldry. This points towards comedy, but it is hard not to feel that Shakespeare has deliberately defied and reversed expectations even in the play's last moments. The two poems' designations as 'songs' as well as a 'dialogue' leave their status paradoxical – they do not have to be sung. But they also enact one of the play's contrary impulses, to lyric but also to argument.

4 Design for a knot from Thomas Hill, *The gardeners labyrinth* (1577)

STYLE

Love's Labour's Lost is a play that delights in the use and abuse of language. Full of parallels and patterns, it is often compared to Armado's '*curious-knotted garden*' (1.1.239) in which arrangement and ornament are ends in themselves (Fig. 4):[1] its subject-matter

---

1 In *The Renaissance Garden in England* (1979), 40–2, Roy Strong cites Gervase Markham's distinguishing between two kinds of knots, 'open and closed':

> Open knots had the pattern set out in lines of rosemary, thyme, hyssop or some other plant, the intervening spaces being filled with different coloured earths and the path, where it was not grass, was sanded. Closed knots had the spaces between filled with flowers of one colour.

On patterns, see also Jane Donawerth, *Shakespeare and the Sixteenth-Century Study of Language* (Urbana and Chicago, Ill., 1984), esp. 149–52.

of affection (2.1.231, 5.1.4) is compounded by a concern with affectation and the infection of ostentation (2.1.229, 5.2.409). Its characteristic style shows a pleasure not just in carefully worked-out and formal structural devices – such as the order of confession and revelation in 4.3[1] – or in playful punning, rhyming and metrical experimentation and linguistic dexterity, but in the verbal texture of repetition and allusion. As the commentary shows, words are repeated, echoed, returned to and played with over long stretches of text – and not just familiar words but unfamiliar neologisms of which the play is particularly full. The repetitions give the play some of its richly allusive feel, but it is an allusiveness that works within, not from outside, the play. It helps create its own self-absorbed world in which it constantly turns its attention in upon itself.

This can be seen in the fondness certain characters have for particular forms of words. For example, Carroll (45) has noted Holofernes' fondness for words ending in '-tion'; in a similar way, Armado finds it hard to resist words which end in '-ate'.[2] Other distinctive linguistic features are not confined to particular characters. The leading examples of these are rhetorical figures, to which Elam devotes a great deal of attention,[3] and compound words, for which see Appendix 5. These last may be so well represented in the play because they were particularly associated with Sidney and with French poetic practice: Joseph

---

1   See William Leigh Godshalk, 'Pattern in *Love's Labour's Lost*', *Renaissance Papers 1968*, 41–8; S. K. Heninger, Jr, 'The pattern of *Love's Labour's Lost*', *SSt*, 7 (1974), 25–53.

2   For Holofernes, see 'intimation' (4.2.13), 'insinuation', 'explication' (4.2.14), 'replication' (4.2.15), 'inclination' (4.2.16), 'motions', 'revolutions' (4.2.67–8), 'instruction' (4.2.77), 'invention' (4.2.125, 157), 'nomination' (4.2.133), 'recreation' (4.2.163), 'salutation' (5.1.34). For Armado, see 'nominate' (1.2.15), 'reprobate' (1.2.59), 'immaculate' (1.2.87), 'situate' (1.2.131), 'passionate' (3.1.1), 'festinately' (3.1.5), 'inconsiderate' (3.1.75), 'captivated' (3.1.122), 'illustrate' (4.1.65), 'indubitate' (4.1.66), 'preambulate' (5.1.74), 'educate' (5.1.75), 'congratulate' (5.1.81), 'importunate' (5.1.92), 'potentates' (5.2.674). Holofernes may be mocking this affectation when he uses 'peregrinate' (5.1.13), insinuateth (5.1.24) and 'illustrate' (5.1.113) in relation to Armado; cf. also Nathaniel's 'nominated' (5.1.8).

3   See Elam, 15–17, 81, 119, 241, 244, 249–50, 252–6, 258, 261, 263, 267, 270, 272–3.

Hall in his satires, *Virgidemiarum*, of 1598 referred to the joining of 'two wordes in one' as 'that new elegance, / Which sweet *Philisides* fetch't of late from *France*'.[1]

Another factor which contributes to this introverted and self-referential world is that well over a third of its lines rhyme: it is, in fact, the most heavily rhymed of all of Shakespeare's plays. No scene is entirely conducted in rhyme; there are no rhymes in the play's two prose scenes (1.2 and 5.1) apart from Moth's poem (1.2.94–101). On the other hand, there are long passages written almost entirely in couplets (4.3.71–209, 5.2.43–156) or in alternating rhymes (4.3.218–85). Characters regularly pick up others' rhymes and often complete them. Some identical rhymes occur four, five or more times (*adieu/you, lord/word, now/brow, part/heart*) and some of these, like *eyes/lies, lord/word* or *oath/troth*, reflect directly on the play's subject-matter (see Appendix 4). Words like *eye* and *wit* in singular and plural forms are rhymed again and again with other words – *eye(s)* with seventeen other words and *wit(s)* with seven. When they speak in verse Boyet is the major character most addicted to rhyme, the Princess and then Rosaline the least. Shakespeare's sophisticated use of rhyme in the play emphasizes its comic playfulness, contributing to its courtly aesthetic and its artistic self-consciousness. The couplets and rhymes tie lines together and suggest the play's dual concern with closed systems of thought and with pairings. Rhyme allows him to bury poems within its dialogue to complement the more easily recognizable inset pieces.

There is a similar delight with metrical experimentation, the verse ranging from doggerel couplets to poulter's measure to formal alexandrines and including large numbers of trimeter couplets and irregular lines. The witty and playful effects Shakespeare achieves can be seen from looking at one passage, a characteristic exchange between Rosaline and Berowne:

---

1   *The Collected Poems of Joseph Hall*, ed. A. Davenport (Liverpool, 1949), 95.

ROSALINE

    Alack, let it blood.

BEROWNE

    Would that do it good?

ROSALINE

    My physic says ay.

BEROWNE

    Will you prick't with your eye?

ROSALINE

    Non point, with my knife.

BEROWNE

    Now God save thy life.

ROSALINE

    And yours from long living.

BEROWNE

    I cannot stay thanksgiving.

             (2.1.185–92)

They begin the rhyming couplets with lines of five syllables each until Berowne moves up one syllable in line 188: Rosaline will not keep up with him in her next line and Berowne moves back to five syllables; Rosaline then thinks she has the better of him with six in her next line, but Berowne trumps her by leaving on seven syllables. The effect is, perhaps, reminiscent of the singing competitions in the eclogues of Sidney's *Old Arcadia* (for example, in OA poem, 7). Equally, the prose styles of the play – not least Armado's – are susceptible of complex analysis which brings out its delight in rhetoric and playful patterning.[1]

Both prose and verse contain a large number of interruptions (well over thirty of them), beginning, perhaps, with Berowne's breaking off from reading the decrees to question them (1.1.119–23), or Costard's comments made while the King reads out Armado's letter (1.1.218–51), and culminating in the

---

1   See Brian Vickers, *The Artistry of Shakespeare's Prose* (1968), 54–65.

Princess's breaking into Marcadé's news (5.2.714–15). The interruptions suggest the way in which death cuts life short, much as in the Apocryphal story Judith decapitated Holofernes, or as the schoolmaster's performance as Judas leads to jokes about splitting his name (5.2.622). The show of the Worthies is cut short by Marcadé's arrival and the whole comedy is 'dashed' (5.2.462) by having an unresolved or even premature ending.[1] A further type of interruption involves imperfect sexual enjoyment, most obviously represented by the lengthy and digressive discussion of Costard's being 'broken in a shin' (3.1.67–117).

If rhetorical and formal cleverness is supposed to be part of life at court, elegant variation being a sign of self-conscious superiority, so is a fairly punctilious interest in titles and modes of address. So 'grace' is only ever used by characters when talking to or of the King, except when Boyet refers to the Princess by that title (5.2.80);[2] 'lord' appears only with reference to the courtly characters; 'madam' applies only to the Princess; 'master' is used largely by Moth to refer to Armado; 'liege' is used alone by Berowne to refer to the King; Moth is referred to exclusively throughout the play as the 'boy' or 'child' – the term associates him with Cupid, whose boyishness is also insisted on (see 1.2.172, 3.1.174–5, 5.2.11) – and Jaquenetta is the 'damsel' and once 'damosella'. On the other hand, 'Monsieur' is applied twice each to Boyet, Berowne and Holofernes. 'Sir' is scarcely used by the courtiers among themselves, which makes Berowne's use of the word to Boyet twice (at 2.1.212 and more pointedly at 5.2.476) quite telling. The term is more often used by the rustics and fantastics, particularly by Moth to Armado (he

1 See Charles Whitworth, '*Love's Labour's Lost*: aborted plays within, unconsummated play without', 109–25, esp. 122, in *The Show Within: Dramatic and Other Insets. English Renaissance Drama (1550–1642)*, ed. François Laroque (Montpellier, 1992).

2 See Thomas M. Greene, '*Love's Labour's Lost*: the grace of society', *SQ*, 22 (1971), 315–28, esp. 326–8; John Dixon Hunt, 'Grace, art and the neglect of time in "Love's Labour's Lost" ', in *Shakespearian Comedy*, 75–96, and Montrose, 531–8, where he explores the connection between 'grace' and 'shame'.

also heavily favours 'master') and by Costard to Berowne (notably, some fifteen times in 5.2.485–508).

When it comes to more personal forms of address, Armado is by far the heaviest user of the second person singular and its derivatives. As well as 'thee-ing' and 'thou-ing' Jaquenetta, Moth and Costard over and over again, he also twice uses the familiar form with the King, referring to 'thy royal sweet breath' and 'thy royal finger' (5.2.520–1, 870) and once 'thy's' the Princess (5.2.663) – all of these occasions reflect his extravagant, over-excited moods. Similarly, when Berowne reproves the King for breaking his vow he slips into the familiar form:

> Ah, good my liege, I pray thee pardon me.
> Good heart, what grace hast thou thus to reprove
> These worms for loving
>
> (4.3.149–51)

When the Princess slips into the familiar form, it is again at a moment of high emotional tension in her penultimate speech to the King ('And, by this virgin palm now kissing thine, / I will be thine . . . If this thou do deny, let our hands part' (5.2.800–1, 805)). Rosaline addresses the King in this way (5.2.208) and Berowne the Princess (5.2.230, 237), but only when the ladies have exchanged favours and are disguised as each other. The King uses the familiar form to the Princess when he talks to Rosaline thinking she is his love (5.2.205, 210), but otherwise he only uses it to her at the end of their first meeting (2.1.170, 178) and at the end of their penultimate conversation: 'my heart is in thy breast' (5.2.810).

This relative degree of formality about the way people address each other contributes to the play's 'high' style. Among the elements that support its 'low' style is its heavy reliance on proverbs. According to R. W. Dent's figures, only *Romeo and Juliet* and *King Lear* have more proverbs in them than *Love's Labour's Lost*: the respective figures for the plays are 223, 197 and 189 (Dent, 3–4). The play's use of proverbial language, setting courtly against popular culture, can be associated with its interest in the cliché and catch-phrase, with trying to represent some of the ways in which people actually spoke or were expected to speak. These range from the witty banter of the courtiers to the empty phrases Jaquenetta comes out with: 'Lord, how wise you are!', 'With that face?', 'Fair weather after you' (1.2.132–8).[1] Shakespeare sets a fairly formal concern with grammar, logic and rhetoric against these more colloquial elements. Moth's clever exercises in reasoning and his grasp of the elements of grammar (for example, 1.2.9–23, 3.1.38–42) contrast with Holofernes' more laboured use of them, and these in turn present a contrast to Berowne's glib reasoning, seen at its most fluent in his speech ('Have at you then, affection's men-at-arms') towards the end of 4.3.

Coleridge said that Berowne's speech was 'logic clothed in rhetoric' (1.94), yet Swinburne described it as having 'the grace of a light and radiant fancy enamoured of itself, begotten between thought and mirth, a child-god with grave lips and laughing eyes' (Furness, 363). These two different but highly characteristic responses to Berowne's arguments illuminate a paradoxical tension in the play between the argumentative and the lyrical, between reason and rhyme (for the last two, see M. Evans, 118–19). Its intellectual toughness, its concern with the logical and rhetorical uses of language, combine with a lack of plot and a certain lack of interest in individualized characters to produce what Coleridge, again, called a play of 'intellectual action' (1.94). Taken on its own, this would be to misrepresent what the play is actually like (which Coleridge does not do), to neglect its lyrical freshness which turns into an autumnal elegiac mood. The paradoxical nature of the play, its concern with argument and lyric, with the high and the low and so on, can be found in its espousal of the paradox itself. This is clearly announced by Berowne in the play's first scene:

---

1   Wilson, 'Diction', 115, compares these with Silena's empty talk in Lyly's *Mother Bombie* and with Luce's in *The Comedy of Errors*.

So study evermore is overshot.
While it doth study to have what it would,
It doth forget to do the thing it should;
And when it hath the thing it hunteth most,
'Tis won as towns with fire: so won, so lost.
(1.1.140–4)

The winning and losing of towns in battle is like the winning and losing of love: at the end of the play, just when the lords think they have won the love of the ladies, they lose them. Earlier, at the moment when Berowne – 'How well he's read, to reason against reading' (1.1.94) – concludes his revisionary argument to permit the lords to court the ladies, he returns to the paradox, 'Let us once lose our oaths to find ourselves, / Or else we lose ourselves to keep our oaths' (4.3.335–6). The genre gets to the heart not just of the play's humanist concerns and its delight in inversion ('O paradox! Black is the badge of hell', 4.3.250), but to its grappling with closed and open systems of thought. Shakespeare's sense of his own art is well conveyed by the Princess's remark to the King towards the end of the long final scene, 'That sport best pleases that doth least know how', to which the ever acute and perceptive Berowne replies, 'A right description of our sport, my lord' (5.2.514, 519). In true Renaissance fashion, the paradox, far from being a sign of intellectual weakness, allows Shakespeare to resolve the conflicting demands of the play into its final songs which seek to combine the lyrical and the argumentative.

STRUCTURE

Now customarily divided into five acts, the play consists of some nine scenes – the same number as in Shakespeare's other 'sourceless' plays, *A Midsummer Night's Dream* and *The Tempest*, for which see below, p. 61. The play's last scene (5.2) is the longest in Shakespeare's work, but, despite its massive length of just over

900 lines, the scene is undivided and the stage never completely empties. It consists of an extended series of amatory encounters which raise and thwart the audience's expectations; to these are added the broad comedy of the show of the Worthies and the chilling entry of Marcadé. The first half of the scene is taken up with the courtly characters. The Princess's party is joined after line 157 by the King's men, who have come disguised as Muscovites, fulfilling the threatened assault spoken of at the end of 4.3; but, instead of neatly pairing off, the couples are deliberately mismatched, since the ladies put on masks to confuse them. Following some conversation, the lords depart after line 264 and the ladies are left alone on stage with Boyet for under fifty lines. As the ladies leave, the King and his men appear again in their own clothes after line 309, have a few words with Boyet and are almost immediately joined once more after line 336 by the ladies, who have unmasked. Now their conversation continues uninterrupted until the show of the Worthies is announced as ready at lines 485–6. The second half of the scene is itself divided into two parts. The first presents the show with the entrance of Armado, who gives the King the prologue, followed by Costard, Nathaniel and Holofernes with Moth and Armado himself as Worthies. It is brought to an end by the entry of Marcadé after line 710. He delivers his grim news and then the Worthies leave (719): the male and female courtiers are at last left alone with each other, and the Princess's three ladies, who have been silent throughout the show (and before, in fact from line 453 to line 780), have their first chance to speak again. Their exchanges come to an end when first Armado and '*all*' re-enter after lines 866 and 878, respectively. The concluding songs are performed to what is evidently a full stage, including Dull, who last spoke in 5.1, promising to play the drum for the dance of the Worthies, and it may well permit Jaquenetta, previously seen in 4.3, to go off with Armado. Part of the renewed energy of the second half of the long scene comes from a fresh interaction, for it is only just after halfway through the scene that the courtiers at last meet Armado, who was going to

entertain them with stories during their retreat (1.1.168–71); previously they have only had contact with him through his letters.

If 5.2 provides one lengthy series of climaxes and anticlimaxes to the play, a stage which regularly fills and (never quite) empties, it is well prepared for, especially in 4.3, the overhearing scene. Early in the play a parallel is set up between Armado and Berowne, who are reluctant lovers of women they do not think are worthy of their affections. At the end of 1.2 Armado has a prose soliloquy dwelling on his love for Jaquenetta and announcing his intention to 'turn sonnet. Devise, wit; write, pen' (1.2.176). The episode anticipates and provides a commentary on Berowne's final speech in 3.1, the soliloquy 'And I, forsooth, in love', which ends with his saying he will 'love, write, sigh, pray, sue and groan' (3.1.199). Berowne, alone of the lords and ladies, is allowed to appear on stage on his own. This marks the play's halfway point, its natural interval. Berowne's last line, 'Some men must love my lady, and some Joan', anticipates the last line of Hiems's song, 'While greasy Joan doth keel the pot' (5.2.917). When the second half of the play begins in 4.1, it starts with the Princess's party, in contrast to the King's party in 1.1: these two scenes which open the play's first and second halves both contain letters from Armado. After his soliloquy at the end of 3.1 Berowne next appears in 4.3 and he is again talking to himself: 'The King, he is hunting the deer; I am coursing myself'; it is the only long prose speech by one of the courtly lovers in the play. As the scene unfolds, first the King, then Longaville and finally Dumaine are exposed to the ridicule of the others as breaking their initial oaths. With the entry of Costard and Jaquenetta bearing Berowne's love-letter, he joins their number, provides the four of them with an excuse for their oath-breaking and ends the scene alone again on stage (cf. Proudfoot, 23). After that, there are no more soliloquies in the play and its action moves towards an apparent conclusion.

This scene (4.3), which contains the arithmetical centre of the play, provides a fair example of how the play's structure relies to a great extent on one fairly simple device, the entry of Costard. At some point, usually at its halfway mark or towards its end, he thrusts into every scene in the play apart from 2.1, where he is excluded from the Princess's party. His central role is suggested by his short exchange alone on stage at the end of 1.1 with Berowne. The two meet again in 3.1 in a conversation framed by soliloquies (Costard's is 3.1.132–9 and Berowne's 3.1.169–200), but have little to say to each other in 4.3. Here Costard enters, almost exactly halfway through the scene, with Jaquenetta (4.3.185.1). The same event takes place at the same moment in the previous scene (4.2.79.1), and the more or less midway point of 5.2 is marked by Costard's entry (5.2.483.1) to be greeted by another bout of witty exchanges with Berowne (5.2.484–508). Costard's regular entries help drive the play on and provide much of its wit: he also contributes to the impression that the play is made out of meetings and muddle. Yet its amatory and sociable whirl disguises some difficulties, chief among which is that two of the four couples are kept apart until the end of the play. Dumaine and Katherine speak to each other for the first and only time at 5.2.811–20 and are immediately followed by the only exchange between Longaville and Maria, who have the next four lines. On the other hand, Berowne and Rosaline and the King and the Princess have plenty of conversation.

The play also has two quite contrived sets of late entries. The most startling is that of Marcadé almost at the very end of 5.2. His four lines change the whole tone and direction of the scene and his unexpected appearance has been compared to that of the Man in Black in Chaucer's *The Book of the Duchess* (Thompson, 85). Such a sudden arrival of an entirely new character bearing important news within sight of the play's ending is very unusual, although it has similarities with the arrival of Jaques De Boys telling of Duke Frederick's sudden conversion by 'an old religious man' in *As You Like It* (5.4.160), or with a sudden descent by one of the gods, like Hymen's appearance in the same play. The other late entry, that of Holofernes and Nathaniel in 4.2, has some parallels with the introduction of the watch, especially of Dogberry and Verges, in 3.3 of *Much Ado*. The two new characters help to reanimate the play's satirical comedy of humorous types, complementing its constant concern with language. In addition to this Holofernes, the petty-school master who teaches boys and girls the hornbook,[1] and the curate Nathaniel are mocked (like the watch in *Much Ado*) as representatives of parochial authority. They also help to fill the stage and supplement the lords who appeared in 2.1 and looked as if they were going to play a minor part in the proceedings.

In fact the lords have only two half-lines (2.1.39 and 80) – they need not even be assigned to different speakers – and their parts soon disappear, probably assumed in Boyet's. The other very minor parts in the play are Marcadé's and the Forester's with only four or five lines each. They are followed by Jaquenetta and Dull appearing respectively in three and four scenes and speaking under twenty and just over thirty lines each. The parts of the two lesser courtly couples are extremely modest: Longaville has just over seventy lines, Maria under forty; Dumaine has about ninety lines, Katherine about fifty. Their parts are sketchy and, as I have suggested, their characters not always easy to differentiate. Nathaniel has slightly less to say than Longaville, yet he is quite clearly drawn. Berowne's is by far the biggest part in the play with nearly 600 lines in five scenes; the King has just over and the Princess just under half that amount. After them, from around 250 to 200 lines, come (in descending order) Armado, Boyet and Costard, followed by the verbose Holofernes with around 180 lines in his three scenes, Rosaline with just under the same amount in the same number of scenes and Moth just below her role. In casting terms the play can be put on by nine men, with six boys playing Moth's and the women's parts, in addition to four or five minor parts for men.[2]

---

1   On this subject, see T. W. Baldwin, *William Shakspere's Petty School* (Carbondale, Ill., 1943), 137–58.

2   See T. J. King, *Casting Shakespeare's Plays* (Cambridge, 1992), 82, 171.

Unless they are included in '*Enter all*' at 5.2.878.1, Dull and Jaquenetta are not part of the show of the Worthies. If they do not appear in 5.2, there is a possible doubling of the parts of Dull, the Forester in 4.1 and Marcadé in 5.2. Stephen Booth (148–9) has suggested that if the roles of Rosaline and Jaquenetta were taken by the same player this would bring out the parallels between Berowne and Armado.

The longest speech in the play is Berowne's 'Have at you then, affection's men-at-arms' (4.3.285–339) followed by Boyet's 'Under the cool shade of a sycamore' (5.2.89–118). The longest speech by a woman is the Princess's 'A time, methinks, too short' (5.2.782–806), almost her last words in the play. It is clear from these figures that Berowne dominates *Love's Labour's Lost*: he is bound to be the sharp focus for the audience's interpretation of its plot and structure.

DATE

Most scholars date *Love's Labour's Lost* to 1594–5 but, although this date is generally accepted, the evidence for it is fairly thin. The play cannot be later than 1598, since it was mentioned then by Meres and the first surviving quarto has that date on its title-page. It also boasts a performance before the Queen 'this last Christmas'. I examine the nature of that claim below (see Appendix 1, pp. 303–4), but the latest date to which it can refer is the Christmas season of 1597–8 and it could belong to the season of 1596–7 or even 1595–6 and before. Despite the large numbers of topical allusions which have been found to lie within the play – 'Most of this', as E. K. Chambers wrote (1.336), 'is mere beating the air' – little internal evidence helps to date it. The most telling reference probably lies in the appearance of the King and his lords in 5.2 as Muscovites. This and other echoes suggest a direct relationship with the Gray's Inn entertainment *Gesta Grayorum* which describes revels beginning on 20 December 1594 and continuing until about 4 March 1595: they included a performance of *The Comedy of Errors* on 28 December 1594. However, it is impossible to determine whether the Gray's Inn show borrowed from Shakespeare's play or whether he borrowed from the entertainment (see above pp. 13–14). Trying to date the play through its French associations is equally unsatisfactory: Bullough pointed out (1.428–9) that Henri IV, King of Navarre, converted to Roman Catholicism in July 1593 and so would have lost English sympathy until his near assassination towards the end of 1594. During this period a King of Navarre would cut an unattractive figure on the stage, but the play may date from before his apostasy or from after the attempt on his life, when his relations with Queen Elizabeth began to improve. Other attempts to date the play on the basis of topical allusions are not convincing.[1]

On stylistic grounds the play has been linked to *Richard II*, *Romeo and Juliet* and *A Midsummer Night's Dream*, the 'lyrical' plays which are usually dated to 1595–6. It may well have been written earlier than them, but this is by no means certain. The link with *Romeo* is particularly marked, not least because Romeo's first love is the dark-eyed Rosaline (1.2.83, 2.4.14): both plays (like *Much Ado* and in a lesser way *The Merchant of Venice*) also have masked courting scenes. *Love's Labour's Lost* is Shakespeare's most heavily rhymed play, followed by *A Midsummer Night's Dream* and *Richard II*, and the use of rhyme also suggests links with the poems (see Appendix 4). None of this, however, allows the date of the play's composition or of its first performance to be fixed with absolute certainty. There is no need to believe it was Shakespeare's first surviving play, as Charles Gildon did in 1710 ('since it is one of the worst of *Shakespeare*'s Plays, nay I think I may say the very worst, I cannot but think that it is his first' (Vickers, *CH*, 2.242)) and T. W. Baldwin was still trying to do in 1947;[2] but, other than a general consensus, there is little

1 For example, E. A. J. Honigmann, *Shakespeare's Impact on his Contemporaries* (Totowa, NJ, 1982), 68–9, proposes a date of 1592 on the basis of two alleged references to Nashe, of which one (4.2.81–5) has been strongly disputed in Ard², 79–80.
2 T. W. Baldwin, *Shakspere's Five-Act Structure* (Urbana, Ill., 1947), 579, 629–64.

hard evidence with which to date it. Nor does working from analogy with the performance and publication histories of the other 'lyrical' plays with which it is usually grouped help advance the dating of *Love's Labour's Lost* beyond the speculative. If, when he wrote *The Blind Beggar of Alexandria* and *An Humorous Day's Mirth*, Chapman knew of Shakespeare's play, then it must have been written by 1596 or 1597 – but the links between the plays are fairly flimsy (see below, pp. 75–6).

It is, however, possible to construct a narrative of Shakespeare's career around and after the various closings of the theatres on account of the plague between August 1592 and the spring of 1594. During this time he put his energies into writing or revising the narrative poems *Venus and Adonis* and *The Rape of Lucrece*, which were published in 1593 and 1594 with dedications to the Earl of Southampton, and he may well have started work on the Sonnets. The death of Ferdinando Stanley, fifth Earl of Derby, in April 1594 more or less coincided with the reopening of the theatres, and these two events led to the reorganization of the London companies. Shakespeare became a sharer in the Lord Chamberlain's Men and the company is first known to have performed at court on 26 and 27 December 1594, the days before the Gray's Inn production of *The Comedy of Errors*. Depending on the tricky matter of *The Comedy*'s date, *Love's Labour's Lost* might have been Shakespeare's first (or second) new play for the company. In this case it may be dated to 1594 and be thought to precede the other 'lyrical' plays. It may have supplied William Kemp as Costard with his first substantial role in the new company. All this is plausible, but there is nothing with which to prove it correct.

SOURCES AND CONTEXTS

Love's Labour's Lost may well be the earliest of Shakespeare's three plays for which no primary source is known; the others are *A Midsummer Night's Dream* and *The Tempest*. I have already suggested that a major influence on the play came through Shakespeare's reading of Sidney, but he is more by way of an influence on it than a source for it. Similarly, the play is in parts reminiscent of the court comedies and the prose romances of John Lyly, especially in the comic use of scholastic knowledge, the advancement of plot through witty debate rather than through deeds, and the careful ordering and patterning of characters and action.[1] The *commedia dell'arte* appears to have supplied character types like the Braggart and the Pedant, types whose origins were preserved in some of the speech prefixes of the quarto for Armado and Holofernes. Similarly, Nathaniel has some of the elements of the flattering hanger-on of Roman New Comedy. But in all these cases there is no more than a general or generic similarity and what Shakespeare does with the material changes it completely.

Other dramatic types can be related to the relatively sophisticated social comedy of humours which became popular during the 1590s: it poked fun at characters dominated by one particular propensity or trait and often satirized the way in which they spoke. *Love's Labour's Lost* is one of the earliest plays of this kind. It mocks the linguistic abuses of Armado, Holofernes and Nathaniel and contains more about the humours than any other of Shakespeare's comedies (except for *The Merry Wives of Windsor*): in it Shakespeare sets out radically different kinds of character. Older critics found perceptible differences between Longaville and Dumaine, Maria and Katherine (T. R. Price in Furness, 366–7), but later discussions of them have judged them – or the lords at least – 'virtually indistinguishable' and 'shadowy figures' (Roesen, 414, 424). On the other hand, characters like Armado, Holofernes, Nathaniel, Costard and even Boyet may be 'in some sense mere types' (Roesen, 417), but that is to a certain extent the point about them: the world of Navarre is not uniformly realistic or unrealistic, but one which moves violently

---

1 There is a useful summary in David Bevington, '"Jack hath not Jill": failed courtship in Lyly and Shakespeare', *SS*, 42 (1990), 1–13, at 1.

between ciphers and overwhelmingly powerful figures who are themselves subject to truly felt and imaginary impulses. In this way Armado, for example, whose homosexuality is strongly suggested, transforms himself into the fantasy world of heroic romance to accommodate his lack of realism about his love. Such extremes, reflected in the way he speaks and writes, make him both a character completely outside an audience's usual experience and one with which it can sympathize and which it might even find full of pathos. The 'humorous' quality of *Love's Labour's Lost* does not prevent it from allowing 'real' characters like Berowne and Rosaline and to a certain extent the King and the Princess to inhabit it, but it does suggest a degree of theatrical self-consciousness about the play.

There are elements in the play which link it to contemporary masks and entertainments. In particular, the musical entry of the lords disguised as Muscovites and accompanied by Blackamoors in 5.2 points towards the revels put on at Gray's Inn during the Christmas season of 1594–5 and published for the first time as late as 1688 under the title *Gesta Grayorum*. In these wordy and elaborate academic entertainments a Prince of Purpoole was elected and held court, receiving an ambassador from the Inner Temple with great formality. Members of both Inns were sworn Knights of the Helmet, a strict chivalric order, and listened to six speeches (written by Francis Bacon) debating the '*Honour, and the Happiness of Our State, that Our Government be rightly bent and directed*' (*Gesta Grayorum*, 32). The 'Councellors' respectively recommended the exercise of war, the study of philosophy, the winning of '*Eternizement and Fame, by Buildings and Foundations*' (35), the increase of 'Absoluteness of State and Treasure' (37), of virtue and of gracious government, pastimes and sports as the best ways of living. The Prince of Purpoole chose the last of these and inaugurated more revels. After a progress through the City and dinner with the Lord Mayor, the ambassador was recalled. On Twelfth Night six Knights of the Helmet returned from Russia where they had been helping the

Emperor against the Tartars (43). Six more Knights then danced before the Prince. When they had finished, trumpets sounded and 'an Ambassador from the mighty Emperor of *Russia* and *Moscovy*', who had 'some Matters of Weight' to discuss, was announced. The ambassador 'came in Attire of *Russia*, accompanied with two of his own Country, in like Habit' (44). After his letters of credence had been read, the ambassador addressed the Prince, praising his fame, referring also to the Knights who had fought the Tartars. They had 'surprized another Army of *Negro-Tartars*' (*sic*) and the ambassador had come to recruit those Knights and a hundred more to return to Russia to subdue the Tartars (46). After feasting and the reading of various letters, the Prince announced he would go to help the Russian Emperor with an army of knights to fight '*the* Negarian Tartars; *more dreadful, the* Barbarian Tartars' (52); he went and did not return until Candlemas, 2 February (53). In a letter written on board his ship on the way back, the Prince apologized for not being able to greet the Queen because his body '*by length of my Journey, and my Sickness at Sea, is so weakened, as it were very dangerous for me to adventure it*' (54–5).

There are similarities here between the revels and Shakespeare's play, with Muscovites in both, black Tartars in one and Blackamoors in the other. The elaborate statutes of the Order of the Helmet might suggest the details of the decrees to which the King and his lords subscribe: the philosophical debate of the six counsellors is reminiscent of the play's academic background. The Prince's exhaustion from his long journey may even glance at the King's supposed sea-sickness (5.2.393). But in addition to doubts as to whether the play borrows from the revels or vice versa, there are few if any verbal links between the two and the elements they share are generic rather than specific: courts, real and imaginary, enjoyed entertaining ambassadors, and witty debate played a part in the entertainments.

Larger and more specific literary debts within the play have also been suggested. More recently it has been claimed that

Marcadé's name was derived from a comedy by Robert Wilson called *The Cobbler's Prophecy*.[1] This was first printed in 1594 (it was registered on 8 June), but the play may have been written as early as 1588 or 1589 and was perhaps performed at court. At its beginning Ralph the Cobbler is visited by the god Mercury, who gives him the power of prophecy. The god tells Ralph that 'I am Mercurie the Messenger of the Gods' (l. 127), but thereafter Ralph refers to him throughout as 'Markedy' (ll. 129, 169), 'Markedie' (ll. 242, 652) and 'Merkedy' (l. 1356).[2] In a play in which 'The words of Mercury are harsh after the songs of Apollo' (5.2.918–19) the resonances between Marcadé, Markedy and Mercury seem at first powerful, but there is nothing else in Wilson's play to suggest Shakespeare was indebted to it: their shared themes are commonplaces and their verbal echoes coincidental.[3] Given this, it is hard to see that an audience, especially a popular one, would have been able to make much of a connection between Marcadé and Mercury without a fairly detailed knowledge of Wilson's play. The case would be altered if it could be established that 'Markedy' was a common error for Mercury, but no other instance of this version of the god's name has so far come to light: as the god of trade, Mercury can be related to the French 'Mercader', which Cotgrave defined as '*A Marchant, or Tradesman*', but he gives 'Mercure' as his French name.

On the other hand, Marcadé's sudden appearance does suggest he is meant to remind the audience of the Roman god Mercury or the Greek Hermes. His many roles as the inventor of letters, the god of rhetoric and of language who marries Philology, the god of interpretation (hermeneutics), the spring god (Mercurius Ver), the father of the Hesperides, the leader of

---

1 Anne Barton, 'A source for *Love's Labour's Lost*', *TLS*, 24 November 1978, 1373–4, and J. M. Nosworthy, 'The importance of being Marcadé', *SS*, 32 (1979), 105–14.
2 *The Cobler's Prophecy 1594*, ed. A. C. Wood, MSR, 1914.
3 In another play, *The Three Ladies of London*, first printed in 1584 and reprinted in 1592, Wilson has an Italian merchant use the phrase 'No point' twice (sig. F1r) in a similar way to its use by Rosaline and Maria (2.1.189, 5.2.277), but the phrase was in use earlier than 1584 (see *OED* point *sb.*[1] 6b).

the Graces, and so on, fit in rather well with the play's concern with words and their significance, with the songs at the end of the play and with the labours of Hercules (see M. Evans). As the messenger of the gods, he is well chosen to announce the French King's death, and this function ties in with his being a psychopomp or conductor of the souls of the dead. This is his role in Marston's *The Malcontent*, probably written in 1603, where he makes a late arrival in the play's last scene as the presenter of a masque of the dead (5.4.66–9, 5.6.56–61).

If at first sight the play's historical background appears to supply a firmer source for it, then it is only so at first sight (cf. Lamb). In 1586 Thomas Bowes published his translation of Pierre de la Primaudaye's *L'Académie française* (Bullough, 1.427–8, 434–5). The work was popular in England – there were further editions in 1589 and 1594 – and had an important influence on English political thinking,[1] being, for example, one of the books prescribed for the Knights of the Helmet in *Gesta Grayorum* (29). It is a bulky compilation of political and moral thought, set in the form of a dialogue between four young gentlemen from Anjou who have withdrawn from the world to study. They are to discuss 'the institution in good manners, and of the means how all estates and conditions may live well and happily'. In addition to their learned discussions under the guidance of a good scholar, they are made to practise chivalric exercises and to go hunting. When the French Wars of Religion break out again, they are ready physically and intellectually to fight in them under their Prince and they return to their discussions when the wars end. La Primaudaye was a follower of the great constitutional theorist Jean Bodin and a proponent of limited monarchy; his work is representative of the contemporary French interest in formal academies which in the end looked back to the fifteenth-century Florentine Neo-Platonic Academy.[2]

---

1   J. H. M. Salmon, *The French Religious Wars in English Political Thought* (Oxford, 1959), 21–2.
2   Frances A. Yates, *The French Academies of the Sixteenth Century* (1947).

La Primaudaye dedicated his book, which provides an analogy rather than a source for Shakespeare's play, to Henri III, who promoted the academic movement through attending his Palace Academy from 1576 to 1579.

Henri III, the son of Catherine de Medici, had succeeded to the French throne in 1574. Since he was a devout Roman Catholic, an effort had been made in 1572 to reconcile the warring religious factions by marrying his sister, Marguerite de Valois, to Henry of Navarre, the leader of the Huguenot or Protestant forces. Along with the French King's rebellious younger brother, François, Duc d'Alençon, Navarre was an important figure in English political circles. While Alençon had a sporadic courtship with Queen Elizabeth which lasted until just before his death in 1584, Navarre had a similarly intermittent relationship with English public opinion. In both 1589 and 1591 English troops were sent out to aid him in his military campaigns; on the second occasion, at the siege of Rouen, the English were led by the Earl of Essex. For a time, Navarre appeared a very attractive figure to the English, but rumours began to spread that he was thinking of converting to Roman Catholicism. Henri III had been assassinated in 1589 but before his death had recognized Navarre as his successor. The Roman Catholic Leaguers agreed to accept Navarre as king, so long as he undertook to protect their faith and to take instruction in it. By the spring of 1593 he had announced his decision to become a Roman Catholic and by the summer had abjured his old faith: he entered Paris and attended mass at Notre-Dame on 22 March 1594. To English eyes his new-found enthusiasm for Roman Catholicism was partly offset by his decision to free France from Spanish occupation. He declared war on Spain in January 1595, successfully defeating the enemy forces in Burgundy in June 1595. As a result of this, his old antagonist Charles de Lorraine, Duc de Mayenne, a leader of the League, made peace with Henri in September.

Navarre's turbulent political and religious life was matched by his unhappy relationship with his wife, Marguerite de Valois.

Their marriage was not a success and they lived apart, with Marguerite taking an active part in the political intrigues of the time. Navarre's court was at Nérac and in 1578 Marguerite, accompanied by her ladies-in-waiting and her mother Catherine de Medici, met Navarre there to discuss her dowry and to try to sort out their marriage: the garden setting and the courtly entertainments were evidently brilliant (Fig. 5). Other meetings took place to try to solve the problems of Navarre's relationship with his wife, including one at Saint-Bris in 1586 between him and his mother-in-law.

These French events were watched with great interest in England. A substantial pamphlet literature made them and the political thinking behind the French Wars of Religion available to English readers. Shakespeare may have read some of these writings or heard other accounts of contemporary French events. But if he seemed to be alluding to current history, writing 'a work of imaginative journalism', his version of it is far from straightforward.[1] Navarre may have been a familiar name to his audience, but his real name was Henri, not Ferdinand. Dumaine's name probably is related to that of the Duc de Mayenne, but the Duc was a bitter opponent of Navarre's until 1595, not his follower. On the other hand, both Henri d'Orléans, Duc de Longueville, and Charles de Gontaut, Duc de Biron (or his father Armand de Gontaut), were loyal adherents of Navarre's. Navarre's oath-taking and oath-breaking were notorious in England, as was his reputation as an unfaithful husband, womanizer and keen huntsman. The names of other characters in the play can be compared to Frenchmen of the time and there were Spaniards in France in the mid-1590s (they took Calais in 1595), yet Armado is not much of a military threat. None of this suggests Shakespeare was writing an allegorical, a political or a topical play. Far from plunging its audience into the middle of a debate about the French Wars of Religion and their worrying

1   Hugh M. Richmond, 'Shakespeare's Navarre', *Huntington Library Quarterly*, 43 (1978–9), 193–216, at 214.

5   The meeting of Henry of Navarre and Marguerite de Valois: *A tournament at the court of France*, Valois tapestry after François Quesnel the elder (1543–1619)

implications for English national security, *Love's Labour's Lost* constantly evades any perceived notion of a relationship between the personal and the political.

Instead of contemporary French politics, critics have sought a source for the play in current English courtly, literary and philosophical circumstances. According to this interpretation the play was part of a complex battle between different factions at court and their followers.[1] Two principal strains of satire can be detected: first, that the play was an attack on the 'School of Night' (the phrase is used by the King, 4.3.251); and, secondly, that it could be related to the quarrel between the Cambridge academic Gabriel Harvey and his foe the London pamphleteer Thomas Nashe. The School of Night was supposed to be a secret atheistical, philosophical and scientific academy, the chief source for English Copernicanism and a precursor of Baconian scientific investigation. It was run by Sir Walter Ralegh under the patronage of Henry Percy, Earl of Northumberland, and his friend Ferdinando Stanley, Lord Strange, fifth Earl of Derby. Others supposed to be involved were writers like Christopher Marlowe, George Chapman and Matthew Roydon as well as the mathematician and astronomer Thomas Harriot, the translator John Florio, the Spanish educationalist Juan Luis Vives and the Italian intellectual Giordano Bruno. Shakespeare, it was supposed, belonged to an opposing group allied to the Earls of Essex and Southampton; it included the writers John Eliot and Thomas Nashe. *Love's Labour's Lost* became a defence of aristocratic women, especially of the Earl of Essex's sisters, Penelope Devereux (Sidney's 'Stella') and Dorothy Devereux, the Countess of Northumberland. Shakespeare was maintaining their beauty against the implied imputations of the 'advanced' philosophers whose minds were allegedly set on higher things. Where personal allegory or satire was sought, it was found:

1   The most convenient listing of the different theories is in Lamb, 49, 53; the classic studies are M. C. Bradbrook, *The School of Night* (Cambridge, 1936), Yates, and R. W. David's Ard².

Moth was Nashe and Holofernes his antagonist Gabriel Harvey or, as Warburton had suggested as long ago as 1747, John Florio, in which case Harvey was Armado, who has also been identified with the Spanish exile and correspondent of the Earl of Essex, Antonio Perez, and so on.[1]

The effect of all this was to turn the play into an enigma, a riddle, which only those in the know could solve: and those in the know inevitably turned out to be factions at court and London's literary elite. The nearest the play's hidden mysteries were allowed to come to the truly popular were the Martin Marprelate controversies (Ard[2], xxxiv–xxxvii). Stirred into the secret society of the School of Night were enigmatic and mysterious figures such as Henry Percy, the 'Wizard' Earl, his brilliant follower, Harriot, and Bruno, whose reputation as a sinister character linked to the world of espionage and treachery still survives.

Of course, it is easier to put forward elaborate theories about what is really going on in the play than to disprove them. The play's language and its often obscure (and obscene) jokes have allowed critics to feel that something other than its ostensible subject is being discussed. For example, when Armado calls Moth 'my tender juvenal' (1.2.8) commentators have pointed out that the satirist Nashe was associated with the Roman writer and that Holofernes' puzzlement about 'Person' and 'pierce-one' (4.2.81) could be taken as an allusion to Nashe's pamphlet *Pierce Penniless his Supplication to the Devil* (1592). Similarly, the verses on the fox, the ape and the humble-bee in 3.1, the reference to Holofernes' school as the 'charge-house on the top of the mountain' (5.1.75–6), the continuous jokes about counting and arithmetic, the idiosyncratic style of Armado's writings and speeches and the whole business of the Nine Worthies and their composition have always been ripe for elucidation by theorists. Older approaches which have sought to establish one-to-one and

---

1   Gustav Ungerer, *A Spaniard in Elizabethan England: The Correspondence of Antonio Pérez's Exile*, 2 vols (1974–6), 2.377–98.

consistent identifications and explanations have been joined by less rigid and more glancing interpretations.

There has also been a movement against such approaches to the play, one which argues from the specific – that 'the school of night' is no more than a misprint in quarto and Folio – to the general: that Elizabethan allegory, satire and topicality do not work in the ways in which commentators have explained the play.[1] Plays on the stage were not understood by such obscure allusions. When dramatists, such as Thomas Middleton in *A Game at Chess*, sought to satirize contemporary political events the satire is unmissable, was widely recognized as such and provoked a marked response. Critics have been able to find correspondences between Shakespeare's play and contemporary circumstances, including literary works, such as Chapman's *The Shadow of Night*, not because Shakespeare was alluding to or was 'replying' to them, but because they come out of the same social, political, philosophical and literary culture. The shifting sands of Elizabethan court intrigue and literary rivalry provide an attractive foundation on which to build theories about the play and about Shakespeare's early career, but they distract attention from the play's far more bracing engagement with its own art and ideas. And just as it is possible to find correspondences with Lyly's plays (which also seem to supply tempting glimpses of political and religious allegory), the *commedia dell'arte*, the Gray's Inn revels, the French Wars of Religion, and so on, there is a difference between Shakespeare's drawing on these elements in a general or diffused way and his consciously deciding at this point in his career that he would write a play that directly alluded to or even was 'about' them.

Instead of trying to turn these alleged contemporary associations into direct sources for the play, it is perhaps more profitable to look at some of the more obvious relations between *Love's*

---

1   See Lamb, but also Ernest A. Strathmann, 'The textual evidence for "The School of Night"', *MLN*, 56 (1941), 176–86, and John W. Shirley, *Thomas Harriot: A Biography* (Oxford, 1983), 358–79, for a detailed account of the myths and facts concerning Northumberland's household.

Labour's Lost and Shakespeare's other works from this period. As is often the case, he borrowed and reused material quite freely from his own writing, so much so that with the Sonnets it is impossible to determine whether the play stimulated the composition of the poems or the poems the play. I have already discussed some of the links between the play and the later *All's Well*, but other relationships – beyond the merely verbal – can be made out, especially with the 'lyrical' plays. The dark Rosaline, perhaps related to the Dark Lady of the Sonnets, and masking also appear in *Romeo and Juliet*, Berowne's and Boyet's courtly elegance provides a parallel to Mercutio's gentlemanly conversation. The growing darkness, literal and metaphorical, which envelops the court of Navarre as the play progresses is linked to a concern with the light which shines within the dark Rosaline. The association between love and darkness in the play finds a fuller expression in *Romeo and Juliet*, where 'love is entirely a thing of the night' and is morbidly bound up with death.[1]

The comedy's concern with the power of language and the arbitrariness of words is shared with much of *Richard II* ('How long a time lies in one little word!', 1.3.213). Whereas almost all of *Love's Labour's Lost* can be played in daylight until 'It grows dark' and then 'The scene begins to cloud' (5.2.624, 716), most of another park play, *A Midsummer Night's Dream*, takes place at night. Both conclude with shows put on to entertain well-born audiences. At the end of what may be the earlier comedy 'Jack hath not Jill' (5.2.863), but in the middle of the later one (3.2.461–3) Puck assures the audience:

> Jack shall have Jill;
> Nought shall go ill:
> The man shall have his mare again, and all shall be well.

Titania is smitten by the transformed Bottom in a comic and troubling meeting of the high and the low, which was perhaps

1   Philip Parsons, 'Shakespeare and the mask', *SS*, 16 (1963), 121–31, at 124.

anticipated by the knight Armado's passion for the dairymaid Jaquenetta: such unusual *de haut en bas* relationships also play a part in *As You Like It*. It is hard to avoid seeing Dull with his malapropisms as a precursor to Dogberry in *Much Ado* and equally possible to find, as Coleridge among others did (2.108), something of Berowne's and Rosaline's sharp wittiness in the combative and playful exchanges between Beatrice and Benedick.

Some of the other elements which go to make up the play, especially the structural ones, like the use of mistaken identity, overhearing, the misdirected letter, of the self-contained scene or play within the play, and of the sudden, late and unexpected entrance, occur regularly elsewhere in Shakespeare's plays. Character types can also be said to recur: Armado's poor command of English is mocked in a way which provides a foretaste of the comedy caused by Dr Caius' French in *The Merry Wives of Windsor*, and the melancholy traveller Armado looks forward to Jaques in *As You Like It*. The clash of the unrealistic scheme against human nature in which the scourge of sexual transgressors finds himself a guilty party anticipates elements in *Measure for Measure*.[1] Even Ferdinand, King of Navarre, dispatched to a hermitage, may look forward to Ferdinand in *The Tempest*, sentenced to carry logs.[2]

EARLY HISTORY

The first surviving edition of the play is a quarto published in 1598 without entry in the Register of the Stationers' Company. The title-page of this printing, which attributes the play to Shakespeare by name, boasts that it was 'presented before her Highnes this last Christmas' and that it was 'Newly corrected and augmented'. These two last claims need to be treated with

---

1 Cf. Roesen, 413–14, and Cyrus Hoy, '*Love's Labour's Lost* and the nature of comedy', *SQ*, 13 (1962), 30–40, at 33, 35–7.
2 Stanley Wells, 'Shakespeare without sources', in *Shakespearian Comedy*, 58–74, at 66.

caution. It may have been acted at court, but that does not necessarily mean that it was written with a courtly audience in mind
or that it was revised for such a royal occasion; it may have begun
life in the public theatre. Similarly, the statement that it was
acted at court 'this last Christmas' (which can be related to the
'Christmas comedy' Berowne refers to at 5.2.462) need not fix
the performance to 1597–8. The question of authorial correction and augmentation also deserves some scepticism. The
title-page formula may imply an earlier shorter version of the
play, but does not have to. There may have been a previous edition with a text significantly different from the one published in
1598, but it may have been more or less identical; or there may
never have been an earlier edition. I discuss the evidence, which
is by no means easy to interpret, in Appendix 1.

The play's earliest known admirer was probably George
Chapman. In his first two comedies, *The Blind Beggar of
Alexandria* of 1596 and *An Humorous Day's Mirth* of 1597, he
seems to show some knowledge of *Love's Labour's Lost.*
Chapman's two comedies are more developed as humours plays
than Shakespeare's is and anticipate the genre which was fully
launched by Jonson's *Every Man in his Humour* of 1598. *The
Blind Beggar* has one scene featuring a 'Martiall Spaniardo'
called Bragadino whose affected way of speaking ('I loue few
wordes') is reminiscent of the braggart Armado: like him,
Bragadino, 'that neuer before drempt of a womans concauitie'
(Sc. 2.23, 37–8, 65), falls in love with a lady. This brief appearance suggests Chapman may have been exploiting Armado's
risibility. In *An Humorous Day's Mirth* his debt to Shakespeare
appears to be slightly more extensive. The play features a show
in its last scene, presented by a Boy who is extensively interrupted (5.2.129ff.), during which a maid is revealed to be already
pregnant (5.2.249). The maid is called Jaquina, which is reminiscent of Jaquenetta, and the play also features a courtier called
Lemot, whose name, like Moth's, allows for jokes about words
and motes (1.5.55–64): 'we shall not haue one mot of Monsieur

Lemot, but it shal be as it were a mote to drown al our conceit in admiration'. There are a few verbal echoes of *Love's Labour's Lost* in Chapman's play (see the commentary to 1.2.92–3 and 5.1.74) and he makes use of the proverbial title in the line 'my labor is not altogether lost' (2.1.102), but the correspondences are not extensive.

The publication of the quarto text of Shakespeare's play in 1598 coincided with, and contributed to, the vogue for satire and the comedy of humours. Its treatment of speech manners and of affectation made it a natural companion piece for Jonson's *Humour*s plays. Looked at in this way it also suggests something about Shakespeare's own reputation as a humorist at the end of the century. The title-pages of Shakespeare's three Falstaff plays (*1* and *2 Henry IV* and *The Merry Wives of Windsor*), published respectively in 1598, 1600 and 1602, advertise themselves as depicting Sir John's '*humorous conceits*', or simply his 'humours', and the 'sundrie variable and pleasing humors, of Syr *Hugh* the Welch Knight, Iustice *Shallow*, and his wise Cousin M. *Slender*'. The contemporary appetite for this sort of comedy was also fed by the popularity of verse satire and the epigram, whether printed or circulated in manuscript: the 'fondling motley humorist' of Donne's first satire, for example, or the individuals hidden behind Latinate names and mocked in John Harington's epigrams could be said to belong to the same or at least to a world similar to that of *Love's Labour's Lost*.

In 1598, the year of its first known publication, there are three important contemporary allusions to the play. In that year Robert Tofte published his poem *Alba: The month's mind of a melancholy lover*, a sequence of poems written in the six-line stanzas also used in *Venus and Adonis*. The object of Tofte's affections, Alba, was a married lady whose love he fails to win, and he ends up turning his mind to higher things, resolving his earthly love into a Platonic one. One of the poems alludes directly to Shakespeare's play:

LOVES LABOR LOST, I once did see a Play,
Ycleped so, so called to my paine,
Which I to heare to my small Ioy did stay,
Giuing attendance on my froward Dame,
 My misgiuing minde presaging to me Ill,
 Yet was I drawne to see it gainst my Will.

This *Play* no *Play*, but Plague was vnto me,
For there I lost the Loue I liked most:
And what to others seemde a Iest to be,
I, that (in earnest) found vnto my cost,
 To euery one (saue me) twas *Comicall*,
 Whilst *Tragick* like to me it did befall.

Each Actor plaid in cunning wise his part,
But chiefly Those entrapt in *Cupids* snare:
Yet All was fained, twas not from the hart,
They seemde to grieue, but yet they felt no care:
 Twas I that Griefe (indeed) did beare in brest,
 The others did but make a show in Iest.

Yet neither faining theirs, nor my meere Truth,
Could make her once so much as for to smile:
Whilst she (despite of pitie milde and ruth)
Did sit as skorning of my Woes the while.
 Thus did she sit to see LOVE lose his LOVE,
 Like hardned Rock that force nor power can moue.
        (*Alba*, sig. G5r)

Tofte had travelled in Italy and was still there in February 1594; it is not known when he got back to England, but he was certainly there by Trinity term (31 May to 19 June) and by January 1598 was living in Holborn, probably near to Barnard's Inn.[1] There is no evidence that he was ever at the court and so, if the episode were based on a real occasion, it seems likely the play was per-

1   Franklin B. Williams, 'Robert Tofte', *RES*, 13 (1937), 282–96, at 288, 290, 292.

formed in the public theatre: as Hibbard pointed out (Oxf[1], 2), this is not the only reference to the theatre in the volume, for Tofte 'refers to Tamburlaine, echoes *The Spanish Tragedy* twice, and *Romeo and Juliet* at least once'.

A second allusion in 1598 occurs in a pamphlet called *A Health to the Gentlemanly Profession of Servingmen* by one I. or J. M. and consists of an extended version of Costard's joke about a guerdon being better than a remuneration as a reward (3.1.165–8): the joke refused to lie down and die, appearing in print as late as 1654 in Alexander Brome's *The Cunning Lovers* (*Allusion-Book*, 2.33). *A Health*, which was entered in the Stationers' Register on 15 May, is a lament for the decline of the servingman's position and the decay of liberality; it has been strongly attributed to Gervase Markham.[1] Markham was closely involved with the Earl of Southampton and the tract was printed by William White, who was also responsible for the first quarto of the play. If it is by Markham, he might have come across Shakespeare's play through his aristocratic friend, or through the printer White, or he might simply have seen the play at the theatre.

The third reference from 1598 is the most famous. On 7 September Francis Meres's *Palladis Tamia: Wit's Treasury* was entered in the Stationers' Register; its dedication was dated 19 October. Its publisher was Cuthbert Burby, who also published the first quartos of *Love's Labour's Lost* and *Romeo and Juliet*. Then living in London, Meres showed he knew of six of Shakespeare's comedies: 'his *Gentlemen of Verona*, his *Errors*, his *Loue labors lost*, his *Loue labours wonne*, his *Midsummers night dreame*, & his *Merchant of Venice*'.[2] The order in which Meres listed the plays is similar to that in which they were arranged in the First Folio, although they are interspersed there with plays written later; the one early comedy Meres does not mention is *The Taming of the Shrew*, nor does he mention *Much Ado About*

1   F. N. L. Poynter, *A Bibliography of Gervase Markham 1568?–1637*, Oxford Bibliographical Society, NS, 5 (1962), 66–9.

2   The passage is reproduced in facsimile in S. Schoenbaum, *William Shakespeare: A Documentary Life* (Oxford, 1975), 140.

Nothing, which may possibly have been written by the time he was drawing up his lists. While Meres was at work on his book, the only quarto of a comedy he could have seen in print was that of *Love's Labour's Lost*. His knowledge of the other plays may have been by report or directly from a manuscript or from the theatre. It would be wrong to try to make anything much out of the form he gave to the play's title – '*Loue*', not '*Loues*' – or to suggest he supplies evidence either way for the existence (or non-existence) of an earlier quarto. But something must be said about what is evidently meant to be a companion piece, the equally grammatically unpossessive *Loue labours wonne*. If there is a relationship between the Folio order and Meres's list, it is not clear where it should come in the Folio, since *A Midsummer Night's Dream* follows directly on from *Love's Labour's Lost*.

Nothing more was known for certain about *Love's Labour's Won* until the discovery in 1953 of a list of books on a leaf of paper which formed part of the binding of a volume of later sermons. T. W. Baldwin, who published the list, argued that it came from an Exeter stationer's accounts of what he had in stock and what he had sold during August 1603.[1] Under the heading '[inte]rludes & tragedyes' the stationer, whom Baldwin argued was one Christopher Hunt, set down the titles of sixteen English plays. These included pieces by Lyly, Thomas Heywood and Greene, in addition to 'marchant of vennis', 'taming of a shrew', 'knak to know a knave' and 'knak to know an honest man', 'loves labor lost' and 'loves labor won'. Before the finding of this document it was just possible to argue that Meres's reference to the last play was made up to provide a symmetrical list in which the titles of six comedies were balanced against the titles of six tragedies. Reviewing Baldwin's book, G. K. Hunter called the identity of the stationer and the purpose of the list into question.[2] He suggested that, rather than representing a stationer's stock,

1   T. W. Baldwin, *Shakspere's 'Love's Labor's Won': New Evidence from the Account Books of an Elizabethan Bookseller* (Carbondale, Ill., 1957).
2   *RES*, NS, 10 (1959), 412–13.

the list, with its symmetrical organization, pointed towards its being a note of books the compiler would like to see or to buy. Of course, its writer could have made up the play's title to set against the previous item and as a parallel to the preceding matching pair of titles. However, the two *Knack* comedies certainly exist and there is little reason to suppose he was merely being playfully imaginative. The list also specifies two copies of four plays, four copies of *Enough is as Good as a Feast* and three copies of *Friar Bacon*. These quantities suggest it represents items the compiler had rather than ones he wanted. Equally, there are objections to supposing he was copying out Meres's account here, since 'taming of a shrew' is not in his group of comedies. Furthermore, as Baldwin pointed out (14), the forms 'loves labor lost' and 'loves labor won' differ from those used by Meres and from those in the 1598 quarto; instead, they agree with the form used in the catalogue of plays in the First Folio, *Loues Labour lost*.

There therefore seems to be strong if not incontrovertible evidence for the existence of a play by Shakespeare with the title *Love's Labour's Won*. A play of this name existed by 1598 and had reached print by the summer of 1603 although like *Love's Labour's Lost* it was apparently not entered in the Stationers' Register. It may be the title of a lost play which for some reason was not included in the Folio or the alternative title for an extant play: not surprisingly, the second possibility has attracted most comment. At first sight the title would fit *The Taming of the Shrew* rather well, but since Hunt included 'taming of a shrew' in his list this seems unlikely, unless there was a lost printing of *The Taming of the Shrew* under the title *Love's Labour's Won* and Hunt had copies of both *Shrew* plays. If *Much Ado About Nothing* is earlier than has generally been thought, then it could be that comedy under a different title. There is also the possibility that it represented a later play in a different form under a different title. Again, *Much Ado* might fit this bill, and other scholars have suggested *All's Well That Ends Well* and, more surprisingly, *Troilus and Cressida*. The alliterative nature of *Love's Labour's Lost*'s title might indicate it preceded *Love's Labour's Won*, which acted as some sort of sequel. Yet, beyond the obvious interpretation of love's labours being rewarded, it is not easy to understand what that title means: it was proverbial to lose one's labour, but one wins a prize, not one's labour. Leslie Hotson saw this difficulty and, citing *The Two Gentlemen of Verona*, 1.1.33 ('If [the object of love be] lost, why then a grievous labour won'), argued that the title means 'Love's sorrow is gained', 'trouble, unhappiness, or grief' are earned or gained.[1] Whatever the title means, the topic is finally indeterminable. But if there is a link between *All's Well* and *Love's Labour's Lost*, as I have suggested above, then perhaps *All's Well* should be also associated with *Love's Labour's Won*.

If no more was heard of that play in print after 1598, its companion piece did gain some attention. William Jaggard took three of the lords' four poems and reprinted them – along with versions of two of the Sonnets – in his unauthorized collection *The Passionate Pilgrim*: the exact date of the first edition is not known, but it was probably published in the same year as the second edition, 1599. In the next year, 1600, one of the three poems from the play, Dumaine's verses to Katherine, was printed for a third time in the anthology *England's Helicon*. Two collections of poetical quotations were published in the same year: Robert Allott's *England's Parnassus* and John Bodenham's *Belvedere*, edited by Anthony Munday, both contain passages from *Love's Labour's Lost*.[2] There are three quotations from the play in the first of these with a total of five lines but without significant variations. The second has five quotations of five lines in all, of which three contain the sorts of substantive differences which are common in the two collections.

---

1 Leslie Hotson, 'Love's Labour's Won', in *Shakespeare's Sonnets Dated and Other Essays* (1949), 37–56, at 38–42.
2 *'Englands Parnassus' Compiled by Robert Allot, 1600*, ed. Charles Crawford (Oxford, 1913), nos 576, 594, 1292; *Allusion-Book*, 2.493.

In the same year John Weever published his long and curious poem, *Faunus and Melliflora, or the Original of our English Satires*. Weever was a Cambridge graduate, born in 1575 or 1576, who came down to London probably in 1598. In 1599 he published a volume of *Epigrams*, one of which was addressed to Shakespeare (sig. E6r) and in which he implied some knowledge of *Venus and Adonis*, *The Rape of Lucrece*, '*Romea Richard*; more whose names I know not'. By the next year his knowledge had expanded to include *Love's Labour's Lost*. In addition to echoes from the play, the long poem is indebted to *Venus and Adonis*, Sidney's *Arcadia* and Marlowe's *Hero and Leander*.[1] Two passages are clearly derived from Shakespeare's comedy:

> With that in his he tooke her moisty hand,
> (How white God knowes) and gently did demand . . .
>
> (861–2)

and

> to what end were you borne?
> Remember but, and you wil be forsworne . . .
> A Votaresse, a Secluse, and a Nunne,
> Nay you must be forsworne when all is done:
> For, can you study, fast, and pray among?
> No no, (faire nymph) your stomacke is too yong,
> Your beautie will dispense with this decree,
> You must be periurde of necessitie.
>
> (915–16, 919–24)

The first passage derives from 5.2.411 and simply adapts Berowne's line 'By this white glove – how white the hand, God knows!', but the second, where Faunus is reproving Melliflora for swearing that she will die a virgin ('It is not lawfull you should make a vow, / The which Religion cannot wel allow' (909–10)), is

---

1 See E. A. J. Honigmann, *John Weever: A Biography of a Literary Associate of Shakespeare* (Manchester, 1987); John Weever, *Faunus and Melliflora (1600)*, ed. A. Davenport, (Liverpool, 1948).

more interesting. Weever's language here and in the surrounding lines is steeped in that of the play, with its parallel oaths to study and to fast, its stress on the breaking of vows, of being forsworn and perjured. Davenport pointed all this out and also that lines 915–16 are related to Berowne's couplet at 4.3.214–15 (with the same rhyme), line 922 comes in part from 4.3.290, lines 923–4 echo the King at 1.1.145–6 and 'flat treason gainst all Deitie', line 933, comes from 4.3.289. It is equally important that the whole passage shows that Weever interpreted the vow of virginity as an irreligious one, something that the Princess states explicitly, ''Tis deadly sin to keep that oath' (2.1.105), but which is also alluded to elsewhere (1.1.151–2 and 4.3.359).

Weever's use and understanding of the play are distinctive and suggest a keen interest in Shakespeare and his work. He might have read the play or, probably like Tofte, seen it at the public theatre. Its next known performance was in a rather more exclusive setting. In the Revels Accounts it is listed as one of the pieces – the others included *Othello*, *The Merchant of Venice*, *The Merry Wives of Windsor*, *Measure for Measure*, *The Comedy of Errors*, *Henry V* and Jonson's *Humour* plays – put on for the Christmas season of 1604–5. The accounts state that *Love's Labour's Lost* was performed 'Betwin Newers Day And Twelfe Day', that is between 2 and 5 January, but there is no corresponding entry for it, as there should be, in the Chamber Accounts. This discrepancy remains unexplained – the scribe may simply have written the wrong dates down.[1] Yet there seems to have been a performance planned for around this time, attended by the Queen, at the Earl of Southampton's house, formerly the Bishop of Lincoln's London residence. In an undated letter, written '*from your library*', Sir Walter Cope, who lived in the Strand, wrote to his friend Robert Cecil, Lord Cranborne:

---

1 *Collections Volume XIII: Jacobean and Caroline Revels Accounts, 1603–1642*, ed. W. R. Streitberger, Malone Society (1986), 9.

Si*r*, I haue sent and bene all thys morning huntynge for players Iuglers & Such kinde of Creaturs but fynde them harde to fynde, wherfore leavinge notes for them to seeke me, burbage ys come, & Sayes ther ys no new playe that the quene hath not seene, but they haue Revyved an olde one, *Cawled Loves Labore lost* whi*c*h for wytt & mirthe he sayes will please her excedingly And Thys ys apointed to be playd to Morowe night at my Lord of Sowthamptons vnless yow send a wrytt to Remove the Corpus *Cum Causa* to yor howse in strande. Burbage ys my messenger Ready attendyng yor pleasure.

Further information about the event was supplied by Dudley Carleton in a letter to John Chamberlain written on 15 January 1605:

But it seemes we shall haue Christmas all the yeare, and therfore I shall neuer be owt of matter. The last nights reuels were kept at my L*o*rd of Cranborns, where the Q: wi*t*h the D: of Holst and a great part of the court were feasted. and the like two nights before at my L*o*rd of Southamptons. The Temples haue both of the*m* done somewhat since twelftide, but nothing memorable, saue that at middle-temple it was obserued on friday last at night the greatest part of the femal audience was of the sisterhoode of blackfriers, and not so much as owr frends in the whitefriers or those wi*t*howt newgate were absent. but theyr ill luck was that by reason of the press of people nothing could be done that night. onely m*aste*r Ross made an extemporal speach in excuse.[1]

As Chambers argued, Carleton's point was that the festivities extended beyond their traditional close on Twelfth Night and

---

1 Hatfield House, The Marquess of Salisbury MS 189/95; Public Record Office, London SP/14/12, f. 32r. The fullest version of Cope's letter is printed in the Third Report of the Royal Commission on Historical Manuscripts (1872), Appendix, 148; cf. Chambers, 2.332, and his *The Elizabethan Stage*, 4 vols (Oxford, 1923), 4.139–40.

therefore he was talking about the period from 6 to 14 or 15 January. Since Jonson's *Mask of Blackness* was performed on 6 January, when Charles was made Duke of York, and performances of *Henry V* and *Every Man Out of his Humour* took place on 7 and 8 January, the likelihood is that Shakespeare's play was put on either at Cecil's house in the Strand or at Southampton House between 9 and 14 January. Cope praised its 'wytt & mirthe', but he also suggested the play made a reasonable alternative to players and jugglers. Nevertheless, the choice of *Love's Labour's Lost* for performance before Queen Anne seems appropriate: if it was put on at Southampton House, not in the Strand, it provides a further link between Shakespeare and his early patron and may reveal something about the new queen's relations with her courtiers.

Nothing more is known for certain about the play's stage history until the publication of the second quarto, itself a reprint of the Folio text of 1623, in 1631. Its title-page announced that the play had been 'Acted by his Maiesties Seruants at the Blacke-Friers and the Globe' (Fig. 6). The King's Men moved into the Blackfriars theatre from the Globe in 1609, so, if its information is correct, the second quarto supplies evidence that the play was put on in both the public and the private theatres: the new edition of 1631 might even suggest the play was still being acted by the King's Men in the reign of Charles I. Quartos of Shakespeare's plays went on being published during the 1630s, but only the 1630 edition of *Othello* and the 1631 edition of *The Taming of the Shrew* have similar claims on their title-pages about performance at both theatres, and *Othello*'s may simply have been inherited from the first quarto of 1622.

Although the stage history of *Love's Labour's Lost* in the early seventeenth century is otherwise a blank, it went on being referred to by other writers. There are echoes of it in *The Fair Maid of the Exchange* (1607) – principally of Berowne's 'And I, forsooth, in love' speech at the end of 3.1.[1] In the same year

---

1 *The Fair Maid of the Exchange (1607)*, ed. Peter H. Davison, MSR, 1962 (1963), ll. 489–517.

Loues Labourslost.

A WITTIE AND.
PLEASANT
COMEDIE,

As it was Acted by his Maiesties Seruants at
the Blacke-Friers *and the* Globe.

Written

By WILLIAM SHAKESPEARE

LONDON,

Printed by *W.S.* for *Iohn Smethwicke*, and are to be
fold at his Shop in Saint *Dunstones* Churchyard vnder the Diall.
1631.

6 Title-page of Q2

Thomas Walkington in *The Optic Glass of Humours* adapted Longaville's lines (1.1.26–7) about 'Fat paunches' – already quoted in *England's Parnassus* – and the lines turn up again in John Clarke's *Parœmiologia Anglo-Latina: Or Proverbs, English, and Latin* (1639): by then they had become proverbial. It is possible that in his comedy *The History of the Two Maids of More-clack* (1609), Robert Armin had parts of 4.2 in mind when, in separate episodes in his play, he quotes (sigs. A2v, C4v) the opening lines of Mantuan's first eclogue and uses the tag '*omne bene*'. However, Armin may not be echoing Shakespeare's play, since the Latin lines were familiar from school-books and the phrase little more than a common tag. The only other contemporary reader of the play who can be identified for certain is William Drummond of Hawthornden, who noted he read 'loues labors lost comedie' in 1606; his own copy of the quarto of 1598 survives in Edinburgh University Library.[1]

LATER HISTORY

Whatever the demands of casting and the possibilities of doubling (see above, pp. 58–9), there are few problems in staging the play once its textual tangles have been sorted out. Despite the dominance of Berowne's role, it is an ensemble piece which calls for detailed rehearsals and close attention to the company's working together. One feature that makes it attractive to the contemporary theatre is that the only scene which requires a setting other than the open stage is 4.3 in which Berowne may have to sit above while he watches his companions (4.3.75–7, 162) come in and read their poems; the King and Longaville may also need hiding places in this scene (Fig. 7). Berowne could hide either in the gallery above the stage or in a property tree like Henslowe's 'baye tree' (319) or of the kind that Marston specified in his comedy *The Fawn* of

---

1 *The Library of Drummond of Hawthornden*, ed. R. H. MacDonald (Edinburgh, 1971), 228 and no. 907.

7 Berowne, the King and Longaville all hide while Dumaine reads his sonnet, 4.3; Royal Shakespeare Company production directed by Terry Hands, 1990

1605 or Jonson used in *The Case is Altered* of 1609. The obvious place for the King and Longaville is behind the pillars which held up the canopy over the stage. If he did hide in the gallery, Berowne may have got there by climbing the tree into it, rather than by going through the tiring house to it. Even here, though, it is not absolutely necessary for Berowne actually to be above and for the King and Longaville really to be hidden; the scene could be played without much physical awkwardness.

The other production demands the play makes were not beyond the resources of Shakespeare's company. During the show of the Worthies Boyet calls for a light because 'It grows dark' (5.2.624), and soon after Marcadé's entrance Berowne says, 'The scene begins to cloud' (5.2.716): at the Globe as the afternoon wore on the stage would naturally (except in summer) have got darker. When it came to costumes, the most exotic outfits would be worn by the lords when they appear disguised as Muscovites 'in shapeless gear' (5.2.303) and by their attendant

8 The arrival of the lords dressed as Muscovites, accompanied by Blackamoors, before the masked ladies, 5.2; Royal Shakespeare Company production directed by Ian Judge (1993)

musical Blackamoors; the Princess and her ladies have to be masked to greet them (Fig. 8). The Nine Worthies needed shields and armour and Act 4 might allow the Princess and the King and their entourages to appear in hunting costumes: the Forester in 4.1 would certainly have to wear a suitably sylvan costume, perhaps like the 'grene cottes' or coats used in Robin Hood plays (Henslowe, 317). Sir Nathaniel and Holofernes might appear in costumes suitable for a curate and a schoolmaster and Marcadé might well wear black in mourning, but Armado's lack of a shirt and 'want of linen' beneath his 'thin-belly doublet' (3.1.17, 5.2.707–10) suggest a certain shabbiness in his appearance as a knight – a shabbiness which he shares with Parolles in *All's Well*.[1]

1   Jean MacIntyre, *Costumes and Scripts in the Elizabethan Theatres* (Edmonton, Alberta, 1992), 147, 199, 202.

Otherwise, there are few essential items called for. In 2.1 Maria must wear white and Rosaline a cap. There has to be some music for the entry of the lords disguised as Muscovites in 5.2, which is anticipated by the sounding of a trumpet. In addition to the various letters and poems with which the characters litter the stage, Nathaniel needs a table-book (5.1.15 SD) and Holofernes might be supplied with more modern educational aids – there is scope for clowning with, for example, a blackboard to illustrate his poem in 4.2. There is little obvious guidance as to how the characters in the play are meant to speak. Armado and the Muscovites presumably have foreign accents but this is nowhere indicated in the text, unless perhaps at 5.2.247. Dull appears to have some difficulty with Armado's name at 1.1.185.

These relatively modest theatrical demands allow producers a great deal of scope in the play's staging, especially for theatrical business, but they give little indication about whether it was intended initially for the popular theatre or for a courtly audience. The play's reliance on linguistic brilliance may have been complemented, especially if it was played before Queen Elizabeth, by elaborate and fantastic costumes. However, its performance history, excellently described by Miriam Gilbert from whom much of the following account has been taken, is largely a blank until this century.

There is no known performance between the first decade of the seventeenth century and 1800: it was the only one of Shakespeare's plays not performed in the eighteenth century (Gilbert, 21). The nearest the play came to the stage appears to have been in 1771, when David Garrick commissioned a musical version, cutting 800 lines and removing the Nine Worthies, but the production was never staged (Gilbert, 21). Nor is there any evidence that an anonymous adaptation, *The Students*, was ever performed. It was published in 1762, cut the play considerably and supplied it with a happy ending (Gilbert, 21–6). Shakespeare's play was next performed at Covent Garden in 1839, when Madame Eliza Vestris staged it as her first production there (Gilbert, 27–9): the evening ended in a near-riot because the shilling gallery had been closed and the play, despite its costumes by the antiquarian J. R. Planché, had only eight more performances. Its acting text was cut and rearranged but it was recognizably Shakespeare's play, performed for the first time in two centuries. It did not, however, inaugurate a flood of productions and it was not revived again until the actor-manager Samuel Phelps put it on at Sadler's Wells in 1857 (Gilbert, 29–36). In the words of a contemporary critic, quoted by Gilbert (33), 'the costumes and the groupings all carry us back to that atmosphere of sylvan aristocracy of which we may read at large in the *Arcadia* of Sir Philip Sydney'.

The play did not disappear entirely during this period. The critical contempt to which it was subject (Johnson is a notable exception) was tied up with the belief that it was Shakespeare's earliest play or at least one of his first. Its particular type of humour was far from popular: Dryden, for example, commented that *Love's Labour's Lost*, *The Winter's Tale* and *Measure for Measure* 'were either grounded on impossibilities, or at least, so meanly written, that the Comedy neither caus'd your mirth, nor the serious part your concernment' (Vickers, *CH*, 1.145). It did, however, allow commentators to use it as a quarry in debates about Shakespeare's learning and about his relations with his contemporaries. Furthermore, its very oddity made some writers question its authenticity – which led others, like Edward Capell, to defend it and try to show how it could be related to Shakespeare's other works (Vickers, *CH*, 5.317–18). Even those most devoted to the study of Shakespeare, such as Edmond Malone, held it in fairly low regard – he wrote of 'the gems that sparkle through the rubbish' (Vickers, *CH*, 6.298) – and the Irish actor Francis Gentleman who contributed introductions and notes to Bell's 1774 edition of Shakespeare could be even more brutal, writing of the dramatist's 'tacking together the scenes of this piece' and describing the language as 'cramp' and the sentiments as 'much laboured' (Vickers, *CH*, 6.106).

A relatively more favourable view of the play can be gathered from its use by Charles Johnson in 1723 to create *Love in a Forest*. This highly unsuccessful piece (it ran for only six perfor-mances) was based mainly on *As You Like It*, but borrowed speeches and lines from other early comedies including *Love's Labour's Lost*. It also supplied several composers with words for settings of songs. One of the earliest of these appears to have been by Thomas Arne, who set versions of Hiems's and Ver's songs: these were performed at Drury Lane in 1740 and proba-bly both were published in the following year (*SMC*, 6495, 6667). The two final songs were relatively popular with com-posers, but there are also early settings of other parts of the play. For example, part of Berowne's great speech at the end of 4.3 ('A lover's eyes will gaze an eagle blind', 308–19) was set by Joseph Kemp and published in about 1810. At around the same time Matthew Peter King published a song based on the end of Dumaine's poem (4.3.112–17). The whole poem was a relative favourite with composers: there are three and possibly four known eighteenth-century settings (*SMC*, 6338, 6342, 6357, 6361, 6365, 6366). More suggestively, the play's concern with academic life and the renunciation of love can be traced in works which appear to have been influenced by it. Tennyson's *The Princess* (1847), for example, is about a similar academy to the one the King of Navarre wishes to set up, but one for women only. Although the poem's plot is different from Shakespeare's play, Tennyson acknowledged his debt to it, and the statutes of the women's college echo those of Navarre's.[1] Tennyson's poem was the main source for W. S. Gilbert's play *The Princess* (1870), which itself was the model for the operetta *Princess Ida* (1884), written with Arthur Sullivan. These literary and musical responses to the play were echoed by the way it was treated by critics such as Pater, Edward Dowden ('a satirical extravaganza'), Swinburne ('a lyrical farce') and so on (Furness, 361, 363). It is

1 *The Poems of Tennyson*, ed. Christopher Ricks (1969), 742–3, and see 2.53–60.

not clear whether these writers had ever seen a production of the play, and even when in 1886 George Bernard Shaw saw one – admittedly an amateur one – he was not greatly impressed by its theatrical potential. In what seems to have been his first Shakespeare review, Shaw tellingly associated the play with Gilbert's comic operas, adding that 'Much of Love's Labor Lost is as objectionable and more tedious'. Although he found it 'full of that bewitching Shakespearean music which tempts the susceptible critic to sugar his ink and declare that Shakespear can do no wrong', he also wondered whether the play was 'worth reviving at this time of day; but I am bound to add that if it were announced to-morrow with an adequate cast, I should make a point of seeing it'.[1]

Phelps's 1857 version of the play was evidently subtle and intelligent, with an ambiguous ending in which the King and his lords may have bidden farewell to the Princess and her ladies with kisses or with more formal bows. His promptbook passed to the Memorial Theatre at Stratford-upon-Avon and was used in short runs of the play, celebrating Shakespeare's birthday, in 1885 and 1907. It was not put on again professionally in London until 1918, when it was staged at the Old Vic, but was performed in New York in 1874 and 1891 (Cam[1], lxi; Gilbert, 37). The subsequent history of the play is to an extent tied up with critical reactions to it. From this point of view, the most important essays on it which have influenced directors and themselves been influenced by productions are Harley Granville-Barker's rehabilitatory preface of 1930 ('Here is a fashionable play; now by three hundred years, out of fashion'), Bobbyann Roesen's (Anne Barton's) brilliant article published in 1953 when she was still an undergraduate, and William Carroll's 1976 book on the play. The important editions of the play by John Dover Wilson (1923), by Richard David (1951), by G. R. Hibbard (1990) and, especially, by John Kerrigan (1982) have also contributed much

---

1 *Shaw on Shakespeare*, ed. Edwin Wilson (Harmondsworth, 1969), 134–5.

to its understanding and current popularity.

Gilbert discusses five important productions in detail, beginning with the 1946 Stratford one by Peter Brook which established a darker, more melancholy and elegiac, reading of the play than had been seen before. She continues with Elijah Moshinsky's not very successful television version of 1984 for the BBC Shakespeare, before describing what was clearly an acute and amusing reading of the play as a 1960s political satire (the King as the Maharishi Mahesh Yogi, his courtiers as the Beatles, Boyet as Truman Capote, Holofernes as Gandhi, the Forester as Ernest Hemingway, and so on) directed by Michael Kahn at Stratford, Connecticut, in 1968. John Barton's two important productions at Stratford-upon-Avon, a relatively ponderous one in 1965 and a more challenging one in 1978, marked an important development in the play's stage history, moving it away from a concern with pure elegance towards an attempt to explore the play as a story of real but uncertain loves: 'Think Chekhov', Barton is reported to have said, 'not Elizabethan' (Gilbert, 99, 112–13).

From these different accounts of productions, including ones by Tyrone Guthrie in 1932 at the Westminster Theatre and then again at the Old Vic in 1936, by Hugh Hunt at the Old Vic in 1949, by David Jones at Stratford-upon-Avon in 1973, by Robin Phillips at Stratford, Ontario, in 1978, when the play was set in 1914 with the rumbling of distant guns, to less impressive productions such as those by Barry Kyle in 1984 and by Terry Hands in 1990, both at Stratford-upon-Avon, it is possible to distinguish several different ways of approaching the play. It can be presented as Michael Kahn did, as a broadly satirical work, with its targets updated from those canonized by Richard David, or it can be turned into a fashionable and amusing comedy of manners in which style and elegance are all-important. If this pushes it into a Restoration or Enlightenment comedy *avant la lettre* – as was done with the BBC Shakespeare version (Fig. 9), partly set in the King's library, and in which the wigs did a lot of

9 The King, the Princess and her ladies in the King's library; BBC television
   production (1984)

the work of the men's acting – a rather different reading takes it
to be a more purely Renaissance work, a meditation on the
nature of pastoral and the inevitable presence of death. In this
view of the play, which was broadly Peter Brook's and which
owed something to an interest in Renaissance iconography, the
play is a series of diversions to distract the audience from the
sudden and unnoticed arrival of death, represented by Marcadé.
In the process the humanity and the feelings of the main characters are in danger of being lost. It was John Barton who sought
to restore the balance by exploring the painful realities about
love which the play presents. By doing this he also brought out
its formal qualities, and this approach suggests that the play is
deeply rooted in its own self-enclosed world. It is a play 'about'
the theatre and its arts of illusion: the key moment is, to a certain extent, moved away from the entrance of Marcadé to the
dialogue of Ver and Hiems, spoken (not sung) in Barton's 1978

version on a raised platform by Nathaniel and Holofernes using small puppets of a cuckoo and an owl (Gilbert, 111–12).

Successful productions of the play depend to a great extent on ensemble playing: the men and women do not have to appear genuinely in love with each other, but there must be some sort of romance, a sexual or erotic charge, between them. An audience is bound to focus on the courtly lovers and look to the fantastics for comic relief. Even so the two worlds of the play are by no means separate – that is part of its point – and they must be integrated. However, that is not to say it is impossible for a particular actor to dominate the stage and set the tone for what happens. Part of what makes it so challenging to put on is that the centre of dramatic power is by no means self-evident. There have been Berownes, like Ian Richardson in David Jones's 1973 Stratford production, who dominate the stage; but equally it is possible for a Boyet, such as Brewster Mason in Barton's 1965 version, his rival who has a far smaller part, to leave his impress on the comedy (Gilbert, 65–6, 124–5). When it comes to the King and the Princess, in Barton's 1978 production a plump Richard Griffiths as the King was well matched with Carmen Du Sautoy's Princess who was fully aware that she was no great beauty (both wore spectacles), yet Maureen Lipman's grown-up anti-romantic Princess in the BBC version was far more arresting than Jonathan Kent's King (Gilbert, 66–8, 95–8, 120–1). The minor parts, especially that of Armado, who has been played by a string of notable actors such as Paul Scofield, Paul Rogers, Michael Hordern, David Warner and Edward Petherbridge, can also attract a great deal of the audience's attention. Kenneth Tynan evidently achieved this when he played Holofernes, in an OUDS production directed by Anthony Besch in Merton College garden in June 1947: he was offered a permanent job at Windsor on the strength of his performance.[1]

---

1   Kenneth Tynan, *Letters*, ed. Kathleen Tynan (1994), 141–2.

The self-conscious theatricality of *Love's Labour's Lost* (for which, see also Carroll, chapter 2) poses problems for actors and directors, but these are relatively minor when placed against the more general difficulty of judging the play's tone. It is, Caryl Brahms wrote, 'less a play with a beginning, a middle and an end, than a pervasive atmosphere', although she acknowledged that it has 'the most beautiful last scene that any play could boast'.[1] For example, how seriously is an audience to take the play's opening vows? Are the King and his courtiers to be portrayed as ridiculous from the start? If so, should the Princess and her party be seen as the centre of sense and order? It is not easy to determine how foolish the fantastics are meant to be or to what extent they are merely types. Armado is clearly intended to be satirized for the way he speaks and for his crush on Jaquenetta, yet he alone finishes the play with his love and he has its last lines. Similarly, a production with a Holofernes who is not (unintentionally) funny in himself, and the cause of laughter in others, would be dreary, but his telling comment about the behaviour of his supposed betters during the show of the Worthies (5.2.623) will lose its considerable force if he is made to appear quite silly. Finally, there is the problematic nature of the play's ending. If the play is Arcadian, does Marcadé's arrival destroy or fulfil the audience's expectations of the setting? The play's performance history can, up to a point, be written around the change that his arrival on stage has on its tone and atmosphere.[2] A director may want to indicate that the royal and courtly couples will come together again after a year and a day or that they will not: equally, this leading question may be deliberately left open.

This theatrical and formal self-consciousness finds some of its expression in the play's concern with the nature of art and the

---

1   'Love's Labour's Won', *The Spectator*, 4 September 1964, 312.
2   See Arthur Colby Sprague, 'Monsieur Marcadé', *Theatre Notebook*, 28 (1974), 102–5.

question of beauty and the eyes. The comedy has been interpreted as one of Shakespeare's more painterly works. Directors
have cast characters (Longaville and Berowne, see Gilbert, 54) as
artists, and designers have looked for an appropriate visual style
derived from several painters. These have included Velázquez
for the melancholy Spanish knight Armado (Paul Scofield in
Brook's production, Fig. 10) and Monet's and Manet's different
interpretations of *Déjeuner sur l'herbe* for the open-air aspects of
the play (Gilbert, 48, 53–4). However, the presiding artistic
genius of the play, beginning with Brook's production, has been
Watteau. Brook claimed the inspiration in particular of what he
called the 'autumn springtime' of Watteau's *Age of Gold*; other
writers have pointed out the similarities between the huge urn
dominating the characters in Brook's garden scenes (Fig. 11) and
the similar urn in Watteau's *Fête Vénitienne* and the sylvan setting for fashionable lovers in the *Pilgrimage to the Island of
Cythera* (Fig. 12) (Gilbert, 44). Indeed, the last of these may well
have served as a model for William Hamilton's painting for the
Boydell Shakespeare Gallery, illustrating the Princess with her
ladies and the Forester at the beginning of 4.1.

   Jean-Antoine Watteau (1684–1721) and his contemporary
Nicolas Lancret (1690–1743) depict a vision of aristocratic
leisure and amusement: Watteau's fantastics are *commedia dell'arte*
figures sent to entertain the courtiers. Their world of *fêtes
galantes*, in which musicians and gardens populated by statues
play a notable part, is animated by love and its pursuit. It is not
far removed from the world of the operas of Mozart.[1] These in
turn, especially in the last act of *The Marriage of Figaro*, can be
connected with the erotic intrigues, exchanges of partners and
night-time encounters of Sidney's *Arcadia*. Although the powerful influence Watteau exercises over modern productions of
the play may be a way of suggesting the autumnal richness of
what has been lost, set against the high-spiritedness of young

---

1   John Dover Wilson, *Shakespeare's Happy Comedies* (1962), 65, compares *Love's
    Labour's Lost* to *Così fan tutte*.

10 Paul Scofield as Don Armado; Shakespeare Memorial Theatre production
by Peter Brook (1946)

11 Set design for the last scene from the Shakespeare Memorial Theatre production by Peter Brook (1946)

love, it may also be a way of evoking the comedy's musical qualities. In the play itself Armado demands that Moth sings to him, since 'My spirit grows heavy in love' (1.2.116–20), but he is interrupted by the arrival of Costard, Dull and Jaquenetta. He gets to sing his enigmatic piece 'Concolinel' to Armado at the beginning of 3.1. Holofernes sings a snatch of a scale (4.2.99: this supplied Anthony Burgess with the theme for the finale of his third symphony (see *SMC*, 6647, 6662)) and Dull promises to play on the tabor for the Worthies, who can 'dance the hay' (5.1.144–5). There is real music when the lords enter as Muscovites and then try to dance with the ladies (5.2.157.1, 211). None of this, however, really adds up to Apollonian song (5.2.918–19), and, although contemporary settings for Rosaline's 'Thou canst not hit it' (4.1.124–5) may exist, the play is not suffused with music (the settings are discussed and illustrated by John Caldwell in Oxf[1], appendix C).

This makes W. H. Auden's belief 'that the only Shakespeare play that is written like an opera and can readily be turned into

12 Jean-Antoine Watteau (1684–1721), *Pilgrimage to the Island of Cythera*, or *The Embarkation for Cythera*

an opera libretto is *Love's Labour's Lost* rather surprising. It was, he believed, 'structured like an opera and so much of it is already rhymed verse'; he saw it 'as an *opera buffa* in a fast tempo, a kind of perpetual allegro going through to the last scene'. He and Chester Kallman wrote a libretto based on the play in 1969 and their friend Nicolas Nabokov (1903–78, cousin of the novelist Vladimir Nabokov) worked on the musical score from 1970. It was first performed by the Deutsche Oper at the Théâtre de la Monnaie in Brussels on 7 February 1973, but was not notably successful (Fig. 13) (Auden, 716–17). The main changes Auden and Kallman made to the play involved cutting out Longaville and Maria, Holofernes, Nathaniel, Dull, Costard, Marcadé and the Forester. They strengthened the relationship between Armado (now Secretary to the Court) and Jaquenetta (its laundrymaid), who became a rather more interesting character than she is in the play – but that is not hard to achieve – and turned Moth 'into a mischievous Cupid who misdelivers [the letters], not out of ignorance, but on purpose to make trouble' (Auden,

13 Scene from the opera *Love's Labour's Lost*, written by W. H. Auden and Chester Kallman, with music by Nicolas Nabokov

732). The opera was scored for ten voices, five of each sex, for, in a tradition which went back as far as Phelps's 1857 production, Moth was played by a woman (cf. Gilbert, 35, 40). Although the cast was cut, the original nine scenes reduced to six and its time-span expanded to fill a year, much of the original play and its language survives in the libretto, which is characteristically witty and playful: Katherine has some fine muddled Latin and Italian and Berowne rhymes 'epanorthosis' with 'A boy supposes' and 'paranomasia' with 'what could be crazier' (Auden, 350–1: the coincidence of the two rhetorical figures suggests a debt to E.K.'s gloss to January in Spenser's *The Shepheardes Calender*). It is Boyet who announces that the Princess's father is dead; the four couples separate for a year and a day and as they leave the stage Moth sings 'When icicles hang by the wall', just as he had begun it with 'When daisies pied and violets blue'; by the end of his song he has become '*a half-frozen Cupid*' who '*draws his cloak about tightly and shivers*' (Auden, 358).

Auden, Kallman and Nabokov were not the first to see the operatic possibilities of the play. Its *opera buffa* qualities link it to Mozart's great collaborations with Da Ponte. Indeed, in the nineteenth century unhappiness with Da Ponte's licentious libretto for *Così fan tutte* grew to such a level that Jules Barbier and Michel Carré set *Love's Labour's Lost* to Mozart's music as adapted by Delibes and Prosper Pascal: this was performed under the title of *Peines d'amour perdues* at the Théâtre Lyrique in Paris in March 1863 (*SMC*, 6675). Two further projects to write operas based on Shakespeare's play unfortunately came to nothing. In 1953 Igor Stravinsky had set Ver's song as part of *Three Songs from William Shakespeare*; when he read the libretto for the Auden–Kallman–Nabokov opera he wrote that he 'became very envious' and that he 'wanted to compose the music' himself (*SMC*, 6479, 6334). Twelve years later Hans Werner Henze reported that when he 'felt like writing a comic opera' he had wanted to set *Love's Labour's Lost* (*SMC*, 6327). It would be extremely interesting to know what these two composers would have made of Shakespeare's comedy.

Thomas Mann was another author who thought about its operatic qualities in his novel *Doctor Faustus* (1947). Mann was Auden's father-in-law and the English poet certainly knew the German novelist's work. The subject of Mann's novel is a composer called Adrian Leverkühn (the choice of first name is immediately suggestive), who enters into a pact with the devil to gain fresh inspiration for his music: the novel looks back and responds to Marlowe's and Goethe's plays about the Faust legend. In writing *Love's Labour's Lost*, Shakespeare drew on Marlowe's play (see above, p. 17, and commentary to 1.1.55–60, 2.1.1), and Goethe and his circle paid the comedy some attention.[1] Leverkühn's only opera, and among his first important compositions, is based on Shakespeare's comedy. Begun in the

---

1 See Goethe's *Dichtung und Wahrheit*, Book 11, and Simon Williams, *Shakespeare on the German Stage*, volume 1: *1586–1914* (Cambridge, 1990), 22–3.

novel's chronology in 1910 and finished in 1912, it has a libretto by Serenus Zeitblom and takes the form of an anti-Wagnerian *opera buffa*; at its first performance at Lübeck it does not succeed. In writing his allegorical novel about German history Mann drew heavily on Shakespeare's play, quoting parts of it in the course of the novel as well as borrowing from its patterning and imagery.[1] The focus of the opera is undoubtedly the relationship between Berowne and Rosaline, which echoes that between Leverkühn and Marie Godeau.

In writing the opera, Leverkühn was possessed by 'the tendency to marriage [of music] with the word' (163), in which he wishes 'to glorify this bond with the word' (165). The anti-Wagnerian wanted

> a revival of opéra bouffe in a spirit of the most artificial mockery and parody of the artificial: something highly playful and highly precious; its aim the ridicule of affected asceticism and that euphuism which was the social fruit of classical studies. [Leverkühn] spoke with enthusiasm of the theme, which gave opportunity to set the lout and 'natural' alongside the comic sublime and make both ridiculous in each other. Archaic heroics, rodomontade, bombastic etiquette tower out of forgotten epochs in the person of Don Armado, whom Adrian rightly pronounced a consummate figure of opera.
>
> (166)

The narrator, Zeitblom, says that he did not altogether approve of the subject ('I have always been rather unhappy at any mockery of humanistic extravagances') and sought to dissuade the composer

---

1   See, for example, Jeffrey Meyers, 'Shakespeare and Mann's *Doctor Faustus*', *Modern Fiction Studies*, 19 (1973–4), 541–5, Patrick Carnegy, *Faust as Musician: A Study of Thomas Mann's Novel 'Doctor Faustus'* (1973), esp. 74–5, and Michael Beddow, *Thomas Mann: Doctor Faustus* (Cambridge, 1994), 36–7. All the following quotations from the novel are taken from the translation by H. T. Lowe-Porter (Everyman's Library, 1992).

from having an English libretto which would accommodate 'the plays on words and the old English verse with doggerel rhyme' (167). Leverkühn finds the music hard to write on account of its 'parodistic artificiality'; it needed 'a supply of whimsicality constantly fresh and sustained' (213). He seeks always to preserve 'the atmosphere of the comic and grotesque', and for Berowne's opening speech in 4.3 he has 'to invent musical accents of quite peculiar fantasticality' (218). The composer – or at least his librettist – believes that there is something autobiographical about the depiction of Berowne's relationship with Rosaline ('an urge to bring in his own experiences', 219), something which Mann may have taken from Frank Harris's *The Man Shakespeare and His Tragic Life-Story* (1909).[1] The opera contributes to the novel's consideration of art and nature: Leverkühn produces 'a witty and melancholy work of art, an intellectual achievement which deserved the name of heroic, something just barely possible, behaving like arrogant travesty' (221). During its first performance two-thirds of the audience leave the theatre and there were only two or three more performances of it. The reviewers dislike Leverkühn's music, but one describes the opera as 'a work of the future, full of profound music', adding that 'the writer was of course a mocker but a "god-witted man"' (267).

The publication of Mann's novel the year after Brook's production at Stratford showed the play's extraordinary imaginative power in the post-war world. Despite its oddity and difficulty, a work with a conclusion in which nothing is concluded, one which deals so effectively with words as open and closed systems of meaning and with the endings we expect from life and from art, the comedy has appealed particularly strongly to modern audiences. Like Mozart's great romantic operas, its mixture of the comic and the profound speaks deeply to people. *Love's Labour's Lost* is in some ways Shakespeare's most 'Elizabethan' play, rooted in its

---

1 See Gunilla Bergsten, *Thomas Mann's Doctor Faustus: The Sources and Structure of the Novel*, tr. Krishna Winston (Chicago, Ill., and London, 1969), 63–4.

LOVE'S LABOUR'S LOST

LIST OF ROLES

KING Ferdinand of Navarre		
BEROWNE		
LONGAVILLE	*lords attending the King*	
DUMAINE		
PRINCESS of France		5
ROSALINE		
MARIA	*ladies attending the Princess*	
KATHERINE		
BOYET	*a lord attending the Princess*	
Monsieur MARCADÉ	*a messenger*	10
Don Adriano de ARMADO	*a Spanish knight and braggart*	
MOTH	*his page, a boy*	
HOLOFERNES	*a schoolmaster*	
NATHANIEL	*a curate*	
Anthony DULL	*a constable*	15
COSTARD	*a clown*	
JAQUENETTA	*a dairymaid*	
Forester		
Lords attending the Princess		
Blackamoors and others attending the King		20

Love's Labour's Lost

LIST OF ROLES Rowe first included a list, expanded by later editors, in his edition of 1709. Elam (263) points out that the list of roles can be 'arranged schematically over a span of the alphabet – A: Adriano de Armado; B: Berowne, Boyet; C: Costard; D: Dumain, Dull; F: Forester; H: Holofernes; J: Jaquenetta; K: Katherine; L: Longaville; M: Maria, Marcade; N: Navarre, Nathaniel; (O: Rowe's "Officers and Others"); P: Princess of France (sometimes given in the First Quarto as Q: Queen); R: Rosaline.' The King could also appear under K or F for Ferdinand.

1 **Ferdinand** This is closer to the Italian, Ferdinando, than Ferrand, the French form of the name. The Italian form became popular in England in the mid-sixteenth century and was given to Ferdinando Heybourne and Ferdinando Stanley, later fifth Earl of Derby, who were born respectively in 1558 and 1559. Shakespeare used it for Alonso's son in *Tem.* The name is not spoken in the play and only appears in the opening SD to 1.1. The King is only referred to by his title 'Navarre' at 1.1.12 and in 2.1.

2 **BEROWNE** For the historical Duc de Biron, see the Introduction, p. 68. At 4.3.228 *Berowne* rhymes with *moon* (as in 'Beroon') and there may be a pun on his name and 'brown' at 2.1.66n. His name is first spoken at 1.1.15 and consistently spelled in full in Q as 'Berowne'. Nashe (2.182.9) has the name 'Beroune' for Biron in the address to the reader before *Christ's Tears Over Jerusalem* (1594).

3 **LONGAVILLE** For the historical Duc de Longueville, see the Introduction, p. 68. His name is made to rhyme with *ill* (4.3.121), with *compile* (4.3.131) and with *mile* (5.2.54); for a pun on 'long veal', see 5.2.247n. His name is first spoken at 1.1.15 and is spelled in full in Q usually as 'Longauil(l)' but twice as 'Longauile'.

4 **DUMAINE** His name rhymes with *pain* (4.3.169) and *twain* (5.2.48). The brothers Dumain are abused by Parolles in

AW (see 4.3.175–291), where their name is spelled 'Dumaine' on three occasions and 'Dumain' once in F. For the historical Duc de Mayenne, see Introduction, pp. 67–8. His name is first spoken at 1.1.15 and is spelled in full in Q as 'Dumaine' and on three occasions in SPs as '*Duman.*'.

5 **PRINCESS** She is not given a first name in the play. She is addressed as *your majesty* by the King as soon as she has heard of her father's death (5.2.720n.), but is referred to several times as a queen before then in dialogue and regularly as such in her SPs.

6 **ROSALINE** Her name rhymes with *mine* (4.1.55, 103, 5.2.441) and *thine* (4.3.216, 5.2.132). For her darkness, see 3.1.192n., 4.3.3n., 243n. Rosaline is the name of Romeo's love at the beginning of *RJ* and, as a variant of Rosalind, the name of Spenser's love in *SC* (1579) and of the heroine of *AYL*. Her name is first spoken at 3.1.162 and is consistently spelled in full in Q as 'Rosaline' and once as 'Rosalin'.

7 **MARIA** As in *TN*, Shakespeare uses the Italian or Spanish form of the name. Her name is first spoken at 4.3.53 and is consistently spelled in full in Q as 'Maria' but appears twice in SPs (5.2.53, 57) as '*Marg.*'.

8 **KATHERINE** The name occurs again as Katharina for the heroine of *TS* and for Henry V's bride. Her name is first spoken at 2.1.194 and is spelled in full in Q once as 'Katherine' and once as 'Katherin'; she is called Kate at 4.3.80.

9 **BOYET** His name rhymes with *debt* at 5.2.333. His name is first spoken at 2.1.13 and is consistently spelled in full in Q as 'Boyet'.

10 **MARCADÉ** The scansion of 5.2.711, where he is named, suggests that his name is trisyllabic. In sixteenth-century Fr. his name signified the *danse macabre*: see René Graziani, 'M. Marcadé and the Dance of Death: *Love's Labour's Lost*, V.ii.705–11', *RES*, NS, 37 (1986), 392–5. For the theory that his name is a version of Mercury, see Introduction, pp. 65–6, and that it suggests 'marred Arcadia', p. 34.

11 **Don Adriano de** ARMADO His first
name is the Spanish version of English
Adrian, itself a translation of the Lat.
Hadrianus, meaning 'of the Adriatic'.
There are Adrians in *Tem* and *Cor* and
Shakespeare had used its female form
for Adriana in *CE*. His second name is
a commonly used but erroneous form
of the Spanish 'armada' (cf. *OED* 1α),
known most famously from the
Spanish attack on England in 1588.
Apart from Blanch of Spain in *KJ* and
Queen Katherine in *H8*, Armado is the
only Spaniard to appear in
Shakespeare's plays. His surname is
first spoken at 1.1.168, and Christian
and surname at 1.1.264: the former
appears once as 'Adriana' in Q , the latter as either 'Armado' or as 'Armatho'.
For Costard's corruption of his name,
'Dun Adramadio', see 4.3.195n. From
the beginning of 3.1 the SDs and SPs
regularly refer to him as '*Braggart*'.

12 MOTH See Appendix 3. There are
pages in *TGV* (Speed), *MW* (Robin),
2H4, *RJ* and *AYL*. His name is first
spoken at 1.2.74: at the beginning of
the scene he enters as Armado's 'page'
and his SP varies between that and
'*Boy*'.

13 HOLOFERNES The story of Judith and
Holofernes is told in the Apocryphal
Book of Judith. Master Thubal
Holofernes was one of Gargantua's
tutors in Rabelais (1.14). His name is
first spoken at 4.2.8 and is spelled consistently in full in Q as 'Holofernes': at
the beginning of the scene he enters as
'*Holofernes*, the *Pedant*' and his SPs
regularly refer to him by both titles.

14 NATHANIEL from the Hebrew, meaning
'God has given'. One of Petruchio's servants has the same name in *TS*. He is
the only curate to appear in the plays,
although Feste pretends to be 'Sir Topas
the curate' in *TN* (4.2.21) to mock
Malvolio; Sir Oliver Martext is a vicar in
AYL and Sir Hugh Evans a Welsh parson in *MW*. His name is first spoken at
4.2.11 and is spelled consistently in full
in Q as 'Nathaniel'; his SPs occasionally
refer to him as a curate.

15 **Anthony** DULL In its Italian form,
Antonio, Dull's Christian name, is one
of Shakespeare's favourites in his
comedies. As a surname, Dull belongs
to the same category as Thomas Wart
in *2H4*, Toby Belch in *TN*, Oliver
Martext in *AYL*, and so on. As a constable he can be related to Dogberry in
MA and to Elbow in *MM*: constables
were proverbially stupid; cf. 'You
might be a constable for your wit',
Dent, C616. His full name is first spoken at 1.1.256 and only once more at
258, which also has a unique SP
'*Antho.*'; when he first enters at
1.1.178.1 and occasionally in SDs and
SPs he is identified as a constable.

16 COSTARD A costard was a kind of
large apple (cf. 'costermonger' and see
'pomewater', 4.2.4n.) and also slang
for the head, see *KL* 4.6.241. As a
clown he is a simple rustic figure
rather than a courtly fool. His name is
first spoken at 1.1.177, where he is also
called 'the swain', and is consistently
spelled in full in Q as 'Costard' except
at 1.1.218, where it appears as
'*Costart*'. He is regularly identified as a
clown in SDs and SPs.

17 JAQUENETTA is presumably related to
the French Jacquetta, itself a diminutive of Jacques or James; her name in
this form is not in Cotgrave. If her
name is a female form of Jacques, then
she can be related to Jaques in *AYL*,
with attendant puns on 'jakes' – one
definition Cotgrave supplies for
'Iaquette', '*(A proper name for a
woman)*', is that it is '*a filthie dungeon,
or loathsome hole in a prison*'. She is
called 'the dey-woman' at 1.2.125: in
TGV Launce is in love with a milk-
maid (3.1.265–79). Her name is first
spoken at 1.1.199 and is consistently
spelled in full in Q as 'Jaquenetta'; her
SPs regularly refer to her as '*Maid*'.

18 **Forester** Oberon is identified with a
forester in *MND* (3.2.390, 4.1.103,
108) and F calls for lords dressed as
foresters in *AYL* at the beginning of
2.1 and 4.2 (see also Introduction,
p. 89). His name is not given in *LLL*,
but the Princess identifies him by his
job at 4.1.7.

LOVE'S LABOUR'S LOST

1[.1]   *Enter* Ferdinand, KING of Navarre, BEROWNE,
LONGAVILLE *and* DUMAINE.

KING

Let fame, that all hunt after in their lives,
Live registered upon our brazen tombs,

TITLE The form of the title and its meaning are uncertain: the title-page to Q has
'Loues labors lost', but its running title is
'*Loues Labor's lost*', which is close to F's
head and running titles. If the apostrophe
in '*Labor's*' is correct, then the title means
'the labour of love is lost' rather than 'the
lost labours of love'. For other forms of
the title, see Introduction, pp. 78–9.

Cf. the proverbial 'You lose your
labour' or 'To lose your labour', Dent,
L9; John Florio, *Florio his First Fruits*,
1578, sig. S3r, 'We neede not speak so
much of loue, al books are ful of loue,
with so many authours, that it were labour
lost to speake of Loue'; and the motto for
a ring in a manuscript collection of about
1596, '*Loue unloued, labor ill lost*' (see J.
Evans, 75). 'Love' suggests Cupid, who as
Oxf¹ points out is mentioned more often
in this than in any other play by
Shakespeare. 'Labours' suggests the
twelve labours of Hercules. After
Hercules had killed his wife and children
in his madness, the Oracle at Delphi
ordered him to serve Eurystheus, King of
Tiryns; the king imposed twelve labours
on him and three are referred to in the
play: the Nemean Lion (4.1.87n.), the
Golden Apples of the Hesperides
(4.3.315n.) and the Descent to the
Underworld for Cerberus (5.2.583n.); see
also Carroll, appendix B, and cf. *AW*

4.3.251–3, where Parolles says of Captain
Dumaine, 'He professes not keeping of
oaths; in breaking 'em he is stronger than
Hercules'. 'Labour' suggests the labour of
giving birth (*OED sb.* 6a), which is lost
because of the play's lack of resolution –
cf. 5.2.518, 'When great things labouring
perish in their birth'. The word also
implies sexual activity. *OED*'s earliest
citation for 'labour of love', love *sb.* 8b, is
from 1673: the phrase occurs in the
Bishops' Bible, 1 Thessalonians, 1.3, and
Hebrews, 6.10.

1.1.1–7 There are parallels in the opening
speech with *Son* 19, 55, 63–5, 100 and
with *R3* 3.1.84–8.

1   **fame** renown; personified as '*Fame*' in
F, cf. *H5* 4.1.45, *MA* 2.1.214; see also
92n., 2.1.21n., 4.1.32n., 5.2.830n.
hunt Cf. 1.1.143, the real hunting
which takes place in 4.1 and Berowne's
opening words to 4.3.

1–2 **lives, / Live** The repetition is striking.

2   **registered** set down, recorded (*OED
v.* 1a)
brazen tombs tombs with inscrip-
tions on plates of brass; cf. Horace's
Exegi monumentum aere perennius, 'I
have built a monument more lasting
than brass', *Odes*, 3.30.1. *Brazen* tombs
could also be shameless tombs, as in
'brazen-faced' (*OED* brazen *a.* 3).

TITLE] *F3; A* PLEASANT Conceited Comedie CALLED, Loues labors lost. *Q (title-page); A
pleasant conceited Comedie: / called Loues Labor's lost. Q (running titles); Loues Labour lost. F (table of
contents);* Loues Labour's lost. *F (head title and running titles)*
1.1] *Rowe; F (Actus primus.); act and scene not in Q*   0.1 Navarre] *F (Nauarre);* Nauar *Q*   0.2
LONGAVILLE] *QF (Longauill)*   DUMAINE] *Q (subst.); Dumane F*   1+ SP KING] *Rowe; Ferdinand
(Ferd., Fer.) QF*   1 fame] *Q (*Fame*); Fame F*

111

And then grace us in the disgrace of death;
When, spite of cormorant devouring time,
Th'endeavour of this present breath may buy   5
That honour which shall bate his scythe's keen edge,
And make us heirs of all eternity.
Therefore, brave conquerors – for so you are,
That war against your own affections
And the huge army of the world's desires –   10
Our late edict shall strongly stand in force.

3–4 **then . . . When** an inversion of the usual formula; see 3.1.161n. and Introduction, p. 15.

3 **grace . . . death** We shall have grace even when we are disfigured by death's decay; we shall have grace when we shame death through our surviving fame. Cf. the tag *Vivit post funera virtus*, 'Only virtue never dies' (Dent, V74), and *Tit* 1.1.390, 'He lives in fame, that died in virtue's cause'. Cf. Sidney, *NA*, 63, 4–6, 'In sum, he left nothing unassayed which might disgrace himself to grace his friend'. Shakespeare plays on *grace . . . disgrace* again at 4.3.64 and in *Luc* 1319–20 and on *grace . . . grace* at 5.2.72.

4 **spite** in spite
cormorant . . . time 'Time eats all up as ravenously as a cormorant'; 'Time even devours the ravenous cormorant.' The cormorant's greed was traditional. Cf. *tempus edax rerum*, Ovid, *Met.*, 15.234, and the proverb 'Time devours all things' (Dent, T326); and see 5.2.749n.

5 **Th'endeavour . . . breath** i.e. 'what we try to do while alive'; 'what I am trying to say in this speech'. The theme of *endeavour* is returned to by Rosaline at 5.2.841 and of *breath* by Longaville at 4.3.65 and by the Princess at 5.2.729.

6 **bate** blunt: *OED v.*[2] 3, which suggests a link with bait *v.*[1] II, to satisfy the hunger of. Cf. the different sort of baiting of Holofernes, 5.2.626n.
scythe's keen edge Father Time's scythe was traditional. The juxtaposition of the sharp scythe and *present breath* looks forward to more in the play about the keenness of tongues; see 122–3n., 5.2.256–8n. and Berowne's being cut to pieces by Rosaline's sharp wit, 5.2.399n.

7 i.e. they will inherit everlasting eternity; everlasting eternity will remember them. The phrase *make us heirs* also suggests begetting children and there may be a hint of the political question of France's heir, for which cf. *CE* 3.2.122–4. Both Katherine and Maria are later identified as heiresses; see 2.1.194, 204.

8 **brave conquerors** The King assumes they have won before the war has begun. Alexander the Conqueror appears later as one of the Nine Worthies.

9 **affections** passions (*OED sb.* 3); cf. 5.2.407n.

10 **army** Cf. *MV* 3.5.67.

11 **late** recent
stand in force be binding, be in effect (*OED* force *sb.*[1] 8c)

5 Th'endeavour] *Q* (Thendeuour), *F*   buy] *F2;* buy: *QF*   10 desires –] *Rowe (subst.);* desires. *QF*
11 force.] *Theobald;* force, *QF*

Navarre shall be the wonder of the world,
Our court shall be a little academe,
Still and contemplative in living art.
You three, Berowne, Dumaine and Longaville,   15
Have sworn for three years' term to live with me,
My fellow-scholars, and to keep those statutes
That are recorded in this schedule here.
Your oaths are passed, and now subscribe your names,
That his own hand may strike his honour down   20
That violates the smallest branch herein.
If you are armed to do as sworn to do,

12 **Navarre** the place and himself as king of it
  wonder . . . world The Emperor Frederick II (1215–50) was called *stupor mundi* for his greatness as a king, soldier and patron. Marlowe's Dido (3.1.94–5) asks 'To be more modest than her thoughts admit / Lest I be made a wonder to the world'. Nashe (2.281) refers to the nine wonders of the world; the Nine Worthies might also be associated with them.

13 **academe** academy: a unique Shakespearean form, with which cf. 4.3.326. The Academy was originally the name of Plato's school in Athens. It was taken up in the mid-fifteenth century by the Medici, rulers of Florence, and imitated at other courts, esp. in France, where academies held formal discussions of matters relating to philosophy and to the arts. In 1577 Pierre de la Primaudaye published his fictional account of *L'Académie française*, containing the discussions of four French courtiers: the work was translated into English by Thomas Bowes in 1586. See Introduction, pp. 66–7.

14 **Still . . . in** calmly and constantly meditating on: cf. *still* at 2.1.228n., 3.1.188n., 4.3.315n., 325n., 5.2.215n. *Still* is opposed to the *living* of the same line.

Still and contemplative a hendiadys, or a way of saying one thing in two words, for which see also 286–7n., 1.2.18n., 4.1.66n., 4.3.306n.
  living art the art of living, the *ars vivendi* of Stoic philosophers; practical learning, knowledge, which has to do with the business of life; the living quality of art. The *art* associated with the King and his courtiers contrasts with the *Nature* of the Princess's party, 2.1.10. Nevo (72) identifies the phrase as an oxymoron with *living* derived from 'life' which is opposed to *art*. Hazard, 181–98, points out that Spenser uses the phrase twice in the Proem to *FQ*, 3. Cf. 1.1.159n.

16 **term** Cf. the one year's term of separation, 5.2.838.

17 **keep** observe, obey
  statutes laws, rules, articles of agreement

18 **schedule** a piece of paper or vellum containing writing; the word had legal associations. The QF forms are variant spellings.

19 **passed** pledged

20 **his . . . hand** the witness of his own handwriting, as well as his own hand

21 **branch** clause, detail

22 **armed** prepared for (sexual) action
  do . . . do For the possible sexual connotation of the verb, see 3.1.193n.

13 academe] *QF (Achademe)* 16 me,] *F2;* me: *QF* 18 schedule] *Q (sedule), F*

Subscribe to your deep oaths, and keep it too.
LONGAVILLE
I am resolved: 'tis but a three years' fast.
The mind shall banquet though the body pine.   25
Fat paunches have lean pates, and dainty bits
Make rich the ribs, but bankrupt quite the wits. *[He signs.]*
DUMAINE
My loving lord, Dumaine is mortified.
The grosser manner of these world's delights
He throws upon the gross world's baser slaves.   30
To love, to wealth, to pomp, I pine and die,
With all these living in philosophy.   *[He signs.]*
BEROWNE
I can but say their protestation over.
So much, dear liege, I have already sworn,
That is, to live and study here three years.   35
But there are other strict observances:
As not to see a woman in that term,

23 **it** the subscription to the vow
24 **fast** For more about fasting, see esp.
1.1.284–6n., 1.2.123n., 4.3.288, 5.2.795,
and, for meals, see 4.2.151n., 5.1.3n., 35.
25 **pine** starve, languish. In *Son* 75.13 and
VA 602 pining is opposed to surfeiting.
26 **Fat . . . pates** Fat people are dim: *pates*
are heads. Despite the example of
Falstaff, the phrase became proverbial
(Tilley, P123). See 5.2.268n.
dainty Cf. 4.3.313n.
bits morsels
28 **mortified** dead to worldly pleasures.
The word had a definite religious association.
29 **grosser** coarser, more indelicate (*OED*
A. *adj.* 15b*)
manner sort, kind
30 **throws upon** i.e. throws away upon
gross whole (*OED* A. *adj.* 6a)

31 **pomp** Cf. 5.1.109–10n.
32 'I suppose he means that he finds
"love, pomp, *and* wealth *in* philosophy"' (Johnson); philosophy makes the
three unnecessary; he will live in philosophy with his three companions.
33 **say . . . over** repeat their formal decla-
ration or promise again
34 **liege** Berowne's favourite way of
addressing the King: all eight uses of
the word and one of *liege's* in the play
are his. On three other occasions
(1.1.111, 4.3.201, 5.2.510) he calls the
King 'my (good) lord'.
36 **observances** ordinances, rules (*OED* 2a)
37 **not . . . woman** In *The Royal
Exchange* (1590) Robert Greene
(7.314) says, '*Plato* admitted no
Auditour in his *Academie* but such as
while they were his schollers woulde

24 three] *F*; thee *Q*   27 bankrupt quite] *Q* (bancrout quite*)*; bankerout *F*   SD] *Kerrigan*
28 mortified.] *Collier*; mortefied, *QF*   29 delights] *Pope*; delyghts: *Q*; delights, *F*   30 slaves.] *F*
(slaues*:)*; slaues *Q* (*an indistinct mark may represent a stop*)   31 pomp] *F*; pome *Q*   32 SD] *Capell*
(*subst.*)   33 over.] *Johnson*; ouer, *QF*

Which I hope well is not enrolled there;
And one day in a week to touch no food,
And but one meal on every day beside,   40
The which I hope is not enrolled there;
And then to sleep but three hours in the night,
And not be seen to wink of all the day,
When I was wont to think no harm all night
And make a dark night too of half the day,   45
Which I hope well is not enrolled there.
O, these are barren tasks, too hard to keep:
Not to see ladies, study, fast, not sleep.

KING

Your oath is passed to pass away from these.

BEROWNE

Let me say no, my liege, an if you please.   50
I only swore to study with your grace
And stay here in your court for three years' space.

LONGAVILLE

You swore to that, Berowne, and to the rest.

BEROWNE

By yea and nay, sir, then I swore in jest.
What is the end of study, let me know?   55

abstaine fro*m* women: for he was wont
to say, that the greatest enemie to the
memorie was venerie'.

38, 41, 46 **enrolled** enrollèd; written upon
a roll or parchment, given legal form

43 **wink of all** close one's eyes during the
whole of

44 **think . . . night** sleep all night; cf. 'He
that drinks well sleeps well and he that
sleeps well thinks no harm' (Dent,
H169).

49 **to . . . from** to renounce

50 **an if** if

51 **grace** Except at 5.2.80 where Boyet
uses it of the Princess, the title is
always used in reference to the King.

54 **By . . . nay** a common oath derived
from Matthew, 5.37: 'let your communication be yea, yea, nay nay' (*OED* yea
B. 3b*). Berowne equivocates: he
swore and he did not.
sir the most commonly used form of
address in the play. See Introduction,
pp. 51–2.

55–60 The exchange, esp. with its questioning of 'the end of study', echoes
Marlowe's *Dr Faustus*, A-Text, 1.1.8,
10, 17–18; see also 2.1.1n.

55 **end** purpose; final limit

39 food,] *Pope²;* foode: *QF*   40 beside,] *Collier;* beside: *QF*   43 day,] *Rowe (subst.);* day. *QF*
50 please.] *F4;* please, *QF*

KING

Why, that to know which else we should not know.

BEROWNE

Things hid and barred, you mean, from common sense?

KING

Ay, that is study's god-like recompense.

BEROWNE

Come on then, I will swear to study so,

To know the thing I am forbid to know: 60

As thus, to study where I well may dine,

  When I to feast expressly am forbid;

Or study where to meet some mistress fine,

  When mistresses from common sense are hid.

Or, having sworn too hard-a-keeping oath,   65

Study to break it, and not break my troth.

If study's gain be thus, and this be so,

Study knows that which yet it doth not know.

Swear me to this, and I will ne'er say no.

KING

These be the stops that hinder study quite   70

And train our intellects to vain delight.

---

57 Cf. Ovid's account (*Met.*, 15.60–272) as translated by Arthur Golding (1565) of Pythagoras' teaching of 'his silent sort' of disciples '(Which woondred at the heavenly woordes theyr mayster did report) / The first foundation of the world: the cause of every thing: / What nature was: and what was God: whence snow and lyghtning spring: / And whither *Jove* or else the wynds in breaking clowdes doo thunder: / What shakes the earth: what law the starres doo keepe theyr courses under: / And what soever other thing is hid from common sence' (74–80).

common sense ordinary or untutored perception (*OED* 2c*, the only citation)

59 **Come on** possibly punning on *common* in 57 and 64

60 The line evokes Adam in the Garden of Eden.

61–6 Berowne's lines form a verse like the one used in *VA*; there are further examples at 74–9, 147–58 (two verses), 4.1.87–92 (Armado's poem), 4.3.210–15, 5.2.242–7, 256–61, 474–9, 582–7 (Holofernes' lines as Judas).

65 **too . . . oath** an oath which is too hard to keep; for the construction of *hard-a-keeping*, see Abbott, 422.

66 **troth** faith

70 **stops** obstacles (*OED sb.*² 7a)

71 **train** entice, lure (*OED v.*¹ 4a)

59 Come on] *F;* Com'on *Q*   62 feast] *Theobald;* fast *QF*   63 fine,] *F;* fine. *Q*   65 hard-a-keeping] *Theobald*²*;* hard a keeping *QF*   68 know.] *Collier;* know, *QF*   70 quite] *F;* quit *Q*

BEROWNE

Why, all delights are vain, but that most vain
Which, with pain purchased, doth inherit pain:
As painfully to pore upon a book
  To seek the light of truth, while truth the while   75
Doth falsely blind the eyesight of his look.
  Light seeking light doth light of light beguile;
So, ere you find where light in darkness lies,
Your light grows dark by losing of your eyes.
Study me how to please the eye indeed   80
  By fixing it upon a fairer eye,
Who dazzling so, that eye shall be his heed,
  And give him light that it was blinded by.
Study is like the heaven's glorious sun,
  That will not be deep-searched with saucy looks;   85

72 **delights are vain** a commonplace; cf. Spenser, *FQ*, 2.5.27.2.

73 ¹**pain** effort; physical suffering
purchased acquired, obtained
inherit pain come with suffering and difficulty. For more about inheriting, see 2.1.5n., 4.1.20n.

74–9 See 61–6n.

74 **As** for example
painfully with effort, painstakingly
pore Cf. Appendix 2.1, line 3: these are the only occurrences of the word in Shakespeare.

75 **light of truth** The phrase translates Cicero's *lux veritatis* in his commendation of history, *De Oratore*, 2.9.36, a favourite Renaissance passage, quoted e.g. by Sidney, *DP*, 84.

76 **falsely** treacherously
his the looker's, or his eyesight's

77 Eyes in search of illumination make themselves lose their ability to see; 'a man by too close study may read himself blind' (Johnson). Eyes were thought to create (and project) the light by which they saw. These lines introduce the first of the play's many references to eyes: see esp. 2.1.233–46, 4.3.25n., 5.2.374–6n.

78 **light in darkness** illumination in obscure knowledge

80–93 These lines form a sonnet; there are further examples at 160–74, 4.3.23–38, 57–70, 5.2.343–56, 402–15.

80 **Study me** let me study; an ethic dative: see Abbott, 220.

81 **a fairer eye** a woman's eye

82–3 'when he "dazzles", that is, has his eye made weak, "by fixing his eye upon a fairer eye, that *fairer* eye shall be his heed", his "direction" or "lodestar . . . and give him light that was blinded by it"' (Johnson). *Dazzling* means losing the ability to see clearly, esp. from looking at too bright lights (cf. Sidney, *OA* poem, 35.6); *heed* means what one heeds or pays attention to.

84–5 Cf. the proverb 'He that gazes upon the sun shall at last be blind' (Dent, S971.1) and 5.2.374–6n.

85 **saucy** insolent, presumptuous

72 but] and *F*   85 searched] searcht *Q;* search'd *F*

Small have continual plodders ever won,
  Save base authority from others' books.
These earthly godfathers of heaven's lights,
  That give a name to every fixed star,
Have no more profit of their shining nights   90
  Than those that walk and wot not what they are.
Too much to know is to know naught but fame,
  And every godfather can give a name.

KING

How well he's read, to reason against reading.

DUMAINE

Proceeded well, to stop all good proceeding.   95

LONGAVILLE

He weeds the corn, and still lets grow the weeding.

BEROWNE

The spring is near when green geese are a-breeding.

---

86 **Small** little; for adjectives used as nouns, see Abbott, 5.
  plodders See Appendix 2.1, line 10n.
87 **base authority** commonplace material thought to settle disputed questions; for *base*, see 1.2.160–2n.
88 **earthly godfathers** i.e. astronomers who name stars
89 **name** On names and naming in the play, see Elam, 120–2, 126–8.
  fixed fixèd
90 **profit of** benefit from
91 **wot** know
  they the stars; the people who walk
92 i.e. people who know too much, or more than they can use, do so for vainglory; to know too much is only to know things by report; for *fame*, see also 1n.
93 i.e. it is easy for godparents to give names to the person being baptized; Berowne's point is that this kind of learning brings *fame* of one kind, but that sort of fame is only a *name* which anyone can acquire.
95 **Proceeded** argued (*OED v.* 2b)
  proceeding advancement (of learn-

ing) (*OED vbl. sb.* 4a). To proceed (*OED v.* 4a) also meant to take a second degree at university or to be admitted a barrister at the Inns of Court.
96 He pulls up the wheat, leaving the weeds to grow. *OED* weeding *vbl. sb.* 1c* is the only citation: the *OED* gloss, 'That which is weeded out', is incorrect. The line may be related to the proverbial 'The weeds overgrow the corn', Tilley, W242, and cf. also 4.3.357n.
97 When geese lay their eggs, spring is near. *Green geese* feed on grass etc., not on corn, and lay their eggs between late February and May; the phrase also suggests inexperienced fools or prostitutes and that Berowne is mocking his companions' rhyming. The geese in these four rhyming lines anticipate the goose of Armado's and Moth's similar rhyme; see 3.1.86–9n. and see also 4.3.72n.: like sheep, geese are by reputation stupid followers of each other. Booth (71–3) comments on all these passages and argues (72, 168–9) that 'goose' was slang for buttocks.

DUMAINE

How follows that?

BEROWNE   Fit in his place and time.

DUMAINE

In reason nothing.

BEROWNE   Something then in rhyme.

KING

Berowne is like an envious sneaping frost,   100

That bites the first-born infants of the spring.

BEROWNE

Well, say I am. Why should proud summer boast

Before the birds have any cause to sing?

Why should I joy in any abortive birth?

At Christmas I no more desire a rose   105

Than wish a snow in May's newfangled shows,

But like of each thing that in season grows.

So you, to study now it is too late,

Climb o'er the house to unlock the little gate.

98 **Fit in his** appropriate to its
99 Rhyme and reason are traditionally opposed (Dent, R98.1); see 1.2.102–3n.
100–1 The opposition of frost and spring here, like that of Christmas and May in 105–6, anticipates the songs of Ver and Hiems at the end of the play. For frost, see also 5.2.795.
100–3 The passage echoes *Luc* 330–3.
100 **envious** malicious, spiteful
   sneaping frost nipping, biting frost (*OED* sneaping *ppl. a.**); the King takes *rhyme* (99) as 'rime'.
101 **first-born . . . spring** spring's young buds and flowers; for 'infants of the spring', cf. *Ham* 1.3.39.
102 **proud summer** Cf. 'summers' pride', *Son* 104.4.
104 **any** Pope's emendation may be correct: Cam¹ suggests eye-skip from *any cause* in 103.
   abortive premature, unnatural (*OED*

A. 1a)
   birth Unless an emendation, like 'earth', is adopted in 106, *birth* has no rhyme word, but is followed by a triplet in 105–7 rhyming *rose/shows/grows*.
105–6 Christmas and May anticipate Hiems and Ver at the end of the play; May also features in Dumaine's lyric at 4.3.99 and Berowne refers to a *Christmas comedy* at 5.2.462.
106 **newfangled shows** the ground that has been newly dressed by the flowers of the spring
107 **like of** like, enjoy; see Abbott, 177.
109 do something pointless: no parallel has been found for this line, but compare the proverb 'To leap over the hedge before you come at the stile' (Tilley, H363) in which 'hedge' and 'stile' were interchangeable. F's version of the line is curious; see Appendix 1, p. 332.

102 am.] *Rowe* (am;*)*; am, *QF*   104 any] *QF*; an *Pope*   abortive] *F;* abhortiue *Q*   109] That were to clymbe ore the house to vnlocke the gate *F*

KING

Well, sit you out. Go home, Berowne: adieu.   110

BEROWNE

No, my good lord, I have sworn to stay with you,

And though I have for barbarism spoke more

   Than for that angel knowledge you can say,

Yet confident I'll keep what I have sworn

   And bide the penance of each three years' day.   115

Give me the paper, let me read the same,

And to the strictest decrees I'll write my name.

KING

How well this yielding rescues thee from shame.

BEROWNE [*Reads.*] *Item, That no woman shall come within*
a mile of my court – Hath this been proclaimed?   120

LONGAVILLE   Four days ago.

BEROWNE   Let's see the penalty – *On pain of losing her*
tongue. Who devised this penalty?

LONGAVILLE   Marry, that did I.

BEROWNE   Sweet lord, and why?   125

LONGAVILLE

To fright them hence with that dread penalty.

110 **sit you out** do not take part (*OED* sit *v.* 24a**); the phrase suggests keeping out of a dance, a meal, a hand of cards, etc.
112 **barbarism** anti-intellectualism
114 **sworn** F2's 'swore' preserves the rhyme.
115 **each . . . day** every day of the three years
118 **yielding** giving way to persuasion, consent (*OED vbl. sb.* 5b*); cf. 2.1.150n.
122–3 *losing her tongue* The proposed punishment evokes the story of Philomela, told by Ovid (*Met.*) and on which Shakespeare had drawn in *Tit*: Tereus, the tyrant of Thrace, married Progne, but lusting after her sister Philomela raped her in a wood and cut

out her tongue so she could not say who had attacked her. The punishment is a distinctively foreign one – English law generally only allowed for cropping of ears (for sedition) and branding – and anticipates Boyet's speech about the razor-sharp tongues of women at 5.2.256–8n. and see 5.2.399n.
123 *tongue* Of the many uses of the word in the play, Marcadé's at 5.2.714 is especially pregnant with meaning; in Lat. *lingua* meant both the tongue and speech or language. See also 165n., 1.2.91n., 2.1.237–8n., 3.1.10–11n., 4.3.313n., 5.1.10n., 5.2.242n., 256–8n., 334n., 731n., 830n.
124 **Marry** indeed; a weakened form of 'by the Virgin Mary'

110 sit] fit *F*   114 sworn] *QF*; swore *F2*   119 SD] *Pope (subst.)*

BEROWNE

A dangerous law against gentility.

Item, If any man be seen to talk with a woman within the
term of three years, he shall endure such public shame as the
rest of the court can possible devise.   130

This article, my liege, yourself must break,
  For well you know here comes in embassy
The French King's daughter with yourself to speak –
  A maid of grace and complete majesty –
About surrender up of Aquitaine   135
  To her decrepit, sick and bedrid father.
Therefore this article is made in vain,
  Or vainly comes th'admired Princess hither.

KING

What say you, lords? Why, this was quite forgot.

BEROWNE

So study evermore is overshot.   140
While it doth study to have what it would,
It doth forget to do the thing it should;
And when it hath the thing it hunteth most,
'Tis won as towns with fire: so won, so lost.

127 **gentility** good manners, polite behaviour; cf. 5.2.623n.
129 *public shame* Such punishment in Elizabethan England might extend from appearing, carrying a white wand, and asking for forgiveness in public, to the pillory or stocks, carting and whipping; cf. Berowne's claim that the lords are *shame-proof*, 5.2.510n.
130 *possible* possibly (*OED* possible C.)
132 **in embassy** as an ambassador
134 **complete** stressed on the first syllable; absolute, perfect
135 **Aquitaine** an area in south-west France; see Introduction, p. 26.
136 **decrepit ... father** Cf. *Son* 37.1, 'As

a decrepit father takes delight'.
138 **admired** admirèd
139 **forgot** The theme of memory and oblivion, evoked in the King's opening speech and returned to in his description of the stories Armado will tell (171), is here made one of the pivots of the play's plot.
140 **overshot** missing the mark by shooting over the target. 'To overshoot oneself' was proverbial; see Dent, O91.1, and 4.3.157n.
143 **hunteth** searches eagerly for; cf. 1.1.1n.
144 a paradox: in the course of capturing a town using fire, it is destroyed; cf. 4.3.70n., *AW* 1.1.124–6.

127 SP] *Theobald; continued to Longaville QF ('Ber.' before 131)* gentility] *F;* gentletie *Q*   129 *public*] *F (*publique*);* publibue *Q*   130 *can possible*] shall possibly *F*   132 embassy] *Q (*Embassaie*), F*
134 complete] *Q (*complet*), F*   136 bedrid] *Q (*bedred*), F*

KING

We must of force dispense with this decree.   145
She must lie here on mere necessity.

BEROWNE

Necessity will make us all forsworn
   Three thousand times within this three years' space;
For every man with his affects is born,
   Not by might mastered, but by special grace.   150
If I break faith, this word shall speak for me:
I am forsworn 'on mere necessity'.
So to the laws at large I write my name,
   And he that breaks them in the least degree
Stands in attainder of eternal shame.   155
   Suggestions are to other as to me;
But I believe, although I seem so loath,
I am the last that will last keep his oath.   [*He signs.*]
But is there no quick recreation granted?

KING

Ay, that there is. Our court, you know, is haunted   160

---

145 of force perforce, necessarily
146 lie stay, lodge. Berowne's *forsworn* in the next line suggests the possibility of a pun on *lie* as telling an untruth. **mere** absolute, sheer
147–58 form two verses like the one used in *VA*; see 61–6n.
149 affects inclinations, passions; cf. *R2* 1.4.30.
150 Cf. the Catechism in the Book of Common Prayer: 'My good Child, know this, thou art not able to do these things of thyself, nor to walk in the Commandments of God, and to serve him, without his special grace.'
151 word phrase
153 at large as a whole, in general (*OED* large C. 5e*)
155 in attainder of condemned to,

accused of (*OED* 2a*). The sense of dishonour attached to this is very strong; cf. *attaint* in Appendix 2.2, line 3. **eternal shame** Cf. *H5* 4.5.10.
156 I am as prone to temptations as any other man (*OED* suggestion 1a).
158 Berowne equivocates: although I am the last to swear, I shall keep my oath the longest; I am the least likely to keep my oath the longest.
159 quick recreation lively amusement; cf. 4.2.163n. *Quick recreation* may be intended to echo the King's *living art* 1.1.14n.
160–74 These lines form a sonnet of 15 lines with a concluding triplet; cf. 1.1.80–93n.
160–1 haunted / With frequented by

---

151 speak] breake *F*   152 'on mere necessity'] *Cam (subst.)*; on meere necessitie *QF*   156 other] others *F*   158 SD] *Capell (opp. 153)*   159–60 granted . . . haunted] *Q (graunted . . . haunted)*, *F (granted . . . hanted)*   160 is.] *Collier*; is, *QF*

With a refined traveller of Spain,
A man in all the world's new fashion planted,
    That hath a mint of phrases in his brain,
One who the music of his own vain tongue
    Doth ravish like enchanting harmony,   165
A man of compliments, whom right and wrong
    Have chose as umpire of their mutiny.
This child of fancy, that Armado hight,
    For interim to our studies shall relate
In high-born words the worth of many a knight   170
    From tawny Spain, lost in the world's debate.
How you delight, my lords, I know not, I,
    But I protest I love to hear him lie,
And I will use him for my minstrelsy.

161 **refined** refinèd; polished, cultivated in his manners (*OED ppl. a.* 2a*)
162 **fashion** whatever is fashionable – not just clothes; see 176.
planted set up, established. The collocation of *world's new . . . planted* might suggest the settling of colonists in America.
163 **phrases** short, pithy expressions; cf. Berowne's renunciation of them at 5.2.406.
164–5 Cf. Dent, L563, 'He loves to hear himself speak'. On the play's Orphic elements, see esp. Elam, 144–5, and cf. 2.1.72–6, 4.3.313–23.
164 **who** whom
165 **ravish . . . enchanting** The verb suggests ecstatic rapture (*OED* ravish *v.* 3c), while the participle implies the tongue's power is magical. See 123n. **harmony** See also 4.3.319.
166 **compliments** formal politeness, courtesy; accomplishments
167 **chose** For the shorter form of the past participle, see *OED* choose *v.* A. 6c and Abbott, 343.
mutiny discord, contention
168 **child of fancy** product of fantasti-

calness. In 'L'Allegro' Milton called Shakespeare 'fancies childe' (line 133). **hight** is called. The word was archaic. See 89n.
169–70 The King is thinking of the Spanish chivalric romances of which *Amadis de Gaule*, the Palmerin cycle and *The Mirror of Knighthood* were the most famous.
169 **For interim** as an interlude, to provide a break
170 **high-born** noble; 'high-borne' (*OED**) would suggest high-flown, lofty; cf. *high words* 190.
worth high personal merit, attainments (*OED sb.*[1] 3a): the choice of word looks forward to the Nine Worthies later in the play.
171 **tawny** yellowish-brown (because of the sun); cf. 4.3.195n.
debate fighting, quarrelling
172 **How you delight** what pleases you
173 **lie** Poets (and painters) are proverbially liars.
174 **minstrelsy** company of minstrels who sang and told stories, hence entertainment; cf. 4.3.155n.

164 One] *F;* On *Q*   165 enchanting] *Q (inchannting), F*   170 knight] *Theobald;* Knight: *QF*

BEROWNE

   Armado is a most illustrious wight,   175

   A man of fire-new words, fashion's own knight.

LONGAVILLE

   Costard the swain and he shall be our sport,

   And so to study three years is but short.

      Enter [DULL,] *a Constable, with a letter, and* COSTARD.

DULL   Which is the Duke's own person?

BEROWNE   This, fellow. What wouldst?   180

DULL   I myself reprehend his own person, for I am his
grace's farborough. But I would see his own person in
flesh and blood.

BEROWNE   This is he.

DULL   Señor Arm . . . Arm . . . commends you. There's   185
villainy abroad. This letter will tell you more.

---

175 **illustrious** eminent, renowned
(*OED a.* 3a*)
  wight person. Like *hight* (168) this
was archaic.
176 **fire-new** freshly coined; cf. *TN*
3.2.22, 'some excellent jests, fire-new
from the mint', and the proverbial
'New out of the mint', Dent, M985.
OED's earliest citation is from *R3*.
  fashion See 162n.
177 **swain** person of low rank, a rustic
179 **Duke's own person** Dull calls the
King a Duke again at 1.2.121, and so
too do Armado at 1.2.36 and the
Princess at 2.1.38. These discrepan-
cies, as well as Holofernes' over the
Princess's title (see 4.2.129 and 137),
suggest they are Shakespeare's and not
the characters': *duke* (Lat. *dux*) could
be used to refer to any sovereign ruler

(*OED sb.* 2a), and cf. Sidney's references in the *Arcadia* to King Basilius as
the 'duke'. For Dull's entry, see also
4.2.79.1n.
181 **reprehend** Dull should say 'represent', but muddles it with 'apprehend'.
His misuse of language anticipates the
errors of other constables, Dogberry
in *MA* and Elbow in *MM*.
182 **farborough** Dull's incorrect version
of 'thirdborough' (F has 'Tharborough'), the petty constable of a
township or manor
185 ***Señor** The Q ('Signeour') and F
('Signeor') forms may suggest Dull
mispronounces Armado's title as well
as his name.
  commends you Dull should say
'commends himself to you'.

---

176 fire-new] *Q (*fier new*)*; fire, new *F*   178.1] *Malone (subst.); Enter a Constable with Costard with
a letter. QF*   179 SP] *Rowe*; Constab. *Q*; Const. *F*   182 farborough] Tharborough *F*   185 Señor]
Oxf; Signeour *Q*; Signeor *F*   Arm . . . Arm] *Warburton (subst.); Arme Arme QF (subst.)*   186 abroad.]
*Rowe (*abroad;*); abroad, Q (*abrod,*), F*

124

COSTARD   Sir, the contempts thereof are as touching me.

KING   A letter from the magnificent Armado.

BEROWNE   How low soever the matter, I hope in God for
high words.   190

LONGAVILLE   A high hope for a low heaven. God grant us
patience!

BEROWNE   To hear, or forbear hearing?

LONGAVILLE   To hear meekly, sir, and to laugh moder-
ately, or to forbear both.   195

BEROWNE   Well, sir, be it as the style shall give us cause to
climb in the merriness.

COSTARD   The matter is to me, sir, as concerning
Jaquenetta. The manner of it is, I was taken with the
manner.   200

BEROWNE   In what manner?

COSTARD   In manner and form following, sir, all those

187 **contempts** Costard means 'contents'. The error is a good one, since in 244 Armado's letter denounces the *shallow vassal* Costard. Slender muddles content and contempt in *MW* 1.1.250.

188 **magnificent** splendid, ostentatious (*OED* A. 4); cf. 3.1.173n.

191 **A . . . heaven** '*high words* are a *low* sort of *heaven* to *hope* highly for' (Kerrigan)

193 **hearing** Although Capell's emendation 'laughing' is attractive and seemingly required by 194–5, it is not absolutely necessary.

196 **style** with a play on 'stile'. The joke concerns the appropriateness of a high style (*to climb*) for a low or merry subject: there may be a pun on *style* as a sharp pointed instrument, as penis, climbing or swelling, in pleasure. The Princess makes the same pun on style/stile at 4.1.96n., as does Benedick in *MA* 5.2.6–7 where

Margaret picks up a sexual innuendo.

198–9 **matter . . . manner** These two terms are usually opposed to express the substance of a subject against the form of words or style by which it is expressed (*OED* matter *sb.*[1] 11a). *Matter* may also have sexual connotations (as in Hamlet's 'country matters', 3.2.116): see 3.1.113–16n., and 116n.

198 **is to** relates to
as concerning legal language, translating the Lat. tag *in re* (*OED* concerning *prep.* 3b)

199–200 **taken . . . manner** caught in the very act; cf. the proverbial 'To take one with the manner', Tilley, M633. *Manner* here derives from the Anglo-Fr. law-term *mainoure*, itself deriving from Fr. *mainœuvre* ('handwork'), meaning 'thing stolen' and later any criminal act.

202 **In . . . following** a legal tag which became proverbial; cf. Dent, M631.1.

187+ SP COSTARD] *Rowe; Clowne. (Clow.) Q; Clow. (Clo.) F (except at 218, 220, where QF read 'Cost.')*   contempts] *F;* Contempls *Q*   192 patience!] *F (*patience.*);* patience *Q*   193 hearing] *QF;* laughing *Capell*   199 manner] *QF;* matter *Bevington*

three. I was seen with her in the manor-house, sitting
with her upon the form, and taken following her into
the park, which, put together, is 'in manner and form   205
following'. Now, sir, for the manner: it is the manner of
a man to speak to a woman; for the form: in some form.

BEROWNE   For the 'following', sir?

COSTARD   As it shall follow in my correction, and God
defend the right!   210

KING   Will you hear this letter with attention?

BEROWNE   As we would hear an oracle.

COSTARD   Such is the simplicity of man to hearken after
the flesh.

KING [*Reads.*]   *Great deputy, the welkin's vicegerent, and*   215
sole dominator of Navarre, my soul's earth's god and
body's fostering patron –

COSTARD   Not a word of Costard yet.

KING   *So it is –*

COSTARD   It may be so; but if he say it is so, he is, in   220
telling true, but so.

KING   Peace!

COSTARD   Be to me and every man that dares not fight.

---

204 **form** bench
205 **park** an enclosed area of land, often
used for hunting
206 **manner** custom, fashion
207 **speak to** talk to; have sex with: cf. 'to
speak to gallants in bay-windows',
Second Maiden's Tragedy, 1.1.41.
209 **correction** punishment
209–10 **God . . . right** the formal prayer
said before a trial by combat; cf. *R2*
1.3.101. In similar circumstances
Armado challenges Costard to a duel
at 5.2.689.
213 **simplicity** ignorance, stupidity. Q's
'sinplicitie' has been defended as a

Freudian slip (see Kerrigan, 24).
hearken after enquire after; go in
pursuit of
215 *deputy . . . vicegerent* The terms are
synonymous and suggest the King
represents God's or the heavens'
(*welkin's*) ruler on earth (*OED*
vicegerent A. 2d); cf. the proverbial
'Kings are gods on earth', Dent,
G275.1.
216 *dominator* ruler, lord
earth's god god on earth
220–1 **in . . . so** to tell the truth, only
so-so, not worth much; for *telling true*,
cf. 4.1.18.

207 form:] *Oxf;* forme *QF*   213 simplicity] *F;* sinplicitie *Q*   214 flesh.] *F;* flesh *Q*   215 SD]
Rowe (subst.)   welkin's] F; welkis *Q*   216 dominator] *F;* dominatur *Q*   217 fostering] *QF (fostring)*
218 Costard] *Qc, F;* Costart *Qu*

KING No words!

COSTARD Of other men's secrets, I beseech you. 225

KING *So it is, besieged with sable-coloured melancholy, I did*
commend the black oppressing humour to the most
wholesome physic of thy health-giving air; and, as I am a
gentleman, betook myself to walk. The time, when? About
the sixth hour, when beasts most graze, birds best peck and 230
men sit down to that nourishment which is called supper. So
much for the time when. Now for the ground, which?
Which, I mean, I walked upon. It is ycleped thy park.
Then for the place, where? Where, I mean, I did encounter
that obscene and most preposterous event that draweth from 235
my snow-white pen the ebon-coloured ink, which here thou
viewest, beholdest, surveyest or seest. But to the place,
where? It standeth north-north-east and by east from the

225 **secrets** private affairs; private parts

226–8 *So . . . air* The association between melancholy and constipation (cf. 'the melancholy Jaques' or 'jakes' in *AYL* 2.1.26 and Rubinstein, 158) may suggest allusions here to excretion (*besieged, air*) and excrement (*sable-coloured, black oppressing*), induced by a purge (*physic*). Cf. 263n.

226 *besieged* In this figurative sense *OED v.* 1b cites *Son* 2.1 and more strikingly *AW* 2.1.9–10, 'the malady / That doth my life besiege'. There is probably a pun on *beseech/besieged*.

 sable-coloured black: melancholy, one of the four humours (for which see 1.2.76n.), was thought to be the product of too much black bile.

227 *commend* commit, entrust (*OED v.* 1a)

 oppressing crushing, weighing down (*OED ppl. a.***)

228 *physic* medicine

 health-giving (*OED* health *sb.* 8b*)

 as on my word as; cf. *R2* 3.3.119.

229–38 Armado's questions suggest both

legal indictments and rhetorical formularies, for which see Baldwin, 2.310–15, and cf. Berowne's questions 5.2.386.

231 *supper* evening meal, with implication of sexual feeding; cf. *RJ* 2.4.129.

233 *ycleped* called. Shakespeare uses this archaism only here and at 5.2.592.

235 *obscene* disgusting, repulsive (*OED a.* 1). See also 4.1.142n.

 preposterous against the natural order of things. For a lengthy commentary on this passage and its (sexual) implications, see Parker.

236 *snow-white pen* a white goose-quill pen; *snow-white* was proverbial: cf. Dent, S591.1.

 ebon-coloured ink black ink. 'As black as ebony' was proverbial: see Dent, E56a, and cf. 4.3.243n.

238 **north-north-east . . . east** North-north-east lies midway between north and north-east; *by east* adds a further minute detail. The precise direction suggests the garden would be sheltered by the trees in the park (*Shakespeare's England*, 1.371).

230 *sixth*] *QF* (*sixt*) 233 *ycleped*] *QF* (*ycliped*) 235 *preposterous*] *F; propostrous Q*

> *west corner of thy curious-knotted garden. There did I see*
> *that low-spirited swain, that base minnow of thy mirth –*   240

COSTARD   Me?

KING   *That unlettered small-knowing soul –*

COSTARD   Me?

KING   *That shallow vassal –*

COSTARD   Still me?   245

KING   *Which, as I remember, hight Costard –*

COSTARD   O, me!

KING   *Sorted and consorted, contrary to thy established*
> *proclaimed edict and continent canon, which with, O,*
> *with – but with this I passion to say wherewith –*   250

COSTARD   With a wench.

KING   *With a child of our grandmother Eve, a female, or, for*
> *thy more sweet understanding, a woman. Him I, as my*

---

239 *corner* secret or remote place (*OED sb.*[1] 6a), hence with a sexual innuendo; cf. *MM* 4.3.156–7, 'the old fantastical Duke of dark corners'.
curious-knotted garden garden laid out with intricately patterned flower-beds; see Introduction, p. 47.

240 *low-spirited* base (*OED* low-spirited *a.* a*)
minnow . . . mirth thing so small and insignificant as to be laughable; a minnow is a small fish (*OED* 1b*).

241–7 *In QF Costard's interruptions are printed with SPs within brackets as part of the King's reading of Armado's letter: Simpson, 95–7, compares other settings in *Oth* and Jonson's *Sejanus*, but his examples are not strictly the same. For a similar dramatic effect, Elam, 78, compares Sir Andrew's interruptions while Malvolio reads from the letter in *TN* 2.5.72–82.

242 *unlettered* illiterate *OED* 1b; cf. 4.2.18, *Son* 85.6.

244 *vassal* base wretch, slavish fellow

248 *Sorted* associated
established fixed, settled (*OED***)

249 *continent canon* law or rule restricting or restraining behaviour, esp. sexual behaviour (*OED* continent *a.* 3a*)
which with Although *which* is otiose, it may reflect Armado's passionate fury, perhaps picking up from the *Which* in 246. Oxf[1]'s argument that a shortened form of 'where' was misread as 'which', to produce the correct reading 'wherewith', is unlikely: more probably, there was some confusion about w^{ch}/wth, involving deletion or dittography.

250 *passion* sorrow, grieve

252 *grandmother Eve* The phrase was common; for Eve, see also 5.2.322n.

253 *understanding* comprehension; those who stand under the stage to watch the play from the theatre yard; the penis which stands under the woman and results in carnal knowledge (see Proudfoot, 22–3)

240 *minnow*] *QF; minion Sisson (Johnson)* ets within the body of the King's speech in QF with*] *QF; with, with / Theobald*   241, 243, 245, 247] *Hanmer; Costard's lines are in brackets*   245 me?] *F; mee. Q*   249 *continent*] *Continet, F which*

ever-esteemed duty pricks me on, have sent to thee, to
receive the meed of punishment, by thy sweet grace's officer,   255
Anthony Dull, a man of good repute, carriage, bearing and
estimation.

DULL   Me, an't shall please you. I am Anthony Dull.

KING   *For Jaquenetta, so is the weaker vessel called which I*
apprehended with the aforesaid swain, I keep her as a vessel   260
of thy law's fury, and shall, at the least of thy sweet notice,
bring her to trial. Thine in all compliments of devoted and
heartburning heat of duty,

Don Adriano de Armado.

BEROWNE   This is not so well as I looked for, but the best   265
that ever I heard.

KING   Ay, the best for the worst. But, sirrah, what say you
to this?

COSTARD   Sir, I confess the wench.

KING   Did you hear the proclamation?   270

COSTARD   I do confess much of the hearing it, but little of
the marking of it.

KING   It was proclaimed a year's imprisonment to be
taken with a wench.

254 *duty . . . on* The ambiguity of
Armado's language, evident in *understanding* and *pricks*, is strengthened if
duty includes a sense of what is owed
sexually.

255 *meed* reward

256 *good repute* like the authorities
Armado calls for at 1.2.67
carriage Cf. the description of
Samson at 1.2.68–70 and of the
Muscovites at 5.2.306n. Like *bearing*
this refers to ability to bear burdens on
the back and hence may have connotations of suitability for sodomy (Ellis).

257 *estimation* reputation

258 *an't* if it

259 *the weaker vessel* Cf. the proverbial

'A woman is the weaker vessel' deriving from 1 Peter, 3.7, Tilley, W655.

261 *at . . . notice* with very little notice at
your command

262 *bring . . . trial* try her in a legal and,
perhaps, sexual sense

263 *heartburning* i.e. inflaming, distress-
ing the heart (*OED ppl. a.*) through
zealousness or indigestion, for which
cf. *MA* 2.1.3–4.

267 *the best . . . worst the best example
of something completely bad; cf. the
proverbial 'The better the worse',
Tilley, B333.

269 confess admit to the charge concerning; cf. 1.2.43.

272 marking paying attention to

258 SP] *Rowe; Antho. Q, F (Anth.)*   260 *keep*] *keeper F*   262 *compliments*] *QF (complements)*
264 *Adriano*] Adriana *F*   267 worst] *F;* wost *Q*

COSTARD   I was taken with none, sir; I was taken with a   275
damsel.

KING   Well, it was proclaimed damsel.

COSTARD   This was no damsel neither, sir; she was a virgin.

KING   It is so varied too, for it was proclaimed virgin.

COSTARD   If it were, I deny her virginity: I was taken with   280
a maid.

KING   This maid will not serve your turn, sir.

COSTARD   This maid will serve my turn, sir.

KING   Sir, I will pronounce your sentence: you shall fast a
week with bran and water.   285

COSTARD   I had rather pray a month with mutton and
porridge.

KING

And Don Armado shall be your keeper.
My lord Berowne, see him delivered o'er;
And go we, lords, to put in practice that   290

275–6 Costard's equivocations echo Armado's synonyms in 252–3.

276 **damsel** The word is used in the play here, at 1.2.124 and, in the form *damosella*, at 4.2.127 exclusively for Jaquenetta. It had French associations – Shakespeare only certainly uses it elsewhere in *1H6* to refer twice to Joan of Arc.

279 SP *Q's '*Ber.*' is changed in F to '*Fer.*'; Berowne's intrusion into the King's dialogue with Costard would draw attention to the clown's role and to his wit, but seems wrong.
varied expressed in different words (*OED v.* 9); cf. 4.2.9, 4.3.97n. and *Son* 105.10. Variation was a means of achieving the copiousness of language valued by Renaissance humanists.

282 Resorting to calling her *maid* will not get you out of trouble or will not do the trick.

283 She will do what I want her to do, sat-

isfy my needs; cf. *OED* turn *sb.* 30b (*a*) and *AC* 2.5.58–9, where the sexual connotation of 'the best turn i' th' bed' is made explicit.

284–5 **fast . . . water** Cf. the common phrase 'to fast bread and water' (*OED* fast *v.*[2] 1b).

284–6 **fast . . . pray** The two commonly went together; cf. *CE* 1.2.51, *Oth* 3.4.40. See 1.1.24n.

285 **bran** bread made from the coarsest grain

286–7 Elam, 110, notes that Costard 'takes the King's new pronouncement as a "sentence" more in the syntactic than in the legal sense'.
mutton and porridge mutton broth, a hendiadys, see 14n. *Mutton* was also slang for a prostitute and *porridge* may have had a similar connotation (possibly a pun on 'partridge'), in which case *pray* might refer to a man's traditional position during intercourse (Ellis).

276 damsel] *Q (*Demsel); Damosell *F*   277, 278 damsel] Damosell *F*   279 SP] *F (Fer.);* Ber. *Q* 284, 288 SP] *F (Kin.);* Fer. *Q*

Which each to other hath so strongly sworn.

[*Exeunt the King, Longaville and Dumaine.*]

BEROWNE

I'll lay my head to any goodman's hat
  These oaths and laws will prove an idle scorn.
Sirrah, come on.

COSTARD   I suffer for the truth, sir, for true it is, I was   295
taken with Jaquenetta, and Jaquenetta is a true girl.
And therefore welcome the sour cup of prosperity!
Affliction may one day smile again, and, till then, sit
thee down, sorrow.   *Exeunt.*

[1.2]   *Enter* ARMADO *and* MOTH, *his Page.*

ARMADO   Boy, what sign is it when a man of great spirit
grows melancholy?

292 'I'll bet my head against any yeo-
man's hat'; cf. the proverbial 'My cap
(hat) to a noble', Dent, C63.1, and
Berowne's later bet involving hats,
5.2.556n.
293 **idle scorn** worthless matter for
scorn (*OED* scorn *sb.* 3a). Rosaline
sentences Berowne to utter *idle scorns*
to *sickly ears* in 5.2.851–3; the phrase
does not occur elsewhere in
Shakespeare.
295 **I . . . truth** As the King and his companions seek *the light of truth* in 75, so
Costard is a martyr to truth.
296 **true** honest
    girl As with *damsel* (276n.) only
Jaquenetta is called a girl in the play,
here and at 1.2.112, 4.2.144. However,
the Princess and her ladies are called
girls at 4.3.345, 5.2.58.
297 **prosperity** Costard means 'adversity'.

298 ***Affliction** Usually in Shakespeare
it is the heavens or fortune which smile
on people.
298–9 **sit . . . sorrow** Substantially
repeated at 4.3.4, the phrase is used by
earlier writers (see *Brittons bowre of
delights* (1591), sig. C3r) and sounds
proverbial with the implication of
being patient, but its precise meaning
is uncertain.
1.2.1–2 Oxf[1] states that the answer
Armado expects is ' "It is an infallible
sign that he is in love" ' and cites
Ovid's *Ars amatoria*, 1.737–8.
1   **Boy** Armado's (and others') characteristic way of addressing Moth
    spirit Armado repeats the word in
relation to himself (40, 116): a pun on
penis or semen – as in *Son* 129.1 –
seems likely.

291 SD] *Capell*   294 Sirrah] *F* (Sirra); Surra *Q*   297 prosperity] *F;* prosperie *Q*   298 Affliction]
F; affliccio *Q*   till] vntill *F*   298–9 sit thee] sit *F*   299 SD] *Exit. F*
1.2] *Capell*   0.1 MOTH] *QF;* Mote *Kerrigan, Oxf*   1+ SP ARMADO] *Q (subst.); Arma. F (at 1, but
thereafter 'Brag.', 'Bra.' or 'Br.')*

Love's Labour's Lost

MOTH   A great sign, sir, that he will look sad.

ARMADO   Why, sadness is one and the selfsame thing,
dear imp.   5

MOTH   No, no, O Lord, sir, no.

ARMADO   How canst thou part sadness and melancholy,
my tender juvenal?

MOTH   By a familiar demonstration of the working, my
tough señor.   10

ARMADO   Why tough señor? Why tough señor?

MOTH   Why tender juvenal? Why tender juvenal?

ARMADO   I spoke it, tender juvenal, as a congruent
epitheton appertaining to thy young days, which we
may nominate tender.   15

MOTH   And I, tough señor, as an appertinent title to your

3–4 **sad . . . sadness** sorrowful, unhappy
. . . sorrowfulness, unhappiness
5 **imp** child, lit. a sprig or offshoot. Oxf¹
points out that Shakespeare uses the
noun only here, at 5.2.582, and in two
speeches by Pistol, *2H4* 5.5.42 and *H5*
4.1.45.
6 **O Lord, sir** certainly, indeed: this
empty, evasive and fashionable phrase
is used several times by the Clown and
once by Parolles in *AW* (2.2.41–62,
4.3.309).
7 **part** distinguish between
8 **tender** young, immature
juvenal youth, punning on the name
of the Roman satirist Juvenal (*OED*
B.*). Although 'juvenile' as an adjective is not recorded in *OED* before
1625 and as a noun before 1733, the
word would have been familiar from
the Lat. adjective *juvenilis*. The sharp-
penned satirist Nashe was particularly
associated with Juvenal. Like 'imp', on
the few occasions Shakespeare used
the word it was in comic circum-

stances; see 3.1.63, *MND* 3.1.95 and
2H4 1.2.19.
9 **familiar** easily understood (*OED* A. 6c)
demonstration proof by argument or
logical demonstration (*OED* 3a): a
technical term
working emotional activity, operation
of the heart; cf. 'the working of the
heart', 4.1.33.
10 *señor** with a pun on 'senior' as at
3.1.175n.
13 **congruent** suitable, proper; see
5.1.85n.
14 *epitheton** description. Shakespeare
uses this form only here, preferring
'epithet(s)': see 4.2.8n., 5.1.15,
5.2.171; its only other occurrences are
in *MA* 5.2.66 and *Oth* 1.1.14.
15 **nominate** call, name; another rare
word repeated in the play: see 4.2.133
and 5.1.8. For Armado's fondness for
forms of words incorporating the suf-
fix -ate, see Introduction, p. 48 n.2.
16 **appertinent** suitable, appropriate

3+ SP MOTH] *Rowe; Boy. QF;* Mote *Kerrigan (subst.)*   4 Why,] *Theobald;* Why? *QF*   8, 12, 13 juve-
nal] *Q (subst.); Iuuenall F*   10, 11, 16 señor] *Oxf;* signeor *Q;* signeur *F*   14 epitheton] *F2;* apethaton
Q; apathaton *F*

132

old time, which we may name tough.

ARMADO   Pretty and apt.

MOTH   How mean you, sir? I pretty and my saying apt, or
  I apt and my saying pretty?   20

ARMADO   Thou pretty, because little.

MOTH   Little pretty, because little. Wherefore apt?

ARMADO   And therefore apt, because quick.

MOTH   Speak you this in my praise, master?

ARMADO   In thy condign praise.   25

MOTH   I will praise an eel with the same praise.

ARMADO   What, that an eel is ingenious?

MOTH   That an eel is quick.

ARMADO   I do say thou art quick in answers. Thou heatest
  my blood.   30

MOTH   I am answered sir.

ARMADO   I love not to be crossed.

MOTH [*aside*]   He speaks the mere contrary: crosses love
  not him.

ARMADO   I have promised to study three years with the   35
  Duke.

MOTH   You may do it in an hour, sir.

ARMADO   Impossible.

---

18 **Pretty and apt** pretty apt. A hendiadys (see 1.1.14n.), which Moth wilfully misinterprets.
21 Cf. the proverbial 'Little things are
pretty', Tilley, T188.
25 **condign** well-deserved (*OED a*. 3a)
26 **praise an eel** Like Erasmus in *The
Praise of Folly*, Moth is proposing the
paradoxical praise of a worthless thing.
Moth may be punning sexually here:
the shape, wetness and slipperiness of
the eel might suggest a penis and there
may be a homophonic pun on eel/ell
(cf. 4.2.58n.). For an emblematic interpretation of the eel, see Elam, 154–5.

27 **ingenious** clever, intellectually quick.
'Ingenious' and 'ingenuous' (the F
reading) were frequently confused; see
OED ingenuous 6 and cf. 3.1.55n.,
4.2.76n.
28 The phrase was (or became) proverbial; see Tilley, E59.
29–30 **Thou . . . blood** 'Your misinter-
preting what I say is making me angry.'
32 **crossed** contradicted (*OED v*. 14c)
33 **the mere contrary** quite the reverse
33–4 **crosses . . . him** coins are not
attracted to him. Coins often had
crosses stamped on one side of them
(*OED* cross *sb*. 20).

22 apt?] *F*; apt. *Q*   27 ingenious] ingenuous *F*   33 SD] *Hanmer*   35 three] iij. *F*

MOTH   How many is one thrice told?

ARMADO   I am ill at reckoning. It fitteth the spirit of a   40
tapster.

MOTH   You are a gentleman and a gamester, sir.

ARMADO   I confess both. They are both the varnish of a
complete man.

MOTH   Then I am sure you know how much the gross   45
sum of deuce-ace amounts to.

ARMADO   It doth amount to one more than two.

MOTH   Which the base vulgar do call three.

ARMADO   True.

MOTH   Why, sir, is this such a piece of study? Now here is   50
three studied ere ye'll thrice wink. And how easy it is to
put 'years' to the word 'three', and study three years in
two words, the dancing horse will tell you.

ARMADO   A most fine figure!

MOTH [*aside*]   To prove you a cipher.   55

ARMADO   I will hereupon confess I am in love. And as it is
base for a soldier to love, so am I in love with a base
wench. If drawing my sword against the humour of

---

39 **told** counted

40 **ill** not good, poor
   reckoning calculations, sums (*OED vbl. sb.* 1a); cf. 5.2.496, 792n.

41 **tapster** tavern-keeper, the man who drew drink from the tap or barrel

42 **gamester** gambler; male prostitute (*OED* 5**); cf. *AW* 5.3.188.

43 **confess** Cf. 1.1.269n.
   varnish finishing gloss

44 **complete** accomplished, consummate

46 **deuce-ace** in the dice game of hazard, a throw of two and of one, which – like 'ames-ace' in *AW* 2.3.79 – lost the game, hence suggesting bad luck

48 **vulgar** common people (*OED sb.* 2a)

50 **piece** task, difficult business (*OED sb.* 7b)

51 **studied** worked out by studious application

52 **put . . . word** Cf. 'put "l" to sore', 4.2.58.

53 **the dancing horse** probably a performing horse called Morocco, in England by 1591 and frequently referred to by writers of the time. He could dance and could count, *tell*, by stamping his hoofs.

54 **figure** figure of speech, form of rhetoric or logic; numeral: cf. 4.2.66n., 5.1.59n., 5.2.408n.

55 **cipher** nothing, nonentity; cf. the proverbial 'He is a cipher among numbers', Dent, C391.

57 ²**base** lowly born

58–9 **humour of affection** inclination, disposition to be in love

40 fitteth] fits *F*   48 do] *om. F*   50 here is] here's *F*   51 ye'll] *Q (*yele*);* you'll *F*   55 SD] *Hanmer*

affection would deliver me from the reprobate thought
of it, I would take desire prisoner and ransom him to   60
any French courtier for a new-devised curtsy. I think
scorn to sigh; methinks I should outswear Cupid.
Comfort me, boy. What great men have been in love?
MOTH   Hercules, master.
ARMADO   Most sweet Hercules! More authority, dear boy,   65
name more. And, sweet my child, let them be men of
good repute and carriage.
MOTH   Samson, master. He was a man of good carriage,
great carriage, for he carried the town-gates on his back
like a porter, and he was in love.   70
ARMADO   O well-knit Samson, strong-jointed Samson! I
do excel thee in my rapier as much as thou didst me in
carrying gates. I am in love too. Who was Samson's
love, my dear Moth?
MOTH   A woman, master.   75
ARMADO   Of what complexion?

---

59 **reprobate** depraved, corrupt (*OED a.* 2a)
61 **new-devised curtsy** newly invented bow (*OED* new-devised*)
61–2 **think scorn** think it disgraceful, disdain
62 **outswear** renounce, swear to do without, cf. 2.1.104n. *OED** defines it as to overcome with swearing.
64–5 **Hercules** the classical hero who was captured and humiliated by the Amazon Omphale; the mention anticipates his being one of the Nine Worthies. Cf. 5.2.872n.
65 **authority** See 4.3.283n.
67 **good repute** See 1.1.256n.
carriage demeanour, behaviour (*OED* 14a)
68 **Samson** the biblical hero, in love with Delilah, who tricked and betrayed him to the Philistines

carriage carrying power (*OED* 6*); cf. 1.1.256n.
69–70 **he carried . . . love** Judges, 16.3, tells how he carried off the gates of Gaza.
70 **porter** one who carries burdens on his back, hence the passive partner in homosexual acts (Rubinstein, 200)
71 **well-knit** well-constructed (*OED* 2**); Shakespeare's only use of the compound
72 **rapier** a long thin sword, fashionable from the 1590s in England
76 **complexion** *Complexion* or temperament was determined by the mixture of the four humours: blood, phlegm, choler and melancholy (the product of black bile). Moth answers Armado's question on the basis that the humours determined the colour of skin.

61 curtsy] *F (*curtsie); cursie *Q*

MOTH   Of all the four, or the three, or the two, or one of
the four.

ARMADO   Tell me precisely of what complexion?

MOTH   Of the sea-water green, sir.   80

ARMADO   Is that one of the four complexions?

MOTH   As I have read, sir; and the best of them too.

ARMADO   Green indeed is the colour of lovers. But to
have a love of that colour, methinks Samson had small
reason for it. He surely affected her for her wit.   85

MOTH   It was so, sir, for she had a green wit.

ARMADO   My love is most immaculate white and red.

MOTH   Most maculate thoughts, master, are masked
under such colours.

ARMADO   Define, define, well-educated infant.   90

MOTH   My father's wit and my mother's tongue assist me!

ARMADO   Sweet invocation of a child, most pretty and
pathetical!

MOTH

If she be made of white and red,

80 **sea-water green** Moth says that
Delilah looked ill, but his phrase also
suggests she suffered from 'green-
sickness' or chlorosis, an anaemic condition affecting young women (*OED*
sea-water 1c*).

83 **Green . . . lovers** Ard[1] refers to the
song 'Greensleeves'; the association
between the greenness of spring and
the coming of love is commonplace.

85 **affected . . . wit** loved her for her
cleverness

86 **she . . . wit** She had an immature,
childish intelligence. 'To have a green
wit' was proverbial, Dent, W563.1.

87 **immaculate** pure, unblemished

88 **maculate** defiled, polluted

89 **under such colours** The colours may
be artificial ones – the phrase recalls
'under colour of', meaning 'under pre-
text of' – and they may be rhetorical

ones, ornaments of style and diction
(*OED* colour *sb.* 13).

90 **Define** explain the meaning (*OED v.*
6b): the word is a term from logic.
well-educated *OED** and educated
ppl. a. a**; Shakespeare's only use of
the compound

91 **father's . . . tongue** Cf. the proverbial
'Mother-tongue' and 'Mother-wit',
Dent, M1208.1 and .2; cf. 1.1.123n.

92–3 **pretty and pathetical** fine and
moving or affecting; for *pathetical* in
this sense, see 4.1.147n. and cf. *Pretty
and apt*, 18. *Pretty* may be used here
adverbially as an intensifier, with the
phrase meaning 'considerably moving
or affecting' (*OED* pretty *a*. 5c), and cf.
CE 3.1.110. Chapman particularly
liked the phrase and used it in *An
Humorous Day's Mirth*, 1.1.36, and
The Widow's Tears, 3.1.120–1.

88 maculate] immaculate *F*   masked] *Q (*maskt*), F*

Her faults will ne'er be known,   95
For blushing cheeks by faults are bred,
And fears by pale white shown.
Then if she fear or be to blame,
By this you shall not know,
For still her cheeks possess the same   100
Which native she doth owe.
A dangerous rhyme, master, against the reason of white
and red.

ARMADO   Is there not a ballad, boy, of the King and the
Beggar?   105

MOTH   The world was very guilty of such a ballad some
three ages since, but I think now 'tis not to be found, or,
if it were, it would neither serve for the writing nor the
tune.

ARMADO   I will have that subject newly writ o'er, that I   110
may example my digression by some mighty precedent.
Boy, I do love that country girl that I took in the park
with the rational hind Costard. She deserves well.

99 **By this** i.e. by her complexion
100 **still** always
   possess the same i.e. keep the same
   colour
101 **native . . . owe** she has naturally:
   owe, own
102–3 The poem warns against the dan-
   gers of trusting to white and red,
   which may be cosmetics. Moth plays
   on the proverbial 'Rhyme and reason',
   see 1.1.99n.
104–5 **ballad . . . Beggar** Armado probably refers to the same ballad relating
   to King Cophetua and the beggar-
   maid Zenelophon at 4.1.65–79. The
   earliest surviving version is in Richard
   Johnson's *A Crown-Garland of Golden
   Roses* (1612).
108 **serve** be acceptable
110 **writ o'er** written out again (*OED v.*
   17a)

111 **example** justify (*OED v.* 3)
   digression moral lapse, going astray;
   elsewhere, Shakespeare only used it in
   this sense in *Luc* 202.
112–13 *Q's comma after 'love' in 112
   might suggest that Armado does not
   suddenly reveal the object of his love
   to Moth, but instead that *I do love* is
   parenthetical and *She deserves well* a
   dependent clause, in which case the
   passage might read 'Boy: I do love.
   That country girl that I took in the
   park with the rational hind Costard,
   she deserves well'.
113 **rational hind** rustic capable of using
   his reason. Armado may also utter a
   contradiction in terms, since a hind
   was a female deer (of the kind to be
   found in a park) and hence incapable of
   reason.

96 blushing] *F2;* blush-in *QF*   101 owe.] *F (*owe:*);* owe *Q*   112 love] *F;* love, *Q*

MOTH [*aside*]   To be whipped: and yet a better love than
    my master.   115
ARMADO   Sing, boy. My spirit grows heavy in love.
MOTH [*aside*]   And that's great marvel, loving a light
    wench.
ARMADO   I say sing.
MOTH   Forbear till this company be passed.   120

Enter [COSTARD, *the*] *Clown,* [DULL, *the*] *Constable,*
        and [JAQUENETTA, *a*] *wench.*

DULL   Sir, the Duke's pleasure is that you keep Costard
    safe; and you must suffer him to take no delight, nor no
    penance, but 'a must fast three days a week. For this
    damsel, I must keep her at the park: she is allowed for
    the dey-woman. Fare you well.   125
ARMADO [*aside*]   I do betray myself with blushing. –
    Maid –
JAQUENETTA   Man.
ARMADO   I will visit thee at the lodge.
JAQUENETTA   That's hereby.   130
ARMADO   I know where it is situate.

114 **whipped** Prostitutes were punished
by whipping.
117 **light** the opposite of heavy in 116;
wanton, unchaste. Katherine puns in
the same way at 5.2.14–15.
123 **penance** in error, perhaps for 'pleas-
ance'. *Penance* occurs again at 1.1.115
and 5.2.706.
'a he; a common colloquial form
fast . . . week Statutes commanding
fish-days on Wednesday, Friday and
Saturday were enforced during Queen
Elizabeth's reign to help promote the
fishing industry. See 1.1.24n.
124–5 *****allowed . . . dey-woman**

approved to serve as the dairy-woman
(*OED* dey-woman*)
126 **betray myself** reveal my true feelings (*OED* betray *v.* 6*)
blushing Armado returns to the theme
of Moth's rhyme: see 96; Dumaine is
accused of blushing later: see 4.3.128n.
129 **lodge** a house in a forest used during
the hunting season; a gatehouse to a
park
130 **hereby** near this place; Shakespeare's
only other use of the word in this sense
is in 4.1.9. Some sort of put-down is
probably intended – perhaps 'That's
by the way', i.e. 'You must be joking'.

114 SD] *Hanmer*   whipped] *Q (*whipt*), F*   116 love] *Q (*loue*);* ioue *F*   117 SD] *Cam¹*   121 SP]
Rowe; Constab. QF (subst.)   122 suffer him to] let him *F*   123 'a] *Q (*a'*);* hee *F*   125 dey-woman]
*F (*Day-woman*);* Day womand *Q*   well.] well. *Exit. F*   126 SD] *Kerrigan*   128+ SP JAQUENETTA]
Rowe; Maide. (Maid., Ma.) QF (subst.)   130 hereby] here by *F*

JAQUENETTA   Lord, how wise you are!

ARMADO   I will tell thee wonders.

JAQUENETTA   With that face?

ARMADO   I love thee.   135

JAQUENETTA   So I heard you say.

ARMADO   And so farewell.

JAQUENETTA   Fair weather after you.

DULL   Come, Jaquenetta, away.   *Exeunt [Dull and Jaquenetta].*

ARMADO   Villain, thou shalt fast for thy offences ere thou   140
be pardoned.

COSTARD   Well, sir, I hope when I do it I shall do it on a
full stomach.

ARMADO   Thou shalt be heavily punished.

COSTARD   I am more bound to you than your fellows, for   145
they are but lightly rewarded.

ARMADO   Take away this villain. Shut him up.

MOTH   Come, you transgressing slave, away!

COSTARD   Let me not be pent up, sir, I will fast being
loose.   150

MOTH   No, sir, that were fast and loose. Thou shalt to prison.

133–4 **tell . . . face** The words suggest
the telling or counting of coins which
have a face on one side of them.
134 **With that face** Really!
136 The phrase became proverbial; see
Tilley, T89.
138 proverbial: see Dent, W217.
139 SP *QF assign the line to Costard,
reading '*Clo.*', and follow it with the
SD '*Exeunt.*', but Armado, Moth and
Costard must remain on stage to continue their dialogue. Theobald was
therefore correct to assign the line to
Dull, who had already shown he wanted to leave with *Fare you well* in 125, at
which point F even gives him an '*Exit.*'
It is possible that the error arose from
a confusion between an SP '*Clo.*' or
even '*Co[stard].*' and '*Co[nstable].*'

140 **Villain** peasant; rogue
142–3 **on . . . stomach** Cf. the proverb
'The belly that is full may well fast',
Dent, B289; the phrase also suggests
doing something courageously.
145 **fellows** servants
149 **pent up** imprisoned; constipated
150 **loose** free; loose in the bowels: cf.
3.1.123–4n.
151 **fast and loose** unfair; more correctly,
a cheating game played by gypsies in
which, according to Reginald Scott, *The
Discovery of Witchcraft* (1584), 13.29,
either a handkerchief appears to be
knotted fast but can be shaken loose or
three beads can be pulled loose from a
piece of string while it is held fast by
hand; mentioned again at 3.1.100. The
phrase was proverbial; see Tilley, P401.

132 are!] *F;* are. *Q*   134 that face?] *Q (*that face.*);* what face? *F*   139 SP] *Theobald; Clo. QF*   SD]
Theobald; Exeunt. QF   142+ SP COSTARD] *Rowe; Clo. QF*   147 SP] *Q (Ar.); Clo. F*

139

COSTARD   Well, if ever I do see the merry days of desolation that I have seen, some shall see –

MOTH   What shall some see?

COSTARD   Nay, nothing, Master Moth, but what they   155
look upon. It is not for prisoners to be too silent in their words and therefore I will say nothing. I thank God I have as little patience as another man and therefore I can be quiet.   [*Exeunt Moth and Costard.*]

ARMADO   I do affect the very ground, which is base,   160
where her shoe, which is baser, guided by her foot, which is basest, doth tread. I shall be forsworn, which is a great argument of falsehood, if I love. And how can that be true love which is falsely attempted? Love is a familiar; Love is a devil. There is no evil angel but   165
Love. Yet was Samson so tempted, and he had an excellent strength. Yet was Solomon so seduced, and he

153 **desolation** in error, perhaps for 'jubilation' (although the word does not occur in Shakespeare) or 'consolation'

156 **silent** in error, probably for a word similar to 'free'

157 **words** There may be a pun intended on 'wards', meaning imprisonment (*OED sb.*[2] 3).

158 **little** in error, probably for 'much', but *patience* (for 'passion(s)') may be incorrect instead

160 **affect** love; cf. 5.2.407n.

160–2 **affect . . . tread** Cf. the proverbial 'To love (hate) the ground another treads on', Tilley, G468.
   base . . . baser . . . basest Armado takes the adjective (cf. 1.1.87n.) through its positive, comparative and superlative forms; cf. 4.3.15–16n.

161 **shoe** The reference anticipates Longaville's insult about Rosaline at 4.3.273–5: the erotic associations of shoes may be relevant in both instances, and see also 4.1.82–3, 5.2.664n.

162 **be forsworn** break my oath

163 **argument** proof

164 **falsely attempted** undertaken or tried under false premises

165 **familiar** attendant evil spirit

166 **Samson so tempted** by Delilah to reveal the secret of his great strength

167–9 **Solomon . . . Hercules** The two occur again together in a different context at 4.3.164–5.

167 **Solomon   so   seduced** For Solomon's love of sexual and sensual pleasures, see 1 Kings, 11.1–3, and the Song of Solomon: his love of women turned him to heathenism, for which God punished him.

155 Master] *F*; M. *Q*   156 too] *om. F*   159 SD] *Pope (subst.); Exit. QF*   166 was Samson] *Q (was Sampson); Sampson* was *F*

had a very good wit. Cupid's butt-shaft is too hard for
Hercules' club, and therefore too much odds for a
Spaniard's rapier. The first and second cause will not   170
serve my turn. The *passado* he respects not; the *duello*
he regards not. His disgrace is to be called boy, but his
glory is to subdue men. Adieu, valour; rust, rapier; be
still, drum, for your manager is in love. Yea, he loveth.
Assist me, some extemporal god of rhyme, for I am   175
sure I shall turn sonnet. Devise, wit; write, pen; for I
am for whole volumes in folio.   *Exit.*

168 **butt-shaft** an unbarbed arrow (*shaft*)
used for short-range target practice,
the target standing on a mound of
earth (a *butt*). Shakespeare's only other
use of the word, *RJ* 2.4.16, in a passage
which echoes this one (see *passado*,
171) is also in the context of Cupid's
shooting.
169 **club** In the context of the hardness
of the butt-shaft – *butt* meaning its
diminutive 'buttock' (*OED sb.³* 3) –
Hercules' club may pun on his penis;
see also 5.1.119–20n.
  odds superiority
170 **first . . . cause** Armado refers to the
codification of chivalric behaviour wit-
nessed in books such as Sir William
Segar's *The Book of Honour and Arms*
(1590). 'Triall of Armes', he wrote,
may take place first 'whensoeuer one
man doth accuse another of such a
crime as meriteth death' or, secondly,
when the 'cause of Combat is Honor,
because among persons of reputation,
Honor is preferred before life' (22–3).
First and secondary causes can be
related to Aristotelian philosophy and
suggest, as Ard² points out, that
Armado is thinking like Subtle when

he speaks to Kastrill in Jonson's *The
Alchemist*, 4.2.21–4, of the '*Grammar*',
'*Logick*' and 'rhetoric of quarrelling':
'You must render causes, child, / Your
first, and second *Intentions*, know your
canons, / And your *diuisions*, *moodes*,
degrees, and *differences*' (Jonson, 5.366).
171 *passado* 'A forward thrust with the
sword, one foot being advanced at the
same time' (*OED* 1*). The term occurs
twice in *RJ* 2.4.26 and 3.1.85.
  **duello* the established code of duel-
lists (*OED* 1*)
174 **manager** one who wields or is in
charge (*OED* 1*)
175 **extemporal . . . rhyme** god of
unpremeditated verse; Holofernes'
poem on the death of the deer is *an
extemporal epitaph*: see 4.2.49–50.
Nashe was particularly associated with
extemporal writing.
176 **turn sonnet** write a sonnet (any sort
of short lyrical or love poem), become
a love poet. For a poem by Armado, see
4.1.87–92.
177 **folio** a large-format book (*OED sb.*
5a); Shakespeare's only use of the
word

171 *duello*] F (*Duello*); Duella Q   177 SD] *Exit. / Finis Actus Primus.* F

2[.1] *Enter the* PRINCESS *of France, with three attending ladies*
[ROSALINE, MARIA *and* KATHERINE] *and three lords* [BOYET
and two others].

BOYET

Now, madam, summon up your dearest spirits.
Consider who the King your father sends,
To whom he sends and what's his embassy:
Yourself, held precious in the world's esteem,
To parley with the sole inheritor   5
Of all perfections that a man may owe,
Matchless Navarre; the plea of no less weight
Than Aquitaine, a dowry for a queen.
Be now as prodigal of all dear grace
As Nature was in making graces dear   10
When she did starve the general world beside
And prodigally gave them all to you.

PRINCESS

Good Lord Boyet, my beauty, though but mean,

2.1.1 madam throughout the play, used
only to address the Princess
summon . . . spirits call upon your
most hearty, strongest, energies; the
terms suggest physiological rather than
supernatural elements in Boyet's command and can be compared to Boyet's
further exhortation to the Princess to
Muster your wits, 5.2.85. On the other
hand, the line suggests a further association with *Dr Faustus*: see 1.1.55–60n.
For *dearest*, see *OED* dear *a.*[1] 7a*.
2–3 who . . . whom . . . what's Boyet's
analytical style is reminiscent of
Armado's letter 1.1.229–38.
3 **embassy** message (*OED* 2**)
5 **inheritor** owner, possessor; cf. 1.1.73n.
6 **owe** own
7 **Matchless** without an equal, but possibly
also punning on the King's single status,
without a match, and cf. *OED* match *sb.*[1]

7, 'A contest or competitive trial of skill in
some sport, exercise, or operation'.
Navarre King of Navarre: apart from
at 1.1.12, it is only in this scene that
the King is referred to in this way.
plea what is claimed, pleaded for
(*OED sb.* 5*)
8 **dowry** The word hints at a possible match
between the King and the Princess.
9 i.e. in your discussions use all the grace
you've got
prodigal lavish (*OED* A. 3b*)
9–10 **dear grace . . . graces dear** precious pleasing quality . . . costly (and
therefore scarce) pleasing qualities
10 **Nature** See 1.1.14n.
11 **did . . . beside** deprived the rest of the
world of grace apart from you
13–19 The speech contains some parallels
to Berowne's at 4.3.230–7.
13 **mean** moderate, middling

2.1] *Rowe; F (Actus Secunda.); act and scene not in Q* 2 Consider] *Q (*Cosider*), F* 13 SP] *F2
(*Prin.*); Queene QF*

Needs not the painted flourish of your praise.
Beauty is bought by judgement of the eye, 15
Not uttered by base sale of chapmen's tongues.
I am less proud to hear you tell my worth
Than you much willing to be counted wise
In spending your wit in the praise of mine.
But now to task the tasker. Good Boyet, 20
You are not ignorant all-telling fame
Doth noise abroad Navarre hath made a vow,
Till painful study shall outwear three years,
No woman may approach his silent court.
Therefore to's seemeth it a needful course, 25
Before we enter his forbidden gates,
To know his pleasure; and in that behalf,
Bold of your worthiness, we single you
As our best-moving fair solicitor.

14 **painted flourish** specious, unreal gloss or varnish. Cf. the proverbial 'A good face needs no paint', Dent, F7, and see *OED* flourish *sb.* 3*, citing 4.3.234, and cf. 2.1.78–9.
16 **uttered** spoken; put on sale: see *RJ* 5.1.67.
chapmen's traders', pedlars'
17 **proud** elated, gratified; cf. *R2* 3.3.191.
tell recount, tell of; count up
18 **much** greatly; see Abbott, 51.
counted accounted
19 **spending your wit** The metaphor is repeated at 4.3.144, 5.2.64.
20 **task the tasker** impose a task on, or reprove, the man who sets tasks (*OED* tasker*); cf. 5.2.126n.
21 F's redundant SP '*Prin.*' may, according to Wells, 'Copy', reflect a cut before these lines. It is possible that at some stage the scene began with these lines: the reference to *fame*, here meaning rumour, would provide a neat parallel with 1.1.1.

all-telling With one OE exception, compound 'all' with a present participle was rare before 1600 (*OED* all E. 7 and telling *ppl. a.***).
22 **noise abroad** report, rumour
23 **painful** exact, precise; physically uncomfortable
outwear wear out; only in *H5* 4.2.63, also with reference to time
24 **silent** noiseless, still (*OED* A. 4*)
25 **to's** to us
27 **in that behalf** in respect of that (*OED* behalf 2c)
28 **Bold of** confident as a result of; see Abbott, 168.
single pick out (*OED v.*¹ 4*)
29 **best-moving** most persuasive (*OED* best B. 2a*)
fair The word is used often without any distinctive sense more frequently in *LLL* than in any other work by Shakespeare.
solicitor petitioner, advocate (*OED* soliciter 3a β)

20 tasker.] *F3 (*tasker:*);* tasker, *QF* 21 You] *Prin.* You *F*

Tell him the daughter of the King of France,   30
On serious business craving quick dispatch,
Importunes personal conference with his grace.
Haste, signify so much, while we attend,
Like humble-visaged suitors, his high will.

BOYET

Proud of employment, willingly I go.   35

PRINCESS

All pride is willing pride, and yours is so.   *Exit Boyet.*
Who are the votaries, my loving lords,
That are vow-fellows with this virtuous Duke?

LORD

Longaville is one.

PRINCESS   Know you the man?

MARIA

I know him, madam. At a marriage feast   40
Between Lord Perigort and the beauteous heir
Of Jaques Falconbridge, solemnized
In Normandy, saw I this Longaville.

---

32 *Importunes stressed on the second
  syllable
  conference conversation, discourse
33 attend wait for, expect
34 *humble-visaged Elsewhere Shakespeare has 'grim-', 'pale-' and 'triple-
  visaged'.
34–5 will . . . willingly a convenient pun
36 pride In contrast to the pride or honour she feels in her previous speech
  (17) and Boyet's pride in his employment, the Princess here casts pride in
  the role of a vice.
37 votaries people bound by a special
  vow (OED 1b*); see also 4.2.135,
  5.2.871.
38 vow-fellows OED vow 7*, the only
  citation. Elsewhere, in H5 and KL,
  Shakespeare has 'yoke-fellow(s)'.

39, 80 SP The lines could be spoken by
  either of the two lords accompanying
  Boyet.
39 Although Capell's emendation regu-
  larizes the metre, it is unnecessary.
41 Perigort Périgord includes the area of
  the Dordogne in south-west France.
  heir heiress: the term applied equally
  to men and women; see 204n.
42 Jaques Falconbridge In verse Jaques
  in AYL is once disyllabic (2.1.26) and
  three times monosyllabic, and disyllabic on both occasions in AW: here it may
  be pronounced 'Jakwis'. Characters
  with the name of Falconbridge or
  Fulconbridge appear or are referred to
  in KJ, MV (1.2.66), H5, 1H6 and 3H6.
  solemnized solemnizèd; stressed on
  the second syllable

32 Importunes] F; Importuous Q   34 humble-visaged] F (humble visag'd); humble visage Q   36 SD]
Exit. F (both opp. 35)   37–8] *Rowe; prose QF*   39 LORD Longaville] QF (Lor. Longauill); LORD
Lord Longaville *Capell (subst.)*   40 SP] *Rowe; 1. Lady. QF*   madam.] *Capell (subst.);* Maddame QF
42 solemnized] *Capell (subst.);* solemnized. QF

A man of sovereign parts, he is esteemed,
Well fitted in arts, glorious in arms.   45
Nothing becomes him ill that he would well.
The only soil of his fair virtue's gloss –
If virtue's gloss will stain with any soil –
Is a sharp wit matched with too blunt a will,
Whose edge hath power to cut, whose will still wills   50
It should none spare that come within his power.

PRINCESS
Some merry mocking lord belike: is't so?

MARIA
They say so most that most his humours know.

PRINCESS
Such short-lived wits do wither as they grow.
Who are the rest?   55

44 ***sovereign parts** supreme, most
notable personal qualities or attributes
(for *parts* cf. 4.2.114n.). This is the F
reading; Q reads 'soueraigne peerelsse'
and some editors combine the two as
'sovereign parts, peerless' on the
assumption that, in correcting Q, F
made a further error: the line would
then have six rather than five feet (cf.
the metrical awkwardness of the next
line). But if F did correct Q here, it
might have done so simply by substituting 'parts' for 'peerless', which
Shakespeare had intended to be delet-
ed. The comma after *parts* makes *he is
esteemed* mean he is highly valued, but
it could be removed.

45 **Well . . . arts** fully furnished in intellectual pursuits (*OED* fit *v.*[1] 11a and
well(-)fitted 1*); the line's metrical
awkwardness may suggest some textual corruption.
arts . . . arms The arms are limbs,
weapons and heraldic devices; as Oxf[1]
observes, this is reminiscent of the
poet George Gascoigne's motto '*Tam*

Marti quam Mercurio' ('By Mercury as
much as by Mars').

46 'Whatever he does he does well and
looks good doing it.'

47 **soil** stain
gloss lustre; the word usually suggests
something that is only superficial or
skin deep, an implication perhaps chal-
lenged by the next line. Cf. *TC*
2.3.117–19, 'yet all his virtues . . .
begin to lose their gloss'.

49 **sharp wit** The phrase occurs again at
5.2.398.
matched with allied to, married to
blunt a will unfeeling, unsparing a will
to use it (*OED* blunt A. 4b); cf. *VA* 884.

50 **whose . . . wills** whose will continually
demands

51 **his** its

52 **merry mocking** Cf. *mockery merriment*, 5.2.139.

53 **most . . . know** know his moods best

54 Cf. the proverbial 'Soon ripe soon rotten', Tilley, R133.
short-lived with 4.1.15, unique in
Shakespeare (*OED a.* 1*)

44 sovereign parts, he is] *F (subst.)*; soueraigne peerelsse he is *Q*; sovereign parts, peerless *Alexander*
50 wills] *Rowe*; wils, *QF*   53 SP] *Rowe; Lad. Q; Lad.* 1. *F*

KATHERINE

The young Dumaine, a well-accomplished youth,
Of all that virtue love for virtue loved;
Most power to do most harm, least knowing ill,
For he hath wit to make an ill shape good,
And shape to win grace, though he had no wit.   60
I saw him at the Duke Alençon's once;
And much too little of that good I saw
Is my report to his great worthiness.

ROSALINE

Another of these students at that time
Was there with him, if I have heard a truth.   65
Berowne they call him, but a merrier man,
Within the limit of becoming mirth,
I never spent an hour's talk withal.

---

56 **well-accomplished** *OED**
57 **Of** by
58 Being the most innocent of men, Dumaine has the greatest scope for doing harm, but he is quite unaware of the harm he does. The line is, perhaps, related to the proverbial 'To be able to do harm and not to do it is noble', Dent, H170, deriving from Sidney's *Arcadia* and varied in *Son* 94.1, 'They that have pow'r to hurt, and will do none'.
59–60 For he is clever enough to make something that looks bad look good, and his own appearance would make up for any lack of cleverness. Katherine's own speech is, of course, a good example of the transforming power of wit on a few words.
61 ***Alençon's** To most contemporaries *Alençon* would have suggested the French King Henri III's younger brother François Hercule, Duc d'Alençon (1554–84), famous for his

unsuccessful courtship of Queen Elizabeth, esp. in the late 1570s and early 1580s.
62 **much too little** far too short
63 **to** compared to (*OED* A. 18)
65 **if . . . truth** Rosaline is perhaps being coy and evasive about her acquaintance with Berowne; even with different punctuation, the phrase seems excessively weighty to qualify his name ('If I have heard a truth, / Berowne they call him').
66 **Berowne . . . but** The *but* can be explained by Rosaline's punning on Berowne's name sounding like 'brown' and so suggesting sadness or thoughtfulness (as in the phrase 'to be in a brown study').
67 **becoming** fitting
68 **an hour's talk** a generalized period of time; the phrase also occurs in *MW* 1.4.151, 2.1.166–7, *JC* 2.2.121. *Hour's* may be disyllabic.
withal with

---

56 SP] *Rowe*; 2. *Lad. QF*   60 he] she *F*   61 Alençon's] *Steevens*; *Alansoes QF*   64 SP] *F (Rossa.)*; 3. *Lad. Q*   65 if] as *F*

His eye begets occasion for his wit,
For every object that the one doth catch   70
The other turns to a mirth-moving jest,
Which his fair tongue, conceit's expositor,
Delivers in such apt and gracious words
That aged ears play truant at his tales
And younger hearings are quite ravished,   75
So sweet and voluble is his discourse.

PRINCESS

God bless my ladies! Are they all in love,
That every one her own hath garnished
With such bedecking ornaments of praise?

LORD

Here comes Boyet.

Enter BOYET.

PRINCESS   Now, what admittance, lord?   80

BOYET

Navarre had notice of your fair approach,
And he and his competitors in oath
Were all addressed to meet you, gentle lady,

69 **begets occasion** finds opportunities
70 **object** thing he sees or comments on (*OED sb.* 3a)
   catch manage to see (*OED v.* 35*)
71 **mirth-moving** laughter-causing (*OED* mirth *sb.* 5*)
72 **conceit's expositor** the declarer of clever ideas
73 **Delivers** utters, brings forth (like a baby); cf. 4.2.69.
74 The old abandon what they should be doing to listen to him; *aged ears* occurs again in *Tit* 4.4.96. See also Introduction, p. 10.
   aged agèd
75 **ravished** ravishèd; see also 4.3.322.

76 **voluble** fluent, quick-witted; cf. Armado's description of Moth, 3.1.63.
78 **garnished** garnishèd
78–9 **garnished . . . ornaments** Oxf[1] compares *H5* 2.2.134, 'Garnish'd and deck'd in modest complement'; *OED* bedecking*. The Princess distrusts the rhetorical *ornaments of praise* as earlier (14) she had distrusted Boyet's 'painted flourish of your praise'. Cf. 4.1.17, 32, 4.3.236.
80 **admittance** permission to enter
82 **competitors** associates, partners (*OED* 2); rivals (*OED* 1a)
83 **addressed** prepared, made ready

71 jest,] *F4;* iest. *QF*   74 tales] *F (*tales,*);* tales. *Q*   75 ravished,] *Collier;* rauished. *QF*   80 SP
LORD] *Ma. F*

Before I came. Marry, thus much I have learned:
He rather means to lodge you in the field,　　　　　85
Like one that comes here to besiege his court,
Than seek a dispensation for his oath,
To let you enter his unpeopled house.

Enter [the KING *of]* Navarre[, BEROWNE, LONGAVILLE *and*
DUMAINE *and attendants].*

Here comes Navarre.

KING　Fair Princess, welcome to the court of Navarre.　　　90

PRINCESS　'Fair' I give you back again, and 'welcome' I
have not yet. The roof of this court is too high to be
yours, and welcome to the wide fields too base to be
mine.

KING

You shall be welcome, madam, to my court.　　　　　95

PRINCESS

I will be welcome then. Conduct me thither.

KING

Hear me, dear lady: I have sworn an oath.

PRINCESS

Our Lady help my lord! He'll be forsworn.

KING

Not for the world, fair madam, by my will.

PRINCESS

Why, will shall break it; will, and nothing else.　　　100

84 **Marry** See 1.1.124n.
85 **lodge** encamp
　　field open country; battleground; cf.
　　2H6 1.1.80. See 5.2.345n.
88 ***unpeopled house** house or house-
　　hold lacking servants; for *unpeopled*, cf.
　　R2 1.2.69, *AYL* 3.2.126.
92 **roof . . . court** i.e. the sky

93 **welcome . . . fields** The phrase may
　　have been proverbial; cf. Dent, W257.
99 **Not . . . world** *OED* world *sb.* 7f (*b*)*
　　by my will of my own accord
100 **will . . . will** desire, lust; with the
　　Princess's puns on the word, cf.
　　210–11n., *Son* 135–6.

88 unpeopled] *F;* vnpeeled *Q*　88.1–2] *QF (subst.) (*Enter Nauar, Longauill, Dumaine, *&* Berowne.*)*
88.2 *and attendants]* Rowe　89 Here] *F; Bo.* Heere *Q*　90+ SP KING] *Rowe; Nauar. (Nau.) Q*
Nau. F　100 it; will,] *Capell;* it will, *QF*

KING

Your ladyship is ignorant what it is.

PRINCESS

Were my lord so, his ignorance were wise,

Where now his knowledge must prove ignorance.

I hear your grace hath sworn out housekeeping.

'Tis deadly sin to keep that oath, my lord,   105

And sin to break it.

But pardon me, I am too sudden bold;

To teach a teacher ill beseemeth me.

Vouchsafe to read the purpose of my coming

And suddenly resolve me in my suit.   110

[*She gives the King a paper.*]

KING

Madam, I will, if suddenly I may.

PRINCESS

You will the sooner that I were away,

For you'll prove perjured if you make me stay.

[*The King reads.*]

BEROWNE [*to Rosaline*]

Did not I dance with you in Brabant once?

ROSALINE

Did not I dance with you in Brabant once?   115

103 **Where** whereas
  prove show itself to be
104 **sworn out housekeeping** renoun-
  ced, sworn to do without hospitality
  (*OED* housekeeping *sb*. 2a); cf. *outswear*
  1.2.62n. For the Christian duty of hospitality, see e.g. Romans, 12.13.
105–6 Cf. the proverbial 'An unlawful oath
  is better broken than kept', Tilley, O7.
107–10 **sudden . . . suddenly** The repetition may suggest annoyance.
107 **sudden** rashly
108 **To . . . teacher** Kerrigan points out
  that the King has become an academic

and compares 20, *task the tasker.*
110 **suddenly** at once
  resolve me answer (*OED v.* 11b)
112 i.e. you will do it more quickly so that
  you can get rid of me.
113 **perjured** There is more about perjury and being perjured in *LLL* than in
  any other of Shakespeare's works.
114–27 *On the positioning of these lines
  and the SP for the woman's part, see
  Appendix 1, pp. 309–11.
114 **dance** There is more about dancing
  in 5.2.185ff. and see esp. 400.
  Brabant in the Low Countries

106–7] *F; one line Q*   110 SD] *Halliwell (subst.)*   113 SD] *Collier MS (subst.)*   114 SD] *Bevington*
115–26 SP ROSALINE] *F (Rosa.); Kather. (Kath.) Q*

BEROWNE

I know you did.

ROSALINE How needless was it then
To ask the question!

BEROWNE You must not be so quick.

ROSALINE

'Tis long of you that spur me with such questions.

BEROWNE

Your wit's too hot, it speeds too fast, 'twill tire.

ROSALINE

Not till it leave the rider in the mire. 120

BEROWNE

What time o'day?

ROSALINE

The hour that fools should ask.

BEROWNE

Now fair befall your mask.

ROSALINE

Fair fall the face it covers.

BEROWNE

And send you many lovers. 125

ROSALINE

Amen, so you be none.

---

117 **quick** hasty, impatient (*OED* A. 22a); sharp, caustic (*OED a.* 18b). Cf. 5.2.283.

118–20 Cf. the proverbial 'Do not spur a willing horse', 'A free horse will soon tire', 'To leave in the mire', Dent, H638, H642, Tilley, M989, and 4.3.183–4.

118 **long of** owing to, on account of (*OED* long *a.*²)

   spur me drive me on; Oxf¹ detects a spelling variant of 'speer' (*OED v.*¹), meaning to interrogate.

121 Berowne's commonplace question is meant to change the topic of conversation.

122 **fools** Although the lords are regularly called fools or told they behave like them (4.3.160, 203, 329–30, 5.2.59, 68–78, 302, 371–2), Berowne is especially associated with being one; see also 2.1.183, 4.3.5, 203, 5.2.68, 380, 384).

123 **fair befall** good luck to (*OED* befall *v.* 4e); cf. *R2* 2.1.129.

124 **Fair fall** may good befall (*OED* fall *v.* 46d)

126 **Amen** Cf. 4.3.91n.
   so provided, if only

116–17 How . . . question] *Capell; one line QF*

BEROWNE

  Nay, then will I be gone.   [*He leaves her.*]

KING

  Madam, your father here doth intimate

  The payment of a hundred thousand crowns,

  Being but the one half of an entire sum   130

  Disbursed by my father in his wars.

  But say that he or we – as neither have –

  Received that sum, yet there remains unpaid

  A hundred thousand more, in surety of the which

  One part of Aquitaine is bound to us,   135

  Although not valued to the money's worth.

  If then the King your father will restore

  But that one half which is unsatisfied,

  We will give up our right in Aquitaine

  And hold fair friendship with his majesty.   140

  But that, it seems, he little purposeth:

  For here he doth demand to have repaid

128–52 As a result of the wars the King of France owes Navarre 200,000 crowns; the Princess brings a letter in which France claims to have paid off half the amount, but the King of Navarre disputes this. Even so, as Navarre points out, he is still owed another 100,000 crowns raised against a part of Aquitaine, land not even worth that amount of money. Navarre has offered to restore Aquitaine to France for 100,000 crowns, but France is now claiming back his 100,000 crowns from Navarre ('that which hath so faithfully been paid', 156). Navarre would rather have the money than the land and thinks the King of France is behaving outrageously.

128 **intimate** refer to

130 *The QF variants indicate the difficulty of scanning this line: if *Being* is not monosyllabic, *the one* should probably be elided; if *Being* is monosyllabic and *the one* is elided, then *entire* may be trisyllabic, 'entiër'.
  entire stressed on the first syllable

131 **Disbursed** disbursèd
  his the King of France's

132 **he** Navarre's father, called Charles at 162
  as neither have which neither of us has; see Abbott, 111 and 12.

135 **bound** contracted

136 **not . . . worth** The land is not worth the money involved (*OED* money's-worth 2*).

138 **unsatisfied** not settled by payment (*OED* 4*)

142 **doth demand** claims he is legally entitled to (*OED* demand *v.* 1b*)

127 SD] *Bevington (subst.)*   128 SP] *F; Ferd. Q*   130 the . . . an] *F* ('th'one halfe, of an*);* the one halfe of, of an *Q*

A hundred thousand crowns, and not demands,
On payment of a hundred thousand crowns,
To have his title live in Aquitaine,   145
Which we much rather had depart withal,
And have the money by our father lent,
Than Aquitaine, so gelded as it is.
Dear Princess, were not his requests so far
From reason's yielding, your fair self should make   150
A yielding 'gainst some reason in my breast
And go well satisfied to France again.

PRINCESS
You do the King my father too much wrong
And wrong the reputation of your name,
In so unseeming to confess receipt   155
Of that which hath so faithfully been paid.

KING
I do protest I never heard of it.
And, if you prove it, I'll repay it back
Or yield up Aquitaine.

PRINCESS   We arrest your word.
Boyet, you can produce acquittances   160
For such a sum from special officers
Of Charles, his father.

KING   Satisfy me so.

BOYET
So please your grace, the packet is not come

---

143 **not demands** i.e. does not demand although he is entitled to
146 **had depart withal** would give up
148 **gelded** deprived of an essential part (*OED v.*[1] 2a); cf. 'gelded of his patrimony', *R2* 2.1.237, and 'gelded the commonwealth', *2H6* 4.2.165.
150 **reason's yielding** giving way to commonsense, sound argument; cf. 1.1.118n.

155 **unseeming** not seeming to be willing (*OED pres. pple.**); see Abbott, 442.
159 **arrest your word** take you at, hold you to (*OED* arrest *v.* 12**) your word; cf. *MM* 2.4.134. Ard[1] cites Sidney, *NA*, 93, where Artesia 'took the advantage one day upon Phalantus' unconscionable praisings of her . . . to arrest his word as soon as it was out of his mouth'.
163–5 a convenient delaying device

143 A] An *F*   144 On] *Theobald;* One *QF*   157–66 SP KING] *F; Ferd. Q*

Where that and other specialties are bound.
Tomorrow you shall have a sight of them.   165

KING

It shall suffice me; at which interview
All liberal reason I will yield unto.
Meantime, receive such welcome at my hand
As honour, without breach of honour, may
Make tender of to thy true worthiness.   170
You may not come, fair Princess, within my gates,
But here without you shall be so received
As you shall deem yourself lodged in my heart,
Though so denied fair harbour in my house.
Your own good thoughts excuse me, and farewell.   175
Tomorrow shall we visit you again.

PRINCESS

Sweet health and fair desires consort your grace.

KING

Thy own wish wish I thee in every place.
                    [*Exeunt the King, Longaville and Dumaine.*]

BEROWNE   Lady, I will commend you to mine own heart.

ROSALINE   Pray you, do my commendations; I would be   180
glad to see it.

---

164 **specialties** sealed contracts or bonds
(*OED* 7); cf. *TS* 2.1.126–7.
bound ready, prepared (*OED ppl. a.*[1]
1); wrapped up (*OED ppl. a.*[2] 4**)
165–76 **Tomorrow . . . Tomorrow** See
4.1.6n.
167 **All liberal reason** any socially polite
and reasonable behaviour
169 **without . . . honour** The King means
'without breaking my oath' (*OED* breach
sb. 3a), but the phrase *breach of honour*
could also have a sexual association,
referring to the woman's sexual parts.
170 **Make tender of** offer

173 **As** that; see Abbott, 109.
174 **harbour** shelter, lodgings (*OED sb.*[1]
2a)
175 **Your . . . me** i.e. may your own good
thoughts excuse me; for the imperative
subjunctive, see Abbott, 364.
177 **consort** attend (*OED v.* 1*)
179 **commend you** commit, entrust you;
remember you kindly
180 **do my commendations** i.e. give it
my respects.
180–1 **I . . . it** i.e. I'd like to know the true
state of your feelings; drop dead
(which you would be, if I could see it)!

167 I will] would I *F*   169 may] *F;* may, *Q*   171 within] in *F*   173 heart,] *F;* hart. *Q*   174 fair]
farther *F*   house.] *F (*house:*);* house, *Q*   176 shall we] we shall *F*   178 SP] *F; Na. Q*   SD] *Capell*
(subst.); Exit. QF   179–90 SP BEROWNE] *Boy. F*   179 mine own] *Q (*my none*);* my owne *F*

BEROWNE   I would you heard it groan.

ROSALINE   Is the fool sick?

BEROWNE   Sick at the heart.

ROSALINE

  Alack, let it blood.   185

BEROWNE

  Would that do it good?

ROSALINE

  My physic says ay.

BEROWNE

  Will you prick't with your eye?

ROSALINE

  Non point, with my knife.

BEROWNE

  Now God save thy life.   190

ROSALINE

  And yours from long living.

BEROWNE

  I cannot stay thanksgiving.   *Exit.*

Enter DUMAINE.

DUMAINE

  Sir, I pray you a word. What lady is that same?

---

183 **fool** poor thing (*OED sb.*[1] 1c); see 122n.

185–92 On this exchange, see the Introduction, pp. 49–50.

185 **blood** *OED*'s earliest citation for 'to blood' in the sense of 'To cause blood to flow from' is from 1633; *blood* may be a noun and *it* an indirect object, hence 'let blood from it', but 'it' could also be used for 'its' (*OED* 10), hence 'let its blood'.

187 **physic** knowledge of healing

188 Berowne (deliberately) misinterprets Rosaline's *ay* and challenges her to bleed his heart with her eye: the com-

bination of *prick* and *eye* suggests a needle, but also a hopeless attempt to 'prick' with a vagina, for which see also 3.1.193n., 4.3.8–10n., 5.2.475n.
't Berowne's heart

189 *Non point not a bit, not at all – with the implication that she has not got a penis; i.e. the eye has no point or is blunt. The phrase is italicized in Q and F to display its being in French. See also 5.2.277n.

192 **stay thanksgiving** remain to thank you (*OED* stay *v.*[1] 19b); cf. 4.2.140n.

183 fool] soule *F*   189 *Non point*] Kerrigan; *No poynt QF*

BOYET

The heir of Alençon, Katherine her name.   194

DUMAINE

A gallant lady. Monsieur, fare you well.   *Exit.*

[*Enter* LONGAVILLE.]

LONGAVILLE

I beseech you a word. What is she in the white?

BOYET

A woman sometimes, an you saw her in the light.

LONGAVILLE

Perchance light in the light. I desire her name.

BOYET

She hath but one for herself; to desire that were a
  shame.

LONGAVILLE

Pray you, sir, whose daughter?   200

BOYET

Her mother's, I have heard.

LONGAVILLE

God's blessing on your beard!

BOYET

Good sir, be not offended.
She is an heir of Falconbridge.

195 **gallant** good-looking, handsome (*OED* A. 2)
196 **What** who
197 **an** if
198 **light . . . light** unchaste when seen properly
199 **desire** Boyet takes Longaville's request as meaning he wants to have her name instead of wanting to know it.
202 **God's . . . beard!** 'Grow up!'
204 If Maria is 'an heir of Falconbridge',

it is surprising and confusing that earlier (40–3) she says she saw Longaville at the marriage feast of Lord Perigort and 'the beauteous heir / Of Jaques Falconbridge': Boyet may mean that she is an heir of the Falconbridge family rather than of an individual member of the family. Cf. the question of the Faulconbridges and their inheritance in *KJ* 1.1.

194 Katherine] *Singer (Capell); Rosalin QF* 195 lady. Monsieur] *Rowe (subst.);* Lady *Mounsir Q;* Lady, Mounsier *F* SD] *om. F* 195.1] *F2* 197 an] *Q (*and*);* if *F* 198 name.] *F;* name? *Q* 202 on] a *F* 203–6] *F; Q lines* Falconbridge. / Ladie. /

LONGAVILLE

> Nay, my choler is ended. 205
> She is a most·sweet lady.

BOYET

> Not unlike, sir, that may be. *Exit Longaville.*

Enter BEROWNE.

BEROWNE

> What's her name in the cap?

BOYET

> Rosaline, by good hap.

BEROWNE

> Is she wedded or no? 210

BOYET

> To her will sir, or so.

BEROWNE

> You are welcome, sir. Adieu.

BOYET

> Farewell to me, sir, and welcome to you. *Exit Berowne.*

MARIA

> That last is Berowne, the merry madcap lord.
> Not a word with him but a jest.

BOYET And every jest but a word. 215

PRINCESS

> It was well done of you to take him at his word.

---

207 **unlike** unlikely
210–11 Cf. the proverbial 'To be wedded to one's will', Tilley, W392, and 100n., esp. for the sexual connotations of 'will'.
211 **or so** or something like that
212 **You are welcome** Q's prefix 'O' was probably picked up from the SP '*Bero*[*wne*].'; cf. 3.1.140n.
213–48 Boyet's speeches make use of ana-

paestic lines in which the feet are made up of two short or unstressed syllables followed by a long or stressed syllable.
213 **welcome to you** you are welcome to go; cf. the proverbial 'Welcome when you go', Tilley, W259.
214 **madcap** engagingly crazy (*OED* B*)
216 **take . . . word** accept what he says; take him on at his word-play

207 SD] *opp. 206 F* 209 Rosaline] *Singer; Katherin QF* 212 You] *F;* O you *Q* 213 SD] *Exit. F*
214 SP] *Q (Lady Maria.), F (La.Ma.)*

BOYET

I was as willing to grapple as he was to board.

KATHERINE

Two hot sheeps, marry!

BOYET   And wherefore not 'ships'?

No sheep, sweet lamb, unless we feed on your lips.

KATHERINE

You sheep, and I pasture. Shall that finish the jest?   220

BOYET

So you grant pasture for me.   [*He tries to kiss her.*]

KATHERINE   Not so, gentle beast.

My lips are no common, though several they be.

BOYET

Belonging to whom?

KATHERINE   To my fortunes and me.

PRINCESS

Good wits will be jangling; but, gentles, agree.

This civil war of wits were much better used   225

---

217 **grapple . . . board** In a naval
engagement grappling-irons would be
thrown to fasten ships so that they
could be boarded; like *grapple*, *board*
(*OED v.* 4), meaning to accost, to make
advances to, had sexual connotations.

218 **hot sheeps** ardent, passionate sheep.
Katherine mocks the battle of wit between the two men – sheep are hardly
noted for their *hot* natures.
sheeps . . . ships Cf. 4.3.46n.; the pun
also appears in *TGV* 1.1.72–3 and *CE*
4.1.93–4.

219 **feed . . . lips** kiss; cf. *VA* 232–3,
'Feed where thou wilt . . . / Graze on
my lips'.

220 **pasture** presumably punning on
'pastor', i.e. shepherd

221 **So** so long as

222 My lips are not common ground where

all may graze their sheep, since they are
enclosed pasture in private ownership
(*OED* several C. 2a); cf. *Son* 137.9. For
'though' meaning 'since' or 'because' – a
sense not recorded in *OED* – cf. *Tim*
4.3.308. If differently punctuated as
'common though, several', *though* would
mean 'however'. *Several* also carries the
meaning that her lips are separated,
apart and that she has more than one.

224 **jangling** squabbling, wrangling
gentles gentlefolk (*OED* B. 1b); often
used to address a play's audience, e.g.
MND 5.1.127; cf. 4.2.162.

225 **civil . . . wits** Elsewhere Shakespeare
uses 'civil war' only figuratively in *Son*
35.12, meaning a domestic conflict
between citizens of the same state; but
here it could also suggest a well-bred
or 'polite' war of wits.

---

218 SP KATHERINE] *Q (Lady Ka.); La.Ma. F*   sheeps, marry!] *Pope (subst.); Sheepes marie. Q; Sheepes
marie: F*   218–19 BOYET And . . . lips.] And . . . Ships? / *Boy.* No . . . lips. *F*   220–3 SP KATHERINE]
Capell; La. (Lad.) QF   221 SD] *Capell (subst.)*   224 but, gentles,] *Theobald; but gentles QF*

On Navarre and his bookmen, for here 'tis abused.

BOYET

If my observation, which very seldom lies
By the heart's still rhetoric disclosed with eyes,
Deceive me not now, Navarre is infected.

PRINCESS   With what?   230

BOYET

With that which we lovers entitle 'affected'.

PRINCESS   Your reason?

BOYET

Why, all his behaviours did make their retire
To the court of his eye, peeping thorough desire.
His heart, like an agate with your print impressed,   235
Proud with his form, in his eye pride expressed.
His tongue, all impatient to speak and not see,

---

226 **bookmen** scholars; Shakespeare uses
the word elsewhere only at 4.2.34, but
cf. *book-mates* 4.1.99.
abused misapplied
227–8 **lies / By** is wrong about
228 **still rhetoric** silent eloquence – an
oxymoron, which can be extended,
since orators were supposed to enforce
their arguments with gestures: cf.
1.1.14n. Malone cited Daniel,
Rosamond, sig. I1v, 'Sweet silent
rhetorique of perswading eyes: /
Dombe eloquence'. There is more
about rhetoric in *LLL* than in any
other of Shakespeare's works.
disclosed with eyes disclosèd; cf. 250.
229 **infected** See 5.2.420.
231 **affected** being in love; cf. *VA* 157.
233–4 i.e. his whole demeanour avoided
others and withdrew or retreated to
the royal dwelling of his eye which put
forth desire.
233 **behaviours** The plural is not uncommon in Shakespeare; see *OED* 1b.
retire withdrawal, avoidance of others

(*OED sb.* 1a); military retreat (*OED sb.*
3a); retiring (cf. *OED sb.* 2a and *Luc* 573
'to his borrowed bed he make retire').
234 **court** a figurative use for the royal
dwelling. Sisson, *Readings* (1.108–9),
suggests an elliptical form of 'court of
guard', a corruption of Fr. *corps de
garde*, meaning a guardroom; cf. *1H6*
2.1.4, *Oth* 2.1.218.
thorough through
235 **agate . . . impressed** precious stone
with your image engraved in it. The
simile is slightly confused, since
impressed (*OED v.*[1] 5a*) and *print* suggest not the agate seal itself, but the
image which it produces when applied
to hot wax. Cf. 3.1.167n.
236 **Proud . . . form** was made proud by
being stamped with the Princess's
image; *proud* may also carry the implication of standing out, of not being
smooth or flush, hence of being erect.
237–8 i.e. longing to see as well as to
speak, his tongue spoke confusedly
and too fast; cf. 1.1.123n.

227–8 observation, which . . . eyes,] *F* (obseruation (which . . . eyes))*; obseruation (which . . . eyes. *Q*
227 lies] *Qc, F;* lyes? *Qu*   232 reason?] *Rowe;* reason. *QF*   233 did] doe *F*

Did stumble with haste in his eyesight to be.

All senses to that sense did make their repair,

To feel only looking on fairest of fair.   240

Methought all his senses were locked in his eye,

As jewels in crystal for some prince to buy;

Who, tendering their own worth from where they
    were glassed,

Did point you to buy them along as you passed.

His face's own margin did quote such amazes   245

That all eyes saw his eyes enchanted with gazes.

I'll give you Aquitaine, and all that is his,

An you give him for my sake but one loving kiss.

PRINCESS

Come, to our pavilion. Boyet is disposed.

BOYET

But to speak that in words which his eye hath disclosed.   250

I only have made a mouth of his eye

By adding a tongue which I know will not lie.

239 **did . . . repair** i.e. made their way to
that place (*OED sb*[1]. 4b)

240 **looking** i.e. what it was like to look

242 **crystal** crystal glass; the jewels seem
to be carried in some sort of glass container or behind a glass cover of some
kind, but crystal was also used to refer
to the eyes; see *VA* 963.

243 **Who** and they

    tendering (tend'ring) presenting,
offering (*OED v.*[1] 2a *fig.**)

    from where Although the F reading
'from whence' is more common in
Shakespeare, 'from where' occurs elsewhere, e.g. in *Son* 51.3, and *Tit* Q1
1.1.68, where F again has 'From
whence'.

    glassed enclosed in glass (*OED v.* 2a*)

244 **point** direct

245 The King's face gave away what he
felt about the Princess. Elizabethan
books often contained marginal mater-

ial which could be printed or handwrit-
ten and consisted of cross-references,
comments on or summaries of the text,
and marginal marks such as numbers or
hands with pointing index fingers
(*OED* quote *v.* 2a *fig.**, the only citation – but cf. *RJ* F 1.4.30–1, 'what care
I / What curious eye doth quote defor-
mities', and *Ham* Q1 TLN 1240–1,
'and Gentlemen quotes his ieasts
downe / In their tables'). Kerrigan
suggests the imagery of glossing and
index fingers of this line was picked up
from *glassed* and *point you* in 243–4.

    amazes extreme astonishment, won-
der

246 **gazes** Cf. 4.3.308n.

249 **pavilion** large and stately tent; cf.
5.1.81, 5.2.649.

    disposed in a jolly mood (*OED ppl. a.*
4b); cf. 5.2.466n.

250 **But** only

243 where] whence *F*   244 point you] point out *F*   245 quote] *QF (*coate*)*   250 SP] *Q (Bo.); Bro. F*

159

MARIA

Thou art an old love-monger, and speakest skilfully.

KATHERINE

He is Cupid's grandfather, and learns news of him.

ROSALINE

Then was Venus like her mother, for her father is but
    grim.   255

BOYET

Do you hear, my mad wenches?

MARIA   No.

BOYET   What then, do you see?

MARIA

Ay, our way to be gone.

BOYET   You are too hard for me.

Exeunt omnes.

3[.1] *Enter* [ARMADO, *the*] *Braggart, and* [MOTH,] *his Boy.*

ARMADO   Warble, child, make passionate my sense of
    hearing.

253–5 *For the distribution of these SPs,
see Appendix 1, pp. 309–11.
253 **love-monger** dealer in love affairs
(*OED* love *sb.* 15b*); the implication is
that Boyet is a pander.
255 i.e. if Boyet is Venus' father (and so
Cupid's grandfather), Venus must get
her beauty from her mother, since
Boyet is ugly (*OED* grim A. 4a).
256 **Do you hear** Will you listen; cf. *TC*
5.3.97 and see Rasmussen, 71–3, for its
occurrence in *Dr Faustus* and in Henry
Porter's *The Two Angry Women of
Abington* (*c.* 1585–9).
   mad high-spirited; cf. the proverbial
'To be mad wenches', Dent, W274.1,
and 5.2.264.

257 **to be gone** to go away, but also to be
pregnant, as at 5.2.668: Boyet's final
exchange with Maria contains some
sexual undercurrents.
   too . . . me too much for me to deal
with (*OED* hard *a.* 7*); for the sexual
sense of *hard*, see 4.1.137n.
3.1.0.1 The F direction implies either
that the scene opens with a song,
which Armado then encourages Moth
to go on singing, or that 'Song.' anticipates or glosses 'Concolinel'.
1 **Warble** sing
1–2 **make . . . hearing** Make what I hear
be affected by the passion of love
(*OED* passionate *a.* 4).

---

253 SP] *Capell; Lad. Q; Lad.Ro. F*   254 SP] *Capell; Lad. 2. Q; Lad.Ma. F*   255 SP] *Rowe; Lad.
3. Q; Lad.2. F;* Katharine *Bevington (subst.)*   256 SP MARIA] *Rowe; Lad. Q; La.1. F;* Rosaline
Bevington (subst.)   257 SP MARIA] *Kittredge; Lad. Q; Lad.2. F;* Rosaline *Bevington (subst.)*
3.1] *Rowe; F (Actus Tertius.); act and scene not in Q*   0.1] *Q (subst.); Enter Broggart and Boy. / Song.
F*   1–63 SP ARMADO] *Rowe; Bra. (Brag.) QF*

MOTH [*Sings.*]   Concolinel.

ARMADO   Sweet air! Go, tenderness of years, take this key,
give enlargement to the swain, bring him festinately   5
hither. I must employ him in a letter to my love.

MOTH   Master, will you win your love with a French
brawl?

ARMADO   How meanest thou? Brawling in French?

MOTH   No, my complete master; but to jig off a tune at   10
the tongue's end, canary to it with your feet, humour it
with turning up your eyelids, sigh a note and sing a
note, sometime through the throat as if you swallowed
love with singing love, sometime through the nose as if
you snuffed up love by smelling love, with your hat   15
penthouse-like o'er the shop of your eyes, with your
arms crossed on your thin-belly doublet like a rabbit on

3   **Concolinel** usually explained as the
title of Moth's song, either the Irish
lyric '*Can cailin gheal*', pronounced
'Con colleen yal', meaning 'Sing,
maiden fair', or a French song beginning '*Quand Colinelle*'.
4   **air** music, melody (*OED* 18); cf. *MND*
1.1.183.
5   **enlargement** freedom
    festinately speedily, *OED*'s only
example, but cf. *KL* 3.7.9–10, 'a most
[festinate] preparation': both come
from Lat. *festinare*, to hasten, as in *fes-
tina lente*, make haste slowly.
8   **brawl** a type of dance, Shakespeare's
only usage of the word in this sense; cf.
Sidney, *NA*, 472.20.
9   **Brawling** noisy quarrelling, rowing;
dancing; masturbating: all pun on Fr.
branler
10–23 Moth's speech (his longest in the
play) is reminiscent of Nashe's style,
esp. of Jack Wilton's description of
himself in *The Unfortunate Traveller*,

1594 (Nashe, 2.227). Cf. also Speed's
description of Valentine in love, *TGV*
2.1.18–32.
10   **jig . . . tune** sing a tune in the style of
a jig (*OED* jig *v.* 1a*)
10–11 **at . . . end** Cf. the proverbial 'To
have it at one's tongue's end', Tilley,
T413, and 1.1.123n.
11   **canary** dance the canaries, a lively
Spanish dance (*OED v.**)
    humour it suit yourself to it (*OED v.*
2*)
15–19 **hat . . . painting** the conventional
poses of the melancholy lover: crossed
arms occur again at 176 and 4.3.132.
16   **penthouse-like . . . shop** a sloping
canopy or covering used to protect
goods on sale in front of a shop – the
eyes where Armado's goods are on display. The penthouse simile for a hat was
not new: see Wilson, 'Diction', 102.
17   **thin-belly doublet** a doublet with no
padding over its lower part, intended
to bring out the wearer's leanness

3–62, 103 SP MOTH] *Rowe; Boy. QF*   3 SD] *Theobald (Singing.)*   7 Master, will] Will *F*   11 your]
the *F*   12 eyelids] *Q* (eylids)*; eie *F*   13 throat as if] *Theobald (subst.);* throate, if *Q;* throate: if *F*
14 singing love,] *Theobald (subst.);* singing loue *Q;* singing, loue *F*   through the nose] *F2;* through: nose
QF   15 love, with] *F2;* loue with *QF*   17 thin-belly] *F (*thinbellie)*;* thinbellies *Q;* thin-bellied *Riv*

a spit, or your hands in your pocket like a man after the
old painting; and keep not too long in one tune, but a
snip and away. These are compliments, these are   20
humours, these betray nice wenches that would be
betrayed without these; and make them men of note –
do you note me? – that most are affected to these.

ARMADO   How hast thou purchased this experience?

MOTH   By my penny of observation.   25

ARMADO   But O – But O –

MOTH   'The hobby-horse is forgot.'

ARMADO   Call'st thou my love 'hobby-horse'?

MOTH   No, master. The hobby-horse is but a colt, and
your love perhaps a hackney. But have you forgot your   30
love?

ARMADO   Almost I had.

MOTH   Negligent student! Learn her by heart.

18–19 after . . . painting No particular
painting need be intended; as Kerrigan
points out, Borachio refers in the same
way to 'the reechy painting' and 'the
smirch'd worm-eaten tapestry' in *MA*
3.3.134–7.

19–20 a . . . away a snatch and then on to
the next (*OED* snip *sb.* 3a (*a*)*); cf. the
proverbial 'A snatch and away', Dent,
S587, and see 5.1.55n. The phrase suggests casual sex (cf. Rubinstein, 248).

20 compliments gentlemanly actions

21 humours fanciful ways of behaving,
whims
betray seduce, lead astray
nice wanton, lascivious

22 of note of distinction or eminence
(*OED* note *sb.*[1] 19b*)

23 *do . . . me? do you follow me? QF's
'men' for 'me' can be retained by adding
a comma before it: a direct address to the
men in the audience may be intended.
affected disposed, given

24 purchased got hold of, without the
financial sense that Moth immediately
assumes (*OED v.* 4a)

25 *penny *Purchased* in the previous line
suggests that QF's 'penne' is a misprint for 'pennie'.

27 Moth takes Armado's sighs in the previous line for part of a popular song;
apart from the comparable line in *Ham*
3.2.135, 'For O, for O, the hobby-horse
is forgot' (which also appears in other
writers of the time), no more is known
of it for certain. The hobby-horse had
a leading role in popular entertainments, but a hobby (*OED sb.*[1] 1) was a
pony and perhaps the line relates to a
familiar joke.

28 hobby-horse slang for a prostitute
(*OED* 3b*)

29 colt young horse; lascivious person
(*OED sb.* 2c)

30 hackney horse for hire (*OED sb.* 2a);
slang for prostitute (*OED sb.* 4)

22–3 note – do you note me? – that] *Hanmer (subst.)*; note: do you note men that *QF*; note, (do you
note, men?) that *Malone*   25 penny] *Hanmer;* penne *QF*   29 and] and / and *F*   33 Negligent] *Q*
(Necligent), *F*

ARMADO   By heart and in heart, boy.

MOTH   And out of heart, master. All those three I will   35
prove.

ARMADO   What wilt thou prove?

MOTH   A man, if I live; and this 'by', 'in' and 'without'
upon the instant. 'By' heart you love her, because your
heart cannot come by her; 'in' heart you love her, because   40
your heart is in love with her; and 'out' of heart you love
her, being out of heart that you cannot enjoy her.

ARMADO   I am all these three.

MOTH   And three times as much more, and yet nothing at
all.   45

ARMADO   Fetch hither the swain. He must carry me a
letter.

MOTH   A message well sympathized: a horse to be
ambassador for an ass.

ARMADO   Ha, ha, what sayest thou?   50

MOTH   Marry, sir, you must send the ass upon the horse,
for he is very slow-gaited. But I go.

ARMADO   The way is but short. Away!

MOTH   As swift as lead, sir.

36, 37 **prove** demonstrate; but in 38
Moth understands it in the sense of
'turn out to be'.

38 **'by'** ... **'without'** *By, in* and *with* were
cited by contemporary grammars as
three signs of the ablative case
(Baldwin, 1.570).

40 **come by** possess, get hold of (*OED v.*
39b)

44–5 Moth returns to the joking about
three begun at 1.2.39, which proved
him a *cipher* at 1.2.55. Here Moth says
that Armado can multiply his three by
another three, but the result will still
be nought.

46 **the swain** i.e. Costard

48 **well sympathized** fittingly contrived
(*OED* sympathize *v.* 3c*)

48–52 The point of this exchange is
obscure. Costard is to be Armado's
ambassador or messenger and the message and the manner of its delivery fit
each other. Costard may be a horse
because he is strong but silent. Armado
seems to object to being called an ass;
the joke may involve the ass's actually
riding on top of the horse, or it may
mean the ass is to be sent after or
towards the horse, because it is so slow.

52 **slow-gaited** *OED* slow *a.* 16a* and
gaited *ppl. a*

54 Moth elides two proverbial phrases,
'As heavy as lead' and 'As swift as a
bullet', Dent, L134 and B719.1, and cf.
5.2.261n. On this Renaissance commonplace, see also Elam, 152–4.

38 and this] *Qc, F* ((and this)); (and) this *Qu*

ARMADO   The meaning, pretty ingenious?   55
    Is not lead a metal heavy, dull and slow?
MOTH
    Minime, honest master; or rather, master, no.
ARMADO
    I say lead is slow.
MOTH   You are too swift, sir, to say so.
    Is that lead slow which is fired from a gun?
ARMADO   Sweet smoke of rhetoric!   60
    He reputes me a cannon; and the bullet, that's he.
    I shoot thee at the swain.
MOTH   Thump then, and I flee.   [*Exit.*]
ARMADO
    A most acute juvenal, voluble and free of grace!
    By thy favour, sweet welkin, I must sigh in thy face.
    Most rude melancholy, valour gives thee place.   65
    My herald is returned.

Enter [MOTH, *the*] *Page, and* [COSTARD, *the*] *Clown.*

MOTH
    A wonder, master! Here's a costard broken in a shin.

55 **pretty ingenious** clever or handsome and talented one; the adjective 'ingenious' is used as a noun. Cf. 1.2.27n.
56 **lead** Cf. 4.3.295n.
57 *Minime* Lat. for 'certainly not'; Moth speaks more Lat. at 5.1.64.
60 **smoke of rhetoric** 'mist' of talk, idle expressions; cf. *Luc* 1027, 'This helpless smoke of words'.
62 **Thump** go 'bang'
63 **acute** clever, shrewd (*OED a.* 7*), cf. 4.2.71: both uses are unique in Shakespeare.
    juvenal See 1.2.8n.
    ***voluble** See 2.1.76n.; Q's 'volable' is

presumably a compositorial error.
    free of grace liberal, lavish with his charm, attractiveness (*OED* free *a.* 21a)
64 **welkin** sky, heaven; cf. 4.2.5.
65 **gives thee place** gives its place to you
67–131 For the change in Moth's SPs, see Appendix 1, p. 308.
67–124 Booth (68–70) has a useful commentary on this passage.
67 i.e. a wonder that a head (*costard*) should have a wounded shin; cf. the proverbial 'To break one's shins', Dent, S342.1. The phrase also suggests sexual or amatory disappointment and borrowing money (*OED* shin *sb.* 2d and Rubinstein, 238).

55–6] *Pope; prose QF* 55 The] *Thy F* 57 *Minime*] *Q* (*Minnime); Minnime F* 62 SD] *F2*
63 voluble] *F;* volable *Q* 67–96 SP MOTH] *Rowe; Pag. QF* 67 costard] *QF (Costard)*

ARMADO

Some enigma, some riddle. Come, thy l'envoy – begin.

COSTARD   No egma, no riddle, no l'envoy, no salve in the
mail, sir! O, sir, plantain, a plain plantain! No l'envoy,   70
no l'envoy, no salve, sir, but a plantain!

ARMADO   By virtue, thou enforcest laughter; thy silly
thought, my spleen; the heaving of my lungs provokes
me to ridiculous smiling. O, pardon me, my stars! Doth
the inconsiderate take *salve* for l'envoy, and the word   75
'l'envoy' for a salve?

---

68 **enigma** only in Shakespeare here and
at *Cor* 2.3.90: the word, which suggests
an enema to Costard, introduces a
series of jokes (68–124) about purges
(*l'envoy . . . egma . . . salve in the mail
. . . argument . . . bound . . . purgation
. . . loose*) (Ellis).
   *****l'envoy** the concluding part or post-
script to a poem or piece of prose in
which the author sends it on its way;
unique in Shakespeare to this scene. In
Armado's view (79–80) it explains
what has gone before.

69 **No egma . . . l'envoy** Costard, misunderstanding *enigma* as 'an egma',
declines what he takes to be remedies
for his injury: *egma* suggests some sort
of medicament made from eggs; *riddle*
is obscure, but may refer to 'ruddle',
the red ochre used to mark sheep (as in
Thomas Hardy's *The Return of the
Native*). Kerrigan believes *l'envoy* 'has
something to do with the verb "to leni-
fy" (that is, "to purge gently")'.
Costard, he points out, refers to *purgation* at 123.

69–70 *****salve . . . mail** ointment or remedy in a bag (*OED* mail *sb.*³ 1a);
Costard may mean 'salvo in the male',
i.e. a discharge (of firearms or of physical matter) from himself. For *salve*,

see also 4.3.285.

70 **plantain** A plant or herb whose leaves
were supposed to have healing qualities; cf. *RJ* 1.2.51–2.

72 **By virtue** This sounds like a mild
oath, may glance jokingly at Costard's
not very virtuous character, but probably means 'by your own physical properties, by your own power' (*OED sb.* 8).
The healing powers of plants were
often described (*OED sb.* 9b) as
'virtues'.
   silly simple

73 **spleen** fit of laughter, merriment; the
spleen was believed to be the seat of
both anger and of laughter. Cf.
5.2.117n.
   spleen; the heaving Cf. *TC* 2.2.196,
'our heaving spleens', Shakespeare's
only other use of the word 'heaving'.

74 **ridiculous smiling** smiling with
amused contempt; silly smiling

74–6 **Doth . . . salve** Since *salve* is the
Lat. for 'hail', the opposite of the
farewell of *l'envoy*, Armado is right
and Costard has got the two muddled
up.

75 **inconsiderate** unthinking person
(*OED* B*), unique in Shakespeare as a
noun

---

68 l'envoy –] *Capell (l'envoy;); Lenuoy QF*   69–141, 150–65 SP COSTARD] *Rowe; Clo. (Clow.,
Clown.) QF*   69–70 salve in the mail] *Malone;* salue, in thee male *QF*   70 O] Or *F*   plain] *Q
(*pline*), F*

MOTH   Do the wise think them other? Is not l'envoy a
salve?

ARMADO

No, page; it is an epilogue or discourse to make plain
Some obscure precedence that hath tofore been sain.   80
I will example it:
The fox, the ape and the humble-bee
Were still at odds, being but three.
There's the moral. Now the l'envoy.

MOTH   I will add the l'envoy. Say the moral again.   85

ARMADO

The fox, the ape and the humble-bee
Were still at odds, being but three.

MOTH

Until the goose came out of door,
And stayed the odds by adding four.
Now will I begin your moral, and do you follow with   90
my l'envoy.

The fox, the ape and the humble-bee
Were still at odds, being but three.

77–8 **Is . . . *salve*** Moth may be returning to
his initial confusion caused by Armado's
seeming to tell him to begin with *thy*
l'envoy (68), so that 'l'envoy' is the same
as a '*salve*', an opening greeting.
79–80 poulter's measure (alternating
lines of fourteen and twelve syllables)
80 **precedence . . . sain** A *precedence* is a
thing that has been said before (*OED*
2*), to which Armado adds a tautolog-
ical gloss: *tofore* was distinctly archaic
at the time (but cf. Shakespeare's only
other use in *Tit* 3.1.293), as was *sain*,
whose use here is unique in
Shakespeare. *Precedence* should be
accented on the second syllable.
81 **example** supply an example of
82–3, 86–9 The significance – topical or
personal – of this four-line verse is

obscure. It comprises a very brief beast
fable of the kind Spenser wrote in *SC*
(1579) and Sidney in OA poem, 66.
82 **humble-bee** bumble-bee
83 **still** always
at odds quarrelling; an odd number
84 **moral** practical lesson, point, meaning (*OED sb.* 2a–c); cf. *R2* 4.1.290.
86–9 See 1.1.97n. and 4.3.207n.; discussions about geese also occur between
Romeo and Mercutio in *RJ* 2.4.71–87
and more briefly between Theseus and
Demetrius in *MND* 5.1.232–6. *Goose*
was slang for a prostitute or for vene-
real disease and perhaps for buttocks.
89 **stayed the odds** sorted the quarrel
out (*OED* stay *v.*[1] 28); stopped the odd
number
adding four becoming the fourth

---

80 sain] *Q* (saine); faine *F*   81–9] *om. F*   82–3, 86–9, 92–5] *Q indents and further indents even lines*

ARMADO

    Until the goose came out of door,

    Staying the odds by adding four. 95

MOTH   A good l'envoy, ending in the goose. Would you
desire more?

COSTARD

    The boy hath sold him a bargain, a goose, that's flat.

    Sir, your pennyworth is good, an your goose be fat.

    To sell a bargain well is as cunning as fast and loose. 100

    Let me see: a fat l'envoy – ay, that's a fat goose.

ARMADO

    Come hither, come hither. How did this argument

      begin?

MOTH

    By saying that a costard was broken in a shin.

    Then called you for the l'envoy.

COSTARD   True, and I for a plantain: thus came your 105
argument in. Then the boy's fat l'envoy, the goose that
you bought; and he ended the market.

ARMADO   But tell me, how was there a costard broken in a
shin?

MOTH   I will tell you sensibly. 110

96, 101 **l'envoy . . . goose** *l'envoy* ends in
'*oie*', the Fr. for 'goose'. Moth mocks
Armado for being the goose by taking
his part.

98 **sold . . . goose** made a complete fool
of him; cf. the proverbial 'To sell one a
bargain', Dent, B80.
  that's flat that's the undeniable truth
(*OED* flat A. 6b*); Tilley, F345

100 **fast and loose** See 1.2.151n.

102 **argument** matter for discussion

106 **argument** Costard appears confused, but he may be referring to a

clyster for administering purges to
make what is fast loose (100): Ellis
cites Florio for *argoménto*: 'also a
remedy. also a glister'; see also
4.3.58n.

107 **ended the market** referring to the
proverbial 'Three women and a goose
make a market', Tilley, W690

108 **how** in what sense

110 **sensibly** in a commonsense way
(*OED adv.* 3a); feelingly, with real
emotion

---

102 ARMADO Come . . . argument] *Qc, F (Ar.* Come . . . argument*); Arm.* Come . . . argumet *Qu*
103, 108 costard] *QF (Costard)* 105–7] *Kerrigan; verse Q, lined* in, / market. /; *verse F, lined*
Plantan: / in: / bought, / market. / 110, 131 SP] *Rowe; Pag. QF*

COSTARD   Thou hast no feeling of it, Moth. I will speak
that l'envoy.
    I, Costard, running out, that was safely within,
    Fell over the threshold, and broke my shin.

ARMADO   We will talk no more of this matter.   115

COSTARD   Till there be more matter in the shin.

ARMADO   Sirrah Costard, I will enfranchise thee.

COSTARD   O, marry me to one Frances! I smell some
l'envoy, some goose in this.

ARMADO   By my sweet soul, I mean setting thee at liberty,   120
enfreedoming thy person. Thou wert immured,
restrained, captivated, bound.

COSTARD   True, true, and now you will be my purgation,
and let me loose.

ARMADO   I give thee thy liberty, set thee from durance,   125
and in lieu thereof impose on thee nothing but this:
[*giving Costard a letter*] bear this significant to the
country maid Jaquenetta. There is remuneration

---

111 **feeling** physical sensation of the pain
of the wound
113–16 Costard's banter and rhyme suggest that his sexual activity has been
interrupted: he runs out of matter and
matter runs out of him.
114 **Fell . . . threshold** 'To stumble at the
threshold' was proverbial: Tilley, T259.
threshold doorway, point of entry;
vagina (Rubinstein, 274)
broke my shin See 67n.
116 **matter** pus (*OED sb.*[1] 4); semen: see
1.1.198–9n.
117 **enfranchise** release
118–19 *Frances* was a conventional name for
a prostitute – Ard[2] points out that the
whore whom the narrator visits in
Nashe's 'The Choice of Valentines' is
called 'Francis' (3.406, line 56) – and
goose was slang for one (*OED sb.* 3).
Costard hears *en-* in *enfranchise* 'both as
"one" ("one Frances") and – obscenely –

as "in" ("in Frances me")' (Booth, 167).
121 **enfreedoming** *OED* en- *prefix*[1] 2a*
immured imprisoned (*OED v.* 2a); cf.
4.3.302n.
123–4 **purgation . . . loose** Clear me of
guilt and free me; give me a purge
and make my bowels loose (cf.
1.2.150n.), taking *bound* (122) to refer
to constipation.
125 **set thee from** Although a missing
'free' has often been conjectured, for
'from' meaning 'away from' or 'apart
from' without a verb of motion, see
Abbott, 158.
durance confinement
127 **significant** something which signi-
fies, a sign (*OED* B.); cf. the plural in
1H6 2.4.26.
128 **remuneration** Armado's usage starts
a series of jokes which extend beyond
this scene to 5.1.67 and which became
celebrated; see Introduction, p. 78.

---

111 Moth. I] *Warburton; Moth,* I *QF*   121 immured] *QF (*emured*)*   127 SD] *Dyce*

[*giving Costard a coin*],   for the best ward of mine   129
honour is rewarding my dependants. Moth, follow.   [*Exit.*]

MOTH

Like the sequel, I. Signor Costard, adieu.   *Exit.*

COSTARD

My sweet ounce of man's flesh, my incony jew!
Now will I look to his remuneration. 'Remuneration'!
O, that's the Latin word for three farthings. Three
farthings – remuneration. 'What's the price of this   135
inkle?' 'One penny.' 'No, I'll give you a remuneration.'
Why, it carries it! 'Remuneration'! Why, it is a fairer
name than French crown. I will never buy and sell out
of this word.

Enter BEROWNE.

BEROWNE   My good knave Costard, exceedingly well met.   140

129–30 **ward . . . rewarding** A pun is
intended.
129 **ward** guard, protection
130 **dependants** retainers, servants
(*OED sb.* 2*)
131 **sequel** continuation of a literary
work, the *l'envoy* (*OED sb.* 7); Moth
may also compare himself to a train of
followers (*OED sb.* 1a).
132 **incony** a popular word meaning
something like 'Rare, fine, delicate'
(*OED*). Shakespeare's only other use
of the word is at 4.1.141. It was apparently meant to be pronounced to
rhyme with 'money'.
jew another term of affection, possibly a
diminutive of 'juvenal' (cf. *MND* 3.1.95)
or of 'jewel': there is perhaps a pun in
the rhyme on *adieu* and *jew*; cf. 5.2.620.
134 **three farthings** three-quarters of a
penny; coins of this value were issued

between 1561 and 1581.
136 **inkle** a kind of linen tape
137 **it carries it** it's a winner (*OED* carry
v. 15b)
138 **French crown** a French coin, the *écu*
(*OED**); a bald head caused by
syphilis, the 'French disease'
buy and sell Cf. the proverbial 'To be
bought and sold', Tilley, B787, meaning to be deceived.
138–9 **out of** without using
140, 143, 145, 147, 151, 153 *Q and F
(except at 143) begin each of these lines
with the exclamation 'O'. Berowne does
not greet anyone elsewhere with the
exclamation and, as at 2.1.212, it may be
a hangover from the SP: in Q Berowne's
SP before a speech beginning 'O' is
'*Ber.*' on thirteen occasions, '*Berow.*'
once (4.3.81), but (although it occurs
some sixty times as an SP) never '*Bero.*'.

---

129 SD] *Steevens (subst.)*   130 honour] honours *F*   SD] *F2*   131 Signor] *Oxf;* Signeur *QF*
132 ounce] *Q* (ouce*),* *F*   incony] *QF* (in-conie*)*   135 remuneration] *F;* remuration *Q*   136 One
penny] *Rowe* (A penny*);* i.d. *QF*   remuneration] *QFc;* remuration *Fu*   137 Why, . . . it!
'Remuneration'!] *Theobald (subst.);* Why? it . . . remuneration: *QF*   138 than] *Q* (then*);* then a *F*
140 My] *Alexander;* O my *QF*

COSTARD   Pray you, sir, how much carnation ribbon may
   a man buy for a remuneration?
BEROWNE   What is a remuneration?
COSTARD   Marry, sir, halfpenny-farthing.
BEROWNE   Why then, three-farthing-worth of silk.   145
COSTARD   I thank your worship. God be wi'you.
BEROWNE   Stay, slave. I must employ thee.
   As thou wilt win my favour, good my knave,
   Do one thing for me that I shall entreat.
COSTARD   When would you have it done, sir?   150
BEROWNE   This afternoon.
COSTARD   Well, I will do it, sir. Fare you well.
BEROWNE   Thou knowest not what it is.
COSTARD   I shall know, sir, when I have done it.
BEROWNE   Why, villain, thou must know first.   155
COSTARD   I will come to your worship tomorrow morning.
BEROWNE   It must be done this afternoon. Hark, slave, it
   is but this:
   The Princess comes to hunt here in the park,
   And in her train there is a gentle lady;   160
   When tongues speak sweetly, then they name her name,
   And Rosaline they call her. Ask for her
   And to her white hand see thou do commend

---

141 **carnation** flesh-coloured
146 **God be wi'you** God be with you, a
   variant form of 'goodbye'; see *OED*
   good-bye 1a, which suggests the
   phrase originated with Shakespeare.
147 **slave** rascal, fellow, an affectionate
   form of address (*OED sb.* 1c)
155 **villain** like *slave* (147), an affectionate form of address (*OED sb.* 1c)
161 **When . . . then** For this formula, see

also 1.1.3–4n., 5.2.817–18, the songs of
Ver and Hiems and Introduction, p.
15.
163 **white hand** Rosaline's pale hand is
   referred to again by Berowne at
   4.2.131 and 5.2.411, but see also
   5.2.230n.; the epithet was conventional: see e.g. *RJ* 3.3.36, *AYL*
   3.2.394.

---

143 What] *F;* O what *Q*   145 Why] *Cam;* O, why *QF*   three-farthing] *Q (*threefarthing*);*
threefarthings *F*   147 Stay] *Cam;* O stay *QF*   151 This] *Cam;* O this *QF*   153 Thou] *Cam;* O
thou *QF*   157–8] *Capell; verse QF, lined* noone, / this: /   *; verse Oxf, lined* slave, / this: /

170

This sealed-up counsel. [*Gives Costard a letter.*]
                                    There's thy guerdon: go.
[*Gives Costard money.*]

COSTARD   Guerdon, O sweet guerdon! Better than   165
remuneration, elevenpence-farthing better. Most sweet
guerdon! I will do it, sir, in print. Guerdon!
Remuneration!   *Exit.*

BEROWNE

And I, forsooth, in love! I, that have been love's whip,
A very beadle to a humorous sigh,   170
A critic, nay, a night-watch constable,
A domineering pedant o'er the boy,
Than whom no mortal so magnificent!
This wimpled, whining, purblind, wayward boy,

---

164 **counsel** confidential or secret business (*OED sb.* 5b)
guerdon reward. The QF spelling 'gardon' in 165–7 as against 'guerdon' in
164 may suggest Berowne pronounces
the word in French, while Costard does
so in English; Cotgrave lists *gardon* as an
alternative Fr. spelling for *guerdon*.
166 **elevenpence-farthing**   Berowne
gives Costard a shilling (twelve pence).
167 **in print** precisely, exactly, to the letter
(*OED sb.* 14a); cf. the proverbial 'A man
(thing, action) in print', Tilley, M239.
The joke is that it is mistaken to rely on
the correctness of print (cf. 2.1.235n.):
Costard delivers this (and Armado's) letter wrongly. Despite its being torn up,
Dumaine identifies its sender first of all
by its being in *Berowne's writing* (4.3.199).
169 The line is probably not a true
alexandrine, in which case *forsooth* is
extrametrical: all Shakespeare's other
uses of the word in verse occur in regular iambic pentameters.
love's whip the scourge of love; cf.

4.3.148n.
170 **beadle** parish officer responsible for
whipping minor offenders, esp. prostitutes
humorous relating to the humours,
moody
171 **critic** censurer, fault-finder (*OED
sb.*[1] 1*); cf. 4.3.167n.
night-watch *OED* 1 *attrib.**
constable i.e. like Dull
172 **domineering** *OED ppl. a.* 1*
pedant schoolmaster, teacher (*OED
sb.* 1*); Holofernes is called a pedant at
5.2.533 and 538 and referred to as one
at his first entry in 5.1.
boy Cupid
173 **Than** as, compared with
magnificent arrogant, proud: the line
as a whole can refer to Cupid or to
Berowne himself; cf. 1.1.188n.
174 **wimpled** blindfolded
purblind completely blind; cf. *RJ*
2.1.12.
wayward boy Cf. the identical epithet
for Adonis in *VA* 344.

164 SD1] *Collier MS*   SD2] *Johnson (subst.)*   165–7 Guerdon . . . guerdon . . . Guerdon] *F2;*
Gardon . . . gardon . . . gardon *QF*   166 elevenpence] *QF (*a leuenpence*)*   169–73] *Pope; Q lines*
whip? / Constable, / magnificent. /; *F lines* loue, / whip? / Criticke, / Constable. / Boy, / magnificent. /
169 And] *Cam;* O and *QF*   171 critic] *Q (*Crietick*), F (*Criticke*)*

This Signor Junior, giant dwarf, Dan Cupid,   175
Regent of love-rhymes, lord of folded arms,
Th'anointed sovereign of sighs and groans,
Liege of all loiterers and malcontents,
Dread prince of plackets, king of codpieces,
Sole imperator and great general   180
Of trotting paritors – O my little heart!
And I to be a corporal of his field
And wear his colours like a tumbler's hoop!
What? I love, I sue, I seek a wife?
A woman that is like a German clock,   185

175 *Signor Junior** senior junior, with
the idea that he is 'Signor' or Mr
Junior (cf. 1.2.10n.): as Oxf[1] points
out, Eros or Cupid was both 'the old-
est of the classical deities, since it was
love that brought order out of chaos,
and simultaneously the youngest of
them, a mere boy'.
  giant dwarf an oxymoron
  Dan sir, master, from the Lat. *dominus*;
Chaucer refers to 'daun Cupido' in *The
House of Fame* (*Riv*, 1.137) and Spenser
to 'Dan *Cupids* powre' at *FQ*, 3.11.46.5,
and to 'Dan *Chaucer*' at 4.2.32.8.
176 **Regent** ruler, governor
  love-rhymes *OED* love *sb*. 15a*
176–8 **lord . . . malcontents** The
description of the melancholy lover is
reminiscent of Moth's in 15–19n.
177 **sovereign** three syllables
179 **plackets** slits in petticoats or skirts
(*OED* 3a**) and by extension women's
sexual organs
  codpieces baggy appendages at the
front of a man's breeches containing
his genitals, and so the genitals themselves. Codpieces were often orna-
mented for display.
180 **imperator** absolute ruler, emperor
(*OED* b*)
181 **paritors** apparitors, officers who
summoned people before ecclesiastical

courts which tried sexual crimes;
unique in Shakespeare, who does not
use the form 'apparitors'
182 **corporal . . . field** field officer to the
general, Cupid (*OED* corporal *sb.*[2]
2**); he acted as an aide-de-camp to
the sergeant-major. Cf. 4.3.83n.
183 **colours** coloured dress or insignia
used to identify members of a party
(*OED sb.* 6a); cf. 4.2.148n.
  tumbler's hoop An acrobat's hoop
with which he did his tricks would be
decorated with ribbons and worn
across his body like a scarf.
184 The line can be punctuated in various
ways. T. W. Craik suggests (privately)
it could be emended to read 'What? I
in love?' and compares 169.
  sue court a woman (*OED v.* 23); see
5.2.426–7n.
185–6 This simile became proverbial; see
Tilley, W658.
185 *German clock** Elaborately made,
often containing moving figures or people and animals, they were more valued
as ornaments than as reliable timepieces
(*OED* German *a.*[2] 4). Clocks, watches
and dials were also suggestive of male
and female sexual organs: cf. *RJ*
2.4.112–13, *AYL* 2.7.20–8. Berowne's
description of the 'regular' woman sus-
tains the sexual innuendo.

175 Signor] *Oxf;* signior *QF;* senior *Hanmer*   Junior] *Hanmer (subst.); Iunios QF*   Dan] *Q (dan);*
don *F*   184 What? I] *QF;* What? I? I *Malone*   185 clock] *F2 (Clocke);* Cloake *QF*

172

Still a-repairing, ever out of frame
And never going aright, being a watch,
But being watched that it may still go right!
Nay, to be perjured, which is worst of all;
And among three to love the worst of all,   190
A whitely wanton with a velvet brow,
With two pitch-balls stuck in her face for eyes;
Ay, and by heaven, one that will do the deed
Though Argus were her eunuch and her guard.
And I to sigh for her, to watch for her,   195
To pray for her! Go to, it is a plague
That Cupid will impose for my neglect
Of his almighty dreadful little might.
Well, I will love, write, sigh, pray, sue and groan.   199
Some men must love my lady, and some Joan.   [*Exit.*]

186 **Still** continually
    out of frame out of order, irregular (*OED* frame *sb.* 5)
187 **going** keeping time (*OED v.* 8d*)
    watch a small clock (*OED sb.* 21)
188 **being** i.e. needing to be
    still go right continually keep time; continually behave as she ought: cf. 1.1.14n.
189 **perjured** i.e. by breaking the oath sworn in 1.1
191 ***whitely** pale, fair-skinned
    velvet brow a brow smooth or soft as velvet (*OED* velvet *sb.* 4b*, citing 4.3.102)
192 **pitch-balls** Cf. the proverbial 'As dark (black) as pitch', Tilley, P357. Berowne returns to pitch when thinking about Rosaline in 4.3.3 where the proverbial association between pitch and being defiled is made explicit. Her dark eyes and hair (4.3.243n.) offend against Elizabethan ideas of beautiful

women being blonde.
193 **one** one of the women; a third 'eye', her vagina; see 2.1.188n.
    do the deed perform the sexual act; cf. 1.1.22n., *Oth* 4.3.64.
194 **Argus** a monstrous herdsman with a hundred eyes whom Juno set to watch Io so that Jupiter could not get near her; see Ovid, *Met.*, 1.625–723.
195 **watch** stay awake at night, be unable to sleep
197 **neglect** disregarding, slighting (*OED sb.* 1a*)
200 **Joan** a conventional name for a lower-class woman (*OED* 1*); cf. *groan for Joan*, 4.3.179, and *greasy Joan*, 5.2.908. She is contrasted to the generalized, upper-class *my lady*, suggesting the proverbial 'Joan is as good as my lady', Dent, J57. Berowne's imputation about Rosaline's social class need not be taken literally.

4[.1]   *Enter the* PRINCESS, *a* Forester, *her ladies*
              [ROSALINE, MARIA *and* KATHERINE] *and her lords*
                        [BOYET *and others*].

PRINCESS

    Was that the King that spurred his horse so hard
    Against the steep-up rising of the hill?
BOYET

    I know not, but I think it was not he.
PRINCESS

    Whoe'er 'a was, 'a showed a mounting mind.
    Well, lords, today we shall have our dispatch;   5
    On Saturday we will return to France.
    Then, forester, my friend, where is the bush
    That we must stand and play the murderer in?
FORESTER

    Hereby, upon the edge of yonder coppice,
    A stand where you may make the fairest shoot.   10
PRINCESS

    I thank my beauty, I am fair that shoot,

4.1 The hunting scene can be compared to
3H6 3.1. Its subsequent references to
archery (107–38) suggest an erotic
undertone and a connection – through
Roger Ascham's *Toxophilus* (1545) –
with the art of rhetoric; see Elam, 238.

2   ***steep-up** precipitous, perpendicular;
cf. *Son* 7.5, 'the steep-up heavenly
hill', and *PP* 9.5.

4   **mounting** lit. climbing, but also aspir-
ing; cf. 'the mounting spirit', *KJ* 1.1.206,
and *Dr Faustus* A-text, Prologue, l. 21.
There may be a pun on mounting/
mountain here, and see 5.1.76–9n.

5   **dispatch** 'Official dismissal or leave to
go, given to an ambassador after com-
pletion of his errand' (*OED sb.* 2)

6   **Saturday** The specific reference to

the day suggests the first two acts are
intended to take place on Friday and
the last three on Saturday. The further
details of the treaty were expected
Tomorrow (2.1.165) and the King and
his lords would visit again *Tomorrow*
(2.1.176). For additional details, see
Furness, 377.

8   **murderer** The Princess's evident dis-
taste for hunting – cf. 'mercy goes to
kill' (24) – may be intended to be revealing and makes her success in killing
a pricket (4.2.56–7) unexpected.

10 **stand** place or station for a hunter; cf.
PP 9.5.
    fairest most favourable, best; the
Princess takes him to mean 'most
beautiful'.

4.1] *Rowe; F (Actus Quartus.); act and scene not in Q* 1+ SP PRINCESS] *F2 (Prin.); Quee. (Que.,
Qu.) QF* 2 steep-up rising] *Hart;* steepe vp rising *Q;* steepe vprising *F* 3 SP] *F; Forr. Q;* First
Lord *Kerrigan (subst.)* 6 On] *F;* Ore *Q*

And thereupon thou speak'st 'the fairest shoot'.

FORESTER

Pardon me, madam, for I meant not so.

PRINCESS

What, what? First praise me, and again say no?

O, short-lived pride! Not fair? Alack for woe!　　　　　　15

FORESTER

Yes, madam, fair.

PRINCESS　　　　　　　Nay, never paint me now.

Where fair is not, praise cannot mend the brow.

Here, good my glass, take this for telling true:

[*She gives him money.*]

Fair payment for foul words is more than due.

FORESTER

Nothing but fair is that which you inherit.　　　　　　20

PRINCESS

See, see, my beauty will be saved by merit!

O heresy in fair, fit for these days!

A giving hand, though foul, shall have fair praise.

But come, the bow. Now mercy goes to kill,

And shooting well is then accounted ill.　　　　　　25

---

15 **short-lived** brief (*OED a.* 2*); cf.
2.1.54n.

16 **paint** flatter (*OED v.*[1] 6b); cf. the
Princess's disapproval of *the painted
flourish* of Boyet's praise, 2.1.13–19.

17 **fair** beauty; cf. *Son* 18.7, 'And every
fair from fair sometime declines'.
praise Cf. 2.1.78–9n.
brow aspect, appearance (*OED sb.*[1]
5c**); cf. 4.3.182.

18 **good my glass** my good mirror
telling true Cf. 1.1.221.

20 **inherit** possess, hold as your own; see
1.1.73n.

21 **by merit** by its own intrinsic worth;
by due reward; by good works, which
Roman Catholics held as the way to

salvation, Protestants believing it lay
through faith alone

22 **heresy** The Princess's word may imply
a heterodox opinion in any subject (cf.
5.1.6), rather than a specifically religious
error, but *by merit* may indicate an inappropriate theological sense is present.
in fair with regard to beauty
for these days The Princess's expos-
tulation may be general rather than
specific.

23 Cf. the proverbial 'The giving hand is
fair', Dent, H68.1.

24 **mercy** The Princess figures herself as
an emblem of mercy.

25 **then** i.e. because the Princess is supposed to be merciful

14 and] & then *F*　18 SD] *Johnson (subst.)*

Thus will I save my credit in the shoot:
Not wounding, pity would not let me do't;
If wounding, then it was to show my skill,
That more for praise than purpose meant to kill.
And out of question so it is sometimes,   30
Glory grows guilty of detested crimes,
When for fame's sake, for praise, an outward part,
We bend to that the working of the heart;
As I for praise alone now seek to spill
The poor deer's blood, that my heart means no ill.   35

BOYET

Do not curst wives hold that self-sovereignty
Only for praise' sake when they strive to be
Lords o'er their lords?

PRINCESS

Only for praise, and praise we may afford
To any lady that subdues a lord.   40

Enter [COSTARD, *the*] *Clown*[, *with a letter*].

BOYET   Here comes a member of the commonwealth.
COSTARD   God dig-you-den all! Pray you which is the

---

26 **credit** reputation
27 i.e. if she fails to hit the deer, she can
claim she misses on purpose
30 **out of question** undeniably
31 This line sounds sententious.
   Glory the habit of claiming honour,
   boastful spirit (*OED sb.* 1a)
   detested detestable, odious
32 **fame's sake** See 1.1.1n.
   praise Cf. 2.1.78–9n.
   outward part superficial, exterior
   thing
33 i.e. we level or direct the heart's emotional activity to gain fame (*OED* working *vbl. sb.* 5d). Here and at 35 there
   may be a pun on heart/hart. Cf. 1.2.9n.
35 **my . . . ill** means me no harm; I feel no

malice towards
36–8 'Don't shrewish wives wilfully
   follow *the working of the heart* precisely
   for praise' sake when they boss their
   husbands about?' (Kerrigan). *Self-
   sovereignty* refers to the power ruling
   in one's self; 'self sovereignty' would
   mean 'the same ruling power': the QF
   reading is hyphenated.
41 **Here comes** Cf. 4.3.17, 5.2.542, 627.
   commonwealth Johnson suggested
   that Boyet means to insult Costard by
   implying he is common; cf. Dent,
   M868.1, *MV* 3.5.34–5 and see 4.2.75.
42 **God dig-you-den** a colloquial form of
   'give you good evening' (*OED* Good even
   a.); this form is unique in Shakespeare.

27 do't] *Q (*doote*), F   40.1 *with a letter*] *Bevington*   42+ SP COSTARD] *Rowe; Clo. (Clow., Cl.) QF*

head lady?

PRINCESS   Thou shalt know her, fellow, by the rest that
have no heads.   45

COSTARD   Which is the greatest lady, the highest?

PRINCESS   The thickest and the tallest.

COSTARD   The thickest and the tallest. It is so, truth is truth.
An your waist, mistress, were as slender as my wit,
One o'these maids' girdles for your waist should be fit.   50
Are not you the chief woman? You are the thickest
here.

PRINCESS   What's your will, sir? What's your will?

COSTARD

I have a letter from Monsieur Berowne to one Lady
Rosaline.

PRINCESS

O, thy letter, thy letter! He's a good friend of mine.   55
[*She takes the letter.*]
Stand aside, good bearer. Boyet, you can carve:
Break up this capon.

BOYET   I am bound to serve.
[*He examines the letter.*]
This letter is mistook; it importeth none here.
It is writ to Jaquenetta.

PRINCESS   We will read it, I swear.

---

45 **no heads** In addition to the obvious
joke, the Princess may be punning on
'maidenheads' here.

48 **truth is truth** proverbial: see Tilley,
T581.

51 **thickest** fattest, stoutest; the only
occasion on which Shakespeare
describes a character generally as
'thick' in this sense.

55 **thy . . . thy . . . He's** The change of
pronouns may suggest the Princess's
excitement.

56 **carve** cut up; the Princess may also
hint at a secondary meaning, make
affected gestures with the hand
(Onions), for which cf. 5.2.323n.

57 **Break up** carve, cut up (*OED* break *v.*
2b)
capon fowl; love-letter (*OED sb.* 4*)
and cf. Cotgrave, 'Poulet', '*A chicken;
also, a loue-letter, or loue-message*'.

58 **mistook** wrongly delivered; cf. 105.
importeth relates to, has to do with
(*OED* import *v.* 7a)

---

49 mistress] *Q (*Mistrs*), F*   50 fit] *Qc, F;* fir *Qu*   52 here.] here? *F*   55 SD] *Cam¹ (subst.)*   57 SD]
Cam¹ (subst.)

Break the neck of the wax, and everyone give ear.   60
BOYET (*Reads.*) *By heaven, that thou art fair is most*
infallible; true that thou art beauteous; truth itself that
thou art lovely. More fairer than fair, beautiful than
beauteous, truer than truth itself, have commiseration on
thy heroical vassal. The magnanimous and most illustrate   65
King Cophetua set eye upon the pernicious and indubitate
beggar Zenelophon, and he it was that might rightly say,
Veni, vidi, vici, *which to annothanize in the vulgar – O*
base and obscure vulgar! – videlicet, *he came, see and*
overcame. He came, one; see, two; overcame, three. Who   70
came? The King. Why did he come? To see. Why did he
see? To overcome. To whom came he? To the beggar. What
saw he? The beggar. Who overcame he? The beggar. The

---

60 **neck . . . wax** i.e. the wax seal, but
referring back to the *capon*
62 *infallible* certain (*OED a.* 2c**)
64 *truer . . . itself* Cf. the proverbial 'It is
as true as truth itself', Tilley, T565.
commiseration pity, compassion
65 *illustrate* illustrious; see also 5.1.113.
66 *King Cophetua* See 1.2.104–5n.
pernicious destructive, fatal; evil,
wicked. Wilson's emendation 'penurious' is based on minim error.
Shakespeare regularly uses 'pernicious' in a pejorative sense (he uses
'penurious' only once, *Tim* 4.3.93), but
the unusual epithet for the beggar-
maid may be Armado's error.
indubitate certain, undoubted.
Pernicious and indubitate form a hendiadys (see 1.1.14n.).
68 **Veni, vidi, vici** Caesar's famous
words are said by Suetonius (*Divus
Julius*, 37.2) to have been displayed in
his Pontic triumph and by Plutarch to
have been sent in a letter at the end of
the Pontic campaign. As well as being
translated in North's Plutarch (see

Bullough, 5.75), the phrase had been
written on by Erasmus and it had
become proverbial; see Tilley, C540.
annothanize explain analytically; presumably an incorrect fusion of 'anatomize', meaning to analyse, and
'annote', meaning to annotate. Some
editors argue that the QF form is an
unmodernized version of 'anatomize',
but none of the other instances in
Shakespeare suggests this is likely:
'anathomize' (*AYL* 1.1.156); 'anath-
omiz'd' (*AYL* 2.7.56, *AW* 4.3.32, *Luc*
1450); 'anothomize' (*2H4* Q1 Prologue
21); 'anotomize' (*KL* Q1 3.6.76);
'Anatomize' (*KL* F 3.6.76).
vulgar vernacular
69 *obscure* lowly, humble (*OED a.* 6a)
videlicet namely, that is
69–70 *see . . . see* 'See' as a third-person
past indicative for modern 'saw' was
acceptable usage (*OED* see *v.* A. 3a).
70 *overcame conquered; had sex with.
Prooffoot suggests (privately) that the
QF reading 'couercame' may be an
error for '& ouercame'.

---

63 *beautiful*] *QF;* more beautiful *(Tyrwhitt)* 66 *set*] *Qc, F;* sets *Qu;* set's *Oxf pernicious*] *QF;*
penurious *Cam¹* 67 *was*] *Qc, F;* is was *Qu* 68 *annothanize*] *QF;* Anatomize *F2* 69 *see*] *QF (*See*);*
Saw *F2* 70 *see, two*] *QF;* saw two *Rowe overcame*] *F3;* couercame *QF, F2*

178

conclusion is victory. On whose side? The King's. The
captive is enriched. On whose side? The beggar's. The   75
catastrophe is a nuptial. On whose side? The King's? No,
on both in one, or one in both. I am the King, for so stands
the comparison, thou the beggar, for so witnesseth thy
lowliness. Shall I command thy love? I may. Shall I
enforce thy love? I could. Shall I entreat thy love? I will.   80
What shalt thou exchange for rags? Robes. For tittles?
Titles. For thyself? Me. Thus expecting thy reply, I
profane my lips on thy foot, my eyes on thy picture and my
heart on thy every part.

> Thine in the dearest design of industry,   85
> Don Adriano de Armado.

Thus dost thou hear the Nemean lion roar
'Gainst thee, thou lamb, that standest as his prey.

---

74 *conclusion* in logic 'A proposition
deduced by reasoning from previous
propositions' (*OED* 5b)
76 *catastrophe* the denouement or resolution of a dramatic piece; cf. Spenser,
SC, 'May' gloss to l. 174, and
Edmund's 'like the catastrophe of the
old comedy', *KL* 1.2.134.
nuptial Shakespeare regularly used
the singular form (*OED* B. 1).
77 *on both . . . in both* a favourite
Shakespearean theme
79 *lowliness* poverty (*OED* 2**)
79–80 *command . . . entreat* A common
pairing, esp. when used by the more
powerful: cf. Venus to Phao, 'I entreat
where I may command; command
thou, where thou shouldst entreat',
Lyly, *Sapho and Phao*, 4.2.26–8;
Richard to Queen Elizabeth, 'Tell her
the King, that may command,
entreats', *R3* 4.4.345.
81 *exchange* obtain in exchange (*OED v.*
1c*)

for rags? Robes Cf. the proverbial 'Out
of rags into robes', Dent, R6.2.
tittles insignificant or minute
amounts, as in the phrase 'jot and tit-
tle'; the word was also used for the
three points placed at the end of horn-
books: see Nashe, 4.205.
82 *expecting* waiting for
82–3 *I . . . foot* Oxf[1] compares Romeo's
first speech to Juliet, *RJ* 1.5.93–6, for
the collocation of profaning lips; see
also 1.2.161n.
85 *in . . . industry* i.e. in the most loving
purpose, fondest intention, of gal-
lantry, i.e. in love (*OED* design *sb.* 2a*);
for *design*, cf. 5.1.93.
87–92 See 1.1.61–6n.
87–90 Cf. the proverbial 'The lion spares
the suppliant', Dent, L316.
87 *Nemean lion Nemean* is three syllables, stressed on the first. Hercules'
first labour was to kill the Nemean
(*OED* 1*) lion. Cf. *Ham* 1.4.83, *TNK*
1.1.68.

---

74 *King's*] *Q2* (Kings); King *QF* 76 *King's?*] *Rowe*; Kinges: *QF* 81 *What*] *F4*; What, *QF* 83 *picture*] *Qc, F*; pictture *Qu* 86 *Adriano*] *Q2*; Adriana *QF* *Armado*] *F2*; Armatho *QF*

> *Submissive fall his princely feet before,*
> > *And he from forage will incline to play.* 90
> *But if thou strive, poor soul, what art thou then?*
> *Food for his rage, repasture for his den.*

PRINCESS

What plume of feathers is he that indited this letter?
What vane? What weathercock? Did you ever hear
  better?

BOYET

I am much deceived but I remember the style. 95

PRINCESS

Else your memory is bad, going o'er it erewhile.

BOYET

This Armado is a Spaniard that keeps here in court,
A phantasime, a Monarcho, and one that makes sport
To the Prince and his book-mates.

PRINCESS   Thou, fellow, a word.
Who gave thee this letter?

COSTARD   I told you: my lord. 100

PRINCESS

To whom shouldst thou give it?

---

90 *from . . . play* will turn from ravaging to playing (*OED* forage *sb.* 2b*)
92 *repasture* food for a repast (*OED**)
93 **plume of feathers** show-off (*OED* feather *sb.* 8b)
94 ***vane** man who constantly changes like a weathervane (*OED* 1b*)
   weathercock inconstant man (*OED sb.* 2b*)
95 **but I** if I do not
   style literary style; name and title
96 **going o'er** having read; having climbed over: Berowne makes the same pun at 1.1.196.
   erewhile a short while ago
97 **keeps** dwells, lodges
98 **phantasime** fantastic creature, person

full of fantasies. *OED** only records the usage here and at 5.1.18, comparing Florio '*fantasima* or *fantasma*'. Cf. *RJ* 2.4.28–9, 'such antic, lisping, affecting [phantasimes]', where Q1 has 'fantasticoes' and Q2–4, F have 'phantacies', presumably with an omitted tilde over the 'i'.
   Monarcho the title assumed by a mad Italian who claimed to be emperor of the world and frequented Elizabeth's court; see Nashe, 4.339. A poem by Churchyard on his death was published in 1580.
99 **To** for
   book-mates fellow students (*OED* book *sb.* 18, the only citation); cf. *bookmen* 2.1.226n.

94 vane] *Rowe;* vaine *Q;* veine *F*   100 you: my] *Theobald (subst.);* you, my *QF*

COSTARD   From my lord to my lady.

PRINCESS

From which lord to which lady?

COSTARD

From my lord Berowne, a good master of mine,

To a lady of France that he called Rosaline.

PRINCESS

Thou hast mistaken his letter. Come, lords, away.   105

[*to Rosaline*] Here, sweet, put up this; 'twill be thine
another day.

          [*Exeunt all but Boyet, Rosaline, Maria and Costard.*]

BOYET

Who is the shooter? Who is the shooter?

ROSALINE   Shall I teach you to know?

BOYET

Ay, my continent of beauty.

ROSALINE   Why, she that bears the bow.

Finely put off!

BOYET

My lady goes to kill horns, but if thou marry,   110

Hang me by the neck if horns that year miscarry.

Finely put on!

---

105 **mistaken** taken wrongfully; cf. 58.
106 **put up** put away, keep
  'twill . . . day your turn – perhaps,
  more specifically, your letter – will
  come; cf. the proverbial 'Let him mend
  his manners, it will be his own another
  day', Dent, M628.
107 **¹Who . . . ²shooter** As Capell first
  noted, the metre requires some elision
  in *Who is*.
  shooter . . . shooter The QF spelling
  is preferable to Farmer's 'suitor', since
  Boyet seems to be asking who is to

shoot next: both words, 'shooter' and
'suitor', would have been pronounced
in the same way.
108 **continent** container; sum and substance (*OED sb.* 1b)
109 **put off** evaded (*OED v*¹. 45g)
110 **horns** deer (*OED sb.* 1d*)
111 **horns . . . miscarry** cuckolds' horns
  don't grow, are in short supply (*OED
  miscarry v.* 4b*: cf. 4.2.138n.); penises
  don't get what they want.
112 **put on** laid on: a hit

106 SD1] *Capell*   SD2] *Cam¹ (subst.); Exeunt. F; not in Q; Exeunt Princess and Train / Theobald
(subst.)*   107 shooter . . . shooter] *QF;* suitor . . . suitor *Steevens² (Farmer)*   108–9 Why . . . off]
Capell; one line QF

ROSALINE

Well, then, I am the shooter.

BOYET   And who is your deer?

ROSALINE

If we choose by the horns, yourself come not near.

Finely put on indeed!   115

MARIA

You still wrangle with her, Boyet, and she strikes at
    the brow.

BOYET

But she herself is hit lower. Have I hit her now?

ROSALINE   Shall I come upon thee with an old saying that
    was a man when King Pepin of France was a little boy,
    as touching the hit-it?   120

BOYET   So I may answer thee with one as old, that was a
    woman when Queen Guinevere of Britain was a little
    wench, as touching the hit-it.

ROSALINE

               Thou canst not hit it, hit it, hit it,
               Thou canst not hit it, my good man.   125

BOYET

           An I cannot, cannot, cannot,

---

113 **deer** punning on 'dear'
114 Rosaline rejects Boyet as her 'dear' because she claims he has cuckold's horns; alternatively, she claims he is immature and that like a young deer's his horns have not grown.
116 **wrangle** argue, bicker
    strikes . . . brow takes good aim at the deer's head, at the lowest part of its antler; attacks you for being a cuckold
117 **hit lower** wounded lower than the brow: the implication is that she has been hit in her heart, but the innuendo – with *come upon* – is that she has also been 'hit' sexually.
    hit her got to her, 'scored' both as in a game and sexually

118 **come upon** riposte to, fight back against (*OED v.* 48b)
119 **King Pepin** Charlemagne's father, who died in 768; he was a symbol of past times: see also *AW* 2.1.76.
120 **hit-it** a popular song and dance, with the innuendo of 'hitting' as having sex
121 **So** provided that
122 **Queen Guinevere** King Arthur's queen, supposed to have lived long before Pepin, and famous for having cuckolded her husband
124–5 **hit it** hit the mark, guess the right thing (*OED* hit *v.* 20a)
126–7 Cf. the proverbial 'If one will not another will', Tilley, O62.

114–15] *F3; prose QF*   119 Pepin] *Q (Pippen), F (Pippin)*   122 Guinevere] *QF (Guinouer)*   126–7] *F; one line Q*   126 An I] *Q (And I); I F*

                An I cannot, another can.   *Exit* [*Rosaline*].

COSTARD

  By my troth, most pleasant! How both did fit it!

MARIA

  A mark marvellous well shot, for they both did hit it.

BOYET

  A mark! O, mark but that mark! A mark, says my lady.   130
  Let the mark have a prick in't, to mete at, if it may be.

MARIA

  Wide o'the bow hand! I'faith your hand is out.

COSTARD

  Indeed, 'a must shoot nearer, or he'll ne'er hit the clout.

BOYET

  An if my hand be out, then belike your hand is in.

COSTARD

  Then will she get the upshoot by cleaving the pin.   135

MARIA

  Come, come, you talk greasily, your lips grow foul.

128 **fit it** make words, metre and subject-matter go together; have sex: cf. *MW* 2.1.161.

129 **mark** target (*OED sb*[1]. 7d); cf. 4.2.111.

130 **mark but** just note

131 **mark** target; woman's genitals
prick bull's-eye (*OED sb*. 10a); penis (*OED sb*. 17a)
mete measure with the eye, take aim (*OED v*.[1] 2b)

132 **Wide . . . bow hand** wide of the mark, out; the left hand usually holds the bow (*OED* bow-hand 1*). The phrase, of which this is the earliest known example, became proverbial (Tilley, B567), but cf. *STM* 3.2.260, 'O Wit, thou art now on the bow hand'.
your . . . out The phrase became proverbial; see Tilley, H67.

out out of practice (*OED adv.* 20c*); inaccurate

133 **nearer . . . *ne'er** A pun may be intended.
clout a white patch of cloth at the centre of the target fixed by a pin

134 Boyet addresses Maria: if my hand as an archer and in sexual matters is out, then most likely yours is in (in both senses).

135 Then she will get the best shot in the archery competition by splitting the *pin* which holds the *clout*; by holding fast to (*OED* cleave *v*.[2] 1) his penis, she will get the result or conclusion from it, i.e. his ejaculation (*OED* upshoot *sb.* 1*). 'To cleave the pin' was proverbial: Tilley, P336.

136 **greasily** indecently (*OED**); cf. 5.2.908n.
foul disgustingly filthy (*OED* A. 2 *fig.**); cf. 5.2.904n.

127 SD] *Rowe; Exit. Q opp. 125, F opp. 127; Exeunt Rosaline and Katharine. / Kittredge (subst.)*   129 did hit it] *F4;* did hit *Qc, F;* hid hit *Qu*   132 o'the] *Qc* (a'the*), F* (a'th*);* athe *Qu*   133 ne'er] *F* (ne're*);* neare *Q*   135 pin] *F2;* is in *QF*

COSTARD

She's too hard for you at pricks, sir. Challenge her to
bowl.

BOYET

I fear too much rubbing. Good night, my good owl.

[*Exeunt Boyet and Maria.*]

COSTARD

By my soul, a swain, a most simple clown!

Lord, lord, how the ladies and I have put him down!   140

O'my troth, most sweet jests, most incony vulgar wit,

When it comes so smoothly off, so obscenely, as it
were, so fit.

Armado o'th' t'other side – O, a most dainty man!

To see him walk before a lady and to bear her fan!

To see him kiss his hand and how most sweetly 'a will
swear!   145

---

137 **hard . . . pricks** good for you to beat
at hitting bull's-eyes in archery; her
vagina is not soft enough for you to get
your penis into it: cf. 2.1.257n.
to bowl to play at bowls

138 **rubbing** when the bowl meets another
bowl on its way to the jack (*OED* rub
*v.*¹ 14b), but Boyet is also thinking of
masturbation
owl a stupid person who looks wise
and grave (*OED sb.* 2); 'to take owl' is
said to mean to take offence (*OED* owl
sb. 1d, citing Francis Grose, *A
Provincial Glossary* (1787)). 'Owl'
would have sounded like '[h]ole' and
so kept up the sexual banter. It anticipates *the staring owl* of Hiems's song,
5.2.905n.

139 **clown** country fellow

141 **incony** See 3.1.132n.
vulgar common, ordinary: Costard
means the reverse.

142 **obscenely** It is not clear what adverb
Costard intended, but *obscenely*
(*OED**) is apt for the previous dialogue; and cf. Shakespeare's only other
use, *MND* 1.2.107–8, Bottom's 'we
may rehearse most obscenely and
courageously'. See also 1.1.235n.
as it were See 4.2.14n.

143–7 Armado and Moth do not appear
between 3.1.131 and 5.1.29: Costard is
comparing them favourably with
Boyet.

143 ***o'th' t'other side** on the other hand
(*OED* side *sb.*¹ 17b). Although 'th' t'
other' literally means 'the the other',
't'other' as an adjective preceding a
noun (*OED* tother B. 1) was in use; cf.
TNK 4.3.32.
dainty particular, fastidious

144 **bear her fan** as Peter does for the
Nurse in *RJ* 2.4.106

145 The line lacks a rhyme.

---

137 bowl.] *F (*boule.*);* bowle *Q*   138 SD] *Theobald (subst.)*   143 Armado o'th' t'other] *Keightley*
(*a'th't'other); Armatho* ath toothen *Q; Armathor* ath to the *F;* Armado a th' t'one *Alexander;* Armado
o' th' one *Bevington;* Armado to th'one *Kerrigan*   145] *QF; line missing (Oxf)*

And his page o' t'other side, that handful of wit!
Ah, heavens, it is a most pathetical nit! *Shout within.*
Sola, sola!   *Exit.*

[4.2] *Enter* DULL, HOLOFERNES, *the Pedant, and* NATHANIEL.

NATHANIEL   Very reverend sport, truly, and done in the
testimony of a good conscience.

HOLOFERNES   The deer was, as you know, *sanguis*, in
blood, ripe as the pomewater, who now hangeth like a
jewel in the ear of *caelo*, the sky, the welkin, the heaven,   5
and anon falleth like a crab on the face of *terra*, the soil,
the land, the earth.

NATHANIEL   Truly, Master Holofernes, the epithets are

---

146   **handful** small company
147   **pathetical nit** touching, affecting
little fellow (*OED* nit *sb.* 2*). A nit is
either a parasitic insect or its egg, or
could be a gnat or small fly. Armado
admires Moth's *pathetical* invocation,
1.2.92–3n.
 *Shout within QF have 'Shoot(e)
within.' after the SD for the exit and
do not indicate the words are an SD.
Costard is responding to a noise which
a bow shooting an arrow would be
unlikely to make: 'Shoot(e)' is more
probably a spelling variant of 'Shout'.
148   **Sola, sola** holla: shouts to attract
attention, perhaps meant to imitate a
horn; *OED int.**, citing only this passage and *MV* 5.1.39–44
4.2.1   **reverend** worthy of deep respect;
suitable for a clergyman
1–2   **in . . . conscience** with the warrant
of a clear conscience; an allusion to 2
Corinthians, 1.12, 'For our reioycing is

this, the testimonie of our conscience'.
3–4   *sanguis*, **in blood** in prime condition;
cf. *1H6* 4.2.48. The Latin is incorrect
and should read either 'in blood, *sanguis*'
or '*sanguine*, in blood' – either the nom-
inative or the ablative. Compositorial
error, a transposition or a failure to note
the tilde in *sanguīe*, is possible, but the
joke may be that Holofernes' Latin is
not as good as it ought to be.
4   **pomewater** a large juicy kind of apple
 who now which at one moment
4–5   **hangeth . . . *caelo*** Oxf[1] compares *RJ*
1.5.45–6.
5   *caelo Again, the error – for *caelum* –
may be Holofernes' rather than the
compositor's failure to read *celū* correctly.
 welkin See 3.1.64n.
6   **anon** a moment later
 crab crab-apple; cf. 5.2.913n.
8   **epithets** terms, names (*OED sb.* 3*);
see 1.2.14n.

---

146   o' t'other] *Rowe[3]*; atother *QF*   147   a] *F2*; *not in QF*   SD] *F2* (*Showte within*)*; Shoot within.
Q opp. 148*; Shoote within. *F centred on new line*   148   Sola, sola!] *Capell*; Sowla, sowla. *QF*   SD]
Capell; *Exeunt. QF* (*before* 'Shoot within.'*)
4.2] *Pope*   3 SP] *Rowe*; *Ped. QF*   3–4   *sanguis*, in blood] *QF* (*sanguis in blood*)*; in *sanguis*, blood
Kerrigan; *sanguis* – in blood *Oxf*; in blood, *sanguis Oxf[1]*   4 the] a *F*   5   *caelo*] *QF* (*Celo*)*; *cœlum* /
Dyce[2]   8+ SP] *QF* (*Curat Nath., Nath.*)   epithets] *Rowe* (*Epithetes*)*; epythithes *QF*

sweetly varied, like a scholar at the least: but, sir, I
assure ye it was a buck of the first head.   10
HOLOFERNES   Sir Nathaniel, *haud credo.*
DULL   'Twas not a 'auld grey doe', 'twas a pricket.
HOLOFERNES   Most barbarous intimation! Yet a kind of
insinuation, as it were, *in via*, in way, of explication,
facere, as it were, replication, or rather *ostentare*, to   15
show, as it were, his inclination, after his undressed,
unpolished, uneducated, unpruned, untrained, or
rather unlettered, or ratherest unconfirmed fashion, to

9   **varied** Cf. 1.1.279n., 4.3.97n.
    at the least to say the least
9–10   **I assure ye** The phrase is used
    again ('I do assure ye') by Armado at
    5.1.89; it only occurs elsewhere in
    Shakespeare in *Son* 111.13.
10   **buck . . . head** five-year-old male deer,
    with its first antlers. Holofernes' error
    about the deer, which Nathaniel appears
    to correct (*but, sir . . .*), is obscure.
11   **Sir** a conventional title for a priest
    haud credo I do not believe it. The
    Latin phrase occurs in the first part of
    the anonymous play *The Troublesome
    Reign of John King of England* (1591),
    1259 (Bullough, 4.106).
12, 20   ***'auld grey doe'** This version of
    QF's 'a *haud credo*' was proposed by A.
    L. Rowse in 1952, substantially accept-
    ed by Kerrigan, endorsed by Stanley
    Wells and adopted by Oxf. A doe is a
    female deer.
12   **pricket** buck in its second year. There
    are sexual puns on 'prick it' and perhaps
    on 'little prick' present in the scene. The
    usages here are unique in Shakespeare.
13   **intimation** announcement; usually
    glossed as 'intrusion', this sense is not
    in *OED*. For Holofernes' fondness for
    forms of words incorporating the suf-
    fix -tion, see Introduction, p. 48 n.2.
14   **insinuation** rhetorically, a type of
    exordium or introduction to a speech

    designed artfully to win over its hear-
    ers (*OED* 3b); cf. 5.1.24–5n.
    as it were A favourite phrase of
    Holofernes': see 15, 16, 25, 5.1.13n.
    and *quasi*, 4.2.81n. Costard used it at
    4.1.142 and Armado uses it at 5.1.107.
    Cf. also *as they say*, 5.1.71n.
    in way as a means of (*OED* way *sb.*[1]
    35c*)
    explication detailed statement or
    description (*OED* 3)
15   *facere* to make
    replication reply, answer
    or rather another of Holofernes'
    favourite phrases (see 17–18, 100),
    translating Lat. *vel potius* (Thomson,
    69)
16   **after** according to
    undressed inelegant, unkempt (*OED
    ppl. a.* 1b*, the only citation)
17   **uneducated** *OED ppl. a.**
    unpruned unrestrained, uncontrolled
    (*OED ppl. a.*[2] b*); cf. 4.3.180.
    untrained In the context of *unpruned*,
    this means Dull is like a plant or tree
    which has not been managed or
    trained to grow in a particular form or
    direction, as well as uninstructed.
18   **unlettered** See 1.1.242n.
    ratherest most of all: not a nonce-word
    unconfirmed uninstructed, ignorant
    (*OED ppl. a.* 2b*, citing only this use
    and *MA* 3.3.117)

12, 20 a 'auld grey doe'] *Oxf (Rowse);* an awd grey doe *Kerrigan;* a *haud credo QF*   14 explication,]
Theobald (subst.); explication *QF*

186

insert again my *haud credo* for a deer.

DULL   I said the deer was not a 'auld grey doe', 'twas a   20
pricket.

HOLOFERNES   Twice-sod simplicity, *bis coctus*!

O, thou monster Ignorance, how deformed dost thou
look!

NATHANIEL

Sir, he hath never fed of the dainties that are bred in a
book.

He hath not eat paper, as it were; he hath not drunk ink.   25

His intellect is not replenished; he is only an animal,
only sensible in the duller parts.

And such barren plants are set before us that we
thankful should be –

Which we of taste and feeling are – for those parts
that do fructify in us more than he.

For as it would ill become me to be vain, indiscreet, or
a fool,   30

19 **insert** introduce, thrust in. Holofernes
is saying that Dull's confusion of a buck
for a doe makes some kind of sense.
22 Dull's repetition of his error annoys
Holofernes. *Twice-sod* means boiled
twice; cf. the proverbial 'Cabbage twice
sodden', Tilley, C511, often used for a
twice-told tale or a repeated remark; *bis
coctus* means twice cooked, as in 'biscuit'.
23 **monster Ignorance** In some Tudor
moral interludes in which Ignorance
appears (e.g. John Redford's *Wit and
Science* and *The Marriage of Wit and
Science*), he is more often the fool and
Tediousness is the monster: on these
interludes as possible sources for the play,
see Lennam. In his masque *Love Freed
from Ignorance and Folly* Jonson drama-
tizes 'monster ignorance' (Jonson, 7.362)
as a Sphinx who has captured Love.
24–33 Nathaniel's speech begins with an
unrhymed line, moves into paratactic

prose (clauses without connectives, cf.
5.1.2–6) and is followed by three
rhyming couplets: the first two sets of
couplets, like the unrhymed line, are in
irregular sixteeners (29 is particularly
irregular) and conclude with a couplet
in poulter's measure (fourteen and
twelve syllables).
25 **eat** eaten: for the shorter form of the
past participle, see Abbott, 343.
26 **replenished** provided, furnished,
supplied with what it needs (*OED v.*
1b)
27 **sensible** capable of physical feeling,
sensitive
28 **barren plants** Cf. *R3* 4.4.394.
29 **Which** as (*OED* 10b), Abbott, 272
feeling sensibility, tenderness to the
feelings of others (*OED vbl. sb.* 5*)
fructify bear fruit
30 ***indiscreet** *OED a.* 2*; cf. *Oth*
2.3.279.

23] *Dyce; prose QF*   28–9] *Hanmer; prose QF*   29 of taste] *Steevens² (Tyrwhitt); taste, Q; taste F*
30 indiscreet] *F; indistreell Q*

So were there a patch set on learning, to see him in a
school.
But *omne bene*, say I, being of an old father's mind;
Many can brook the weather, that love not the wind.

DULL

You two are bookmen: can you tell me by your wit
What was a month old at Cain's birth, that's not five
weeks old as yet?   35

HOLOFERNES Dictynna, goodman Dull. Dictynna,
goodman Dull.

DULL   What is Dictynna?

NATHANIEL   A title to Phoebe, to Luna, to the moon.

HOLOFERNES

The moon was a month old, when Adam was no more,   40
And raught not to five weeks when he came to five-score.
Th'allusion holds in the exchange.

31 **So . . . learning** it would be like edu-
cating a fool or a dolt; it would be like
putting a different piece of cloth on
the fabric of learning. Fools wore
patchwork clothes: see *OED* patch *sb.*[2]
and cf. *parti-coated*, 5.2.760n.
32 *omne bene* all is well
being . . . mind agreeing with someone who lived long ago; Nathaniel
refers to a *father* again at 146: here (as
there) he may be thinking of a Father
of the Church to whom he mistakenly
attributes a familiar proverb.
33 i.e. 'You have to put up with what you
can't change'; this became proverbial
as 'There is no weather ill when the
wind is still', Tilley, W220.
34 **bookmen** See 2.1.226n.
36 *Dictynna Nathaniel explains this at
39: the word is rare, but was used by
Ovid among others. In *Endymion and
Phoebe* (1595) (lines 823–8), Drayton
gives a list of Phoebe's titles including

Dictynna and Luna: see Drayton,
1.150.
goodman a title given to those not of
gentle birth, like yeomen or farmers
38 *Dictynna The QF reading '*dictima*'
is probably a compositor's error (cf.
'*Dictisima . . . dictisima*' in 36) rather
than Dull's, since the varied form is
neither comic nor suggestive.
39 **Phoebe** the sister of Phoebus Apollo,
the sun
40 **no more** no older
41 *raught reached
five-score i.e. one hundred years old
42 **allusion** riddle; word-play, pun (*OED*
2). Shakespeare uses the word only
here and at 44.
holds remains valid, applies (*OED v.*
23c)
exchange change, transmutation, i.e.
of Adam for Cain, but also in the
changing of the moon (*OED sb.* 6a)

34 me] *om. F* 36 Dictynna . . . Dictynna] *Rowe; Dictisima . . . dictisima QF* 38 Dictynna] *F2
(dictinna); dictima QF* 41 raught] *Hanmer;* rought *Q;* wrought *F*

DULL   'Tis true indeed: the collusion holds in the exchange.

HOLOFERNES   God comfort thy capacity! I say th'allusion
      holds in the exchange.   45

DULL   And I say the pollution holds in the exchange, for
      the moon is never but a month old; and I say beside that
      'twas a pricket that the Princess killed.

HOLOFERNES   Sir Nathaniel, will you hear an extemporal
      epitaph on the death of the deer? And, to humour the   50
      ignorant, call I the deer the Princess killed a pricket.

NATHANIEL   *Perge*, good Master Holofernes, *perge*, so it
      shall please you to abrogate scurrility.

HOLOFERNES   I will something affect the letter, for it
      argues facility.   55

---

43 **collusion** verbal trick or ambiguity in
reasoning; Dull, for once picking the
right word, which is also unique in
Shakespeare, realizes that he is being
fooled by Nathaniel and Holofernes,
who are working together.

44 **comfort** strengthen, invigorate (*OED*
v. 4)
capacity mental ability (*OED* 5)

46 **pollution** corruption, contamination
of what Dull, who again gets *allusion*
wrong but chooses an apt word
instead, has said
exchange If Dull refers to the verbal
exchange between Holofernes and
Nathaniel, this usage antedates *OED*
sb. 1d.

48 **'twas** Corrected Q repeats Dull's formula from 12, 20–1.

49 **extemporal** See 1.2.175n.

50 ***death . . . deer** The deer's/dear's
death suggests orgasm; cf. *WT*
1.2.117–18, 'and then to sigh, as 'twere
/ The mort o' th' deer'.
humour gratify, indulge (*OED v.* 1)

52–5 With the omission of Nathaniel's
address to *good Master Holofernes* the

lines may represent verse, rhyming
scurrility/facility.

52 ***Perge** go on, proceed (*OED**)

53 **abrogate *scurrility** do away with,
abstain from, coarseness or indecency:
Nathaniel is probably thinking of the
possibilities of the word 'pricket'. For
abrogate, see *OED v.* 2*, and for *scurrility*, see also 5.1.4n. and *WT*
4.4.213–14, where Perdita wants
Autolycus to be warned 'that he use no
scurrilous words in 's tunes', which
alerts the audience to the probability of
sexual innuendo to come.

54 **something . . . letter** show some
preference for alliteration (*OED* affect
v.[1] 2b). There may be a hidden pun
here, since to indulge in alliteration
was to hunt or to course the letter; see
OED hunt *v.* 3c and Sidney, *DP*,
117.17, and cf. 4.3.2n. Holofernes'
alliterative verse would have been
comically unfashionable in the 1590s.

55 **argues facility** indicates fluency, ease
of manner (*OED* facility 3b*, citing
122); cf. 91–2n.

---

46 pollution] *QF* (polusion)   48 'twas] *Qc* (twas), *F;* was *Qu*   49 HOLOFERNES Sir] *Q (text of sig.*
E1r), F; Sir *Q (sig. D4v c.w.)*   51 ignorant] *Q* (ignorault), *F*   call I] *Cam;* cald *Q;* call'd *F;* call
Alexander   deer] *Rowe;* Deare: *Q;* Deare, *F*   53 scurrility] *F* (scurilitie); squirilitie *Q*

The preyful Princess pierced and pricked a pretty
  pleasing pricket;
  Some say a sore, but not a sore till now made sore
    with shooting.
The dogs did yell, put 'l' to sore, then sorrel jumps
  from thicket;
  Or pricket, sore, or else sorrel, the people fall a-
    hooting.
If sore be sore, then 'l' to sore makes fifty sores
  o'sorrel: 60
Of one sore I an hundred make by adding but one
  more 'l'.
NATHANIEL   A rare talent!

56 *preyful killing much prey (*OED**);
often glossed as 'intent on' or 'desirous
of' prey. What Holofernes says in his
poem need not be taken as literally
true.
  pierced and pricked *Pierced* may
have been pronounced like 'pursed'
and with *pricked* suggests a conjunction of either vagina or scrotum (*OED*
purse *sb*. 8b) and penis, the 'prick it'.
57 Some . . . ¹sore Some say the pricket
(a buck in its second year) was a buck
in its fourth year.
  but . . . shooting but it was not a sore
until it was made sore by being shot
58 yell . . . sore i.e. either the yelling of
the dogs literally makes a sound like
'ell' (the QF spelling of 'l'); or *yell* and
l can be confused because they sound
alike, so that *l* can be added to *sore*: for
putting '*l*' *to sore*, cf. 1.2.52n. An 'ell'
was a measure of length and could be
used to refer to a penis (cf. 5.2.665n.),
hence a *sorel* is a sore penis, with the
implication that *thicket* refers to a

vagina or to pubic hair.
  sorrel a buck in its third year: this is
the spelling in *OED*, but QF have the
form 'Sorell'.
  thicket Cf. 5.2.94.
59 Or . . . sorrel i.e. whatever kind of
buck it was; Q's 'els' (F '*else*') may add
to the punning.
  fall a-hooting start shouting out
60 If . . .² sore if the deer is hurt
  fifty sores i.e. because *l* is the Roman
numeral for fifty
  *o'sorrel out of one sorrel. Q's 'o
sorell' and F's '*O sorell*' suggest this is
meant to be an exclamation and Q consistently uses 'a' not 'o' to abbreviate
'of', but the context of the next line
indicates that a form 'of sorrel' is
required here.
61 By adding a second *l* and so a further
fifty to sorrel Holofernes can make a
hundred deer.
  more 'l' The rhyme suggests a pun on
'moral'.

56–61] *Capell; QF line* prickt / Pricket, / not a sore, / shooting. / Sore, / thicket: / Sorell, / hoot-
ing. / to Sore, / sorell: / make / more l. / 56 preyful] *Collier;* prayfull *QF* 58 'l'] *Capell (subst.);*
ell *QF* 60 'l'] *Pope;* el *QF* o'sorrel:] *QF (*o sorell:*);* O sore L! *Capell;* one sorel. *Cam;* O-sorel!
Ard²

DULL   If a talent be a claw, look how he claws him with a
talent.

HOLOFERNES   This is a gift that I have – simple, simple;   65
a foolish extravagant spirit, full of forms, figures,
shapes, objects, ideas, apprehensions, motions, revolutions. These are begot in the ventricle of memory,
nourished in the womb of *pia mater* and delivered upon
the mellowing of occasion. But the gift is good in those   70
in whom it is acute, and I am thankful for it.

NATHANIEL   Sir, I praise the Lord for you, and so may my
parishioners, for their sons are well tutored by you, and
their daughters profit very greatly under you. You are a
good member of the commonwealth.   75

---

63 **If . . . claw** *Talent* is an alternative
spelling of 'talon'.
claws him scratches an itch for him
(*OED v.* 3a); flatters, fawns upon him
(*OED v.* 4a); cf. *MA* 1.3.17, the
proverb 'Claw me, and I'll claw thee'
(Tilley, C405), which is related to 'You
scratch my back and I'll scratch yours'
and modern 'claw-back'.

65–145 *For the confusion of SPs here,
see Appendix 1, pp. 312–13.

65–71 Holofernes aligns himself with the
type of Renaissance poet visited by
divine inspiration, as opposed to the
poet who is a 'maker'. Oxf¹ compares
this speech with Falstaff's praise of
sack, *2H4* 4.3.86–125.

66 **foolish** Holofernes may be falsely self-
deprecatory, but he may use the word
in the sense of poor, trifling (*OED* 4).
extravagant astonishingly absurd
(*OED* A. 6b*)
forms Form and matter together create things: in his list Holofernes is
drawing on the languages of scholastic
philosophy, rhetoric and contemporary

ideas about the workings of the mind.
figures rhetorical forms of expression; cf. 1.2.54n.

67 **objects** things that are external to the
mind (*OED sb.* 6)
apprehensions what the mind has
grasped, views, ideas (*OED* 9)
motions inward promptings (*OED sb.*
9a)

67–8 **revolutions** considerations, reflec-
tions (*OED sb.* 5b)

68 **ventricle** belly, used figuratively for
part of the brain (*OED* 3c*, the only
citation)

69 *pia mater* one of the membranes
protecting the brain

69–70 **delivered . . . occasion** born or
spoken when the time is ripe; cf.
2.1.73n.

71 **acute** See 3.1.63n.

74 **profit** make progress; increase in size
(through pregnancy): Nathaniel's
unintentional *double entendre* is
brought out by the phrase *under you*
and by *member*.

75 **commonwealth** See 4.1.41n.

65–103 SP HOLOFERNES] *Rowe³*; Nath. (Nat.) QF   69 pia mater] *Rowe*; prima- / ter *Q*; primater
F   71 in whom] *F*; whom *Q*   72–102 SP NATHANIEL] *Rowe³*; Holo. (Hol.) QF

HOLOFERNES   *Mehercle*! If their sons be ingenious, they
shall want no instruction. If their daughters be capable,
I will put it to them. But *vir sapit qui pauca loquitur*. A
soul feminine saluteth us.

Enter JAQUENETTA [*with a letter*] *and* [COSTARD,] *the Clown.*

JAQUENETTA   God give you good morrow, Master Person.   80
HOLOFERNES   Master Person, *quasi* pierce-one? And if
one should be pierced, which is the one?
COSTARD   Marry, Master Schoolmaster, he that is likest
to a hogshead.

---

76 **Mehercle** By Hercules. The oath is
unique in Shakespeare.
76–7 **ingenious . . . capable** Cf. *R3*
3.1.154–5, 'O, 'tis a perilous boy, / Bold,
quick, ingenious, forward, capable'.
76 *ingenious** intelligent (*OED a.* 2);
although the F form ('ingennous') is
almost certainly meant to represent
'ingenuous', Q's 'ingenous' could
alternatively represent 'ingenious' or
'ingenius': at 1.2.27 Q has 'ingenious',
F 'ingenuous', and at 3.1.55 Q has
'ingenius', F 'ingenious'. See 1.2.27n.
77 **want** lack
    capable able to understand; capable of
    having sex
78 **put . . . them** set them to work on it;
give them some sex (*OED* put *v.*[1] 51b
(*b*); the only citation is from *WT*
1.2.276–8)
    vir . . . loquitur It's a wise man who
    says little; cf. the proverbial 'Few
    words show men wise', Tilley, W799.
    The Latin phrase occurs in Lily and
    Colet's grammar (Baldwin, 1.571).
79 **soul** person, individual (*OED sb.* 12a)
79.1 Kerrigan points out the similarity
    between Jaquenetta's entrance here
    with a letter to Dull's at 1.1.178.1,

where he enters with a letter and at
once asks, 'Which is the Duke's own
person?'
80 *Person** 'Person' and 'parson' are
variant forms for both words, but
Holofernes' objection in the next line
shows that Jaquenetta's pronunciation
is at fault here; see 4.3.191, 5.2.910n.
81 **quasi** as if, as it were; cf. 14n.
    *pierce-one** is intended to sound like
    'Person'. As Oxf[1] points out, the pun-
    ning possibilities of 'pierce' are wit-
    nessed by *1H4* 5.3.56, 'Well, if Percy
    be alive, I'll pierce him', and the title of
    Nashe's pamphlet *Pierce Penniless his
    Supplication to the Devil* (1592). 'On',
    as in 'Person', is a variant form of
    'one'.
83 **he** Costard may be referring specifi-
    cally to one of the characters on stage
    or making a more general point.
    *likest** Q's 'liklest' for 'likeliest',
    meaning 'most like', is possible, but
    Shakespeare uses 'likest' in *MV*
    4.1.196 and 'likeliest' only in the sense
    of 'most likely' or 'most handsome' in
    2H4 3.2.255.
84 **hogshead** large barrel for drink, but
    also suggesting a drunkard

---

76 *Mehercle*] F *(Me hercle)*; Me hercle *Q*   ingenious] *Capell*; ingenous *Q*; ingennous *F*   78 *sapit*]
Q2; sapis *QF*   79.1 *with a letter*] *Rowe (subst.)*   80–1 Person] *QF*; Parson *F2*   81 pierce-one]
Halliwell; Person *QF*; pers-one *Capell*   82 pierced] *QF (perst)*   83 SP] *Rowe*; *Clo. QF*   likest] *F*;
liklest *Q*; likeliest *Cam*[1]

HOLOFERNES   'Of piercing a hogshead' – a good lustre of   85
conceit in a turf of earth, fire enough for a flint, pearl
enough for a swine: 'tis pretty, it is well.

JAQUENETTA   Good Master Parson, be so good as read
me this letter. It was given me by Costard and sent me
from Don Armado. I beseech you read it.   90

HOLOFERNES
Fauste precor, gelida quando pecus omne sub umbra
Ruminat –
and so forth. Ah, good old Mantuan, I may speak of
thee as the traveller doth of Venice:
            Venetia, Venetia,   95
            Chi non ti vede, non ti pretia.
Old Mantuan, old Mantuan, who understandeth thee
not, loves thee not. [*He sings.*]
            Ut, re, sol, la, mi, fa.

85 **'Of . . . hogshead'** concerning the broaching of a barrel. Holofernes' phrase may suggest getting drunk, but also sounds like the title of a book or the heading to a chapter, as in the Latin '*De . . .* '. 'To pierce a hogshead' was proverbial: Dent, H504.1.
85–6 **lustre of conceit** flash of wit
86 **turf** clod
   fire . . . flint Cf. the proverbial 'In the coldest flint there is hot fire', Tilley, F371.
86–7 **pearl . . . swine** Cf. the proverbial 'Cast not pearls before swine', Tilley, P165.
91–2 ***Fauste . . . Ruminat*** 'Faustus, while all the cattle are chewing the cud in the cool shade, I pray you [let us talk a little about our old love affairs].' The opening lines of Mantuan's first eclogue – perhaps set off by Jaquenetta's 'I beseech you' (*precor*) – would have been familiar to many Elizabethans, since his works were read at grammar school (Baldwin,

1.643–52). QF's handling of the Latin probably represents compositorial error rather than an authorial joke, although the form of the first word, '*Facile*', echoes Holofernes' word of praise in relation to poetry, *facility*, see 55, 122.
93 **Mantuan** Baptista Spagnuoli of Mantua (1448–1516)
95–6 *Cf. the proverbial 'Venice, he that does not see does not esteem thee', Tilley, V26. QF's version of the Italian is clearly the result of compositorial error and not an authorial joke: '*perreche*' for '*pretia*' may have resulted from a misreading of 'p' as indicating an abbreviation.
99 **Ut . . . fa** Holofernes, whose duties as a schoolmaster might have included the teaching of singing, may be performing a scale or a snatch of a tune: *ut* and *sol* correspond to modern 'doh' and 'soh'. Shakespeare had already made use of the scale of notes in *TS* 3.1.73–8. In *KL* Edmund sings '*fa, sol, la, mi*', 1.2.137.

85 Of] *QF; om. Alexander*   90 Armado] *QF (Armatho)*   91–2, 95–6] *Capell; prose QF*   91–2] *F2; Facile precor gellida, quando pecas omnia sub vmbra ruminat QF*   95–6] *Cam; vemchie, vencha, que non te vnde, que non te perreche QF*   98 loves thee not] *om. F*   SD] *Kerrigan*

Under pardon, sir, what are the contents? Or rather as   100
Horace says in his – What, my soul, verses?
NATHANIEL   Ay, sir, and very learned.
HOLOFERNES   Let me hear a staff, a stanza, a verse.
Lege, domine.
NATHANIEL [*Reads.*]

'If love make me forsworn, how shall I swear to love?   105
    Ah, never faith could hold, if not to beauty vowed.
Though to myself forsworn, to thee I'll faithful prove.
    Those thoughts to me were oaks, to thee like osiers
        bowed.
Study his bias leaves, and makes his book thine eyes,
    Where all those pleasures live, that art would
        comprehend.   110
If knowledge be the mark, to know thee shall suffice:
    Well learned is that tongue, that well can thee
        commend,
All ignorant that soul, that sees thee without wonder;

100 **Or rather** See 15n.
101 **Horace** Baldwin (2.403–4) argues
    that Holofernes is thinking of the
    Horatian equivalent for 'contents' and
    that this was '*materia*', hence he had
    the third precept from the *Ars Poetica*
    in mind: 'Choose a subject that is
    suited to your abilities'.
103 **staff . . . verse** All mean the same
    thing, a verse; see *OED* staff *sb.*[1] 19c
    and stanza 1α*, with which cf.
    Shakespeare's only other use of the
    word in *AYL* 2.5.18–19.
104 *Lege, domine* read, master
105–18 Berowne's poem, like Longaville's
    (4.3.57–70) and Dumaine's (4.3.98–117),
    was reprinted in William Jaggard's *The
    Passionate Pilgrim* (1599), a collection of
    poems by various authors but attributed

to Shakespeare.
105 If love makes me abandon my oath,
    how can I swear on my oath that I love?
108 Those thoughts which seemed to me
    as strong and unyielding as oaks, look
    to you as flexible and inconstant as
    bending willows or, under your influ-
    ence, bent like willows.
109 i.e. the student abandons the thing
    that draws him on and makes your eyes
    his book. Berowne returns to the
    doubts he had at 1.1.80–3 and ampli-
    fies at 4.3.285–339. Cf. the proverbial
    'To run against the bias', Tilley, B339.
110 **art** scholarship, learning (*OED sb.*
    3b*)
111 **mark** See 4.1.129n.
112 **learned** learnèd

101 his –] *Hanmer;* his, *QF*   103 stanza] *Q (*stauze*), F*   105 SP] *Rowe*[3]*; continued to Nathaniel (for
Holofernes) QF*   SD] *Capell (subst.)*   105–18] *QF, PP*   106 Ah] *QF;* O *PP*   107 faithful] *QF;*
constāt *PP*   108 were] *QF;* like *PP*   bowed.] *F, PP;* bowed *Q*   109 eyes,] *PP;* eyes. *QF*   110
would] *QF;* can *PP*

Which is to me some praise, that I thy parts admire.
Thy eye Jove's lightning bears, thy voice his dreadful
    thunder,   115
Which, not to anger bent, is music and sweet fire.
Celestial as thou art, O, pardon love this wrong,
That sings heaven's praise, with such an earthly
    tongue.'

HOLOFERNES   You find not the apostrophus and so miss
the accent. Let me supervise the canzonet. [*Takes the*   120
letter.] Here are only numbers ratified, but for the
elegancy, facility and golden cadence of poesy, *caret.*
Ovidius Naso was the man; and why indeed 'Naso', but

---

114 **Which . . . that** I deserve some
praise for this, because
parts physical or mental attributes; cf.
2.1.44n.
116 **not . . . bent** not inclined to be angry
117 **pardon . . . wrong** excuse this fault
in my love for you
118 **That** that it (love)
119 ***apostrophus** a variant form of
'apostrophe', meaning a mark of elision
signifying the omission of a letter in a
word (*OED sb.*[2] 2*). Holofernes may be
using the word's Latin form, represented in QF by 'apostraphas'. It is not
clear precisely what Holofernes is complaining about, since there is no obvious word in the poem in need of elision
– 113 has thirteen and 118 may have
ten or eleven syllables. He may simply
be trying to unsettle Nathaniel's perfectly sound reading with a difficult
word or, as some editors suggest, may
be using the rhetorical term for turning
from one audience to address another
to indicate Nathaniel has got the
caesuras in the poem wrong.

120 **accent** stress, emphasis (*OED sb.* 6)
supervise look over (*OED v.* 1a*); cf.
overglance (130n.), *o'er-eye* (4.3.77n.),
over-view (4.3.172n.).
***canzonet** short song or poem
121–7 ***Here . . . you?** QF assign these
lines to 'Nath.', which cannot be correct; it is possible that a compositor
misunderstood 'Sir Nathaniel, here are
. . . ' as containing a new SP. See also
Appendix 1, p. 312.
121 **numbers ratified** lines in which
there is a correct ratio of feet and syllables, hence metrically correct lines
(Baldwin, 2.392–3; *OED* number *sb.*
18b*, citing 4.3.54); see also 5.2.35.
122 **elegancy** unique in Shakespeare,
who never uses 'elegant' either, apart
from the form 'alligant' in *MW* 2.2.68
facility See 55n.
cadence rhythmical flow
caret it is wanting; cf. *MW* 4.1.53.
123 **Ovidius Naso** Ovid's family name
means 'large-nosed'. Holofernes' praise
of Ovid is suggestive, given Shakespeare's
evident admiration for his poetry.

---

115 Thy . . . bears] *QF;* Thin . . . seems *PP* 117 pardon love this] *QF;* do not loue that *PP*
wrong] *Qc, F, PP;* woug *Qu* 118 That sings heaven's] *QF;* To sing heauens *PP;* That sings the
heaven's *Hanmer;* That singeth heaven's *Oxf (Proudfoot, privately)* 119+ SP] *Rowe; Pedan. (Ped.,
Peda.) Q; Ped. (Peda.) F* apostrophus] *Hart (OED);* apostraphas *QF* 120 canzonet] *Theobald;*
cangenct *Q;* cangenet *F* 120–1 canzonet. Here] *continued to Holofernes / Theobald;* cangenct. /
Nath. Here *QF (subst.);* canzonet. Sir Nathaniel, here *Oxf*[1] *(subst.)* 120–1 SD] *Cam*[1]

for smelling out the odoriferous flowers of fancy, the
jerks of invention? *Imitari* is nothing. So doth the   125
hound his master, the ape his keeper, the tired horse his
rider. But, damosella virgin, was this directed to you?

JAQUENETTA   Ay, sir, from one Monsieur Berowne, one
of the strange queen's lords.

HOLOFERNES   I will overglance the superscript. *To the*   130
snow-white hand of the most beauteous Lady Rosaline. I
will look again on the intellect of the letter, for the
nomination of the party writing to the person written
unto: *Your Ladyship's in all desired employment, Berowne.*

---

124 **odoriferous** fragrant
flowers picked, choicest parts
125 **jerks** witty speeches, sallies (*OED*
*sb.*¹ 3*); its primary meaning was a
stroke with a whip or cane.
invention inventiveness, imagination;
see 157.
*Imitari to imitate, hence to follow.
Baldwin (2.234–5) shows that
Holofernes borrows his critical terms
for judging the success of imitation
from Quintilian. Bate, 87, identifies
Quintilian (*Institutiones Oratoriae*,
10.2.4, 10.2.1) as the source of the
doctrines ' "imitatio per ipsa non sufficit"; "invenire primum fuit estque
praecipuum" – imitation by itself is
not sufficient; invention came first and
is all-important'.
126 **ape** For the mimic skills of monkeys,
see also 5.2.325n.
tired usually glossed as the aphetic
form of 'attired', adorned with trap-
pings (Onions), but it may simply
mean that the rider leads the tired
horse by the reins as dogs and monkeys
are kept on leads: cf. *Son* 50.5, 'The
beast that bears me, tired with my woe'.
127 **damosella** *Damosella* may represent a
Latinized version of 'damoiselle', itself
a variant form of 'damsel'. Cf. 1.1.276n.

128–9 Jaquenetta has already said (89–90)
what she knows of the letter's origins,
and Berowne is one of the King's, not
the Princess's, lords. The lines may
represent unrevised material or signal
Jaquenetta's state of confusion which
Holofernes corrects (135–8).
129 **strange** foreign; cf. 137, 5.2.175.
130 **overglance** cast an eye over (*OED*
v.*); cf. *supervise* 4.2.120n.
superscript address, superscription
(*OED* A.*); unique in Shakespeare,
who twice uses 'superscription' elsewhere
131 *snow-white* Cf. the proverbial 'As
white as snow', Tilley, S591, Dent,
S591.1 and 3.1.163n.
132 **intellect** Citing this passage, *OED*
sb. 5 defines the word as 'sense, meaning, signification, purport', but a sense
suggesting 'sign, signature' may be
intended (Schmidt). Baldwin (2.103)
argues that *intellect* and *nomination* are
technical terms relating to the writer
and the person addressed, taken from
the rhetorical work *Ad Herennium*,
attributed to Cicero.
133 **nomination** name; cf. 1.2.15n.
134 *all desired employment* any use you
wish to make of me (*OED* employment 1**)

---

124 fancy,] *Capell;* fancie: *QF*   125 invention? *Imitari*] *Theobald (subst.);* inuention imitarie *QF*
127 damosella virgin] *QF (Damosella virgin); domicella* – virgin *Oxf*   128–9 from . . . lords] *QF;*
om. *Oxf*   130 SP] *Theobald; Nath. QF*   133 writing] *Rowe;* written *QF*

Sir Nathaniel, this Berowne is one of the votaries with   135
the King, and here he hath framed a letter to a sequent
of the stranger queen's, which accidentally, or by the
way of progression, hath miscarried. Trip and go, my
sweet, deliver this paper into the royal hand of the
King; it may concern much. Stay not thy compliment: 140
I forgive thy duty, adieu.

JAQUENETTA   Good Costard, go with me. Sir, God save
your life.

COSTARD   Have with thee, my girl.

[Exeunt Costard and Jaquenetta.]

NATHANIEL   Sir, you have done this in the fear of God,   145
very religiously; and as a certain father saith –

HOLOFERNES   Sir, tell not me of the father, I do fear
colourable colours. But to return to the verses: did they
please you, Sir Nathaniel?

135 **votaries** See 2.1.37n.
136 **sequent** follower (*OED* B. 1*, the only citation)
137 **accidentally** *OED* 1*
137–8 **by . . . progression** as a result of its path (*OED* progression 1b*)
138 **miscarried** failed to reach its right destination (*OED v*. 6a**). The confusion of antecedents – the letter, the queen or the sequent – could suggest one of the women has had a miscarriage. Cf. 4.1.111n.
Trip and go get going: a common phrase (*OED* trip *v*. 3a)
140 **concern much** be of great importance (*OED* concern *v*. 4b)
Stay . . . compliment don't hang around to say a polite farewell (*OED* stay *v*.¹ 19b, cf. 2.1.192n.; complement *sb*. 8b)
141 **I . . . duty** you don't need to pay me

your respects.
144 **Have with thee** I'll go along with you
146–51 **father . . . father . . . father's** Nathaniel suggests an allusion to one of the Fathers of the Church. Holofernes repudiates such an authority, but seems, instead, to allude to God and then to be led into an association with the father of one of his pupils. Cf. 32n.
148 **colourable colours** plausible but specious shows of reason (*OED* colour *sb*. 12a). Holofernes is playing on the proverbial 'To fear no colours', Tilley, C520, where the 'colours' are military ones (cf. 3.1.183n.), and perhaps on 'Truth needs no colours', Tilley, T585. He interprets Nathaniel's *father* as meaning a Father of the Church whose Scholastic logic he rejects.

135 Sir] *continued to Holofernes / Theobald; Ped.* Sir *Q; Per.* Sir *F* Nathaniel] *Capell; Holofernes QF* 139 royal] *om. F* 142 SP] *Rowe; Mayd. Q; Maid. F* 144 SD] *Rowe (subst.); Exit. QF* 145 SP] *Rowe; Holo. QF* 146 saith –] *F2*; saith *QF* 147, 151 SP] *Rowe³; Ped. (Peda.) QF*

NATHANIEL   Marvellous well for the pen.   150

HOLOFERNES   I do dine today at the father's of a certain
pupil of mine, where if, before repast, it shall please you
to gratify the table with a grace, I will, on my privilege
I have with the parents of the foresaid child or pupil,
undertake your *ben venuto*; where I will prove those   155
verses to be very unlearned, neither savouring of
poetry, wit, nor invention. I beseech your society.

NATHANIEL   And thank you too, for society, saith the text,
is the happiness of life.

HOLOFERNES   And certes, the text most infallibly   160
concludes it. [*to Dull*] Sir, I do invite you too: you shall
not say me nay. *Pauca verba.* Away, the gentles are at
their game and we will to our recreation.   *Exeunt.*

150 Nathaniel may simply be saying that
he admires the penning or handwriting
of Berowne's verses, but T. W. Craik
suggests (privately) that Nathaniel is
not by implication unhappy with their
style, but that Holofernes interrupts
him again and the line should be punctuated 'Marvellous well; for the pen –',
although the line ends with a stop in
QF whereas 146 does not in either.
151 **dine** Cf. 1.1.24n., 5.1.3n.
152 **repast** the meal
153 **gratify** please (*OED v.* 4); grace
(*OED v.* 6)
privilege advantageous position
(*OED sb.* 3) in a general rather than a
technical sense
155 **undertake . . . *venuto*** ensure your
welcome; a similar phrase occurs in *TS*
1.2.280.

156 **savouring** having the characteristics
157 **invention** See 125n.
I . . . society I hope you will come
(*OED* society 1b*); cf. 4.3.50n., 125n.
158 **the text** Whether from the Bible or
some other source or proverb, this has
not been identified; Baldwin (2.636–7)
cites the tag *Amicitia inter bonos*, which
can be traced back to Sallust.
160 **certes** indeed, certainly
161 **concludes** settles
162 *Pauca verba* few words; cf. the
proverbial 'Few words are best', Tilley,
W798.
gentles See 2.1.224n.
163 **game** sport; animals being hunted;
amorous play (*OED sb.* 3b)
recreation refreshment, meal (*OED
sb.*[1] 1); entertainment. Cf. 1.1.159n.

152 before] being *F*   155 *ben venuto*] *Rowe; bien venuto Q; bien vonuto F; bien venu too (Cam)*
161 SD] *Theobald*

[**4.3**]   *Enter* BEROWNE *with a paper in his hand, alone.*

BEROWNE   The King, he is hunting the deer; I am
coursing myself. They have pitched a toil; I am toiling
in a pitch, pitch that defiles. Defile, a foul word. Well,
set thee down, sorrow, for so they say the fool said, and
so say I, and I the fool. Well proved, wit! By the Lord,   5
this love is as mad as Ajax. It kills sheep, it kills me – I
a sheep. Well proved again, o'my side! I will not love; if
I do, hang me! I'faith, I will not. O, but her eye! By this
light, but for her eye, I would not love her – yes, for her
two eyes. Well, I do nothing in the world but lie, and lie   10
in my throat. By heaven, I do love, and it hath taught
me to rhyme, and to be melancholy. And here is part of

4.3 The order in which the men come on and reveal their love – Berowne, King, Longaville, Dumaine – is the mirror image of the order in which their love is exposed – Dumaine, Longaville, King, Berowne – with the result that each in turn has one extra witness to his hypocrisy.

2 **coursing** hunting, chasing; beating, cudgelling. There is also probably a pun on 'cursing' intended. Cf. 4.2.54n.

2–3 **They . . . word** In Berowne's thoughts words breed other words.

2 **pitched a toil** set nets into which the game are driven to be killed

2–3 **toiling . . . pitch** i.e. struggling with the black sticky substance that is love, represented by Rosaline's eyes, the *two pitch-balls* of 3.1.192n.

3 **pitch that defiles** Cf. the proverbial 'He that touches pitch shall be defiled', Tilley, P358, deriving from Ecclesiasticus, 13.1.

4 **set . . . sorrow** See 1.1.298–9n.: Berowne was, of course, present when Costard used the phrase.

5 **proved** demonstrated to be true (*OED v.* 5b): by his false logic Berowne has

shown he is a fool; cf. 61n., 280n.

6 **as mad . . . sheep** Mad with fury because Odysseus was awarded the armour of the dead Achilles, Ajax attacked a flock of sheep, thinking they were the Greek enemy; cf. the proverbial 'As mad as Ajax', Dent, A95. The mention of Ajax prefigures his being promoted to being one of the Nine Worthies, see 5.2.571–2n.

8–10 **O . . . eyes** Although Berowne says he is toiling in *a* pitch, the change from one eye to two eyes may allow the 'one eye' to have been Rosaline's vagina, see 2.1.188n.

8 **O . . . eye** Cf. *AS*, 47.13 'O me, that eye'.

10–11 **lie in my throat** tell gross lies; proverbial: see Dent, T268.

12 **rhyme . . . melancholy** Berowne evokes the melancholy love-lorn poet, such as Sidney's persona, Philisides, in the *Old Arcadia*.

12, 13 *****melancholy** The QF form 'mallicholie' may be a variant spelling of melancholy rather than a compositorial error: cf. the corrupt form 'allycholly', *TGV* 4.2.27, and see Appendix 1, p. 318.

4.3] *Steevens*   1–2 The . . . myself] *Pope; verse QF, lined* Deare, / selfe. /   5 and I] *QF;* and I am *Alexander*   8 do,] *F2;* do *QF*   12, 13 melancholy] *Rowe;* mallicholie *QF*

my rhyme, and here my melancholy. Well, she hath one
o'my sonnets already. The clown bore it, the fool sent
it, and the lady hath it. Sweet clown, sweeter fool,   15
sweetest lady! By the world, I would not care a pin if
the other three were in. Here comes one, with a paper.
God give him grace to groan!   (*He stands aside.*)

[*Enter*] *the* KING [*with a paper*].

KING   Ay me!

BEROWNE   Shot, by heaven! Proceed, sweet Cupid, thou   20
hast thumped him with thy birdbolt under the left pap.
In faith, secrets!

KING [*Reads.*]
'So sweet a kiss the golden sun gives not
    To those fresh morning drops upon the rose,
As thy eye-beams when their fresh rays have smote   25
    The night of dew that on my cheeks down flows.
Nor shines the silver moon one half so bright
    Through the transparent bosom of the deep
As doth thy face, through tears of mine, give light.

15–16 **Sweet . . . lady** The grammatical
    formula is characteristic of the play, as
    at 1.2.160–2n.
16 **By the world** a mild oath used twice
    by Armado (5.1.94–5 and 97–8);
    Shakespeare rarely uses it elsewhere
    (*TS* 2.1.160, *R3* 4.4.375, *Oth* 3.3.383).
    I . . . pin proverbial: see Tilley, P333.
17 **in** in the same predicament as I am; in
    love (*OED* in A. 6b*)
18 **God . . . groan** This sounds prover-
    bial.
21 **birdbolt** blunt arrow used for shoot-
    ing birds
    under . . . pap i.e. where the heart lies,
    under the breast
23–38 See 1.1.80–93n.

23 **sweet a kiss** Cf. *Son* 33.1–3, 'Full
    many a glorious morning have I
    seen . . . Kissing with golden face the
    meadows green'.
25 **eye-beams** The *beams* (*OED**) and
    smote in the same line anticipate
    Berowne's comments at 158–9n. Cf.
    1.1.77n. and see 2.1.233–46.
26 **night of dew** i.e. the tears I shed all
    night
    cheeks down Kerrigan suggests
    'cheek's' or 'cheeks' down', may be
    intended here; cf. *Luc* 1271, 'Those
    tears from thee, that down thy cheeks
    are raining'.
28 **the deep** i.e. the night

13 here] *Q* (heare), *F*   18.1] *Capell; The King entreth. (opp. He standes a side.) QF*   23 SD] *Theobald*
25 rays] *QF* (rayse)   smote] *Rowe;* smot. *QF*

Thou shin'st in every tear that I do weep,   30
No drop but as a coach doth carry thee:
　So ridest thou triumphing in my woe.
Do but behold the tears that swell in me,
　And they thy glory through my grief will show.
But do not love thyself: then thou will keep   35
My tears for glasses, and still make me weep.
O Queen of queens, how far dost thou excel,
No thought can think, nor tongue of mortal tell.'
How shall she know my griefs? I'll drop the paper.
Sweet leaves shade folly. Who is he comes here?   40
(*Steps aside.*)

Enter LONGAVILLE [*with a paper*].

What, Longaville, and reading? Listen, ear!
BEROWNE
　Now, in thy likeness, one more fool appear!
LONGAVILLE　Ay me, I am forsworn!
BEROWNE　Why, he comes in like a perjure, wearing
　papers.   45
KING
　In love, I hope. Sweet fellowship in shame.

31–2 **coach . . . triumphing** The imagery
　of the cruel mistress being drawn in a
　Roman triumph is Petrarchan ('coach'
　is repeated by Berowne at 152).
32 **triumphing** stressed on the second
　syllable
36 **glasses** mirrors
　still continually
37 **Queen of queens** Like Longaville
　(53) and Dumaine (80), the King
　makes clear with whom he is in love.
40 **leaves** of trees; of the paper
　shade hide, conceal

42 **in thy likeness** looking like the King;
　looking like yourself (Longaville). 'To
　show oneself in one's own likeness'
　was proverbial: Dent, L293.1.
44 **perjure** perjurer
44–5 **wearing papers** As part of their
　punishment perjurers were made to
　wear papers on their heads or on their
　backs, setting out their guilt. Perhaps
　Longaville, like Dumaine (see 122n.),
　is wearing papers in his hat.
46 **fellowship** The ship/sheep pun of
　2.1.218 is appropriate here.

35 will] wilt *F*　39 paper] *Qc, F;* pa d er *Qu*　40 leaves] *QF;* leaves, *Theobald*　40 SD] *QF (The King steps a side.)*　40.1] *opp. 40 SD QF*　with a paper] *Capell*　46 SP] *Rowe³; Long. QF*

BEROWNE

One drunkard loves another of the name.

LONGAVILLE

Am I the first that have been perjured so?

BEROWNE

I could put thee in comfort: not by two that I know.

Thou makest the triumviry, the corner-cap of society,   50

The shape of Love's Tyburn, that hangs up
    simplicity.

LONGAVILLE

I fear these stubborn lines lack power to move.

O sweet Maria, empress of my love,

These numbers will I tear and write in prose.

BEROWNE

O, rhymes are guards on wanton Cupid's hose: 55

Disfigure not his shop.

LONGAVILLE   This same shall go.

(*He reads the sonnet.*)

'Did not the heavenly rhetoric of thine eye,

---

48 Cf. the proverbial 'I am not the first (and shall not be the last)', Dent, F295.

50 ***triumviry** triumvirate (*OED**); for the QF forms ('triumpherie', 'triumphery') cf. *AC* 3.6.28, 'triumpherate'.

50–1 **corner-cap . . . Tyburn** Tyburn was the principal place of execution for London, near to present-day Marble Arch. Permanent triangular gallows were erected there in 1571 and used for the execution of Father John Story. Roman Catholic priests wore three-cornered caps and the gallows were known as 'Dr Story's corner-cap': see Wilson, 'Diction', 113–14, 127–8.

50 **society** fellowship; cf. 4.2.157–9.

51 **simplicity** foolishness, silliness

52 **stubborn** usually glossed as harsh, rugged; but *OED a*. 2a suggests the word means intractable, hard to make to work.

power to move force to make her love me (*OED* move *v*. 10b); cf. Daniel, *Delia*, sonnet 41.10, 'If loue in her hath any powre to moue', and more generally Sidney, *DP*, 91–4.

54 **numbers** lines, verse; see 4.2.121n.

55 **guards** ornamental borders or trimmings; defences

hose breeches

56 **his shop** The place where Cupid does his work, and so the codpiece in his hose and the genitals in the codpiece (*OED sb*. 3c). Pope's emendation 'slop', prompted by *hose*, means one leg of a pair of loose trousers or baggy breeches (*OED* slop *sb.*[1] 4b).

57–70 See 1.1.80–93n.

---

50 triumviry] *Rowe*[3]; triumpherie *Q*; triumphery *F*   56 shop] *QF (*Shop*);* slop *Pope*[2]   57–70] *QF, PP*

'Gainst whom the world cannot hold argument,
Persuade my heart to this false perjury?
   Vows for thee broke deserve not punishment.   60
A woman I forswore, but I will prove,
   Thou being a goddess, I forswore not thee.
My vow was earthly, thou a heavenly love;
   Thy grace being gained, cures all disgrace in me.
Vows are but breath, and breath a vapour is: 65
   Then thou, fair sun, which on my earth dost shine,
Exhal'st this vapour-vow; in thee it is.
   If broken then, it is no fault of mine;
If by me broke, what fool is not so wise
To lose an oath to win a paradise?'   70

BEROWNE

This is the liver vein, which makes flesh a deity,
A green goose a goddess. Pure, pure idolatry.
God amend us, God amend! We are much out o'th' way.

Enter DUMAINE [*with a paper*].

58 **whom** which
  argument There may be a pun here on *argument* as clyster (see 3.1.106n.), supported by perjury/purgery in the next line.
59 **false perjury** a tautology
61–2 The argument is similar to Chaucer's *The Knight's Tale* (*Riv*, 1155–9), itself close to *TNK* 2.2.162–4.
61 **prove** establish as true; see 5n.
64 **grace** favour, good opinion. The line echoes 1.1.3, 'And then grace us in the disgrace of death'.
65 Cf. the proverbial 'Words are but wind', Tilley, W833. Cf. 1.1.5n.
67 **Exhal'st** draw up, evaporate (*OED v.*¹

4b*). The sun was thought to draw up vapours from the earth and so produce meteors; cf. *RJ* 3.5.13.
69–70 Cf. the proverbial 'To bring one into a fool's paradise', Tilley, F523.
70 **To** as to
  lose Although QF's 'loose' could mean set free or let go, a *lose/win* paradox (cf. 1.1.144n.) is clearly intended; cf. 335.
71 **liver vein** the lover's style: the liver was thought to be the seat of sexual passion.
72 **green goose** silly young woman; new prostitute; see 1.1.97n. and 3.1.88–101.
73 **out o'th' way** mistaken, gone badly wrong

58 cannot] *QF;* could not *PP*   59 perjury?] *QF;* periury; *PP*   65 Vows are but] *QF;* My vow was *PP*   66 which on my] *QF;* that on this *PP*   dost] *QF;* doth *PP*   67 Exhal'st] *Q* (Exhalst*); Exhalest F;* Exhalt *PP*   68 broken then,] *QF;* broken, then *PP;* broken, then, *Kerrigan*   70 lose] *QF* (loose*);* breake *PP*   71 deity,] *Dyce;* deitie. *QF*   72 idolatry] *F;* ydotarie *Q*   73.1 *with a paper*] *Capell*

LONGAVILLE

By whom shall I send this? Company? Stay.
[*He stands aside.*]

BEROWNE

All hid, all hid, an old infant play. 75
Like a demi-god here sit I in the sky,
And wretched fools' secrets heedfully o'er-eye.
More sacks to the mill. O heavens, I have my wish!
Dumaine transformed! Four woodcocks in a dish!

DUMAINE   O most divine Kate! 80

BEROWNE   O most profane coxcomb!

DUMAINE

By heaven, the wonder in a mortal eye!

BEROWNE

By earth, she is not, corporal: there you lie.

DUMAINE

Her amber hairs for foul hath amber quoted.

BEROWNE

An amber-coloured raven was well noted. 85

---

75 **All . . . hid** 'All hid' was the cry used in the game of hide-and-seek or blind-man's buff and so was a name for the game itself (*OED* hide *v.*[1] 1e*). Berowne may be saying that the game the men are playing is an old children's game or that they are behaving like overgrown children.

76 Berowne compares himself to a semi-divine figure who watches over his friends' antics. He may climb a prop-tree of some kind, but his sitting in the sky need not be taken literally, although 162 does imply he was seated. The staging of the scene is not altogether clear; see 4.3.315n. and also Introduction, pp. 87–8.

77 **o'er-eye** *OED* over-eye *v.**; cf. *super-vise*, 4.2.120n.

78 **More . . . mill** proverbial (Tilley,

S12), meaning that there is lots more work to do or, perhaps, that there is more evidence to come

79 **transformed** See also 163.
woodcocks fools

83 **corporal** Berowne at 3.1.182 called himself *a corporal* in Cupid's army and now he includes Dumaine in his forces. But he also states that she is not heavenly but *corporal*, corporeal, flesh and blood.

84 Her amber hair makes amber itself look ugly (*OED* quote *v.* 6a*); cf. 5.2.780n.

85 Berowne takes Dumaine's *foul* as 'fowl', saying sarcastically that he has done well to spot an amber-coloured raven, i.e. done well to see Katherine's black hair as amber. Cf. *AS*, 91.5–6, 'if this darke place yet shew like candle light, / Some beautie's peece, as amber colour hed'.

---

74 SD] *Johnson (subst.)*   82 in] of *F*   83 corporal] *Qc, F*; croporall *Qu*   84 hairs] *Q (heires), F*; hair *Cam*[1] *(Capell)*   quoted] *QF (coted)*

DUMAINE

As upright as the cedar.

BEROWNE   Stoop, I say.

Her shoulder is with child.

DUMAINE   As fair as day.

BEROWNE

Ay, as some days, but then no sun must shine.

DUMAINE

O that I had my wish!

LONGAVILLE   And I had mine!

KING

And I mine too, good Lord!   90

BEROWNE

Amen, so I had mine! Is not that a good word?

DUMAINE

I would forget her, but a fever she

Reigns in my blood and will remembered be.

BEROWNE

A fever in your blood? Why then incision

Would let her out in saucers. Sweet misprision!   95

DUMAINE

Once more I'll read the ode that I have writ.

BEROWNE

Once more I'll mark how love can vary wit.

---

86 **As . . . cedar** The simile was proverbial: Tilley, C207.
Stoop stooping, bent; come down to
earth: this use may derive figuratively
from hawking, for when the bird
returns to its lure (*OED v.*[1] 6).
87 **with child** humped, bulging (as if
pregnant) (*OED* child *sb*. 17c)
As . . . day The simile was proverbial:
Dent, D56.1.
91 **Is . . . word?** Isn't that kind of me?;
isn't *Amen* known to be a good word?
Berowne's dwelling on the word may

derive from his exchange with
Rosaline at 2.1.126.
94 **incision** cutting to let blood out as a
cure for the fever
95 **in saucers** into the saucers used to
collect the blood; by the saucerful
(*OED* saucer 2**)
misprision misunderstanding, mistake (*OED* 3*)
97 **vary wit** change or alter someone who
is normally intelligent and sensible;
make wit express itself in different
words. Cf. 1.1.279n., 4.2.9.

86–7 Stoop . . . child] *Theobald; one line QF*   90 I] *Johnson; not in QF*   95 misprision] *Q (mis-
prison), F*   96 ode] *Q (Odo), F*

205

DUMAINE (*Dumaine reads his sonnet.*)
'On a day – alack the day! –
Love, whose month is ever May,
Spied a blossom passing fair   100
Playing in the wanton air.
Through the velvet leaves the wind,
All unseen, can passage find;
That the lover, sick to death,
Wished himself the heaven's breath.   105
"Air," quoth he, "thy cheeks may blow;
Air, would I might triumph so!
But, alack, my hand is sworn
Ne'er to pluck thee from thy thorn.
Vow, alack, for youth unmeet,   110
Youth so apt to pluck a sweet.

98–117 See 4.2.105–18n.; the poem was also included in *PP* (1599) and in the collection *England's Helicon* (1600). In both later printings 112–13, which connect the poem with the play, were omitted. The anacreontic poem's language and imagery (*wanton . . . velvet leaves . . . passage . . . death . . . cheeks . . . pluck . . . thorn*) allow a strong erotic interpretation.
99 **May** See 1.1.105–6n. and Introduction, pp. 12–13.
100 **passing fair** Cf. *TGV* 4.4.148, *RJ* 1.1.234–6.
  passing exceedingly
101–3 Cf. the proverbial 'As free as the air', Tilley, A88.
101 **wanton air** Cf. *RJ* 2.6.19.
  wanton frolicsome, playful
102 **velvet** velvety smooth or soft (*OED sb.* 4b*); cf. 3.1.191n.
103 **can** did, was able to

104–5 It was conventional for the lover to wish himself transformed (to a dog, sparrow, etc.) so that he could be intimate with his mistress; cf. *AS*, 83.
104 **That** so that
  sick to death made mortally ill by his passion; longing to the point of orgasm
105 ***Wished** Abbott, 368, defended the QF reading of 'Wish' as a subjunctive, but admitted the usage was unique.
109 ***thorn** stalk, stem; cf. *Son* 54.7. Thorns prick people (cf. *AW* 4.2.19), so that plucking the woman from her thorn could mean taking her away from her male lover.
110 **unmeet** unfitting, improper
111 **pluck** may have sexual associations; cf. *VA* 574, *MM* 1.2.96.
  sweet sweetheart; a sweet-smelling flower

98–117] *QF, PP, EH* (*The passionate Sheepheards Song.*)   99 is ever] *is euery F;* was ener *PP;* was euer *EH*   101 air.] *EH; Q* (aire:), *F;* ayre, *PP*   102 velvet] *PP, EH;* Veluet, *QF*   103 can] *QF;* gan *PP, EH*   104 lover] *QF, PP;* Sheepheard *EH*   105 Wished] *PP* (Wisht), *EH* (Wish'd); Wish *QF*   107 Air,] *F, PP, EH* (Ayre,); Ayre *Q;* Ah! (*Johnson*)   108 alack] *QF;* alas *PP, EH*   is] *QF;* hath *PP, EH*   109 pluck] *QF, EH;* pruck *PP*   thorn] *EH* (thorne); throne *QF, PP*   110 alack] *QF, EH;* allcke *PP*

Do not call it sin in me,
That I am forsworn for thee;
Thou for whom Jove would swear
Juno but an Ethiop were,   115
And deny himself for Jove,
Turning mortal for thy love."'
This will I send, and something else more plain,
That shall express my true love's fasting pain.
O, would the King, Berowne and Longaville   120
Were lovers too! Ill, to example ill,
Would from my forehead wipe a perjured note,
For none offend where all alike do dote.

LONGAVILLE [*Comes forward.*]

Dumaine, thy love is far from charity,
That in love's grief desirest society.   125
You may look pale, but I should blush, I know,
To be o'erheard and taken napping so.

KING [*Comes forward.*]

Come, sir, you blush. As his your case is such.
You chide at him, offending twice as much.

---

115 **Ethiop** Ethiopian, black woman: the comparison revolves around her ugliness compared with the standard Petrarchan mistress, rather than around her race: cf. *TGV* 2.6.25–6 and *MND* 3.2.257, where infidelity is also at issue. 'Real' Ethiopians appear at 5.2.157.1.
116 **deny himself for** repudiate his being (*OED* deny *v*. 4b*)
117 Ovid's *Met*. record Jove's frequent changes into mortal shapes to conquer women.
119 **fasting pain** pain caused by abstinence
121 **example** justify by precedent (*OED v*. 3)
122 See 44n. and 44–5n. (*OED* perjured *ppl. a*. 2*).

124 **charity** Christian love (*caritas*) as opposed to erotic love (*amor*). Cf. 4.3.338–9n.
125 **That** you who
   in . . . society Cf. the proverbial 'It is good to have company in trouble', Tilley, C571 and 4.2.157n.
127 **o'erheard** The theme of overhearing is returned to by Boyet at 5.2.95.
   taken napping The phrase was proverbial: cf. Tilley, N36–7.
128 **blush** Cf. Armado at 1.2.126n.
128–9 **As . . . much** Cf. the proverbial 'He finds fault with others and does worse himself', Tilley, F107.
128 **case** situation; face
129 **chide** reprove, tell off, scold; cf. 5.2.326.

112–13] *QF; om. PP, EH* 114 Jove] *QF, PP, EH;* ev'n Jove *Rowe;* great Jove *Collier MS* 117 thy] *QF, PP;* my *EH* 118 plain,] *Rowe;* plaine. *QF* 119 true love's] *Rowe;* trueloues *Q;* true-loues *F* 124, 128, 148 SDs] *Rowe* 127 o'erheard] *Q (*ore-hard*), F*

You do not love Maria? Longaville   130
Did never sonnet for her sake compile,
Nor never lay his wreathed arms athwart
His loving bosom to keep down his heart.
I have been closely shrouded in this bush,
And marked you both, and for you both did blush.   135
I heard your guilty rhymes, observed your fashion,
Saw sighs reek from you, noted well your passion.
'Ay me!' says one, 'O Jove!' the other cries.
One, her hairs were gold; crystal the other's eyes.
[*to Longaville*]
You would for paradise break faith and troth;   140
[*to Dumaine*]
And Jove for your love would infringe an oath.
What will Berowne say when that he shall hear
Faith infringed which such zeal did swear?
How will he scorn, how will he spend his wit!
How will he triumph, leap and laugh at it!   145
For all the wealth that ever I did see,
I would not have him know so much by me.
BEROWNE [*Comes forward.*]
    Now step I forth to whip hypocrisy.

---

131 **compile** compose (*OED v.* 3); there
is more compiling at 5.2.52 and 874,
and cf. *Son* 78.9.
132 **wreathed arms** wreathèd; see
3.1.15–19n.
  athwart across (*OED* B. 1b*)
134 **closely shrouded** secretly hidden
(*OED* shroud *v.*[1] 4a)
136 **fashion** behaviour (*OED sb.* 6)
137 **reek** exhale, emanate; Ard[1] compares
RJ 1.1.190, 'Love is a smoke made
with the fume of sighs'.
140 **faith and troth** a common phrase
141 **infringe** break, transgress (*OED v.*[1] 2)
142 **when that** when
143 The line's metrical irregularity makes

emendation   tempting   but   not
absolutely necessary.
  infringed infringèd
144 **spend his wit** See 2.1.19n.
145 **leap and laugh** The phrase was
proverbial: Dent, L92a.1.
147 **by** about; see Abbott, 145.
148 **step I forth** i.e. I present myself
before the others, advance to do something (*OED* step *v.* 22); see 5.2.661
SDn.
  to whip hypocrisy Berowne had earlier said he used to be *love's whip*,
3.1.169, but now he presents himself as
a satirist whose self-appointed task is to
whip the follies and vices of the age.

---

137 passion] *Q (*pashion*), F*   139 One,] *Malone;* One *Q;* On *F;* One that *(Oxf)*   140, 141 SDs]
Johnson   143 Faith] *QF;* Faith so *(Cam (Walker));* Our faith *(Oxf)*   148 SD] *Capell (subst.)*

Ah, good my liege, I pray thee pardon me.
Good heart, what grace hast thou thus to reprove   150
These worms for loving, that art most in love?
Your eyes do make no coaches; in your tears
There is no certain princess that appears;
You'll not be perjured, 'tis a hateful thing;
Tush, none but minstrels like of sonneting!   155
But are you not ashamed? Nay, are you not,
All three of you, to be thus much o'ershot?
You found his mote, the King your mote did see;
But I a beam do find in each of three.
O, what a scene of foolery have I seen,   160
Of sighs, of groans, of sorrow and of teen!
O me, with what strict patience have I sat,
To see a king transformed to a gnat!
To see great Hercules whipping a gig,
And profound Solomon to tune a jig,   165

---

150 **grace** privilege, dispensation (*OED sb.* 8b)
151 **worms** miserable creatures (*OED sb.* 10a)
152–3 Berowne turns to the King's sonnet, 30–2.
152 ***coaches** Cf. 31–2n.
155 **minstrels** professional entertainers, who might be musicians and storytellers, jugglers or clowns; cf. 1.1.174n. The medieval and romantic associations of the term developed after Shakespeare's time.
   like of are pleased with, approve of
   sonneting composing sonnets (*OED vbl. sb.* 1*)
157 **to be . . . o'ershot** to miss the target, hence to be mistaken, in error (*OED* overshoot *v.* 3b); see 1.1.140n.
158–9 Cf. Christ's attack on hypocrisy in His speaking of motes and beams,

Matthew, 7.3–5, and Luke, 6.41–2. The saying was proverbial: Tilley, M1191, and cf. 4.3.25n. See also Appendix 3.
161 **teen** affliction, grief
162 **strict** absolute, complete, perfect (*OED a.* 13a*)
163–7 For the Lucianic satire of this passage, see Baldwin, 1.732–3.
163 **transformed** transformèd; see also 79.
   gnat i.e. something insignificant; 'straining at gnats' was proverbial (Tilley, G150) from Matthew, 23.24.
164–5 **Hercules . . . Solomon** See 1.2.167–9n.
164–6 **whipping . . . to tune . . . play** For the construction, see Abbott, 349.
164 **gig** top; see 5.1.62n. Shakespeare uses the word only in this play.
165 **tune a jig** play a tune or sing a song

---

152 coaches] *Rowe³*; couches *QF*   coaches; in your tears] *Hanmer*; couches in your teares. *QF*
156 ashamed] *F* (asham'd); a shamed *Q*   158 mote . . . mote] *Q* (Moth . . . Moth), *F*   160 foolery] *Q* (foolrie), *F* (fool'ry)   165 to tune] tuning *F*

209

And Nestor play at push-pin with the boys,
And critic Timon laugh at idle toys.
Where lies thy grief? O, tell me, good Dumaine.
And, gentle Longaville, where lies thy pain?
And where my liege's? All about the breast?   170
A caudle, ho!
KING   Too bitter is thy jest.
Are we betrayed thus to thy over-view?
BEROWNE
Not you to me, but I betrayed by you;
I that am honest, I that hold it sin
To break the vow I am engaged in –   175
I am betrayed by keeping company
With men like you, men of inconstancy.
When shall you see me write a thing in rhyme?
Or groan for Joan? Or spend a minute's time
In pruning me? When shall you hear that I   180
Will praise a hand, a foot, a face, an eye,

166 **Nestor** a Greek commander at the siege of Troy, famed for his great age and wisdom (*OED**)
push-pin a children's game in which each player tries to flick a pin so that it lands across an opponent's (*OED* 1a*)
167 **critic** censorious, carping (*OED a.* 2); cf. 3.1.171n.
Timon Athenian famed for his misanthropy, the subject of Shakespeare's *Tim* (*OED* Timon[1]*)
idle toys foolish trifles, pointless games; cf. 197n.
171 **caudle** a sweet and spicy warm drink made of thin gruel mixed with wine or ale, given to the sick
172 **over-view** overlooking, supervision (*OED sb.**); cf. *supervise*, 4.2.120n.
174 **honest** honourable, morally upright

175 **engaged in** engagèd; pledged to
177 ***men like you, men** F changes Q's 'men like men' to 'men, like men': neither reading is satisfactory and the addition of 'you' is simple, corrects the metre and continues Berowne's comparison of 'I' and 'you'.
178 **thing** piece of writing (*OED sb.*[1] 13)
179 **groan** See 5.2.840.
Joan See 3.1.200n.
180 **pruning me** preening myself; cf. 4.2.17n.
180–3 **When . . . limb** The anatomical catalogue Berowne denies he has made – but which he seems to enter into with some enthusiasm – would in poetry form a blazon like Sidney's OA poem, 62, *AS*, 9.

171 caudle, ho] *Q (Caudle hou)*; Candle hoa *F*   173 to . . . by] *Capell*; by . . . to *QF*   177 men like you, men] *Dyce (Walker)*; men like men *Q*; men, like men *F*; moon-like *Malone (Mason)*   179 Joan] *Qc (Ione)*, *F (Ioane)*; Loue *Qu*   180–3 In . . . limb] *Rowe*; prose *QF*   180 me?] *F3*; mee *Q*; mee, *F*

A gait, a state, a brow, a breast, a waist,
A leg, a limb –

KING   Soft! Whither away so fast?
A true man, or a thief, that gallops so?

BEROWNE

I post from love. Good lover, let me go.   185

Enter JAQUENETTA [*with a letter*] *and* [COSTARD, *the*] *Clown.*

JAQUENETTA

God bless the King!

KING   What present hast thou there?

COSTARD

Some certain treason.

KING   What makes treason here?

COSTARD

Nay, it makes nothing, sir.

KING   If it mar nothing neither,
The treason and you go in peace away together.

JAQUENETTA

I beseech your grace let this letter be read.   190
Our person misdoubts it; 'twas treason, he said.

---

182 **gait, a state** way of walking, posture, attitude: neither is obviously a part of the body and Rubinstein (107) detects puns on *gate*, as in sluice-gate, for the woman's sexual parts (cf. *WT* 1.2.197), and on *state* as what is sat upon, the buttocks.
  brow Cf. 4.1.17n.
183–4 **Soft . . . so** Cf. 2.1.118–20n.
183 **Soft** Be quiet; don't go away.
  Whither . . . fast? The question was proverbial: Dent, W316.1.
184 **true** honest
185 **post** ride quickly, hurry, like a courier

or letter-carrier
186 **present** gift; document, writing (*OED sb.*¹ 2b); thing that is present, affair in hand (*OED sb.*¹ 2a)
187 **makes treason** has treason to do
188 Cf. the proverbial 'To make or mar', Tilley, M48.
191 **person** See 4.2.80n.
  misdoubts has suspicions or misgivings about. It was Holofernes, not Nathaniel, who had doubts about the letter (see 4.2.135–40), but he did not mention treason.

183 limb –] *Capell* (limb? –); limme. *QF*   185.1] *placed here in F, opp. 186,* 'God blesse the King.', *in Q*   187, 188 SP COSTARD] *Rowe; Clow. Q; Clo. F*   191 'twas] *Q* (twas); it was *F*

KING

> Berowne, read it over.   [*Berowne*] *reads the letter.*
>   Where hadst thou it?

JAQUENETTA   Of Costard.

KING   Where hadst thou it?

COSTARD   Of Dun Adramadio, Dun Adramadio.   195

> [*Berowne tears the letter up.*]

KING

> How now, what is in you? Why dost thou tear it?

BEROWNE

> A toy, my liege, a toy. Your grace needs not fear it.

LONGAVILLE

> It did move him to passion and therefore let's hear it.

DUMAINE [*Picks up the pieces.*]

> It is Berowne's writing and here is his name.

BEROWNE [*to Costard*]

> Ah, you whoreson loggerhead, you were born to do me
>   shame.   200
> Guilty, my lord, guilty: I confess, I confess.

KING   What?

BEROWNE

> That you three fools lacked me fool to make up the
>   mess.
> He, he and you – and you, my liege – and I
> Are pick-purses in love and we deserve to die.   205

---

195 **Dun Adramadio** Costard's error or
mispronunciation of 'Don' plays on
Armado's coming from *tawny Spain*: see
1.1.171n. His version of 'Armado' may
confuse his Christian name, Adriano,
but could allow plays on its elements,
such as 'drama', 'mad', 'dio', and so on.
197 **toy** something of no importance, a
trifle; cf. 167n.
200 **loggerhead** blockhead (*OED* 1a*)

203 **mess** group of four eating together
at a table; cf. the proverbial 'Four make
up a mess', Tilley, F621, and see also
5.2.361.
204 ²**and you** that means you
205 **pick-purses** thieves, cheats (in love);
cf. *AS*, 74.8, 'I am no pick-purse of
another's wit'.
deserve to die The punishment for
pickpockets was death.

---

192 SD *Berowne*] Collier; He *QF*   Where] *F2*; *King.* Where *QF* (*subst.*)   195, 199 SDs] Capell
(*subst.*)   200 SD] *Theobald*   204 and you,] *QF* (*and you*); even you, *Dyce²*; e'en you, *Oxf*

O, dismiss this audience and I shall tell you more.

DUMAINE

Now the number is even.

BEROWNE   True, true, we are four.

Will these turtles be gone?

KING   Hence, sirs, away!

COSTARD

Walk aside the true folk and let the traitors stay.

[*Exeunt Costard and Jaquenetta.*]

BEROWNE

Sweet lords, sweet lovers, O, let us embrace!   210
    As true we are as flesh and blood can be,
The sea will ebb and flow, heaven show his face;
    Young blood doth not obey an old decree.
We cannot cross the cause why we were born;
Therefore of all hands must we be forsworn.   215

KING

What, did these rent lines show some love of thine?

BEROWNE

'Did they?' quoth you! Who sees the heavenly Rosaline
That, like a rude and savage man of Ind,

207 Dumaine and Berowne echo Armado's and Moth's rhyme about 'The fox, the ape and the humble-bee' who by adding the goose 'stayed the odds': see 3.1.86–9n.

the . . . even There is an even number of us; we're all square or quits (*OED* even *a*. 10b).

208 turtles turtle-doves, lovers

sirs This polite form of address could be used equally for men or for women.

210–15 See 1.1.61–6n.

211 as . . . be Cf. the proverbial 'To be flesh and blood as others are', Dent, F367.

212 The . . . flow proverbial: see Dent, S182.1.

213 Young . . . decree proverbial: see Dent, Y44.1.

214 cross thwart, go counter to (*OED v.* 14a)

cause . . . born destiny, fate that determines our birth; the sexual passions which caused us to be conceived

215 of all hands in any case (*OED* hand *sb.* 30b); see also Abbott, 165.

217 Who does anyone who; see Abbott, 257.

218 rude and savage ignorant and uncivilized

Ind India. Whether Asian or American, Indians were supposed to be sun-worshippers; cf. 5.2.201–2 and *AW* 1.3.204–7.

207–8 True . . . gone] *Rowe²; one line QF* 209 SP] *Rowe; Clow. QF* SD] *Theobald* 212 show] *Q (shew); will shew F* 214 were] are *F* 218 That, like . . . Ind,] *Capell;* That (like . . . *Inde.*) *QF*

At the first opening of the gorgeous east,
Bows not his vassal head and, strucken blind,   220
   Kisses the base ground with obedient breast?
What peremptory eagle-sighted eye
   Dares look upon the heaven of her brow
That is not blinded by her majesty?

KING

   What zeal, what fury hath inspired thee now?   225
My love, her mistress, is a gracious moon;
   She, an attending star, scarce seen a light.

BEROWNE

My eyes are then no eyes, nor I Berowne.
   O, but for my love, day would turn to night!
Of all complexions the culled sovereignty   230
   Do meet as at a fair in her fair cheek,
Where several worthies make one dignity,
   Where nothing wants, that want itself doth seek.
Lend me the flourish of all gentle tongues –

---

219 **opening** disclosing to the view, i.e. dawning

220 **vassal** *OED* 4c*

222 **peremptory** resolute, obstinate, i.e. unblinking (*OED a.* 3); cf. 5.1.10n.
eagle-sighted The royal eagle was supposed to be able to look directly at the sun (*OED* eagle *sb.* 10c* and see Tilley, E7.1); cf. 5.2.374–6n.

225 **zeal** ardent desire
fury poetic frenzy

226–7 **gracious . . . star** Cf. the proverbial 'To be like the moon to the stars', Dent, S826.2, in which 'moon' and 'stars' were interchangeable, and cf. 5.2.205n.

227 **She** i.e. Rosaline
attending attendant, waiting to do service (*OED ppl. a.* 2*)
scarce . . . light a light only seen with great difficulty. It is possible that QF's 'a light' should read 'alight', in which case the phrase means that it can hardly be seen whether it is alight.

229 **but for** were it not for

230–7 See 2.1.13–19n.

230 **the culled sovereignty** those chosen as supremely excellent (*OED* culled *ppl. a.**); cf. 5.1.86n.

231 **fair . . . fair** a characteristic pun: Berowne talks about fairs again at 5.2.318 and the Princess mentions the *fairings* she and her ladies have received at 5.2.2n.

232 where several kinds of value come together in one thing of supreme excellence
worthies The choice of word anticipates the Nine Worthies in 5.2.

233 **wants** is lacking
want desire

234 **flourish** gloss, varnish (*OED sb.* 3*); see 2.1.14n.
gentle noble

---

219 opening] *Q (*opning), *F*   220 blind,] *F*; blind. *Q*   222 peremptory] *Q (*peromptorie), *F*

Fie, painted rhetoric! O, she needs it not.   235
To things of sale, a seller's praise belongs:
　　She passes praise; then praise too short doth blot.
A withered hermit, five-score winters worn,
　　Might shake off fifty, looking in her eye.
Beauty doth varnish age, as if new born,   240
　　And gives the crutch the cradle's infancy.
O, 'tis the sun that maketh all things shine.

KING

By heaven, thy love is black as ebony!

BEROWNE

Is ebony like her? O word divine!
　　A wife of such wood were felicity.   245
O, who can give an oath? Where is a book?
　　That I may swear beauty doth beauty lack
If that she learn not of her eye to look.
　　No face is fair that is not full so black.

---

235 **painted rhetoric** the painted or arti-
　　ficial language of rhetoric; cf. the
　　proverbial 'Truth has no need of
　　rhetoric', Tilley, T575.
236 Cf. the proverbial 'He praises who
　　wishes to sell', Tilley, P546: the con-
　　nection between rhetoric and things
　　for sale suggests the presence of
　　Mercury, god of language and of mar-
　　kets. See also 2.1.78–9n.
　　of sale for sale
237 She surpasses all praise and, since she
　　does so, all praise being too short is
　　bound to defame her (*OED* blot *v.*[1] 3a
　　absol.*, the only citation).
238 **hermit** See 5.2.789n.
240 **doth varnish** embellishes, improves
241 **the crutch** old age (*OED sb.* 1b)
　　cradle's infancy youth that goes with
　　the cradle

243 **black as ebony** proverbial (Dent,
　　E56a); see 1.1.236n.: like the Dark
　　Lady of *Son* (esp. 127, 130–2, 147) and
　　Sidney's Stella (see *AS*, 7, 47), Rosaline
　　is said to be dark.
244 **word** Theobald's emendation,
　　'wood', has been widely accepted, but
　　is unnecessary; see Wells, *Re-Editing*,
　　44.
246 **oath . . . book** Berowne recalls the
　　oath-taking in 1.1, but here calls for a
　　Bible (*OED* book *sb.* 4a).
247–9 Cf. *Son* 132.13–14 and note the
　　same *black/lack* rhyme.
248 i.e. if beauty does not learn from
　　Rosaline's eye how to appear; or, possi-
　　bly, if beauty does not learn how to
　　look with Rosaline's eye
249 **fair** beautiful

238 hermit] *Q (*Hermight*), F*   244 word] *QF;* wood *Theobald*

KING

O paradox! Black is the badge of hell,   250
The hue of dungeons and the school of night;
And beauty's crest becomes the heavens well.

BEROWNE

Devils soonest tempt, resembling spirits of light.
O, if in black my lady's brows be decked,
It mourns that painting and usurping hair   255
Should ravish doters with a false aspect;

250–1 **Black . . . night** The meaning of the passage is much disputed and is probably best left unemended; see Introduction, pp. 24–6. Oxf[1] quotes part of Sisson's gloss in *Readings* (1.115–16), 'night is the scholar or pupil of blackness', then adds a further explanation, that 'black is the school where night learns to be really black', and goes on to compare *Luc* 615–17 and 4.3.297, where Berowne calls the ladies *beauty's tutors*. 'As black as hell' was proverbial, Tilley, H397, and cf. *Son* 147.14, 'as black as hell, as dark as night'.

250 **badge** sign, emblem, symbol (*OED sb.* 2a); cf. 5.2.748, *2H4* 4.3.102–6, 'The second property of your excellent sherris is the warming of the blood, which before (cold and settled) left the liver white and pale, which is the badge of pusillanimity and cowardice'. In heraldry a badge or cognizance was borne by members of a household, but could be more loosely used for a coat of arms.

251 **school** The school may be of the kind which Holofernes runs, or closer to the university or *academe* which the King and his companions have formed (*OED sb.*[1] 7a).

252 **beauty's crest** i.e. the sun which surmounts, is the height of, beauty. In heraldry the crest is placed above the shield in a coat of arms and a contrast

may be intended between the *badge* of 250 and the *crest* which is superior to it: cf. *KJ* 4.3.45–7, 'This is the very top, / The heighth, the crest, or crest unto the crest, / Of murther's arms'.
becomes adorns, graces

253 Cf. the proverbial 'The Devil can transform himself into an angel of light', Tilley, D231, and 2 Corinthians, 11.14, 'for Satan himselfe is transfourmed into an angel of lyght'. *Devils* (like *devil* at 271) and *spirits* may be monosyllabic.
resembling when they resemble

254–61 Berowne's argument can be paralleled by *Son* 127.7–11.

254 Shakespeare twice has 'black-brow'd night' (*RJ* 3.2.20, *MND* 3.2.387): citing the second of these, *OED* supplies an additional gloss of frowning, scowling, but this does not fit the context. It may rather be that black brows suggested, as Bevington said, 'a rustic, unsophisticated kind of beauty' (Lyly, *Sapho and Phao*, 287), comparing *WT* 2.1.8; cf. also Phoebe's 'inky brows', *AYL* 3.5.46.
decked adorned

255 *i.e. 'she is mourning the fact that cosmetics and false hair'; F4's 'and' may be correct, but so might 'or'.
usurping *OED ppl. a.* 1b

256 **doters** people who are foolishly fond or in love
false aspect misleading appearance

251 school] *QF* (Schoole*); scowl *Theobald*; stole *Hanmer*; style *Oxf (Shapiro)*   252 And] *QF*; A *Cam*[1] *1962*   255 and] *F4*; *not in QF*   256 doters] *Q* (dooters*), *F*

And therefore is she born to make black fair.
Her favour turns the fashion of the days,
    For native blood is counted painting now;
And therefore red, that would avoid dispraise,   260
    Paints itself black, to imitate her brow.

DUMAINE
    To look like her are chimney-sweepers black.

LONGAVILLE
    And since her time are colliers counted bright.

KING
    And Ethiops of their sweet complexion crack.

DUMAINE
    Dark needs no candles now, for dark is light.   265

BEROWNE
    Your mistresses dare never come in rain,
        For fear their colours should be washed away.

KING
    'Twere good yours did; for, sir, to tell you plain,
        I'll find a fairer face not washed today.

BEROWNE
    I'll prove her fair, or talk till doomsday here.   270

KING
    No devil will fright thee then so much as she.

DUMAINE
    I never knew man hold vile stuff so dear.

---

258 Her face completely alters, turns around, what is considered fashionable.
259 **native blood** i.e. a complexion which is naturally ruddy
    counted accounted
260 **red** i.e. what is naturally red
261 **imitate** make itself like (*OED v.* 3*)
263 **colliers** traders or carriers of charcoal or coal
264 **crack** boast (*OED v.* 6a)

266 **come in** i.e. walk in
267 **colours** what little natural colour they have; their painted cosmetics; and, just possibly, badges, crests
269 **not washed** i.e. which has not been washed
271 **then** i.e. on doomsday
272 **vile** cheap, worthless
    stuff here, contemptuously applied to Rosaline (*OED sb.*[1] 7c*)

262 black] *Q* (blake), *F*   264 crack] *QF* (crake)

LONGAVILLE [*Shows his shoe.*]

  Look, here's thy love, my foot and her face see.

BEROWNE

  O, if the streets were paved with thine eyes,
  Her feet were much too dainty for such tread.   275

DUMAINE

  O, vile! Then, as she goes, what upward lies
  The street should see as she walked overhead.

KING

  But what of this? Are we not all in love?

BEROWNE

  O, nothing so sure, and thereby all forsworn.

KING

  Then leave this chat and, good Berowne, now prove   280
  Our loving lawful and our faith not torn.

DUMAINE

  Ay, marry, there; some flattery for this evil.

LONGAVILLE

  O, some authority how to proceed.
  Some tricks, some quillets how to cheat the devil.

---

273 **my foot . . . see** Presumably
Longaville's shoe is black, but perhaps
he is also suggesting that Rosaline is as
ugly as his shoe; cf. 1.2.161n.
274 **paved** pavèd
275 **tread** a path, a track (*OED sb.* 3a); for
the sexual meaning involving copula-
tion, see 5.2.330n. and 5.2.893n.
276–7 The passage is to a certain extent a
parallel for Berowne's description of
Boyet climbing the stairs at 5.2.330. In
one of the most famous portraits of
Queen Elizabeth, the Ditchley Portrait
of about 1592 in the National Portrait
Gallery, the Queen stands with her feet
near Ditchley in Oxfordshire on a map
of southern England, allowing its
inhabitants (who are not shown) to see
up her dress.

276 **goes** walks
  what upward lies what is above it; i.e.
  what could be seen up her dress
280 **chat** The King uses the word again at
5.2.228.
  prove demonstrate by logic: see 5n.
282 **there** that's the point
  some . . . evil i.e. some gratifying
  delusion or deception to put this evil in
  the best possible light (*OED* flattery 2,
  citing *Son* 42.14)
283 **authority** Cf. Armado's plea to
  Moth for *More authority* regarding
  men who have been in love, 1.2.65.
284 **quillets** verbal niceties, subtle dis-
  tinctions (*OED sb.*²)
  how . . . devil Cf. the proverbial 'This
  is the way to catch the old one', Dent,
  W149.

---

273 SD] *Johnson (subst.)*   276 lies] *Rowe*³; lyes? *QF*   279 O, nothing] *QF;* Nothing *F2*

DUMAINE
    Some salve for perjury.
BEROWNE   O, 'tis more than need.   285
Have at you then, affection's men-at-arms.
Consider what you first did swear unto:
To fast, to study and to see no woman –
Flat treason 'gainst the kingly state of youth.
Say, can you fast? Your stomachs are too young,   290
And abstinence engenders maladies.
O, we have made a vow to study, lords,
And in that vow we have forsworn our books;
For when would you, my liege, or you, or you,
In leaden contemplation have found out   295
Such fiery numbers as the prompting eyes
Of beauty's tutors have enriched you with?
Other slow arts entirely keep the brain,
And therefore, finding barren practisers,
Scarce show a harvest of their heavy toil;   300
But love, first learned in a lady's eyes,
Lives not alone immured in the brain
But with the motion of all elements
Courses as swift as thought in every power

285 **salve** See 3.1.69–70n.
  need necessary (*OED sb.* 4a)
286 **Have at you** here goes
  affection's men-at-arms love's war-riors; the men are now the reverse of the King's followers who 'war against your own affections', 1.1.8–10. Cf. 5.2.407n.
288 **fast** See 1.1.24n.
289 **state** status, rank, hence majesty
290 **young** inexperienced
291 For the lines following this in QF, see Appendix 2.1.
295 **leaden** heavy, oppressive; cf. 'Is not lead a metal heavy, dull and slow?', 3.1.56.

296 **fiery numbers** the poems which Berowne previously mocked
  prompting *OED* prompt *ppl. adjs.**
298 i.e. other duller or more serious kinds of learning completely occupy the brain
300 **of their** i.e. from the practisers'
301 **learned** learnèd
302 **immured** immurèd; enclosed, con-fined (*OED v.* 3a); cf. 3.1.121n.
303 **motion . . . elements** i.e. the speed of winds and storms (*OED* element *sb.* 11)
304 **Courses** runs
  as swift as thought proverbial: see Dent, T240.
  power faculty

285 O] *QF; om. Cam (Walker)* 289 'gainst] *Q (*gainst*); against F* 291+] *at this point QF print the lines in Appendix 2.1* 302 immured] *QF (*emured*)* 303 elements] *Q (*elamentes*), F*

219

And gives to every power a double power,   305
Above their functions and their offices.
It adds a precious seeing to the eye:
A lover's eyes will gaze an eagle blind.
A lover's ear will hear the lowest sound
When the suspicious head of theft is stopped.   310
Love's feeling is more soft and sensible
Than are the tender horns of cockled snails.
Love's tongue proves dainty Bacchus gross in taste,
For valour, is not Love a Hercules,
Still climbing trees in the Hesperides?   315
Subtle as Sphinx, as sweet and musical
As bright Apollo's lute, strung with his hair.

305 **every power . . . power** a double
force to every faculty
306 above and beyond their ordinary
functions; a sort of hendiadys; see
1.1.14n.
307 **precious seeing** Cf. *precious eyesight*,
5.2.444–5n.
308 **gaze . . . blind** i.e. by being brighter
than the sun the lover's eyes will blind
the eagle (see 222n.); outstare even an
eagle. See 2.1.246.
310 i.e. when the thief listening out for
the slightest noise can hear nothing.
The sense is strained, but the evident
meaning is clear.
311–12 **more . . . snails** Cf. *VA* 1033–4,
'Or as the snail, whose tender horns
being hit, / Shrinks backward in his
shelly cave with pain'.
311 **sensible** sensitive (*OED* A. 8a)
312 **cockled** having a shell (*OED a.* 1*,
the only citation); Jackson detects a
pun on cockled/cuckold, esp. in relation to the snails' horns.
313 **Love's tongue** Like *Love's feeling*
(311), the phrase has clear erotic overtones. Cf. 1.1.123n.
dainty Bacchus Berowne's epithet

for Bacchus may be intended as a joke,
but it could simply mean that Bacchus
is concerned about the quality of his
(food and) drink: *OED a.* 6, cf. 1.1.26
and 'Plumpy Bacchus', *AC* 2.7.114.
315 **Still climbing** There is a parallel for
the possible oxymoron (cf. 1.1.14n.) in
Marlowe's *1 Tamburlaine*, 2.7.24, 'Still
climbing after knowledge infinite', and
cf. *AS*, 23.10, 'still climing slipprie
place'.
the Hesperides The eleventh of
Hercules' twelve labours was to pick
the golden apples from a tree growing
in the garden of the Hesperides, who
were the daughters of Hesperus: the
tree was guarded by a dragon. Like
other writers, Shakespeare used
Hesperides here for the garden rather
than for the daughters themselves
(*OED sb. pl.* 1c). The imagery of
climbing trees may look back to
Berowne's position in the overhearing
scene: see 4.3.76n.
316 **Sphinx** a monster made up of parts
of a woman, a dog, a serpent, a bird
and a lion: it ate those unable to answer
its riddles.

309 sound] *Rowe (subst.);* sound. *QF*   313 dainty] *F2;* daintie, *QF*   314–15 Hercules, . . . Hesperides?]
Theobald²; Hercules? . . . Hesperides. QF   316 Subtle] *Q (*Subtit*), F*

And when Love speaks, the voice of all the gods
Make heaven drowsy with the harmony.
Never durst poet touch a pen to write   320
Until his ink were tempered with Love's sighs.
O, then his lines would ravish savage ears
And plant in tyrants mild humility.
From women's eyes this doctrine I derive:
They sparkle still the right Promethean fire;   325
They are the books, the arts, the academes,
That show, contain and nourish all the world;
Else none at all in aught proves excellent.
Then fools you were these women to forswear,
Or, keeping what is sworn, you will prove fools.   330
For wisdom's sake, a word that all men love,
Or, for love's sake, a word that loves all men,
Or, for men's sake, the authors of these women,
Or women's sake, by whom we men are men,
Let us once lose our oaths to find ourselves,   335
Or else we lose ourselves to keep our oaths.
It is religion to be thus forsworn,

---

318 **voice** voices; for the omission of the final 's' in words ending in 'ce' and so on, see Abbott, 471.

319 **harmony** See also 1.1.165.

321 **tempered** mixed, blended

322 **ravish** See also 2.1.75.

324 Cf. *Son* 14.9, 'But from thine eyes my knowledge I derive'.

325 **sparkle** throw out fire like sparks (*OED v.*[1] 7a)
still either an adverb meaning 'constantly' or an adjective forming an oxymoron with the sparkling fire, with which cf. 1.1.14n.
right Promethean fire very fire which Prometheus stole from heaven to give to man, so allowing him to become

civilized (*OED* Promethean A. 1*)

326 **academes** Cf. the form at 1.1.13n.

328 i.e. without them nobody can achieve excellence in anything

332 **loves** The sense is strained, but it could mean that the very word love inspires men with love, or that it has a seductive effect upon them, or that it praises or flatters men, gives them some sense of their value (*OED v.*[1] 1a).

334 **women's . . . we men** There may be a pun intended.

335 **lose our oaths** Cf. 70n.

337 **religion** i.e. within the beliefs of our religion

---

319 Make] *QF*; Makes *Hanmer*   326 academes] *QF* (*Achademes*)   333 authors] *Capell*; authour *Q*; author *F*   335 Let us] *Q* (*Lets vs*); Let's *F*

For charity itself fulfils the law,
And who can sever love from charity?

KING

Saint Cupid, then! And, soldiers, to the field! 340

BEROWNE

Advance your standards and upon them, lords!
Pell-mell, down with them! But be first advised
In conflict that you get the sun of them.

LONGAVILLE

Now to plain dealing. Lay these glozes by.
Shall we resolve to woo these girls of France? 345

KING

And win them too! Therefore let us devise
Some entertainment for them in their tents.

BEROWNE

First, from the park let us conduct them thither.
Then homeward every man attach the hand

338–9 Berowne returns to the question of love and charity raised by Longaville at 124: the point is that *caritas* and *amor* are different.

338 **charity . . . law** an allusion to Romans, 13.8, 'For he that loueth another, hath fulfylled the lawe'.

340 **Saint Cupid** Here and 5.2.87 are the only occasions where Shakespeare calls Cupid a saint (*OED* saint A. 2a). The usage is possibly unique to Shakespeare.

341–2 **Advance . . . them** Berowne's exhortations (cf. *R3* 5.3.264, 348) have a sexual strain, where *standards* may be taken for their penises and *upon* and *down* suggest intercourse.

342 **Pell-mell** at close quarters, hand to hand
be first advised first of all, take care

343 **get . . . them** make sure they have the sun in their eyes (*OED* sun *sb.* 1e (*c*)*, the only citation): 'To get the sun of one', Tilley, S987, may have been proverbial; have a son by them.

344 **plain dealing** straightforward behaviour in words and deeds
glozes false or specious arguments (*OED sb.* 2b)

345–6 **to woo . . . them** Cf. the proverbial 'Woo, wed, and bed her', Tilley, W731.

345 **girls** See 1.1.296n.

347 **in their tents** Presumably the King means in front of, or in among, their tents: later (5.2.307), Rosaline refers to their appearance *at our tent*.

348 **thither** Presumably, they are going to lead the women from the park to their tents. Earlier, Boyet had told the Princess that the King meant to 'lodge you in the field' (2.1.85), suggesting the tents were in the park. Later, the Princess and her ladies return to their tents at 5.2.309 and, at 5.2.344, the King proposes to lead them to the court.

349 **attach** seize, grasp (*OED v.* 3b*): the word had legal associations for taking something with authority.

341 standards] *Q (standars), F*

Of his fair mistress. In the afternoon   350
We will with some strange pastime solace them,
Such as the shortness of the time can shape;
For revels, dances, masques and merry hours
Forerun fair Love, strewing her way with flowers.

KING

Away, away! No time shall be omitted   355
That will betime and may by us be fitted.

BEROWNE

Allons, allons!   [*Exeunt the King, Longaville and Dumaine.*]
Sowed cockle reaped no corn:
And justice always whirls in equal measure.
Light wenches may prove plagues to men forsworn;   359
If so, our copper buys no better treasure.   [*Exit.*]

351 **strange** new, unusual; cf. 5.1.6.
pastime Cf. 5.2.360.
solace entertain, amuse (*OED v.* 1a)
354 **Forerun fair Love** run in front of and announce the coming of Venus (*OED* fore-run *v.* 3)
356 ***betime** happen, come to pass; there is a play on 'be time', the reading in QF, meaning that there will be time enough.
*be fitted be used in a fitting manner; there is a play on 'befitted', the Q reading, meaning 'found fitting'.
357 ***Allons, allons** Q reads 'Alone alone' and F has 'Alone, alone': the same reading of 'Alone' in QF occurs at 5.1.143, where it is clear that Holofernes means 'let's go'. The French word was not uncommon in literature of the time.
SD *Q has no SD to clear the stage and F only a general '*Exeunt.*' at the end of the scene. Berowne's dark com-

ments – that, having broken their vow, they may receive the punishment they deserve – seem more appropriately addressed to himself and to the audience than to his fellow suitors.
Sowed . . . corn i.e. you don't get any corn if you sow weeds. *Cockle* was the word sometimes used in the parable of the tares and the wheat, Matthew, 13.24–30; cf. also 1.1.96n.
358 **whirls . . . measure** spins in an even-handed way; cf. *R3* 4.4.105, 'Thus hath the course of justice whirl'd about', and see *OED* whirl *v.* 2a. The imagery seems to be that of the wheel of fortune.
359 **Light** frivolous, wanton
360 i.e. as men who are supposed to have forsworn love, we must take what we can get
copper coins of low value (*OED sb.*[1] 2a*)

355 omitted] *Cam;* omitted, *QF* 356 betime] *Rowe;* be time *QF* be fitted] *F;* befitted *Q* 357 *Allons, allons*] *Theobald;* Alone alone *Q;* Alone, alone *F* SD] *Kerrigan* 359 forsworn] *Q (*forsorne*), F* 360 SD] *Kerrigan; Exeunt. F*

5[.1]   *Enter* [HOLOFERNES,] *the Pedant,* [NATHANIEL,]
            the Curate, and DULL[, *the Constable*].

HOLOFERNES   *Satis quod sufficit.*

NATHANIEL   I praise God for you, sir. Your reasons at
dinner have been sharp and sententious, pleasant
without scurrility, witty without affection, audacious
without impudency, learned without opinion and   5
strange without heresy. I did converse this *quondam* day
with a companion of the King's, who is intituled,
nominated, or called, Don Adriano de Armado.

HOLOFERNES   *Novi hominem tanquam te.* His Humour is
lofty, his discourse peremptory, his tongue filed, his eye   10
ambitious, his gait majestical and his general behaviour

5.1.1 *Satis quod sufficit* lit. '[That is]
enough which suffices.' Holofernes
alludes to the proverbial 'Enough is
enough' and 'Enough is as good as a
feast', Dent, E159, and Tilley, E158.
2–6 *Your . . . heresy* See 4.2.24–33n.
2 **reasons** observations, remarks (*OED*
   *sb.*¹ 3a)
3 **dinner** The invitation to dinner, the
   chief meal of the day, eaten at the time
   around 11 a.m., was issued at 4.2.151.
   Cf. 1.1.24n.
   sententious wise, full of meaning
   (*OED a.* 1): in humanist terms, a word
   of high praise
4 **scurrility** obscene jokiness or coarse
   language; see 4.2.53n.
   affection affectation (*OED sb.* 13); see
   5.2.407n.
   audacious bold, confident; cf.
   5.2.104n.
5 **impudency** shamelessness, immod-
   esty; unique in Shakespeare, who elsewhere uses the form 'impudence'
   opinion arrogance, dogmatism (*OED*
   sb. 5c*)

6 **strange** See 4.3.351n.
   heresy See 4.1.22n.
   quondam former, other (*OED* C. b*)
7 **intituled** entitled, called (*OED v.* 3a)
8 **nominated** See 1.2.15n.
9–14 Holofernes' description may be
   intended to suggest Armado's homosexuality.
9 *Novi hominem . . . te* I know the man
   as well as I know you: the phrase is
   taken from Lily and Colet's grammar
   and, like the later snatches of Latin at
   29–30, 71–3, is reminiscent of
   Erasmus's colloquies (Baldwin, 1.578,
   735–6). The reading '*hominum*' in QF
   is almost certainly a compositorial
   error.
10 **peremptory** arrogant, dogmatic
   (*OED a.* 4); cf. 4.3.222n.
   filed polished, smooth; cf. the proverbial 'To file one's tongue', Dent,
   T400.2, and 1.1.123n.
11 **majestical** an earlier form of 'majestic'. It appears in plays up to and
   including *Ham*; thereafter 'majestic' is
   used (in *JC, Cym, Tem*). Cf. 5.2.102.

5.1] *Rowe; F (Actus Quartus.); act and scene not in Q*   0.1 *the Curate*] Curate F   1+ SP HOLOFERNES]
Rowe; Pedant. (Peda., Ped.) QF   1 *quod*] *Rowe; quid QF*   2+ SP NATHANIEL] *Rowe; Curat. (Cura.)
QF*   4 *affection*] *QF; affectation F2*   8 Armado] *QF (Armatho)*   9 *hominem*] *F3; hominum QF*

vain, ridiculous and thrasonical. He is too picked, too
spruce, too affected, too odd, as it were, too peregrinate,
as I may call it.

NATHANIEL   A most singular and choice epithet.   15

(*Draws out his table-book.*)

HOLOFERNES   He draweth out the thread of his verbosity
finer than the staple of his argument. I abhor such
fanatical phantasimes, such insociable and point-device
companions, such rackers of orthography, as to speak
'dout' *sine* 'b', when he should say 'doubt', 'det' when   20

---

12 **thrasonical** bragging, boastful, from
the braggart soldier Thraso in Terence's
comedy *Eunuchus*; Shakespeare uses the
word again in *AYL* 5.2.31.
picked finical, fastidious (*OED ppl. a.*
2)

13 **spruce** trim, smart in his dress (*OED
a.* 2a**); cf. 5.2.407n.
odd peculiar, eccentric (*OED a.* 9b*):
Holofernes' *as it were* (see 4.2.14n.)
demonstrates his own recognition that
he is stretching the meaning of the
word (*OED* as *adv.* 9c).
peregrinate with the air of one who
has travelled abroad; a Shakespearean
coinage (*OED a.**): the word can be
associated with pilgrimages and astro-
logically (*OED* peregrine A. 2) with a
planet which is in part of the zodiac
where its influence is weak.

15 **singular** remarkable, extraordinary
(*OED a.* 11)
epithet See 1.2.14n.

15 SD *table-book* a book made out of
tablets, used for making notes (*OED* 1)

16–17 **He . . . argument** Holofernes' figure is drawn from spinning: he accuses
Armado of being verbose. All of
OED's examples of 'spinning out' an
argument in this sense (spin *v.* 6a–d)
date from the seventeenth century.

16 **draweth out** extends, prolongs (*OED
draw v.* 87d). The repetition of the
verb 'draw' in this line and the preceding SD is curious.

17 **finer** more thinly (*OED a.* 7d *fig.**)
staple the fibre from which a thread is
made (*OED sb.³* 2*); unique in
Shakespeare

18 **fanatical** extravagant (*OED a.* 2b*,
the only citation)
phantasimes See 4.1.98n.
insociable unsociable, not fit for
social intercourse; *OED a.* 2*, citing
5.2.793, Shakespeare's only two uses of
the word
point-device over-correct, extremely
precise

19 **companions** fellows, used contemp-
tuously, *OED sb.¹* 4, citing *2H4* 2.4.123,
'I scorn you, scurvy companion'
rackers of orthography i.e. people
who torture correct spelling. The QF
form ('ortagriphie') suggests the
word's own orthographic problems: in
MA 2.3.20, Shakespeare's only other
use of the word, Q has 'ortography'
and F has 'orthography'.

20 *sine* 'b' without sounding the letter
'b'. QF both read 'fine', but an f/long
s confusion followed by the omission
of 'b' is easy to posit.

12–13 too spruce] *Q (*to spruce*), F*   13 too odd] *Q (*to od*), F*   15 SD] *Q (*Draw-out his Table-
booke.*), F*   19 orthography] *QF (*ortagriphie*)*   20 sine 'b'] *Cam¹ 1962 (Hertzberg);* fine *QF*
20–1 'det' . . . d, e, b, t] *QF (*det . . . d e b t*);* 'det', 'debt' – when he should pronounce – d, e, b, t
Bevington (subst.)

he should pronounce 'debt': d, e, b, t, not d, e, t. He
clepeth a calf 'cauf', half 'hauf'; neighbour *vocatur*
'nebour', neigh abbreviated 'ne'. This is abhominable,
which he would call 'abominable'. It insinuateth me of
insanie. *Ne intelligis, domine?* To make frantic, lunatic.   25
NATHANIEL   *Laus Deo, bone intelligo.*
HOLOFERNES   *Bone? 'Bone'* for *'bene'*! Priscian a little
scratched; 'twill serve.

Enter [ARMADO, *the*] *Braggart,* [MOTH, *his*] *Boy,* [*and*
COSTARD].

NATHANIEL   *Videsne quis venit?*
HOLOFERNES   *Video et gaudeo.*   30

21–2 **debt . . . calf . . . half** The discussion of the pronunciation of these
three words anticipates further use of
them at 5.2.333–4, where *debt* rhymes
with *Boyet*, and 5.2.43–4, where *debtor*
rhymes with *letter*, and 5.2.246–9,
where *calf* and *half* rhyme.
22 **clepeth** calls; archaic and unique in
Shakespeare
22–3 **neighbour . . . nebour** Presumably,
Holofernes is complaining that
Armado pronounces the 'gh' silently
instead of like 'ich' in German. Cf.
Ham 2.2.12, where Q2 has 'nabored'
and F has 'Neighbour'd'.
22 **vocatur** is called
23 **abbreviated** *OED v.* 3d*
23–4 **abominable . . . abominable** Up
to the mid-seventeenth century 'abominable' was regularly spelled 'abhominable', since it was assumed the word
came from the Lat. *ab homine*, meaning
'away from man', hence 'inhuman' or
'beastly'. The correct etymology for
the word is from Lat. *abominabilis*,
meaning 'deserving imprecation or
abhorrence'. The word and its deriva-

tives are consistently spelled with the
medial 'h' in the quartos and in F.
24–5 **insinuateth . . . insanie* subtly
makes me mad; perhaps, suggests or
implies madness to me. QF read 'infamie'
and, although the emendation to 'insanie'
is graphically easy, so is *insanire* the Lat.
for 'to be mad' or 'to act like a madman'.
But this is not quite the same as his subsequent gloss 'To make frantic, lunatic'.
For *insinuateth*, see 4.2.14n.
25 *Ne . . . domine?* Do you understand, sir?
26 **Laus . . . intelligo* God be praised, I
understand good; the QF reading
'bene', 'well', needs to be corrupted to
make sense of Holofernes' next remark.
27–8 **Priscian . . . scratched* i.e. your
Latin is slightly wrong. The sixth-cen-
tury AD grammars of Priscian were
still in use in the Renaissance and cf.
the proverbial 'To break Priscian's
head', Tilley, P595.
29 **Videsne quis venit?* Do you see who's
coming? See 9n.
30 **Video et gaudeo* I see and I'm glad.
QF read *'gaudio'*, meaning 'with joy',
but Holofernes tends to use parallelism.

21 d, e, t] *Pope;* det *QF*   24 abominable] *Q (*abbominable*);* abhominable *F*   25 insanie] *Theobald
(Warburton);* infamie *QF; insanire / Singer;* insania *Collier MS*   26 bone] *Theobald;* bene *QF*
27 *¹Bone . . .* Priscian] *Theobald; Bome boon for boon prescian QF;* Bon, bon, fort bon! Priscian *Cam*
28.1–2 *and* COSTARD] *Rowe*   29 *Videsne*] *Pope²; Vides ne QF*   30 gaudeo] *F3;* gaudio *QF*

ARMADO Chirrah!

HOLOFERNES *Quare* 'chirrah', not 'sirrah'?

ARMADO Men of peace, well encountered.

HOLOFERNES Most military sir, salutation.

MOTH [*to Costard*] They have been at a great feast of   35
languages and stolen the scraps.

COSTARD [*to Moth*] O, they have lived long on the alms-
basket of words! I marvel thy master hath not eaten
thee for a word, for thou art not so long by the head as
honorificabilitudinitatibus. Thou art easier swallowed   40
than a flap-dragon.

MOTH Peace! The peal begins.

ARMADO [*to Holofernes*] Monsieur, are you not lettered?

MOTH Yes, yes! He teaches boys the hornbook. What is a,

---

31 **Chirrah** Hail. Probably a corruption
of the Greek χαῖρε (*chaere*), used as a
greeting in Erasmus's colloquies,
which were read in Elizabethan
schools.

32 **Quare* why

33 **Men of peace** *OED* man *sb.*¹ 18**;
Armado's phrase is the converse of
'men of war'.

34 **military** soldierly (*OED* A. 2b*)
salutation I greet you (*OED* 2)

35 **feast** See 1.1.24n.

37–8 **lived . . . words** lived on public charity, i.e. on the words others have rejected (*OED* alms-basket, To live . . . *)

38–9 **eaten . . . word** punning on the pronunciation of Moth's name as Fr. *mot*

40 *honorificabilitudinitatibus* Commonly
said to be the longest word, it is the
dative or ablative plural of a medieval
Lat. noun meaning 'the state of being
honoured'. Hutton pointed out that
the word is quoted from a Lat. couplet
in Erasmus's *Adagia* (3.2.69) where it
is associated with Hermes, but

Erasmus's source for the quotation
remains untraced.

41 **flap-dragon** a raisin or plum floating
in burning brandy which had to be
snapped up in the mouth in the game
of snapdragon (*OED* 1c*)

42 **peal** Moth may be referring simply to
a loud outburst of sound (*OED sb.*¹ 6),
or more specifically to the ringing of
bells or the noise made by cannons
which Armado's and Holofernes' conversation resembles. At 3.1.61 Armado
says that Moth 'reputes me a cannon'
and Moth goes *Thump*.

43 **lettered** learned, educated, but also –
as Moth takes it – literate

44 **hornbook** a piece of paper on which
were written the alphabet, numbers,
prayers, and so on, protected by a thin
sheet of horn, mounted on a wooden
block with a handle (*OED a.*)

44–64 **What . . . horn** Kerrigan compares the verbal- and logic-chopping
of *TGV* 1.1.70–109.

31+ SP ARMADO] *Rowe; Brag. (Bra.) QF*   32 Quare] *F2; Quari QF*   33 encountered] *Q
(*incontred*), F (*incountred*)*   35 SP] *Rowe; Boy. QF* SD] *Johnson*   37+ SP COSTARD] *Rowe;
Clow. QF*   37 SD] *Cam*   42+ SP MOTH] *Rowe; Page. (Pag.) QF*   43 SD] *Capell*

b, spelt backward with the horn on his head?   45
HOLOFERNES   Ba, *pueritia*, with a horn added.
MOTH   Ba, most silly sheep with a horn. You hear his
learning.
HOLOFERNES   *Quis*, *quis*, thou consonant?
MOTH   The last of the five vowels, if you repeat them; or   50
the fifth, if I.
HOLOFERNES   I will repeat them: a, e, i –
MOTH   The sheep. The other two concludes it: o, u.
ARMADO   Now, by the salt wave of the *Mediterraneum*, a
sweet touch, a quick venue of wit! Snip-snap, quick and   55
home! It rejoiceth my intellect. True wit!
MOTH   Offered by a child to an old man – which is wit-
old.
HOLOFERNES   What is the figure? What is the figure?
MOTH   Horns.   60

46 *pueritia* childishness, hence child
47 **Ba** Moth turns 'a, b, spelt backward' into 'baa', the cry of the sheep (*OED* baa *sb.* a). 'Ba' was also an onomatopoeic verb for kissing.
silly simple
49 *Quis* who; there may also be a pun on its contemporary pronunciation as 'kiss', referring back to 'ba'.
consonant a sound which, unlike a vowel, cannot form a syllable by itself, hence an insignificant person, a nonentity (Onions). This meaning is not recorded in *OED*.
50–3 **The last . . . o, u** Moth gets Holofernes to repeat the five vowels to identify the *silly sheep*. Moth stops him at 'i', i.e. himself. Moth then tricks Holofernes again with 'o, u', 'Oh, you' or 'Oh, ewe'.
53 **concludes** i.e. brings the list to an

end; proves my point
54 *Mediterraneum Mediterranean. Armado's use of the Lat. form ('*mare Mediterraneum*') may be practical rather than pedantic: *OED*'s earliest citation for the English form of the word (A. 2a) is 1594.
55 **touch** hit, blow (*OED sb.* 4b)
venue thrust, hit (*OED* 2b)
Snip-snap 'to snip-snap' was to indulge in smart repartee (*OED adv.**); see 3.1.19–20n.
55–6 **quick and home** i.e. by being quick you hit the target.
57–8 **wit-old** a pun on 'Wittold', a variant form of 'wittol', meaning a man who knows he is a cuckold and does nothing about it
59 **figure** as at 1.2.54n., rhetorical figure of speech (*OED sb.* 21a); emblem, type (*OED sb.* 12)

46 SP] *Q (Poda.), F   pueritia] QF (puericia)*   50 last] *QF;* third *Theobald*   54 salt wave] *F;* sault wane
Q   Mediterraneum] Rowe (subst.); meditaranium *Q;* mediteranium *F*   55 venue] *Dyce;* vene we *QF*

HOLOFERNES   Thou disputes like an infant. Go, whip thy
gig.

MOTH   Lend me your horn to make one and I will whip
about your infamy *manu cita*. A gig of a cuckold's horn!

COSTARD   An I had but one penny in the world, thou   65
shouldst have it to buy gingerbread. Hold, there is the
very remuneration I had of thy master, thou halfpenny
purse of wit, thou pigeon-egg of discretion. O, an the
heavens were so pleased that thou wert but my bastard,
what a joyful father wouldst thou make me! Go to, thou   70
hast it *ad dunghill*, at the fingers' ends, as they say.

HOLOFERNES   O, I smell false Latin: 'dunghill' for
unguem.

ARMADO   Arts-man, preambulate. We will be singuled

---

61 **disputes** For this form of the second
person singular, esp. in verbs ending in
't' or 'te', see Abbott, 340, and cf. *Thou
now requests*, 5.2.208.
whip spin (*OED v.* 6e*)
62 **gig** See 4.3.164n.; Furness cites
Halliwell as maintaining that tops were
made from the tips of horns.
63 **horn** Ard[1] questioned why Holofernes
should be accused of being a cuckold:
see 5.2.882–917n.
63–4 **whip . . . infamy** There may be a
sexual subtext to this, suggesting that
he will slip quickly about his 'shameful
parts', his genitals; Oxf[1] compares *2H4*
2.1.60, 'I'll tickle your catastrophe'.
64 ***manu cita** with a ready hand; cf.
3.1.57n.
65 **An** if
67 **remuneration** See 3.1.128n.
67–8 **halfpenny purse** small purse for
holding silver halfpennies; cf. *MW*
3.5.146–7, where Falstaff is said to be
unable to 'creep into a halfpenny

purse, nor into a pepper-box'.
68 **pigeon-egg** presumably meant as an
example of something very small
discretion discernment, sound judgement (*OED* 6a)
71–3 ***ad dunghill . . . unguem** Costard's
scatalogical corruption of '*Ad unguem*',
which means 'to the fingernail', i.e.
perfectly: the phrase comes from
sculpture. 'At one's fingers' ends' was
proverbial: see Tilley, F245.
71 **as they say** Costard uses the phrase
again at 5.2.500 and Armado at
5.2.527; cf. *as it were*, 4.2.14n.
74 **Arts-man** scholar, learned man (*OED*
2**); cf. *war-man* 5.2.657n. There may
be a pun on 'arse-man' and Armado's
and Holofernes' exchange (*dunghill . . .
fingers' ends . . . barbarous . . . charge-
house . . . mountain . . . pleasure . . . posteriors . . . culled . . . inward . . . excrement* and the many 'ass' sounds, see
87n.) may suggest banter about
sodomy and excretion.

---

61 disputes] *QF;* disputes't *F2*   64 *manu cita*] *Ard[2] (Cam); vnū cita Q; vnum cita F; circùm circà /
Theobald*   69 wert] *F;* wart *Q*   71 dunghill] *Theobald; dungil QF*   72 dunghill] *Theobald; dunghel
QF*   74 Arts-man,] *Theobald; Arts-man QF*   preambulate] *Cam; preambulat QF; preambulate Oxf*
singuled] singled *F*

from the barbarous. Do you not educate youth at the   75
charge-house on the top of the mountain?

HOLOFERNES   Or *mons*, the hill.

ARMADO   At your sweet pleasure, for the mountain.

HOLOFERNES   I do, *sans question*.

ARMADO   Sir, it is the King's most sweet pleasure and   80
affection to congratulate the Princess at her pavilion in
the posteriors of this day, which the rude multitude call
the afternoon.

HOLOFERNES   The posterior of the day, most generous
sir, is liable, congruent and measurable for the   85

---

74 *preambulate* walk, or go before
(with me). The QF reading '*Arts-man
preambulat*', meaning 'the arts-man
walks forth', is weak, mixing English
and Latin with both in italics and no
comma to separate them. Although the
emendation 'preambulate' antedates
OED's first citation by a decade or so
(*OED***), it is plausible and Oxf[1]
points out an identical usage in
Chapman's *An Humorous Day's Mirth*,
'Mistris will it please you to preambulate?' (1.3.50–1), which was first acted
in May 1597 and published in 1599.
   singuled singled out, distinguished; a
nonce-word, not in *OED* and unique
in Shakespeare: presumably formed
from 'singular'

75 **barbarous** uncultured, uncivilized;
related to buttocks and excrement
(Rubinstein, 21); not recorded as a
noun in *OED*
   educate teach (*OED* 2b*)

76–9 **charge-house ... *question*** Thomson,
72–3, argues that this passage derives
from one of Erasmus's colloquies,
between Georgius and Livinus: 'G. *Unde
prodis?* (Where do you come from?) L. *E
collegio Montis Acuti.* (From the college
with the sharp crest.) G. *Ergo ades nobis
onustus literis.* (So you come laden with
learning.) L. *Immo pediculis.* (No, with
lice).' Erasmus was alluding to his own

unhappy time at the Collège de Montaigu
in Paris. The homosexual drift of the conversation may include a pun on moun-
tain/mounting, for which cf. 4.1.4n.

76 **charge-house** house for the charging,
filling up or burdening, of youth, a
school (*OED* 1*, the only citation)

79 *sans* Fr. without; cf. 5.2.416.

81 **affection** disposition, inclination
(*OED sb.* 5); cf. 5.2.407n.
   congratulate salute (*OED v.* 5)
   pavilion Cf. 2.1.249n.

82 **posteriors** later part (*OED* B. 3*); this
and 84 are the only citations in *OED*,
which does not record 'posterior',
meaning buttocks, in English until 1619,
although the word existed in late Latin.
QF set both instances of the word in
italics, suggesting the word was understood as Latin. Ard[1] notes that in 1596
Harington (69) used 'Posteriorums' for
buttocks. With *posterior* in 111 these
three instances are Shakespeare's only
uses of the word, but cf. *Cor* 2.1.52,
'the buttock of the night'.
   rude multitude Cf. *2H6* 3.2.135.
   rude uneducated, ignorant

84 **generous** nobly born (*OED a.* 1a*); cf.
5.2.623n.

85 **liable** suitable, apt (*OED a.* 6)
   congruent congruous; see 1.2.13n.
   measurable fitting, proportionable
(*OED a.* 4)

82–4 posteriors . . . posterior] *Capell; posteriors . . . posterior QF*

afternoon. The word is well culled, choice, sweet and
apt, I do assure you, sir, I do assure.

ARMADO   Sir, the King is a noble gentleman, and my
familiar, I do assure ye, very good friend. For what is
inward between us, let it pass. I do beseech thee,   90
remember thy courtesy: I beseech thee, apparel thy
head. And among other importunate and most serious
designs, and of great import indeed too – but let that
pass. For I must tell thee it will please his grace, by the
world, sometime to lean upon my poor shoulder and   95
with his royal finger thus dally with my excrement,
with my mustachio. But, sweet heart, let that pass. By

86 **culled** chosen, selected; see 4.3.230n.;
cul in Fr. is defined by Cotgrave as '*An
arse, bumme, tayle, nockandroe, funda-
ment*'.

87 **assure** the first of a dense concentra-
tion (87–120) of 'ass' sounds – *assure*
three times (87, 89), *pass* five times (90,
94, 97, 101, 120), *assistance* twice (108,
112) and perhaps *grace* (94), *mustachio*
(97) – suggesting further puns relating
to sodomy and/or bodily functions

89 **familiar** close friend, intimate: the
word may be a noun on its own or an
adjective as part of *very good friend*.
I . . . ye See 4.2.9–10n.

90 **inward** private, secret

91 **remember thy courtesy** Be covered,
put your hat on again; cf. *Ham* 5.2.104
(*OED* remember *v.* 1d*).

92 ***importunate** burdensome, grave;
urgent. F's 'importunate' may be no
more than a guess to correct Q's
'importunt' and the easier emendation
to 'important' may be correct.

93 **designs** See 4.1.85n.
import consequence, significance
(*OED sb.* 2*)

93–4 **but . . . pass** Armado's use of the
phrase four times in the speech may be

significant: Shakespeare has it again
only in *MW* 1.4.15. Ard[1] points out
that Miso uses it in Sidney, *NA*, 210.
31, and suggests it was 'Probably a
common colloquialism': cf. to pass over
a thing or a matter (*OED* pass *v.* 67e).
In the context *but* and passing may suggest excretion (Rubinstein, 135).

94–5, 97–8 **by the world** See 4.3.16n.

96 **royal finger** The phrase only occurs
again in Shakespeare when Armado
uses it at 5.2.870.
thus For other examples of this kind
of reference (cf. Elam, 54), see esp.
5.2.100, 109, 585.
dally toy, play with (*OED v.* 2a)
excrement what grows out of the
body, i.e. hair, nails (*OED* excrement[2]
1*). The scatological sense of the word
is present.

97 **mustachio** moustache; the Q form
'mustachie' is probably an error, rather
than a variant form. The word derives
from Spanish *mostacho* and Italian
mostaccio. On the only other occasion
Shakespeare uses the word, *1H4*
2.1.75, it appears in QF in the form
adopted here.

86 choice] *F2* (choise*); chose *QF*   89 ye,] *Rowe*; ye *QF*   92 importunate] *F*; importunt *Q*; important *Collier (Capell)*   97 mustachio] *F*; mustachie *Q*

the world, I recount no fable! Some certain special
honours it pleaseth his greatness to impart to Armado,
a soldier, a man of travel, that hath seen the world. But   100
let that pass. The very all of all is – but, sweet heart, I
do implore secrecy – that the King would have me
present the Princess – sweet chuck – with some
delightful ostentation, or show, or pageant, or antic, or
firework. Now, understanding that the curate and your   105
sweet self are good at such eruptions and sudden
breaking-out of mirth, as it were, I have acquainted you
withal, to the end to crave your assistance.

HOLOFERNES   Sir, you shall present before her the Nine
Worthies. Sir Nathaniel, as concerning some enter-   110
tainment of time, some show in the posterior of this
day, to be rendered by our assistance, the King's
command and this most gallant, illustrate and learned
gentleman, before the Princess – I say, none so fit as to
present the Nine Worthies.   115

NATHANIEL   Where will you find men worthy enough to

101 **all of all** sum of everything
103 **chuck** chick, a term of endearment
     (*OED sb.*² 1*, citing 5.2.658)
104 **ostentation** show, display (*OED* 2c*,
     the only citation); cf. 5.2.409.
     antic grotesque pageant (*OED* B.
     3a*); the show of the Nine Worthies is
     not an antic: see 138.
105 **firework** firework display (*OED* 4c*)
106 **eruptions** outbreaks (*OED* 4*)
107 **as it were** Cf. 4.2.14n.
108 **withal** with this
109–10 **Nine Worthies** nine heroes,
     three from the Bible (Joshua, David
     and Judas Maccabaeus), three from the
     classics (Hector of Troy, Alexander the
     Great and Julius Caesar) and three

from romance (Arthur, Charlemagne
and Godfrey of Bouillon). They often
featured in pageants and entertainments. Before Shakespeare's play,
Pompey and Hercules are not known
to have been included among them.
Pompey suggests the pomp of 1.1.31
and the Pompion of 5.2.501; for
Hercules, see note on the play's title.
110–15 **Sir . . . Worthies** The syntax of
     this passage is hard to grasp: perhaps
     Holofernes is meant to be excited by
     his idea.
110–11 **entertainment**   occupation,
     spending (*OED* 7)
111 **posterior** Cf. 82n.
113 **illustrate** See 4.1.65n.

102 secrecy] *F;* secretie *Q*   110 Nathaniel] *Capell; Holofernes QF*   112 rendered] *F (*rendred*);*
rended *Q*   assistance] *Hanmer (Theobald);* assistants *QF*   114–15 as to present] *QF;* to present as
Hudson (Dyce)

present them?

HOLOFERNES Joshua, yourself; this gallant gentleman,
Judas Maccabaeus; this swain, because of his great
limb or joint, shall pass Pompey the Great; the page,　120
Hercules.

ARMADO Pardon, sir, error! He is not quantity enough for
that Worthy's thumb. He is not so big as the end of his
club.

HOLOFERNES Shall I have audience? He shall present　125
Hercules in minority. His enter and exit shall be

117 **present** represent (*OED v.* 7b*); cf.
5.2.531.

118–19 *****Joshua . . . Maccabaeus**
Holofernes' initial casting of the
pageant is clearly unsatisfactory in Q:
'*Iosua*, your selfe, my selfe, and this
gallant Gentleman *Iudas Machabeus*;'.
F tries to improve matters by changing the comma after 'your selfe' to a
semicolon. The Oxf reading, 'Joshua,
yourself; myself, Judas Maccabaeus;
and this gallant gentleman, Hector.', is
based on Proudfoot's suggestion that
either 'and this gallant Gentleman' or
'*Iudas Machabeus*' was misplaced by
the compositor and that '*Hector*' was
omitted – the error arising from inter-
lineation or through its being a marginal addition. Oxf's casting makes
sense, except that in 5.2, while
Holofernes and Armado appear as
Judas and Hector, Nathaniel is
Alexander, not Joshua. It is clear that
at some stage Shakespeare had difficulty with this passage and in the circumstances the omission of 'my selfe,
and' does less violence to the casting
than Oxf's solution. However, the
problem remains that Holofernes
assigns Judas to *this gallant gentleman*,

who is presumably Armado, whereas
Holofernes takes the part himself.
Shakespeare's difficulties with casting
may be connected to the tortuous syntax of 110–15: there may be an unin-
tended repetition in 'this most gallant,
illustrate and learned gentleman' and
'this gallant gentleman'.

Richard Proudfoot (privately) has
suggested a further solution, that F's
changed punctuation is correct, but
that after 'my selfe,' Holofernes pauses
and suppresses the fact that he intends,
as he announces at 134, to take three
roles.

119–20 **great limb . . . joint** Costard is
clearly a large man and there is a hint
here about how big his penis is: see also
1.2.169n., 5.2.505n. The pun on
Pompey/pumpy (cf. the pimp Pompey
Bum in *MM*) suggests his role is
appropriate; see also 5.2.546–55n.

120 **pass** pass for, hence be suitable for
the part of (Onions); this sense is not
properly recognized by *OED*, but see
also 87n.

125 **have audience** be given a hearing

126 **in minority** i.e. when a child
enter entrance; the latest citation in
OED sb. 1

118–19 yourself . . . Maccabaeus;] *Kerrigan;* your selfe, my selfe, and this gallant Gentleman *Iudas
Machabeus; QF (subst.);* yourself; myself, Alexander; this gallant gentleman, Judas Maccabæus;
Alexander; yourself; myself, Judas Maccabeus; and this gallant gentleman, Hector. *Oxf (Proudfoot,
privately)*

strangling a snake; and I will have an apology for that purpose.

MOTH   An excellent device! So if any of the audience hiss, you may cry, 'Well done, Hercules! Now thou crushest   130
the snake!' That is the way to make an offence gracious, though few have the grace to do it.

ARMADO   For the rest of the Worthies?

HOLOFERNES   I will play three myself.

MOTH   Thrice-worthy gentleman.   135

ARMADO   Shall I tell you a thing?

HOLOFERNES   We attend.

ARMADO   We will have, if this fadge not, an antic. I beseech you, follow.

HOLOFERNES   *Via*, goodman Dull! Thou hast spoken no   140
word all this while.

DULL   Nor understood none neither, sir.

HOLOFERNES   *Allons*! We will employ thee.

DULL   I'll make one in a dance, or so; or I will play on the tabor to the Worthies, and let them dance the hay.   145

HOLOFERNES   Most Dull, honest Dull! To our sport, away!   *Exeunt.*

---

127 **strangling a snake** Hercules strangled two snakes sent by Juno to kill him in his cradle.
   apology justification, explanation of the incident (*OED sb.* 2*)
129 **device** arrangement, plan (*OED* 6)
131 **gracious** acceptable, popular (*OED a.* 1)
138 **fadge not** does not succeed, fails to come off (*OED v.* 4)
   antic See 104.
140 *Via* come on, come along; see also 5.2.112 and cf. *3H6* 2.1.182.
143 **Allons* See 4.3.357n.

144 **make one** take part (*OED v.*[1] 26)
145 **tabor** small drum used to accompany a pipe or trumpet
   hay country dance with winding movement
146 **Most Dull** Oxf[1]'s emendation ('Most dull Dull') is attractive but not strictly necessary. An audience will not be able to tell whether Q's '*Dull*' is a name or an adjective. Holofernes may well intend a superlative form of the name as in Lat., for example, in '*Johnsonissimus*'.

143 *Allons*!] *Rowe;* Alone, *QF*   146 Most Dull] *QF;* Most dull Dull *Oxf[1]*   147 SD] *Exit. F*

234

[5.2]   *Enter the ladies* [*the* PRINCESS, ROSALINE, MARIA
                    and KATHERINE].

PRINCESS

Sweet hearts, we shall be rich ere we depart
If fairings come thus plentifully in.
A lady walled about with diamonds!
Look you what I have from the loving King.

ROSALINE

Madam, came nothing else along with that?   5

PRINCESS

Nothing but this? Yes, as much love in rhyme
As would be crammed up in a sheet of paper
Writ o'both sides the leaf, margin and all,
That he was fain to seal on Cupid's name.

ROSALINE

That was the way to make his godhead wax,   10
For he hath been five thousand year a boy.

KATHERINE

Ay, and a shrewd unhappy gallows too.

ROSALINE

You'll ne'er be friends with him: 'a killed your sister.

5.2.2 **fairings** gifts (*OED* 1b*); originally, those given at or brought from a fair. See 4.3.231n.
come . . . in come into hand as revenue or receipts (*OED* come *v.* 59i*)
3 a pendant or brooch with the picture of a lady surrounded by jewels; gifts of this kind were popular in Elizabeth's reign.
9 Navarre has covered every inch of the sheet, so that he was forced (*fain*) to apply his seal where the word *Cupid* was written; for the omission of 'so' before 'that', see Abbott, 283.
seal place or stamp his seal; in a sexual sense, beget, breed

10 **wax** grow, increase, with the suggestion of a growing penis; what the seal is made of
11 He has been a boy ever since the world was (supposedly) made: cf. Sidney, OA poem, 20.9–10.
12 **shrewd** mischievous, naughty (*OED a.* 1b)
unhappy trouble-making (*OED a.* 5a)
gallows gallows-bird, someone deserving to be hanged (*OED* 3*); cf. 507n.
13–15 **'a killed . . . died** The story of the sister who dies for love is not developed, but is reminiscent of Viola's in *TN* (2.4.107–15).

5.2] *Steevens*   0.1–2] *Capell (subst.)*   0.1 *the ladies*] *Q (subst.); Ladies F*   1+ SP PRINCESS] *Rowe; Quee. (Que., Qu.) QF*   3–4] *Pope; prose QF; transposed / Hudson (Walker)*   6 this?] *Rowe;* this: *QF*   8 o'] *Q (a);* on *F*   11 year] *Q (yeere);* yeeres *F*   13 ne'er] *F (nere);* neare *Q*

KATHERINE

He made her melancholy, sad and heavy;
And so she died. Had she been light, like you,   15
Of such a merry, nimble, stirring spirit,
She might ha' been a grandam ere she died.
And so may you, for a light heart lives long.

ROSALINE

What's your dark meaning, mouse, of this light word?

KATHERINE

A light condition in a beauty dark.   20

ROSALINE

We need more light to find your meaning out.

KATHERINE

You'll mar the light by taking it in snuff;
Therefore I'll darkly end the argument.

ROSALINE

Look what you do, you do it still i'th' dark.

KATHERINE

So do not you, for you are a light wench.   25

ROSALINE

Indeed I weigh not you, and therefore light.

KATHERINE

You weigh me not? O, that's you care not for me!

14 **heavy** weighed down with sorrow (*OED a.*[1] 27a)
15 **light** cheerful; wanton, unchaste: see 1.2.117n.
16 **stirring** lively, energetic (*OED ppl. a.* 2a)
17 **grandam** grandmother
18 **a . . . long** proverbial: see Dent, H320a.
19 **dark** hidden
   mouse a playful term of endearment; cf. *Ham* 3.4.183.
   light frivolous
20 **light condition** wanton disposition, unchaste character (*OED* condition *sb.* 11a)

22 **taking . . . snuff** taking offence at it; proverbial, see Tilley, S598. By trimming or snuffing the wick of the candle the light is put out and the burned wick's unpleasant smell is avoided.
24 **Look what** whatever: an indefinite relative, not an imperative
   do it have sex
25 Katherine implies Rosaline is unchaste, but also that she does not even bother to hide her sexual activities.
26 **weigh not you** don't balance you, don't weigh as much as you do. Katherine takes it in the sense of 'esteem', 'value' (*OED v.*[1] 13a).

15–18] *F2; prose QF*   17 been a] *F (*bin a*);* bin *Q*   22 You'll] *F;* Yole *Q*

ROSALINE

Great reason, for past cure is still past care.

PRINCESS

Well bandied both! A set of wit well played.

But, Rosaline, you have a favour too: 30

Who sent it? And what is it?

ROSALINE   I would you knew.

An if my face were but as fair as yours,

My favour were as great. Be witness this:

Nay, I have verses too, I thank Berowne;

The numbers true, and, were the numbering too,   35

I were the fairest goddess on the ground.

I am compared to twenty thousand fairs.

O, he hath drawn my picture in his letter!

PRINCESS

Anything like?

ROSALINE

Much in the letters, nothing in the praise.   40

---

28 *past cure . . . care** It is not worth worrying about what cannot be made better; proverbial: see Dent, C921. Theobald's emendation, reversing QF's 'past care, is still past cure', is generally accepted, but cf. the punning inversion in *Son* 147.9, 'Past cure I am, now reason is past care'.

29 For the Princess the exchanges between Rosaline and Katherine are like a game of tennis or bandy (*OED* set *sb.*[1] 26).

30 **favour** token of love (*OED sb.* 7a). Favours are exchanged at 130–4 and 292; for the jewel on Rosaline's sleeve, see 455ff. and, for another favour, see 710.

31 **I . . . knew** Although she holds it up for the others to see ('Be witness this'), the nature of Rosaline's favour is never made clear: she may imply that it is smaller or less valuable than the Princess's.

33 **favour** appearance (*OED sb.* 9a)

35 **numbers true** metre correct; see 4.2.121n.

numbering reckoning, enumeration (*OED* number *v.* 2a)

37 **fairs** fair women (*OED* B. *sb.*[2] 2)

40 i.e. the lettering, the forms of the letters, are an accurate reflection of Rosaline's appearance, probably because being black ink (41) on white paper they reflect her dark hair against her white skin; but in what is said, *the praise*, the letter's contents are inaccurate. *Nothing* may anticipate Rosaline's subsequent exclamation 'O', her reference to 'O's, with a pun on 'nothing' as the vagina, and the Princess's allusion to the pox.

---

28 cure . . . care] *Theobald (Thirlby)*; care . . . cure *QF*

237

PRINCESS
Beauteous as ink: a good conclusion.
KATHERINE
Fair as a text B in a copy-book.
ROSALINE
'Ware pencils, ho! Let me not die your debtor,
My red dominical, my golden letter.
O, that your face were not so full of O's!   45
PRINCESS
A pox of that jest and I beshrew all shrews.
But, Katherine, what was sent to you from fair Dumaine?

41 **Beauteous as ink** Cf. the proverbial 'As black as ink', Tilley, I73.

42 **text B** a capital B written in a large fine hand (*OED* text *sb.*[1] 5*); since the letter uses a good deal of black ink, Katherine is saying that Rosaline is not at all fair. 'B' is also the first letter of Berowne's name.
copy-book writing manual (*OED* 2a*)

43–4 For the rhyme, see 5.1.21–2n.

43 **'Ware pencils, ho** Rosaline's cry imitates ''Ware riot, ho' used as a hunting cry: see *OED* riot *sb.* 3a and Harington, 222.
'Ware beware
pencils small fine paintbrushes, used by artists and by women to apply cosmetics
Let . . . debtor Let me repay your insult; cf. the proverbial 'I will not die in your debt', Tilley, D165.

44 **red dominical** The dominical letter is one or two of seven letters (A–G) used to denote the days on which Sunday falls in particular years (*OED* dominical B. 2*): in almanacs and suchlike they were printed in red. Rosaline is referring to Katherine's ruddy complexion. As Katherine's choice of 'B' may have stood for Berowne, Rosaline's

alliteration on 'd' (*die . . . debtor . . . red dominical . . . golden*) may hint at Dumaine. There is some joking about dominical letters and what they stand for in *2 Return from Parnassus*, 1065–72 (Leishman, 291).
golden letter It is possible that while her mind is on the calendar Rosaline confuses the golden letter with the golden number, the number of the year in the Metonic cycle used for finding the date of Easter. But it is more likely that the letter is the dominical and that *golden* here means red as in Duncan's 'golden blood', *Mac* 2.3.112 (*OED* red A. 3a–b).

45 **O's** probably smallpox scars (*OED* O *sb.*[1] 2a*)

46 **A pox . . . jest** In cursing the joke, the Princess acknowledges its force (*OED* pox *sb.* 3); cf. the proverbial 'A pox on these true jests', Dent, P537.
I . . . shrews I wish a plague on all scolds; QF 'Shrowes' (a perfectly acceptable variant form) preserves the rhyme with *O's*.

47–8 For the lines to scan correctly *Katherine* must be considered as an extrametrical vocative: the couplet is followed by a short line.

43 pencils] *Q* (pensalls*), F* (pensals*)* ho!] *Hanmer;* How? *QF* 45 not so] *om. F* 46 SP] *QF;* Katharine *Kittredge (subst.)* jest and I] *QF;* jest! and *Capell;* jest; I *Oxf* shrews] *QF* (Shrowes*);* shrows *Kittredge* 47] *Theobald; QF line* you / Dumaine? / Katherine] *QF; om. Theobald*

KATHERINE

Madam, this glove.

PRINCESS   Did he not send you twain?

KATHERINE

Yes, madam, and moreover

Some thousand verses of a faithful lover.   50

A huge translation of hypocrisy,

Vilely compiled, profound simplicity.

MARIA

This and these pearls to me sent Longaville.

The letter is too long by half a mile.

PRINCESS

I think no less. Dost thou not wish in heart   55

The chain were longer and the letter short?

MARIA

Ay, or I would these hands might never part.

PRINCESS

We are wise girls to mock our lovers so.

ROSALINE

They are worse fools to purchase mocking so.

That same Berowne I'll torture ere I go.   60

O that I knew he were but in by th' week!

How I would make him fawn, and beg, and seek,

And wait the season, and observe the times,

51 A 'monstrous transformation of hypocrisy into words, i.e. great pack of lies', Oxf[1] (*OED* translation 2b*)
52 **compiled** heaped together (*OED v.* 5); see 4.3.131n.
    profound simplicity deeply silly (*OED* profound *a.* 3b**); learned silliness, an oxymoron
54 **too . . . mile** perhaps proverbial: cf. Dent, M924.1, and see *OED* mile *sb.*[1] 1d*.
57 Presumably Maria uses the chain, which may have been made up of

pearls or with pearls attached to it, to bind her hands.
59 **purchase** buy, procure
60 **torture** torment, make him suffer (*OED v.* 2*)
61 **in . . . week** ensnared, caught deeply in love; proverbial: see Tilley, W244, and *OED* week *sb.* 6a.
63 **wait the season** i.e. wait until the moment suits me
    observe the times keep to what seems proper to me

53, 57 SP] *F (Mar.); Marg. Q*   53 pearls] *F;* Pearle *Q*   55 not] *om. F*

And spend his prodigal wits in bootless rhymes,
And shape his service wholly to my hests,   65
And make him proud to make me proud that jests!
So pair-taunt-like would I o'ersway his state,
That he should be my fool, and I his fate.

PRINCESS

None are so surely caught, when they are catched,
As wit turned fool. Folly, in wisdom hatched,   70
Hath wisdom's warrant and the help of school
And wit's own grace to grace a learned fool.

ROSALINE

The blood of youth burns not with such excess
As gravity's revolt to wantonness.

---

64 **spend . . . wits** See 2.1.19n.
   bootless fruitless
65 ***hests** QF's 'deuice' does not rhyme:
   the error could possibly lie in *jests*, but
   it is hard to think of a monosyllabic
   verb that rhymes with 'device' to
   replace it. *Hests* fits well here, although
   Shakespeare used the noun only once
   in the plural elsewhere (*Tem*) and three
   times in the singular (twice again in
   Tem and once in *1H4*); the error may
   be compositorial, but may reflect an
   authorial oversight.
66 i.e. to make Berowne so abject that he is
   proud to make Rosaline feel proud about
   her jests aimed against him; there may
   be a sexual pun on *proud* meaning erect.
67 ***pair-taunt-like** Many emendations
   have been proposed for Q's 'perttaunt
   like' and F's 'pertaunt like': these are
   discussed in Wells, *Re-Editing*, 34–5,
   and can be supplemented by Oxf[1]'s
   'fortune-like'. The crux has most commonly been explained by reference to
   the card game Post and Pair (*OED post
   sb.*[4] b), in which a pair-royal is three

cards of the same value and double
pair-royal or pair-taunt is four cards of
the same value (four aces or kings,
etc.). *OED*, however, suggests that Post
and Pair is played only with hands of
three cards and does not record 'pair-
taunt'. If *pair-taunt-like* is correct,
Rosaline means that she will always
hold a better hand than Berowne. The
phrase *taunt pour taunt* (*OED* taunt *sb.*[1]
1), meaning like for like, tit for tat, may
possibly lie behind what Rosaline says.
   o'ersway rule, domineer over (*OED*
   oversway *v.* 1a)
68 **fate** *OED sb.* 1b*
69 **catched** captivated, charmed (*OED v.*
   37a)
70–8 The exchange is reminiscent of the
   subject-matter of Erasmus's *The
   Praise of Folly*.
70 **hatched** originating, deriving (*OED
   v.*[1] 6a)
72 **to grace** to adorn, embellish (*OED v.*
   4a); cf. 1.1.3n.
74 **revolt** change of sides, relapse (*OED
   sb.*[1] 1c**)

---

65 hests] *Dyce (Knight);* deuice *QF*   67 pair-taunt-like] *Q (*perttaunt like*), F (*pertaunt like*);* Pair-
Taunt like *Ard*[2] *(Simpson, TLS);* planet-like *Cam*[1] *(Moore Smith, privately);* pursuivant-like *Oxf;*
fortune-like *Oxf*[1]   70 fool.] *F2 (*foole.*);* Foole, *QF*   hatched,] *F2;* hatcht: *QF*   74 wantonness] *F2*
*(*wantonesse*);* wantons be *QF*

MARIA

Folly in fools bears not so strong a note 75
As foolery in the wise when wit doth dote,
Since all the power thereof it doth apply
To prove, by wit, worth in simplicity.

Enter BOYET.

PRINCESS

Here comes Boyet, and mirth is in his face.

BOYET

O, I am stabbed with laughter! Where's her grace? 80

PRINCESS

Thy news, Boyet?

BOYET   Prepare, madam, prepare!
Arm, wenches, arm! Encounters mounted are
Against your peace. Love doth approach disguised,
Armed in arguments: you'll be surprised.
Muster your wits, stand in your own defence, 85
Or hide your heads like cowards and fly hence.

PRINCESS

Saint Denis to Saint Cupid! What are they
That charge their breath against us? Say, scout, say.

75 **note** stigma
77–8 'i.e. since the wise man turned fool will avail himself of all the intelligence he has to show that folly is true wisdom' (Oxf[1]); since all the misapplied wit proves is the virtue of simplicity. See 2.1.122n.
80 *stabbed i.e. feel as though I have been wounded
    grace See 1.1.51n.
82 **Encounters mounted are** skirmishes are on the way
82–8 **mounted . . . charge** Ard[1] compares *KJ* 2.1.381–2, 'mount / Their battering cannon charged to the

mouths'.
84 **Armed** armèd
    surprised attacked without warning (*OED v.* 2a); taken prisoner (*OED v.* 2b)
85 **Muster your wits** gather up your ideas; gather up your clever companions (*OED* muster *v.*[1] 3b*); cf. 2.1.1n.
87 **Saint Denis** the patron saint of France
    to For *to* meaning against, see Abbott, 187.
    Saint Cupid See 4.3.340n.
88 **charge** Both senses apply to guns: load (*OED v.* 5 *fig.**, the only citation); level, aim (*OED v.* 21a).
    scout spy

79 is] *om. F*   80 stabbed] *F (*stab'd*); stable Q*   83 peace.] *Theobald (subst.); Peace, F; Peace Q*

BOYET

Under the cool shade of a sycamore
I thought to close mine eyes some half an hour,   90
When, lo, to interrupt my purposed rest,
Toward that shade I might behold addressed
The King and his companions. Warily
I stole into a neighbour thicket by
And overheard what you shall overhear: 95
That, by and by, disguised they will be here.
Their herald is a pretty knavish page
That well by heart hath conned his embassage.
Action and accent did they teach him there:
'Thus must thou speak and thus thy body bear.'   100
And ever and anon they made a doubt
Presence majestical would put him out;
'For', quoth the King, 'an angel shalt thou see;
Yet fear not thou, but speak audaciously.'

---

89 **sycamore** *OED* 2*; for the tree's melancholy associations, see Desdemona's
'willow' song in *Oth* 4.3.40, but more
generally sitting under trees was
thought to be a melancholy occupation:
see *AYL* 2.7.111 and Sidney, *OA*, 71.33.
92 **might behold addressed** could see
directing themselves (*OED* address *v.* 6b)
93–5 **Warily . . . overhear** Boyet's overhearing from a thicket is like the overhearing that took place in 4.3.
94 **thicket** Cf. 4.2.58.
95 **overheard** See 4.3.127n.
overhear hear told over again, a
nonce-use (*OED v.* 4*)
96 **by and by** before long, soon
97 **knavish** The epithet is perhaps more
suitable for Costard than for Moth (see
3.1.140, 148), but suggests Moth's
impertinence or cheekiness.
98 **conned his embassage** learned his

message
99 **Action and accent** In rhetoric, *action*
involved the speaker's suiting gesture
to the subject described (*OED* 6a), as
in Hamlet's 'Suit the action to the
word, the word to the action'
(3.2.17–18), while *accent* refers to the
speaker's control of tone and stress.
101 **made a doubt** expressed their fear
that
102 **majestical** See 5.1.11n.
put him out disconcert, confuse,
embarrass him (*OED v.*[1] 47f (*b*)*), with
the implication that he then forgets his
lines. Cf. 5.2.150, 152, 165, 336, 478,
Cor 5.3.40–2, 'Like a dull actor now / I
have forgot my part, and I am out, /
Even to a full disgrace', and the actor in
Son 23.2 who is 'put besides his part'.
104 **audaciously** boldly (*OED adv.* 1*);
cf. 5.1.4n.

---

89 sycamore] *Q (Siccamone)*, *F (Siccamore)*   93 companions. Warily] *F (subst.)*; companions
warely, *Q*   96 they] *F*; thy *Q*   97 page] *Capell (page,)*; Page: *QF*   98 embassage.] *Rowe*; embassage
Q; embassage, *F*   101 doubt] *Collier*; doubt, *QF*

The boy replied, 'An angel is not evil;   105
I should have feared her had she been a devil.'
With that all laughed and clapped him on the shoulder,
Making the bold wag by their praises bolder.
One rubbed his elbow thus, and fleered, and swore
A better speech was never spoke before.   110
Another with his finger and his thumb
Cried, '*Via*, we will do't, come what will come!'
The third he capered and cried, 'All goes well!'
The fourth turned on the toe, and down he fell.
With that they all did tumble on the ground,   115
With such a zealous laughter, so profound,
That in this spleen ridiculous appears,
To check their folly, passion's solemn tears.

PRINCESS

But what, but what, come they to visit us?

BOYET

They do, they do, and are apparelled thus,   120
Like Muscovites, or Russians, as I guess.
Their purpose is to parley, court and dance,
And every one his love-suit will advance

---

109 **rubbed his elbow** a sign of pleasure
and satisfaction (*OED* elbow 4d*); the
phrase became proverbial, Dent, E100,
and cf. *1H4* 5.1.76–8.
fleered grinned
111 **with . . . thumb** snapping his fingers
112 *Via* See 5.1.140n.
come . . . come proverbial: see Dent,
C529.
113 **capered** danced playfully (*OED v.*[1] a*)
117 **spleen ridiculous** ludicrous merriment (*OED* spleen *sb.* 3); cf. 3.1.73n.
121 **Muscovites, or Russians** Shakespeare may anticipate or echo the ambassador 'from the mighty Emperor of
Russia and *Moscovy*' who appeared in

the Gray's Inn revels celebrating
Twelfth Night in 1595, *Gesta Grayorum*,
44; cf. *AS*, 2.10, 'slave-borne *Muscovite*'.
Parolles thinks that his foreign-speaking
captors belong to the 'Muskos' regi-
ment' (*AW* 4.1.69), suggesting that they
are Muscovites. See Introduction, p. 15.
guess The absence of a rhyme-word
for this line may suggest that a line is
missing before or after it; see 215n.
123 ***love-suit** QF's 'Loue-feat', meaning
an act of love, is strained and implausi-
ble; although *love-suit* is not recorded
in *OED*, it may be picked up in the *suit*
of 129; the compound also occurs in
Son 136.4, *H5* 5.2.101, *Cym* 3.4.133.

---

111 thumb] *Q* (thume), *F*   118 folly,] *Pope;* follie *QF*   solemn] *Q* (solembe), *F*   120 apparelled]
Q (appariled), *F*   121] *omission marked before this line Oxf*   122 parley, court] *Rowe;* parlee, to court
QF; parle, to court *Capell*   123 love-suit] *Halliwell;* Loue-feat *QF*

Unto his several mistress, which they'll know
By favours several which they did bestow.　　　　　125

PRINCESS

And will they so? The gallants shall be tasked;
For, ladies, we will every one be masked,
And not a man of them shall have the grace,
Despite of suit, to see a lady's face.
Hold, Rosaline, this favour thou shalt wear,　　　　130
And then the King will court thee for his dear.
Hold, take thou this, my sweet, and give me thine,
So shall Berowne take me for Rosaline.
And change you favours too; so shall your loves
Woo contrary, deceived by these removes.　　　　135

ROSALINE

Come on, then, wear the favours most in sight.

KATHERINE

But in this changing what is your intent?

PRINCESS

The effect of my intent is to cross theirs.
They do it but in mockery merriment,
And mock for mock is only my intent.　　　　140

---

124 **several** respective
126 **gallants** lover, suitors; cf. 308, 363.
　　tasked tried, tested; cf. 2.1.20n.
128 **grace** privilege, permission
129 **suit** asking, suing; wooing, courting
　　(as in *love-suit*); suit of (Russian)
　　clothes
130–1 Oxf omits these lines on the
　　grounds that they are a first version of
　　132–3, but the second modifies the
　　first pair of lines and they undoubted-
　　ly help to make the plan clearer.
134 **change** exchange
135 **removes** exchanges (*OED sb.* 3a)
136 **most in sight** very conspicuously

139 **mockery** mocking (the F reading);
　　cf. *R2* 4.1.260, 'a mockery king of
　　snow'.
　　merriment bit of mirth, fun (*OED*
　　2a*); the word is used for the
　　Muscovite device, the show of the
　　Worthies and more generally for the
　　courtship: see 461, 712, 778. Cf. *merry
　　mocking*, 2.1.52.
140 Cf. the proverbial 'He who mocks
　　shall be mocked', Dent, M1031; the
　　line also includes the sense of *mock*
　　meaning to ridicule by imitation (*OED
　　v.* 4a); see also 887n.

---

127 ladies,] *F4;* Ladies; *QF* 　130–1] *QF; relegated to 'Additional Passages' Oxf (Riv)* 　134 you]
your *F* 　too] *F;* two *Q* 　139 mockery] *Q (mockerie);* mocking *F*

Their several counsels they unbosom shall
To loves mistook, and so be mocked withal
Upon the next occasion that we meet,
With visages displayed to talk and greet.

ROSALINE

But shall we dance if they desire us to't?   145

PRINCESS

No, to the death we will not move a foot;
Nor to their penned speech render we no grace,
But while 'tis spoke each turn away her face.

BOYET

Why, that contempt will kill the speaker's heart
And quite divorce his memory from his part.   150

PRINCESS

Therefore I do it, and I make no doubt
The rest will e'er come in, if he be out.
There's no such sport as sport by sport o'erthrown,
To make theirs ours and ours none but our own.
So shall we stay, mocking intended game,   155
And they, well mocked, depart away with shame.

Sound trumpet.

BOYET

The trumpet sounds. Be masked. The maskers come.

141 **counsels** secret purposes (*OED sb.* 5a)
  unbosom reveal (*OED v.* 1a*)
146 **to . . . not** i.e. we'd rather die than;
  Ard¹ compares *R3* 3.2.55.
147 **penned** written out with a pen for
  the occasion; cf. 305.
  render pay, show (*OED v.* 12)
149 **kill . . . heart** i.e. depress or discour-
  age him completely (*OED* kill *v.* 7c);
  cf. *WT* 4.3.83.
152 **e'er** F2's negative is unnecessary,
  given the force of 'I make no doubt'.
  out nonplussed, puzzled (*OED adv.*
20a*); cf. 102n.
153 For another paradoxical description
  of sport, see 514n.
154 **theirs ours** their sport our sport
157 **Be masked** If the ladies put on their
  masks here, it is not absolutely clear
  where in this part of the scene they
  take them off: *Dismasked* (296) or
  known (301) may suggest moments
  when they remove them – this could
  be done when the lords leave at 264,
  but it need not be done at all.

141 Their] *Q (text of sig. G3v)*, F; The *Q (sig. G3r c.w.)*   142 withal] *Dyce;* withall. *QF*   148 her]
F2; his *QF*   149 speaker's] *Q (*speakers*);* keepers *F*   151 doubt] *Rowe³;* doubt, *QF*   152 e'er] *QF*
*(*ere*);* ne're *F2*   155 stay,] *Theobald;* stay *QF*   156 SD] *Q (Sound Trom.);* Sound. *F*

*Enter Blackamoors with music, [MOTH,] the Boy, with a speech,
and the rest of the lords disguised.*

MOTH

All hail the richest beauties on the earth!

BOYET

Beauties no richer than rich taffeta.

MOTH

A holy parcel of the fairest dames   160
(The ladies turn their backs to him.)
That ever turned their – backs – to mortal views.

BEROWNE

Their eyes, villain, *their eyes.*

MOTH

That ever turned their eyes to mortal views.
Out –

BOYET

True! Out indeed!   165

MOTH

Out of your favours, heavenly spirits, vouchsafe
Not to behold –

BEROWNE

Once to behold, rogue!

MOTH

Once to behold with your sun-beamed eyes –
With your sun-beamed eyes –   170

157.1 **Blackamoors** QF's '*Black-moores*'
are variant forms of 'blackamoor',
which was already in use by 1581,
meaning any very dark-skinned person: see 4.3.115n. The sun-burned
Blackamoors contrast with the frozen
Muscovites. Cf. Queen Helen's coach
in Sidney, *NA*, 58.10, and see
Introduction, p. 14.

159 SP* 5.2.336 explains that it was
Boyet and not QF's Berowne who put
Moth out of his part.
   taffeta The glossy silk material was
used for making masks; cf. 406.
160 **parcel** collection, company (*OED sb.*
6a)
169, 170 **sun-beamed** sun-beamèd; *OED*
sunbeam *adjs.**

157.1 *Blackamoors*] *QF (Black-moores)*   158–73 SP MOTH] *Rowe; Page. (Pag.) QF*   159 SP] *Theobald;
Berow. QF*   160–1] *Theobald; prose QF*   160 SD] *QF in roman, centred and after 161*   161 *their – backs
– to*] *Capell; their backes to QF*   163 *ever*] *F; euen Q*

BOYET

    They will not answer to that epithet.

    You were best call it 'daughter-beamed eyes'.

MOTH

    They do not mark me and that brings me out.

BEROWNE

    Is this your perfectness? Be gone, you rogue!   [*Exit Moth.*]

ROSALINE

    What would these strangers? Know their minds, Boyet.   175

    If they do speak our language, 'tis our will

    That some plain man recount their purposes.

    Know what they would.

BOYET   What would you with the Princess?

BEROWNE

    Nothing but peace and gentle visitation.

ROSALINE

    What would they, say they?   180

BOYET

    Nothing but peace and gentle visitation.

ROSALINE

    Why, that they have, and bid them so be gone.

BOYET

    She says you have it and you may be gone.

KING

    Say to her, we have measured many miles

    To tread a measure with her on this grass.   185

171 **epithet** See 1.2.14n.

172 **daughter-beamed** daughter-beamèd; punning on sun-/son-beamèd

173 **mark** pay attention to
brings puts; see 272n.

174 **perfectness** word-perfectness

175 **strangers** foreigners; cf. 4.2.129.

177 **plain** straightforward, plain-speak-

ing (*OED adj.* 12a)

179, 181 **gentle visitation** courteous and friendly call (*OED* visitation 5a); Ard[1] points out that Shakespeare always uses this word and never 'visit', which *OED* first records as a noun in 1621.

184 **measured** travelled

185 **tread a measure** dance a slow and stately dance (*OED* measure *sb.* 20a)

171 epithet] *Q* (Epythat*)*, *F* (Epythite*)* 174 SD] *Capell (subst.)* 175] *Pope; QF line* stranges? / *Boyet.* / strangers] *Q* (stranges*)*, *F* 185 her] you *F*

BOYET

They say that they have measured many a mile
To tread a measure with you on this grass.

ROSALINE

It is not so. Ask them how many inches
Is in one mile? If they have measured many,
The measure then of one is easily told.   190

BOYET

If to come hither you have measured miles,
And many miles, the Princess bids you tell
How many inches doth fill up one mile.

BEROWNE

Tell her we measure them by weary steps.

BOYET

She hears herself.

ROSALINE   How many weary steps,   195
Of many weary miles you have o'ergone,
Are numbered in the travel of one mile?

BEROWNE

We number nothing that we spend for you.
Our duty is so rich, so infinite,
That we may do it still without account.   200
Vouchsafe to show the sunshine of your face,
That we like savages may worship it.

ROSALINE

My face is but a moon and clouded too.

KING

Blessed are clouds, to do as such clouds do.

---

190 **told** counted; said
194–5 **Tell . . . herself** Berowne's brief taking over of the King's part may provoke Boyet's abandoning the role of interpreter.
197 **travel** Q's 'trauaile' (F 'trauell') includes the sense of weary labour as well as of travelling.
198 **number** reckon up
200 **still** always, ever

account counting
201–2 See 4.3.218n.
203 i.e. Rosaline's light is not her own but only reflected from the sun of the Princess
clouded i.e. masked
204 How lucky are the masks which are so close and so which kiss the ladies' faces; cf. *RJ* 1.1.230, 'These happy masks that kiss fair ladies' brows', and, for the clouds, see 297n.

Vouchsafe, bright moon, and these thy stars, to shine –   205
Those clouds removed – upon our watery eyne.

ROSALINE

O vain petitioner! Beg a greater matter:
Thou now requests but moonshine in the water.

KING

Then, in our measure, do but vouchsafe one change.
Thou biddest me beg: this begging is not strange.   210

ROSALINE

Play music then! Nay, you must do it soon.   [*Music plays.*]
Not yet? No dance! Thus change I like the moon.

KING

Will you not dance? How come you thus estranged?

ROSALINE

You took the moon at full, but now she's changed.

KING

Yet still she is the moon and I the man.   215
The music plays, vouchsafe some motion to it.

---

205 **moon . . . stars** Cf. the proverbial 'To be like the stars to the moon', Dent, S826.2, and the King's imagery at 4.3.226–7n.

206 **watery eyne** tearful, weeping eyes: *eyne* is a common spelling variant; cf. *TS* Ind. 1.128.

208 **Thou now requests** See 5.1.61n.
moonshine . . . water nothing at all, something completely insubstantial; proverbial: see Tilley, M1128.

209 **change** round of dancing (*OED sb.* 1c*, the only citation, but see Marston, *Malcontent*, 5.6.86.2); changing of the moon

210 **strange** odd, abnormal

212 **Thus . . . moon** proverbial: see Tilley, M1111.

213 **estranged** kept apart. The King puns on *strange* in 210.

215 i.e. they are naturally linked like the moon and the man in the moon, who was proverbial: see Dent, M240, and cf. 'You are *ipse* (he, the man)', Dent, I88; *still* implies always, but also that the moon does not change (see 1.1.14n.). The man in the moon had three unfortunate biblical associations: with Isaac, who carried sticks for his own sacrifice (Genesis, 22.1–14); with Cain and his unworthy offering to God (Genesis, 4.3–9); and with the sabbath-breaking gatherer of sticks who was stoned to death (Numbers 15.32–6).
man Again, there is no rhyme-word for this; see 121n.

216 **motion** movement, i.e. dancing; sympathetic response, i.e. the condition of having one's emotions moved by something. The King intends the first of these, but Rosaline understands the second.

---

209 do but vouchsafe] vouchsafe but *F*   211 SD] *Capell (subst.)*   212 yet?] *Theobald;* yet *QF*
214 changed.] *F4;* changed? *QF*   215] *omission marked after this line Oxf*   216–17] *prose F*   216 The]
Theobald; Rosa. The *QF*   it.] *Theobald;* it, *Q;* it: *F*

249

ROSALINE

    Our ears vouchsafe it.

KING   But your legs should do it.

ROSALINE

    Since you are strangers and come here by chance,

    We'll not be nice. Take hands. We will not dance.

KING

    Why take we hands then?

ROSALINE   Only to part friends.   220

    Curtsy, sweet hearts, and so the measure ends. [*Music stops.*]

KING

    More measure of this measure! Be not nice.

ROSALINE

    We can afford no more at such a price.

KING

    Price you yourselves. What buys your company?

ROSALINE

    Your absence only.

KING   That can never be.   225

ROSALINE

    Then cannot we be bought. And so adieu –

    Twice to your visor and half once to you!

KING

    If you deny to dance, let's hold more chat.

ROSALINE

    In private then.

---

219 **nice** shy, coy (*OED a.* 5a)

220–1 **Only . . . ends** Rosaline only lets the dance go as far as the taking of hands and a curtsy at its beginning.

222 **More measure** a larger quantity, i.e. so that they can get on to the kiss which traditionally follows the curtsy

224 **Price you** fix your own value on.

QF's 'Prise' may represent 'Prize' rather than 'Price'.

227 The line's meaning is obscure: perhaps Rosaline curtsies once each to the visor and to the face behind it and more briefly to the King himself.

228 **deny** refuse (*OED v.* 8)

    chat See 4.3.280.

217 SP ROSALINE] *Theobald; not in QF* 219 nice.] *Collier;* nice, *QF* 220 we] you *F* 221 SD] *Oxf¹ (subst.)* 222 ²measure!] *Q (*measue*), F* 224 you] *om. F*

KING   I am best pleased with that.

[*They converse apart.*]

BEROWNE

White-handed mistress, one sweet word with thee.   230

PRINCESS

Honey, and milk, and sugar: there is three.

BEROWNE

Nay then, two treys, an if you grow so nice,

Metheglin, wort and malmsey. Well run, dice!

There's half-a-dozen sweets.

PRINCESS   Seventh sweet, adieu.

Since you can cog, I'll play no more with you.   235

BEROWNE

One word in secret.

PRINCESS   Let it not be sweet.

BEROWNE

Thou griev'st my gall.

PRINCESS   Gall? Bitter.

BEROWNE   Therefore meet.

[*They converse apart.*]

DUMAINE

Will you vouchsafe with me to change a word?

MARIA

Name it.

---

230 **White-handed** *OED* white *a.* 12c*;
see 3.1.163n.

231 All proverbially sweet: see Tilley,
H544, M930.1, Dent, S957.1. Colie,
93–5, points out the literary-critical
terms that lie behind Berowne's
exchange here and in 237: 'Sonnets are
mel, honey, sugar, sweetness; epigrams
are salt, vinegar, or gall'.

232 **treys** threes, a throw of three at dice
nice shy, coy

233 **Metheglin . . . malmsey** three

strong sweet drinks. Metheglin was a
Welsh drink made from honey and
spices; wort was sweet unfermented
beer and malmsey a strong sweet wine.

235 **cog** cheat, esp. associated with cheating at dice

237 **gall** sore or wound produced by rubbing; bile, whose bitterness was
proverbial: see Tilley, G11.
meet fitting, appropriate

238 **change** exchange

229, 237, 241, 255 SDs] *Capell (subst.)*   234–5 Seventh . . . you.] *Rowe³; QF line* cogg, / you. /
237 griev'st] *F (*gree'ust*); greeuest Q

DUMAINE   Fair lady –

MARIA   Say you so? Fair lord!
Take that for your 'fair lady'.

DUMAINE   Please it you,   240
As much in private and I'll bid adieu.
[*They converse apart.*]

KATHERINE
What, was your visor made without a tongue?

LONGAVILLE
I know the reason, lady, why you ask.

KATHERINE
O, for your reason! Quickly, sir, I long.

LONGAVILLE
You have a double tongue within your mask   245
And would afford my speechless visor half.

KATHERINE
'Veal', quoth the Dutchman. Is not veal a calf?

LONGAVILLE
A calf, fair lady.

KATHERINE   No, a fair lord calf.

242–7 See 1.1.61–6n.

242 **tongue** a leather strap inserted in the mouth and designed to hold the mask in place (*OED sb.* 14f); but Katherine is also asking why Longaville is so silent. Cf. 1.1.123n.

245–6 i.e. having your own tongue and the mask's tongue, you are being two-tongued, deceptive or ambiguous, and would do well to give me one of them, which would stop my being so silent – giving him the mask's tongue would reveal who she is

246–9 For the rhyme, see 5.1.21–2n.

247 **Veal . . . Dutchman** 'The Dutchman is trying to say "well", which represents Katharine's sarcastic

judgement on Longaville's *reason*. At the same time, *Veal* puns on "veil" (often spelled "veal"), this being Katharine's substitution for the *speechless visor* of the preceding line. Further, *Veal*, when tacked on to Katharine's last spoken word, *long* (line 244), makes up her wooer's name. By adopting Longaville's *half* (uttering *half* his name to make up the whole), Katharine demonstrates her ability to see through the *Veal* on the suitor's face' (Kerrigan).

Is . . . calf? *Veau* in Fr. means both 'veal' and 'calf'; a *calf* was also a stupid person, a dolt (*OED* calf[1] 1c); cf. 635n.

239–41 Say . . . adieu] *F; prose Q* 240 Take that] Take you that *F* 242–55 SP KATHERINE] *Rowe; Maria. (Mari., Mar.) QF*

LONGAVILLE

Let's part the word.

KATHERINE   No, I'll not be your half.

Take all and wean it; it may prove an ox.   250

LONGAVILLE

Look how you butt yourself in these sharp mocks.

Will you give horns, chaste lady? Do not so.

KATHERINE

Then die a calf before your horns do grow.

LONGAVILLE

One word in private with you ere I die.

KATHERINE

Bleat softly then; the butcher hears you cry.   255

[*They converse apart.*]

BOYET

The tongues of mocking wenches are as keen

    As is the razor's edge invisible,

Cutting a smaller hair than may be seen;

    Above the sense of sense, so sensible

Seemeth their conference. Their conceits have wings   260

Fleeter than arrows, bullets, wind, thought, swifter

        things.

249 **part** share, divide (*OED v.* 10a): i.e. agree that we are both calves. The beginning of *calf*, the word Longaville wants to *part*, forms the beginning of Katherine's name.
half partner, co-sharer (*OED sb.* 5): 'better half' (*OED* better A. 3c) was proverbial; see Tilley, H49. 'Half', pronounced 'alf', is the other part of 'calf' without its beginning. Cf. the discussion of the word's pronunciation 5.1.21–2n.

250 **wean** cease to suckle (*OED v.* 1a)
prove an ox show itself to be a fool (*OED* ox 4a): an ox is a castrated male animal.

251 **butt** strike, thrust

252 **give horns** butt with horns; make

your husband a cuckold

256–61 See 1.1.61–6n.

256–8 Cf. the proverbial 'To have a tongue like a razor' and 'To cut the hair' (Dent, T401.1 and H32) and see 1.1.122–3n.

259–60 **Above . . . conference** Their conversation seems so striking that it goes beyond the power of the senses to perceive it. Cf. 4.3.301–12.

259 **sensible** making a strong impression on the mind, striking (*OED* A. 5)

260 **conceits** clever ideas (*OED sb.* 8a)

261 **arrows . . . thought** four proverbially fast things: see Tilley, A322, Dent, B719.1, Tilley, W411, T240; for bullets, cf. 3.1.54n.

259 sense, so] *Pope;* sence so *QF*

ROSALINE

Not one word more, my maids; break off, break off.

BEROWNE

By heaven, all dry-beaten with pure scoff!

KING

Farewell, mad wenches. You have simple wits.

Exeunt [the King, lords and Blackamoors].

PRINCESS

Twenty adieus, my frozen Muscovites.   265

Are these the breed of wits so wondered at?

BOYET

Tapers they are, with your sweet breaths puffed out.

ROSALINE

Well-liking wits they have; gross, gross, fat, fat.

PRINCESS

O poverty in wit, kingly-poor flout!

Will they not, think you, hang themselves tonight?   270

Or ever but in visors show their faces?

This pert Berowne was out of countenance quite.

ROSALINE

They were all in lamentable cases.

---

263 **dry-beaten** severely beaten, but without drawing blood

scoff contemptuous ridicule, mockery

264 **mad wenches** proverbial: see Dent, W274.1, and 2.1.256.

You . . . wits you are dim; your wits are plain: as opposed to the lords' *Well-liking wits* (268), they are simple fare.

266 **breed** kind, species (*OED sb.* 2c*)

268 Rosaline refers to the traditional opposition between fatness and wit; see 1.1.26n.

Well-liking plump, thriving (*OED ppl. a.* 1 *fig.**)

269 The Princess is either reproving Rosaline for her dismissal of the lords in 268 (perhaps involving a pun on 'Well-

li-king') or, more probably, returning to the feebleness of the King's farewell in 264: a feeble piece of mockery for a king showing the poverty of his wit.

271 **but in visors** except behind masks to hide their faces

272 **out of countenance** disconcerted, abashed (*OED* countenance *sb.* 6b). The phrase became proverbial: see Tilley, C705, and cf. the bringing of Moth out at 173 and the putting of Holofernes out of countenance at 601 and 615.

273 Either a syllable is missing here, or 271 has one too many.

cases states (*OED sb.*[1] 5a); clothes, garments (*OED sb.*[2] 4b); masks (cf. *RJ* 1.4.29), the visors of 227.

---

264 SD] *Theobald (subst.); Exe. Q; Exeunt. F; opp.* 265 *Capell*   266 wondered] wondred *F*   268 have;] *Theobald;* haue *Q;* haue, *F*   273 They] *QF;* O! They *F2;* Ah, they *Oxf*

The King was weeping-ripe for a good word.

PRINCESS

Berowne did swear himself out of all suit.   275

MARIA

Dumaine was at my service, and his sword.

'*Non point*,' quoth I; my servant straight was mute.

KATHERINE

Lord Longaville said I came o'er his heart;

And trow you what he called me?

PRINCESS   Qualm perhaps?

KATHERINE

Yes, in good faith.

PRINCESS   Go, sickness as thou art!   280

ROSALINE

Well, better wits have worn plain statute-caps.

But will you hear? The King is my love sworn.

PRINCESS

And quick Berowne hath plighted faith to me.

KATHERINE

And Longaville was for my service born.

274 **weeping-ripe** ready to weep: cf. Sidney, *NA*, 100.8, *3H6* 1.4.172, *CE* 1.1.77.

275–6 **suit . . . service** the two went together; cf. 827–8.

275 **out . . . suit** beyond the limits of proper behaviour; unsuitably for his courtship; unsuitably for the suit of clothes he was wearing; naked, i.e. that he had no oath left to swear

277 *Non point* not a bit, not at all, with a pun on the point of Dumaine's sword; see also 2.1.189n.

278 **came o'er** took possession of (*OED* come *v*. 43c**)

279 **trow you** do you know

Qualm sudden feeling of faintness which 'comes over' one: Katherine has suggested the answer to her own question.

281 **plain statute-caps** plain woollen caps worn according to the law by people of low social rank on Sundays and holy days (*OED* statute *sb*. 9*). Various laws regulating the wearing of such garments were passed during Elizabeth's reign. Rosaline means that apprentices and people like them have shown themselves to be *better wits* than the lords.

283 **quick** See 2.1.117n.

277 *Non point*] *QF* (No poynt)   servant] *F*; seruant, *Q*   279 perhaps] *Q* (perhapt), *F*

MARIA

   Dumaine is mine as sure as bark on tree.   285

BOYET

   Madam, and pretty mistresses, give ear:

   Immediately they will again be here

   In their own shapes, for it can never be

   They will digest this harsh indignity.

PRINCESS

   Will they return?

BOYET   They will, they will, God knows;   290

   And leap for joy, though they are lame with blows.

   Therefore change favours and, when they repair,

   Blow like sweet roses in this summer air.

PRINCESS

   How 'blow'? How 'blow'? Speak to be understood.

BOYET

   Fair ladies masked are roses in their bud;   295

   Dismasked, their damask sweet commixture shown,

   Are angels vailing clouds, or roses blown.

PRINCESS

   Avaunt, perplexity! What shall we do

   If they return in their own shapes to woo?

---

285 **as sure . . . tree** used proverbially for close relations: see Dent, B83 and H88.

288 **In . . . shapes** i.e. not disguised

289 **digest** put up with, swallow (*OED v.* 6a)

292 **repair** return (*OED v.*¹ 2a)

293 **Blow** blossom, bloom, referring back to the *blows* in 291 and causing the Princess's questions in 294

296 The line is rather a tongue-twister.
Dismasked unmasked (*OED v.**): unique in Shakespeare, who elsewhere (*Luc, Ham, MM*) uses 'unmask'
damask red and white, blush-

coloured (*OED sb.* and *a.* 8*), with an evident pun on 'mask'
commixture complexion, bodily constitution (*OED* 3*), the only citation

297 ***vailing clouds** letting fall, lowering, often as a mark of respect or submission, the clouds which hid them (*OED* vail *v.*² 1–3); the last sense of the verb refers to lowering a sail on a ship: cf. *MV* 1.1.28, 'Vailing her high top', and, for the clouds, see 204n.
blown in bloom, blossomed

298 **Avaunt, perplexity** i.e. go away, riddler, or away with puzzlement

297 vailing] *F;* varling *Q*

ROSALINE

Good madam, if by me you'll be advised   300
Let's mock them still, as well known as disguised.
Let us complain to them what fools were here,
Disguised like Muscovites in shapeless gear;
And wonder what they were, and to what end
Their shallow shows and prologue vilely penned,   305
And their rough carriage so ridiculous,
Should be presented at our tent to us.

BOYET

Ladies, withdraw. The gallants are at hand.

PRINCESS

Whip to our tents, as roes runs o'er the land.

Exeunt [the Princess and ladies].

Enter the KING *and the rest* [,BEROWNE, LONGAVILLE *and*
DUMAINE, *as themselves*].

KING

Fair sir, God save you. Where's the Princess?   310

BOYET

Gone to her tent. Please it your majesty
Command me any service to her thither?

KING

That she vouchsafe me audience for one word.

---

301 **as well . . . disguised** i.e. as much
    when they come as themselves as when
    they came in disguise
303 **shapeless gear** inelegant, shapeless
    clothes (*OED* shapeless *a.* 2)
305 **penned** Cf. 147n.
306 **carriage** behaviour (*OED* 14a); cf.
    1.1.256n.
307 **tent** Cf. 4.3.347n.

308 **gallants** See 126n.
309 **Whip** move quickly, dash
    as . . . land proverbial: see Tilley,
    R158; Kerrigan detects a pun on
    roes/rose, looking back to Boyet's
    remarks in 293, 297.
    runs For the third person plural in -s,
    see Abbott, 333.

---

305 penned] *Capell (*pen'd,*);* pende. *Q;* pen'd: *F*   308 hand.] *F;* hand, *Q*   309 runs] *QF;* run *F4*
o'er the] *F3* (ore the*);* ore *QF;* over *Steevens*   309 SD] *Capell (subst.)*   309.1–2 BEROWNE . . .
themselves] *this edn*   311–12] *Capell; prose Q; F lines* Tent. / her? /   312 her thither?] *Capell;* her
thither, *Q;* her? *F*

BOYET

I will; and so will she, I know, my lord.   *Exit.*

BEROWNE

This fellow pecks up wit as pigeons peas   315
And utters it again when God doth please.
He is wit's pedlar and retails his wares
At wakes and wassails, meetings, markets, fairs;
And we that sell by gross, the Lord doth know,
Have not the grace to grace it with such show.   320
This gallant pins the wenches on his sleeve.
Had he been Adam, he had tempted Eve.
'A can carve too, and lisp. Why, this is he
That kissed his hand away in courtesy.
This is the ape of form, Monsieur the Nice,   325
That when he plays at tables chides the dice
In honourable terms. Nay, he can sing

315–16 These lines became proverbial: see Dent, C333.
316 **utters** speaks; puts for sale; discharges, emits (*OED v.*¹ 6a, 1a, 3b, respectively)
318 **wakes** festivals of sports and entertainments, celebrating the feast day of the patron saint of the parish church
wassails revels, festivals, esp. those involving drink (*OED sb.* 3**)
fairs See 4.3.231n.
319 **by gross** in large quantities, wholesale
321–34 For further commentary on this passage, see Introduction, pp. 35–6.
321 **pins . . . sleeve** makes women absolutely dependent on him, has complete power over them (*OED* pin *v.*¹ 4a); proverbial: see Dent, S534.
322 **Adam . . . Eve** Traditionally, Eve tempted Adam to eat of the fruit of the tree of knowledge and caused him to fall; see also 1.1.252n.

had would have
323 **carve** Following Schmidt, *OED v.* 13* cites this passage and *MW* 1.3.45 for the sense of 'To show great courtesy and affability', but the word's precise meaning, which may include affected behaviour or some sexual innuendo, is not clear. A literal sense may also be present: cf. *TNK* 4.3.87–9. See also 4.1.56n.
lisp Cf. Rosalind's farewell to Jaques, *AYL* 4.1.33–4, 'look you lisp and wear strange suits'.
324 **kissed . . . away** wore his hand out by so much kissing
325 **ape of form** unthinking imitator or follower of polite behaviour; see 4.2.126n.
Nice fastidious
326 **tables** backgammon
chides scolds; cf. 4.3.129n.
327 **honourable** i.e. politely, without excessive swearing (*OED a.* 1c)

315 pecks] *Q (*peckes*); pickes *F*   316 God] *Ioue F*   323 'A] *Q (*A*); He *F*   324 his hand away] *Q (*his hand, a way*); away his hand *F*

A mean most meanly; and in ushering
Mend him who can. The ladies call him sweet.
The stairs, as he treads on them, kiss his feet.   330
This is the flower that smiles on everyone,
To show his teeth as white as whale's bone;
And consciences that will not die in debt
Pay him the due of 'honey-tongued Boyet'.

KING

A blister on his sweet tongue, with my heart,   335
That put Armado's page out of his part!

Enter the ladies [, the PRINCESS, ROSALINE, MARIA *and*
KATHERINE, *with* BOYET].

BEROWNE

See where it comes! Behaviour, what wert thou
Till this man showed thee, and what art thou now?

---

328 **mean** middle part (alto or tenor)
most meanly pretty well
***ushering** acting as an usher, (like
Mercury) conducting ceremonies
(*OED vbl. sb.**): an usher may also have
suggested the sense of woman's male
companion, and hence a penis.
329 **Mend . . . can** Let anyone who
thinks he can do better try it (*OED*
mend *v.* 11).
330 The stairs are figuratively the means
by which someone climbs socially or in
rank (*OED* stair *sb.* 3c), but in collocation with *tread* (see 4.3.275n.,
5.2.893n.) they suggest sexual activity,
for which cf. 'stair-work', *WT* 3.3.74.
331–3 proverbial: see Dent, T430.1,
Tilley, W279, D165.
332 **whale's bone** ivory of some kind;
whale's is two syllables.
333 **consciences** either the moral faculty
of right and wrong itself, or that faculty turned from an abstract to a con-

crete, i.e. people with consciences
333–4 For the rhyme, see 5.1.21–2n.
334 **honey-tongued** sweetly speaking
(*OED a.**); *OED*'s next citation is the
passage from Francis Meres, *Palladis
Tamia* (1598), stating that 'the sweete
wittie soule of *Ouid* liues in mellifluous
& hony-tongued *Shakespeare*'. In the
same year Richard Barnfield in *Poems:
in Divers Humours* praised his 'hony-
flowing Vaine' and in his *Epigrams* of
1599 John Weever called him 'Honie-
tong'd'. See also *VA* 452 and 1.1.123n.
335 Cf. the proverbial 'Report has a blister on her tongue', Dent, R84.
336 **put . . . part** See 102n., 159n.
337 **Behaviour** good manners (*OED sb.* 1e)
338 ***man** Q reads 'mad man' and F 'madman', which may result from eye-skip
and dittography from *madam* in the next
line. Berowne mockingly means that
good manners were nothing until Boyet
showed what they could or should be.

328 ushering] *F;* hushering. *Q*   329 can.] *F (*can:*);* can, *Q*   331 everyone,] *F (*euerie one,*);* euery one. *Q*
332 whale's] *QF (*Whales*);* whalës *Singer*   334 due] dutie *F*   336 Armado's] *QF (*Armathoes*)*   336.1–2]
Rowe (subst.)   337 thou] *F (*thou,*);* thou? *Q*   338 man] *Theobald;* mad man *Q;* madman *F;* map o' man *Oxf*[1]

KING

All hail, sweet madam, and fair time of day.

PRINCESS

'Fair' in 'all hail' is foul, as I conceive.   340

KING

Construe my speeches better, if you may.

PRINCESS

Then wish me better; I will give you leave.

KING

We came to visit you and purpose now

To lead you to our court. Vouchsafe it then.

PRINCESS

This field shall hold me, and so hold your vow.   345

Nor God nor I delights in perjured men.

KING

Rebuke me not for that which you provoke.

The virtue of your eye must break my oath.

PRINCESS

You nickname virtue: 'vice' you should have spoke;

For virtue's office never breaks men's troth.   350

Now, by my maiden honour, yet as pure

As the unsullied lily, I protest,

A world of torments though I should endure,

---

340 The Princess takes the King's *hail* as in 'hailstorm', so that it is *foul* to call such a storm *fair*; cf. *TNK* 3.5.100–1.

341 **Construe . . . better** interpret, take the sense of what I'm saying properly; there may also be a grammatical sense present, i.e. look correctly at the words I'm using to show the meaning of what I'm saying.

343–56 See 1.1.80–93n.

345 **field** where the King *means to lodge you* in 2.1.85

346 **Nor** neither

348 **virtue** power; cf. Daniel, *Rosamond*,

sig. K3v, 'And bade me vse the vertue of mine eyes'. The Princess takes the word in the next line as 'moral goodness', the opposite of vice.

349 **nickname** wrongly assert or mention (*OED v.* 1c*); misname

350 **office** proper function, action

351–2 **pure . . . lily** proverbial: see Dent, L295.3.

352 ***unsullied** *OED ppl. a.* a*; QF's 'vnsallied' is almost certainly a compositorial error, frequently discussed in relation to *Ham* 1.2.129.

---

341 Construe] *Q (Consture), F;* Conster *Riv*   speeches] *Q (spaches), F*   350 men's] *Q (mens);* men *F*   352 unsullied] *F2;* vnsallied *QF*

I would not yield to be your house's guest,
So much I hate a breaking cause to be   355
Of heavenly oaths, vowed with integrity.

KING

O, you have lived in desolation here,
Unseen, unvisited, much to our shame.

PRINCESS

Not so, my lord. It is not so, I swear.
We have had pastimes here and pleasant game: 360
A mess of Russians left us but of late.

KING

How, madam? Russians?

PRINCESS   Ay, in truth, my lord.
Trim gallants, full of courtship and of state.

ROSALINE

Madam, speak true! It is not so, my lord.
My lady, to the manner of the days,   365
In courtesy gives undeserving praise.
We four indeed confronted were with four
In Russian habit. Here they stayed an hour
And talked apace; and in that hour, my lord,
They did not bless us with one happy word.   370
I dare not call them fools, but this I think,
When they are thirsty, fools would fain have drink.

355 **breaking cause** i.e. cause for breaking; for transposed adjectival phrases,
   see Abbott, 419a.
357 **desolation** loneliness, solitariness
   (*OED* 3*)
358 The King maintains the fiction of the
   masque.
   Unseen unknown, unnoticed (*OED*
   2a)
360 **pastimes** Cf. 4.3.351.
361 **mess** group of four; see 4.3.203n.
363 **gallants** See 126n.
   courtship courtliness of manners

(*OED* 1a*); cf. 774.
   state dignified appearance, stately
   bearing (*OED sb.* 18a); cf. 588n.
365 **to . . . days** as is now the practice or
   fashion; see Abbott, 187.
366 **undeserving** undeserved (*OED ppl.
   a.* 3*, the only citation)
369 **talked apace** talked quickly, i.e.
   chattered
370 **happy** apt, felicitous
372 i.e. they are fools; see 2.1.122n.
   fain gladly, willingly

368 Russian] Russia *F*

BEROWNE

This jest is dry to me. My gentle sweet,
Your wits makes wise things foolish. When we greet,
With eyes' best seeing, heaven's fiery eye,   375
By light we lose light. Your capacity
Is of that nature that to your huge store
Wise things seem foolish and rich things but poor.

ROSALINE

This proves you wise and rich, for in my eye –

BEROWNE

I am a fool and full of poverty.   380

ROSALINE

But that you take what doth to you belong,
It were a fault to snatch words from my tongue.

BEROWNE

O, I am yours, and all that I possess.

ROSALINE

All the fool mine?

BEROWNE   I cannot give you less.

ROSALINE

Which of the visors was it that you wore?   385

BEROWNE

Where, when, what visor? Why demand you this?

ROSALINE

There, then, that visor: that superfluous case

---

373 **jest is dry** joke is apparently unintentional; *OED* (dry *a.* 14) cites
Puttenham's calling 'Ironia' as 'the drye
mock' and Maria in *TN* 1.3.76, 'A dry
jest'. Berowne says that Rosaline's jokes
about being *thirsty* are dry or ironic, but
his own comment is equally *dry*.
374–6 **When . . . light** i.e. when we look
directly at the sun, we are blinded; cf.
the proverbial 'He that gazes upon the
sun shall at last be blind', Dent,
S971.1, and 1.1.84–5n., 4.3.222n.

376 **capacity** intellectual power, knowledge (*OED* 4)
377 **to** compared to
379 **eye** organ of sight, looking back to
375; opinion, judgement
386 See 1.1.229–38n.
387–8 Cf. the proverbial 'A well-favoured
visor will hide her ill-favoured face',
Dent, V92.
387 **case** outer covering; used in reference to masks in *RJ* 1.4.29, *MA* 2.1.95

---

373 me. My] *Malone (subst.);* me. *F;* me, *Q;* me. Faire *F2*   374 foolish.] *Rowe (subst.);* foolish *QF*
379 eye –] *F (*eie*);* eie. *Q*   384 mine?] *Pope;* mine. *QF*   385 was] what *F*

That hid the worse and showed the better face.

KING

We were descried. They'll mock us now downright.

DUMAINE

Let us confess and turn it to a jest.   390

PRINCESS

Amazed, my lord? Why looks your highness sad?

ROSALINE

Help! Hold his brows! He'll swoon. Why look you
    pale?

Seasick, I think, coming from Muscovy!

BEROWNE

Thus pour the stars down plagues for perjury.

Can any face of brass hold longer out?   395

Here stand I, lady; dart thy skill at me.

Bruise me with scorn, confound me with a flout,

Thrust thy sharp wit quite through my ignorance,

    Cut me to pieces with thy keen conceit,

And I will wish thee never more to dance,   400

    Nor never more in Russian habit wait.

O, never will I trust to speeches penned,

    Nor to the motion of a schoolboy's tongue,

Nor never come in visor to my friend,

---

391 **Amazed** bewildered
392 **brows** 'The prominences of the fore-
    head on either side above the eyes'
    (*OED sb.*[1] 4a*)
394–415 Berowne's lines form a twenty-
    two-line poem (with a concluding cou-
    plet): 402–15, in which he renounces
    rhetorical artifice, form a sonnet; cf.
    1.1.80–93n.
394 Some diseases were thought to be
    star-blasted.
395 **face of brass** brazen behaviour;
    proverbial: see Dent, F8.

397 **confound** destroy
    flout jeer, scoff; cf. 832n.
398 **sharp wit** See 2.1.49n.
399 **keen conceit** sharp and fanciful wit;
    cf. Boyet's description of the keenness
    of women's tongues at 256–8 and see
    1.1.122–3n.
400 **wish** request, invite (*OED v.* 5b)
401 **wait** attend upon you
402–15 See 1.1.80–93n.
403 **motion** movement (*OED sb.* 2a*)
    schoolboy's *OED* 1*
404 **friend** lover (*OED sb.* 4); cf. 822.

389] *F lines* discried, / downeright. / were] are *F*   392 swoon] *Pope;* sound *QF*

Nor woo in rhyme like a blind harper's song.   405
Taffeta phrases, silken terms precise,
    Three-piled hyperboles, spruce affectation,
Figures pedantical: these summer flies
    Have blown me full of maggot ostentation.
I do forswear them, and I here protest,   410
    By this white glove – how white the hand, God
        knows! –
Henceforth my wooing mind shall be expressed
    In russet yeas and honest kersey noes.
And, to begin: wench, so God help me, law!

405 **blind harper's song** Harpers were proverbially blind: see Dent, H175, and Tilley, H176.
song The QF spelling is clearly intended to mirror the rhyme with 'tongue'.
406–7 **Taffeta . . . silken . . . Three-piled** The materials all suggest fashionable richness.
406 **Taffeta** florid, overblown (*OED* B. 2*); cf. 159n.
phrases See 1.1.163n.
silken soft, flattering (*OED a.* 7a*)
precise over-exact, fastidious
407 **Three-piled** excessive, extreme (*OED a.*[1] 2*); 'three-pile' was applied to velvet of triple thickness: see *MM* 1.2.32, 4.3.10, *WT* 4.3.13–14.
spruce smart (*OED a.* 2e**); cf. 5.1.13.
***affectation** QF read 'affection': the two were muddled in the sixteenth century through a confusion between 'affect' (*OED v.*[1]), meaning 'to like' (cf. 1.1.9n., 1.2.160, 4.3.286n., 5.1.81n.), and 'affect' (*OED v.*[2]), meaning 'to lay hold of'. It is possible that 'affection', meaning affectation (*OED sb.* 13), came to be seen as obsolete, for at 5.1.4, where QF read 'affection', F2 has 'affectation'; similarly in *Ham* 2.2.443, where Q2 has 'affection', F has 'affectation'. Rowe's emendation is necessary here for the metre. Baldwin (2.218–19) draws atten-

tion to Quintilian's warning that too much hyperbole leads to affectation.
408 **Figures** rhetorical figures; see 1.2.54n.
pedantical Ard[2] points out that Shakespeare was anticipated in this usage by Gabriel Harvey in 1589.
408–9 **these . . . ostentation** From the rich fabrics of 406–7 Berowne's imagery moves on to decay and disgust.
409 **blown me** laid their eggs on me (*OED* blow *v.*[1] 28c*); cf. *Oth* 4.2.66–7, 'as summer flies . . . / That quicken even with blowing'.
ostentation pretentious showing-off (*OED* 3); cf. 5.1.104n.
411 **white the hand** See 3.1.163n.
413 **russet** rustic, homely simple (*OED* B. 4*); russet was a homespun woollen cloth of reddish colour worn by country people.
kersey plain, homely (*OED* 4b*, the only citation); kersey was a coarse woollen ribbed cloth.
414 **wench** Berowne's change of linguistic register is reflected in his choice of term.
law la (*OED int.**); an exclamation usually used by comic or low-life figures, such as the Hostess in *2H4*, Macmorris and Fluellen in *H5*, but also once each by Cleopatra in *AC* and by Marina in *Per*

405 song] *QF (*songue*)* 407 hyperboles] *Q (*Hiberboles*), F* affectation] *Rowe;* affection *QF*
414 begin:] *Ard*[2]*;* begin, *Pope;* begin *QF*

My love to thee is sound, *sans* crack or flaw. 415
ROSALINE
Sans '*sans*', I pray you.
BEROWNE   Yet I have a trick
Of the old rage. Bear with me, I am sick;
I'll leave it by degrees. Soft, let us see:
Write 'Lord have mercy on us' on those three.
They are infected; in their hearts it lies; 420
They have the plague and caught it of your eyes.
These lords are visited: you are not free,
For the Lord's tokens on you do I see.
PRINCESS
No, they are free that gave these tokens to us.
BEROWNE
Our states are forfeit. Seek not to undo us. 425
ROSALINE
It is not so; for how can this be true,

416 *Sans* '*sans*' without '*sans*', i.e. without the affected use of French. Cf. 5.1.79n.

416–17 **Yet . . . rage** Bevington compares Virgil, *Aeneid*, 4.23, '*Agnosco veteris vestigia flammae*', 'I recognize the traces of an old fire' (Lyly, *Endymion*, 173).

416 **trick** characteristic trait, touch (*OED sb.* 7); cf. 465n.

417 **rage** madness, mania (*OED sb.* 1a)

419 **Lord . . . us** The phrase was written on the doors of houses with the plague (*OED* lord *sb.* 6b (*a*)). See Wilson, *Plague*, 61–4.

420 **infected** See 2.1.229.
it i.e. the plague of love; but Berowne shifts from the plague of affected language to that of love.

422 **visited** attacked by plague
free uninfected

423 **Lord's tokens** The earliest citation for this sense of *token* as a sign of plague (*OED sb.* 2b) is 1634, but Ard[2] points out comparable phrases from *TC* and *AC* and cites Cotgrave, 'Tac . . . *a Plague-spot, or Gods-token on one*

that hath the Plague': the usage also appears in Dekker, *The Wonderful Year*, 1603 (Dekker, *Plague*, 29.19). It seems these plague spots were so called after the cheap tokens used as coins (Dekker, *Plague*, 224). The *OED*'s earliest citations (God 16c) for 'God's marks' is 1531 and for 'God's tokens' is 1582. Berowne also refers to the tokens or favours which the lords gave the ladies.

424 **free** i.e. free from the tokens of plague; at liberty in love; generous

425 **Our . . . forfeit** We have lost our status as bachelors or as honourable men (*OED* state *sb.* 15a); we have lost our properties, possessions (*OED* state *sb.* 36). The legal associations of *forfeit* are picked up in *sue* (427).
undo ruin

426–7 **how . . . sue?** 'How can those be liable to forfeiture that begin the process' (Johnson). Rosaline puns on two senses of *sue*, to woo, to court (*OED v.* 15 and see 3.1.184n.), to be a suitor to a woman (*OED v.* 23) and to take legal action or to prosecute a suit.

That you stand forfeit, being those that sue?

BEROWNE

Peace! for I will not have to do with you.

ROSALINE

Nor shall not if I do as I intend.

BEROWNE [*to the other lords*]

Speak for yourselves. My wit is at an end.   430

KING

Teach us, sweet madam, for our rude transgression
Some fair excuse.

PRINCESS   The fairest is confession.

Were not you here but even now, disguised?

KING

Madam, I was.

PRINCESS   And were you well advised?

KING

I was, fair madam.

PRINCESS   When you then were here,   435
What did you whisper in your lady's ear?

KING

That more than all the world I did respect her.

PRINCESS

When she shall challenge this, you will reject her.

KING

Upon mine honour, no.

PRINCESS   Peace, peace, forbear!
Your oath once broke, you force not to forswear.   440

KING

Despise me when I break this oath of mine.

---

428 **have . . . you** have anything to do with you; have sex with you

434 **well advised** in your right mind

437 **respect** value, esteem (*OED v.* 4b)

438 **challenge** lay claim to (*OED v.* 5a)

440 i.e. having once broken your oath about the 'academe', you will not care about breaking it again (*OED* force *v.*[1] 14a (*c*))

430 SD] *Capell (subst.)*   433 not you] you not *F*   439–40 Peace . . . forswear] *F; prose Q*

PRINCESS

    I will; and therefore keep it. Rosaline,

    What did the Russian whisper in your ear?

ROSALINE

    Madam, he swore that he did hold me dear

    As precious eyesight and did value me   445

    Above this world; adding thereto, moreover,

    That he would wed me, or else die my lover.

PRINCESS

    God give thee joy of him. The noble lord

    Most honourably doth uphold his word.

KING

    What mean you, madam? By my life, my troth,   450

    I never swore this lady such an oath.

ROSALINE

    By heaven you did! And to confirm it plain,

    You gave me this; but take it, sir, again.

KING

    My faith and this the Princess I did give.

    I knew her by this jewel on her sleeve.   455

PRINCESS

    Pardon me, sir, this jewel did she wear,

    And Lord Berowne, I thank him, is my dear.

    What! Will you have me or your pearl again?

BEROWNE

    Neither of either; I remit both twain.

    I see the trick on't. Here was a consent,   460

    Knowing aforehand of our merriment,

444–5 **dear . . . eyesight** proverbial: see Dent, E249.1, and cf. *precious seeing*, 4.3.307n.

453 **this** presumably a love token or favour

459 **Neither of either** neither of the two (*OED* neither B. 2b)
    remit give up, surrender (*OED v.* 2)

both twain both of them

460 **trick** prank, practical joke (*OED sb.* 2a)
    consent agreement, pact (*OED sb.* 2a)

461 **Knowing** since they knew; for participles expressing a condition, see Abbott, 377.

To dash it like a Christmas comedy.
Some carry-tale, some please-man, some slight zany,
Some mumble-news, some trencher-knight, some Dick
That smiles his cheek in years and knows the trick   465
To make my lady laugh when she's disposed,
Told our intents before; which, once disclosed,
The ladies did change favours and then we,
Following the signs, wooed but the sign of she.
Now, to our perjury to add more terror,   470
We are again forsworn in will and error.
Much upon this 'tis. [*to Boyet*] And might not you
Forestall our sport, to make us thus untrue?

462 **dash** ruin, spoil (*OED v.*[1] 6); usually used in this sense to refer to the failure of a bill in Parliament (cf. *3H6* 2.1.118)
like . . . comedy Cam[1] suggests that spoiling the entertainment (as in *MND*, the Gray's Inn revels and later in *LLL*) 'was a recognized part of the fun'. This is possible, but it is hard to reconcile with the sense that comedies – whether poems, plays or interludes – generally have a happy ending. *A Christmas comedy* may suggest some sort of institutional entertainment; cf. the Cambridge University play, *1 Return from Parnassus*, l. 18, 'A Christmas toy thou haste' (Leishman, 136, and cf. 220), and Sly's asking whether 'a comonty' was 'a Christmas gambold, or a tumbling-trick' (*TS* Ind. 2.137–8). Berowne's precise meaning is obscure; for his earlier reference to Christmas, see 1.1.105–6n.
463 **carry-tale** tale-bearer, tell-tale; cf. *VA* 655–7.
please-man sycophant, toady (*OED**, the only citation)
***slight** low, humble (*OED* A. 4a)

***zany** the pantaloon's rustic assistant in the *commedia dell'arte*
464 **mumble-news** gossip (*OED* mumble *v.* 7*, the only citation)
trencher-knight A trencher was a plate of some kind; *OED* trencher 7a* is the only citation, but on the analogy of 'trencher-chaplain', 'trencher-fly' and 'trencher-friend' Berowne may mean a parasitic hanger-on at someone else's table
Dick fellow, lad; see also 901.
465–83 Much of the sexual banter and innuendo of this passage has been illuminated by Holdsworth.
465 **smiles** *OED** *v.* 6a
in years into looking old with wrinkles
trick device, dodge (*OED* 3), with a sexual innuendo; cf. 416n. and *AW* 5.3.239–40, 'Tricks he hath had in him, which gentlemen have'.
466 **disposed** inclined to be merry; see 2.1.249n.
469 **sign of she** i.e. the identifying device of our respective mistress
472 **Much . . . 'tis** This is pretty much what has happened.

463 slight zany] *F (slight Zanie); sleight saine Q*   465 smiles] *F; smyles, Q*   472 'tis] *QF (tis); it is F2*   SD] *Rowe (opp. 472)*

Do not you know my lady's foot by th' squier,
    And laugh upon the apple of her eye?   475
And stand between her back, sir, and the fire,
    Holding a trencher, jesting merrily?
You put our page out – Go, you are allowed;
Die when you will, a smock shall be your shroud.
You leer upon me, do you? There's an eye   480
Wounds like a leaden sword.
BOYET   Full merrily
Hath this brave manage, this career, been run.
BEROWNE
Lo, he is tilting straight. Peace! I have done.

474–9 See 1.1.61–6n.

474 **know . . . squier** know exactly the size of my lady's foot, i.e. have her measure (*OED* square *sb.* 1b); cf. the proverbial 'To know the length of one's foot', Tilley, L202. *Foot* suggests sexual intercourse from Fr. *foutre*: see 5.2.664n. The variant form *squier* has been retained for the sake of rhyme, but also because of the sexual innuendo suggested by *apple* in the next line: an 'apple-squire' was a whore's attendant or pimp; cf. Nashe, *The Unfortunate Traveller*, 'what proper apple squire is this you bring so suspitiously into my chamber?' (2.308. 29–30).

475 look pleasantly on her pupil, i.e. exchange smiling or knowing looks: see *OED* laugh *v.* 4a, apple 7a, and cf. the proverbial 'As dear as the apple (pupil) of my eye', Tilley, A290. For the sexual implications of *eye*, see 2.1.188n.

476 i.e. and act as her fire-screen; but a sexual innuendo involving *stand* and *fire* for the penis and the vagina is present.

477 **Holding a trencher** i.e. being ready to serve her in a sycophantic way

478 *****allowed** licensed, permitted

479 Whenever you die, you'll be buried like the woman you are. *Die* contributes a further sexual innuendo involving orgasm.

480 **leer upon me** look askance at me

481 **Wounds . . . sword** proverbial; see Dent, S1054, and cf. S1048: leaden or wooden swords were used as stage properties. The leaden sword suggests a penis.

482 *****brave manage** splendid gallop at full speed (*OED* manage *sb.* 2; cf. *AS*, 49.14, in sense 1); there may also be a pun on 'man-age', i.e. stuff about men. **career** charge (*OED* sb. 2a)

483 **tilting straight** going immediately back to his (wit) encounters (*OED* tilt *v.*[1] 5c); thrusting with his penis. Berowne's phrase continues the martial, chivalric and sexual language of 482, but it may also be a contradiction in terms: that Boyet is sloping or leaning forward, but is upright (*OED* tilt *v.*[1] 4a).

478 allowed] *F* (alowd); aloude *Q*   481–2 Full . . . run] *Rowe*[2]; prose *QF*   481 merrily] *Q* (merely), *F*   482 manage] *Theobald (subst.)*; nuage *Q*; manager *F*; manège *Oxf*

Enter [COSTARD, *the*] *Clown.*

Welcome, pure wit! Thou partest a fair fray.
COSTARD
  O Lord, sir, they would know   485
  Whether the three Worthies shall come in or no.
BEROWNE
  What, are there but three?
COSTARD   No, sir, but it is vara fine,
  For every one pursents three.
BEROWNE   And three times thrice is nine.
COSTARD
  Not so, sir – under correction, sir – I hope it is not so.
  You cannot beg us, sir, I can assure you, sir; we know
    what we know.   490
  I hope, sir, three times thrice, sir –
BEROWNE   Is not nine?
COSTARD Under correction, sir, we know whereuntil it
  doth amount.
BEROWNE
  By Jove, I always took three threes for nine.
COSTARD O Lord, sir, it were pity you should get your   495

---

484 **Thou . . . fray** You're breaking up a good fight; the wit has been anything but pure.
  *****partest** Pope's emendation is unnecessary if *fair* is disyllabic.
487 **vara fine** i.e. it's perfectly all right, or even excellent: *vara* is a dialectal form of 'very'.
488 **pursents** Costard's form of 'presents', i.e. represents
490 **You . . . us** You can't take us for fools. The phrase came from the Court of Wards and refers to petitioning it for the custody of a minor, an heiress or an

idiot as a way of getting hold of his or her property (*OED* beg *v.* 5a); cf. the proverbial 'Let him be begged for a fool', Tilley, F496.
  we . . . know Cf. the proverbial 'I know what I know', Tilley, K173.
  [2]**know** The *so / know* rhyme looks back to Costard's *know / no* rhyme in 485–6.
492 **whereuntil** whereunto, to what: a dialectal form (*OED adv. dial.**), only here and at 499 in Shakespeare; for 'till' used for 'to', see Abbott, 184.
495 **were . . . get** would be hard on you if you had to make

484 Welcome] *F; Ber.* Welcome *Q*   partest] *Pope;* partst *Q;* part'st *F*   485+ SP COSTARD] *Rowe; Clow. (Clowne., Clo.) QF*   490–1 You . . . 'sir] *Capell;* prose *QF*   491 sir –] *Rowe (subst.);* sir. *QF*

living by reckoning, sir.

BEROWNE   How much is it?

COSTARD   O Lord, sir, the parties themselves, the actors,
sir, will show whereuntil it doth amount. For mine own
part, I am, as they say, but to parfect one man in one   500
poor man – Pompion the Great, sir.

BEROWNE   Art thou one of the Worthies?

COSTARD   It pleased them to think me worthy of Pompey
the Great. For mine own part, I know not the degree of
the Worthy, but I am to stand for him.   505

BEROWNE   Go bid them prepare.

COSTARD   We will turn it finely off, sir; we will take some
care.   *Exit.*

KING

Berowne, they will shame us. Let them not approach.

BEROWNE

We are shame-proof, my lord; and 'tis some policy   510
To have one show worse than the King's and his
company.

496 **reckoning** See 1.2.40n.
498 **parties** people in question (*OED sb.*
14a); cf. 667. There may be a punning
allusion to people with parts in the
play and also to people with sexual
parts, for which cf. *o'erparted*, 578–9n.
500 **to parfect** Costard's old-fashioned
form of 'perfect' (cf. *OED* A. 5α) is
related to his earlier *pursent*, probably
means 'to perform' and may be related
to *OED v.* 1a, to accomplish, to carry
through.
501 **Pompion** pumpkin; cf. 5.1.109–10n.,
and *MW* 3.3.41, where Mrs Ford refers
to Falstaff as 'this gross wat'ry pumpion'.
504 **degree** rank
505 **stand for** represent, take the place of
(*OED* stand *v.* 71h). There may be a
pun involved here about the size of
Costard's erect penis, his *part*; see
5.1.119–20n.

506 **prepare** may be intended to rhyme
with *care*, in which case the verse dialogue may resume with 'But I am to
stand for him'.
507 **turn . . . off** *OED* (turn *v.* 73) has no
specific sense which fits what Costard
means here, that they will pull off a
fine performance, they will execute it
finely. Two contemporary meanings
were to dismiss or sack somebody
(*OED* 73b; cf. *AW* 5.3.220) or to hang
someone on the gallows, 'to turn off
the ladder' (*OED* 73d), with the earliest citation from Nashe's *The
Unfortunate Traveller*. Costard may be
indulging in some gallows humour
here, for which see also 5.2.12n.
510 **shame-proof** *OED sb.* 17*, the only
citation; cf. 1.1.129n.
some policy a crafty device, a strata-
gem

500 they] *F;* thy *Q*   parfect] perfect *F*   508 SD] *F opp. 506*

KING

    I say they shall not come.

PRINCESS

    Nay, my good lord, let me o'errule you now.

    That sport best pleases that doth least know how –

    Where zeal strives to content and the contents   515

    Dies in the zeal of that which it presents;

    Their form confounded makes most form in mirth,

    When great things labouring perish in their birth.

BEROWNE

    A right description of our sport, my lord.

Enter [ARMADO, *the*] *Braggart.*

ARMADO   Anointed, I implore so much expense of thy   520
royal sweet breath as will utter a brace of words.

[*Armado and the King talk apart.*]

PRINCESS   Doth this man serve God?

BEROWNE   Why ask you?

PRINCESS   'A speaks not like a man of God his making.

ARMADO   That is all one, my fair, sweet, honey monarch;   525
for, I protest, the schoolmaster is exceeding fantastical;
too, too vain; too, too vain; but we will put it, as they say,

---

514 A commonplace related to '*Ars est celare artem*', Tilley, A335; cf. 153n.

515 **zeal** passionate eagerness, enthusiasm
content please, delight (*OED v.* 1b)

515–16 **the . . . presents** i.e. the enthusiasm of those who put on the play overwhelms what it's about and it *dies*.

517 i.e. the ruining of what the play is about brings its own reward by making the audience laugh.

518 Cf. Horace, *Ars poetica*, 139, '*Parturiunt montes, nascetur ridiculus mus*', and its proverbial form, 'The mountains have brought forth a

mouse', Tilley, M1215, and see note on title.

519 **right** fitting
our sport i.e. the Muscovite masque

520 **Anointed** i.e. the King, who has been anointed; unique as a form of address in Shakespeare; cf. 3.1.177.
expense using up (*OED* 1b*)

524 **a man . . . making** proverbial: see Dent, M162.
God his God's

525 **That . . . one** it's all the same to me
sweet, honey Cf. the proverbial 'As sweet as honey', Tilley, H544.

---

514 least] *F;* best *Q*   517 Their] *QF;* There *Capell*   520+ SP ARMADO] *Rowe; Brag. (Braggart.)*
QF   521 SD] *Capell (subst.)*   524 'A] *Q (A);* He *F*   God his] God's *F*   525 That is] That's *F*

to *fortuna de la guerra*. [*Gives the King a paper*.] I wish
you the peace of mind, most royal couplement.   *Exit.*

KING   Here is like to be a good presence of Worthies. He   530
presents Hector of Troy; the swain, Pompey the Great;
the parish curate, Alexander; Armado's page, Hercules;
the pedant, Judas Maccabaeus.
And if these four Worthies in their first show thrive,
These four will change habits and present the other five.   535

BEROWNE
There is five in the first show.

KING
You are deceived: 'tis not so.

BEROWNE   The pedant, the braggart, the hedge-priest,
the fool and the boy.
Abate throw at novum, and the whole world again   540
Cannot pick out five such, take each one in his vein.

KING
The ship is under sail and here she comes amain.

Enter [COSTARD *as*] *Pompey.*

528 **fortuna . . . guerra* the chance of war; cf. the proverbial 'The chance of war is uncertain', Dent, C223.
529 **couplement** couple, pair (*OED* 2a*); cf. *Son* 21.5.
530 **presence** assembly, company (*OED* 3)
531 **presents** See 5.1.117n.
537 The King's inability to count is striking.
538–9 The list of characters is reminiscent of those in the *commedia dell'arte*: Pedant, Braggart and Boy are all used in SPs.
538 **hedge-priest** uneducated country priest, like Sir Oliver Martext in *AYL* 3.3
540 **Abate** set aside, leave out of the

count (*OED v.*[1] 16*)
throw at novum a lucky throw at novum, a dice game in which five and nine appear to have been winning throws, but like those of Post and Pair (5.2.67n.) its rules are obscure (*OED* novum*). Berowne's remarks revolve around the performance of the show of the Nine Worthies with only five actors.
541 **pick out** F's suggestive reading 'pricke out' has no parallel in Shakespeare, who often uses 'pick out', e.g. *1H4* 2.4.367.
take . . . vein i.e. given what each one is like
542 **amain** with all speed

528 *fortuna . . . guerra*] *Theobald; Fortuna delaguar QF*   SD] *Capell (subst.) opp. 521*   529 SD] *om.*
F   534–5] *Rowe³; prose QF*   541 pick] *Q (picke);* pricke *F*   in his] in's *F*

COSTARD

   I Pompey am –

BEROWNE   You lie, you are not he.

COSTARD

   I Pompey am –

BOYET   With leopard's head on knee.

BEROWNE

   Well said, old mocker. I must needs be friends with

      thee.   545

COSTARD

   I Pompey am, Pompey surnamed the Big.

DUMAINE   The 'Great'.

COSTARD

   It is 'Great', sir: *Pompey surnamed the Great,*

   That oft in field, with targe and shield, did make my foe

      to sweat;

   And travelling along this coast, I here am come by chance,   550

   And lay my arms before the legs of this sweet lass of France.

   If your ladyship would say, 'Thanks, Pompey', I had

      done.

PRINCESS   Great thanks, great Pompey.

COSTARD   'Tis not so much worth, but I hope I was

   perfect. I made a little fault in 'Great'.   555

---

544 **With . . . knee** Pompey's arms were traditionally said to be a leopard or a lion holding a sword: if Costard had these painted on his shield and if he held it upside-down, then they might be on his knee. Some editors suspect that Costard falls over on his entry – hence Berowne's *You lie* is a pun – and has his shield on his knee. A further possibility is that Boyet may be referring to '*masquine*' in which a leopard's or a lion's head was represented on the knees or elbows of a garment.

546–55 The joke revolves around Costard's confusion of size (see 5.1.119–20n.) and worth.

549 *targe* light shield

550 *coast* district, region (*OED sb.* 6)

551 Costard may be speaking figuratively or acting literally: at 691–2 he asks to be allowed to borrow the arms again.

553 SP* The QF SPs are inappropriate.

555 **perfect** word-perfect (*OED* B. 2c)

543 *am* –] *Theobald; am. QF*   544 *am* –] *Theobald; am, Q; am. F*   553 SP] *F2; Lady. Q, F (La.)*

BEROWNE My hat to a halfpenny, Pompey proves the best Worthy.

Enter [NATHANIEL, *the*] *Curate, for Alexander.*

NATHANIEL
When in the world I lived, I was the world's commander;
By east, west, north and south, I spread my conquering might;
My scutcheon plain declares that I am Alisander.   560
BOYET
Your nose says no, you are not; for it stands too right.
BEROWNE
Your nose smells 'no' in this, most tender-smelling knight.
PRINCESS
The conqueror is dismayed. Proceed, good Alexander.
NATHANIEL
When in the world I lived, I was the world's commander –
BOYET
Most true, 'tis right: you were so, Alisander.   565
BEROWNE Pompey the Great –
COSTARD Your servant, and Costard.
BEROWNE Take away the conqueror; take away Alisander.
COSTARD [*to Nathaniel*] O sir, you have overthrown

556 **My . . . halfpenny** I'll bet anything; cf. the proverbial 'My cap (hat) to a noble', Dent, C63.1, and Berowne's earlier bet involving hats, 1.1.292.
560 *scutcheon* coat of arms
561 **right** straight. Alexander was supposed by some (including Plutarch) to have had a wry neck which twisted his head to one side.
562 According to Plutarch, Alexander's

skin was supposed to smell sweet: Berowne says that Boyet is able to detect that Nathaniel is not really Alexander, since the curate does not smell sweetly.
tender-smelling having a delicate sense of smell (*OED* A. 10a); cf. *Luc* 694–5, 'Look as the full-fed hound or gorged hawk, / Unapt for tender smell, or speedy flight'.

558–64 SP NATHANIEL] *Rowe; Curat. (Cura., Cur.) QF*   562 'no' in this] *Cam;* no, in this *F;* no in his *Q*   563] *F lines* dismaid: / *Alexander.* /   564 *commander* –] *Cam;* commander. *QF*
566 Great –] *Cam;* great. *QF*   569 SD] *Capell*

Alisander the conqueror. You will be scraped out of the   570
painted cloth for this. Your lion, that holds his pole-axe
sitting on a close-stool, will be given to Ajax. He will be
the ninth Worthy. A conqueror, and afeard to speak?
Run away for shame, Alisander. [*Nathaniel retires.*]
There, an't shall please you, a foolish mild man; an   575
honest man, look you, and soon dashed. He is a
marvellous good neighbour, faith, and a very good
bowler; but for Alisander, alas you see how 'tis – a little
o'erparted. But there are Worthies a–coming will speak
their mind in some other sort.   580

PRINCESS   Stand aside, good Pompey.

Enter [HOLOFERNES, *the*] *Pedant* [, *as*] *Judas, and* [MOTH,] *the Boy* [, *as*] *Hercules.*

HOLOFERNES

Great Hercules is presented by this imp,
Whose club killed Cerberus, that three-headed canus,

---

571 **painted cloth** The Nine Worthies frequently appeared painted on or woven in wall-hangings in Elizabethan buildings.

571–2 **Your . . . Ajax** Alexander's arms traditionally included a lion sitting on a throne holding a battle-axe. Costard transforms the throne into a privy and puns on Ajax, whose name was often rendered as 'a jakes' (*OED* Ajax*), i.e. a privy; cf. Florio's Montaigne cited in *OED* close-stool, 'A commodious ajax or easie close-stoole'. Cf. 4.3.6n.

575–78 **an . . . bowler** Cf. the proverbial 'To lack but a bowl and a besom of being an honest man', Dent, B568.1, which Shakespeare adapts here (using different senses of 'bowl', as a dish and to roll a ball) to make a new proverb,

'An honest man and a good bowler', Dent, M183.

576 **dashed** put to shame, abashed (*OED v.*[1] 7b)

578 **bowler** one who plays at bowls

578–9 **a little o'erparted** having rather too difficult a part to play (*OED* over-parted *a.**); cf. 498n. There may be a joke here and in Costard's reference to his *pole-axe* about the size of Nathaniel's penis.

582–7 See 1.1.61–6n.

582 *imp* See 1.2.5n.

583 *Cerberus* the dog that guarded the entrance to Hades: in his last labour Hercules captured and bound him, took him to his taskmaster king Eurystheus and returned him to the Underworld.

---

573 afeard] *Q (*a feard*)*; affraid *F*   574 SD] *Capell; Exit Curat. opp. 580 Q,F (Exit Cu.)*
575 you,] *F (*you:*); you Q*   577 faith] *Q (*fayth*); insooth F*   581.1–2 *as . . . as*] *this edn; for . . . for QF*

And when he was a babe, a child, a shrimp,
    Thus did he strangle serpents in his manus.   585
Quoniam *he seemeth in minority,*
Ergo *I come with this apology.*
Keep some state in thy exit, and vanish.   [*Moth retires.*]
Judas I am –

DUMAINE   A Judas!   590

HOLOFERNES   Not Iscariot, sir.

Judas I am, ycleped Maccabaeus.

DUMAINE   Judas Maccabaeus clipped is plain Judas.

BEROWNE   A kissing traitor. How, art thou proved Judas?

HOLOFERNES
    Judas I am –   595

DUMAINE   The more shame for you, Judas.

HOLOFERNES   What mean you, sir?

BOYET   To make Judas hang himself.

HOLOFERNES   Begin, sir; you are my elder.

BEROWNE   Well followed: Judas was hanged on an elder.   600

HOLOFERNES   I will not be put out of countenance.

BEROWNE   Because thou hast no face.

---

583 *three-headed* **canus** correctly 'canis',
but it needs to rhyme with 'manus'; the
phrase may recall Ovid's '*tria colla
canis*', *Met.*, 10.65.
585 **manus** hands
586 **Quoniam** since
587 **Ergo** therefore
588 **Keep some state** behave in a dignified manner (*OED* state *sb*. 19a**); cf.
363n.
590 **A Judas** a traitor, betrayer
591 Cf. John, 14.22, 'Iudas sayth vnto
hym, not Iscariot'.
592 *ycleped* called; see 1.1.233n.
593 **clipped** cut short (*OED v.*² 5a*);
embraced, hugged (*OED v.*¹ 1a)

594 **kissing** Judas betrayed Christ with a
kiss (*OED ppl. a*. a**). A Judas kiss was
proverbial: see Tilley, J92.
How . . . Judas How say you – does
that prove you're Judas?
599 i.e. being older than I am, you can be
the first to hang yourself: if taken literally, Boyet may be one of the older
characters in the play.
600 **Judas . . . elder** Traditionally, Judas
was supposed to have hanged himself
on an elder tree.
601 **put . . . countenance** disconcerted
(*OED* countenance *sb*. 6b); cf. 272n.,
614n. and 615.

---

588 Keep . . . vanish] *F; in italic Q*   SD] *Capell (subst.); Exit Boy. QF*   589 *Judas*] *Capell; Peda.*
Iudas *QF   am –*] *Capell (subst.); am. QF*   591] *Cam; in italic QF*   592 *Judas*] *F; in roman Q*
ycleped] *Q (ecliped), F (ycliped)   Maccabaeus*] *F; in roman Q*   593 clipped is plain] *F; in italic Q*
594 proved] *F (*prou'd*); proud Q*   595 *am –*] *Capell (subst.); am. QF*

HOLOFERNES   What is this?

BOYET   A cittern-head.

DUMAINE   The head of a bodkin.   605

BEROWNE   A death's face in a ring.

LONGAVILLE   The face of an old Roman coin, scarce
seen.

BOYET   The pommel of Caesar's falchion.

DUMAINE   The carved-bone face on a flask.   610

BEROWNE   Saint George's half-cheek in a brooch.

DUMAINE   Ay, and in a brooch of lead.

BEROWNE   Ay, and worn in the cap of a tooth-drawer. And
now forward, for we have put thee in countenance.

HOLOFERNES   You have put me out of countenance.   615

BEROWNE   False! We have given thee faces.

HOLOFERNES   But you have outfaced them all.

BEROWNE

An thou wert a lion, we would do so.

---

603 **this** i.e. his face

604 **cittern-head** A cittern was a kind of guitar which often had a grotesquely carved head (*OED* cithern 2*).

605 **bodkin** long hairpin, with a head that might be elaborately decorated (*OED* 3a); Ard¹ quotes Florio, 'Puntarvolo, *a bodkin, a head-needle . . . Also a nice, a coy or selfe-conceited fellow*'.

606 A death's head worn as a *memento mori* was a common gift as a mourning ring; *death's face* is the only citation in *OED*.

607–8 **scarce seen** i.e. because it has been almost entirely worn away

609 **pommel** knob at the end of the handle of a sword or dagger
falchion sword

610 **flask** a powder-flask made of horn or bone (*OED sb.² 2a); cf. *RJ* 3.3.132.

611 **half-cheek** face in profile (*OED* 1*,

the only citation); elsewhere Shakespeare tends to use 'half-face' and 'half-faced'.

612–13 **brooch . . . tooth-drawer** Brooches worn in caps showed the wearer's profession: the tooth-drawer's or dentist's low status is indicated by his badge being made out of lead.

614 **put . . . countenance** stopped you from being disconcerted or abashed (*OED* countenance *sb.* 6c*); cf. 601n.

615 **put . . . countenance** See 601n.

617 **outfaced them all** put them all to shame, mocked them all with your impudence

618–19 **lion . . . ass** In Aesop's fable the ass passed himself off as a lion by wearing his skin until his braying gave him away; 'An ass in a lion's skin' was proverbial: see Tilley, A351.

613–14] *Capell; QF line* Tooth-drawer: / countenance. /   617 outfaced] *Q* (outfaste), *F* (out-fac'd)

BOYET

Therefore, as he is an ass, let him go.

And so adieu, sweet Jude. Nay, why dost thou stay?   620

DUMAINE   For the latter end of his name.

BEROWNE

For the ass to the Jude? Give it him. Jud-as, away!

HOLOFERNES

This is not generous, not gentle, not humble.

BOYET

A light for Monsieur Judas! It grows dark; he may
    stumble.   [*Holofernes retires.*]

PRINCESS   Alas, poor Maccabaeus, how hath he been   625
    baited!

Enter [ARMADO, *the*] *Braggart* [, *as Hector*].

BEROWNE   Hide thy head, Achilles! Here comes Hector
    in arms.

DUMAINE   Though my mocks come home by me, I will
    now be merry.   630

---

620 **adieu . . . Jude** For the possible pun,
see 3.1.132n.
621 **latter end** This sets up the ass/arse
pun in the next line.
623 **generous** appropriate for people of
noble birth, magnanimous (*OED* 2a*);
the only other use of the word in the
play occurs when Holofernes calls
Armado a *most generous sir* (5.1.84n.).
gentle courteous, polite (*OED* A. 3c);
cf. 1.1.127n.
624 'Boyet probably refers to the *Judas
candlestick* once used in parish
churches at Easter. Made of brass, this
candlestick had seven branches, from
the seventh or middle one of which a
tall thick piece of wood, painted like a
candle, and called *the Judas of the*

Paschal, rose nearly to the roof, and on
the top of this was placed at Eastertide
the paschal candle of wax (*OED* Judas
2). Boyet thus completes the list of
carved or painted objects with which
the courtiers identify Holofernes'
(Oxf[1]). The practice appears to have
been a pre-Reformation one.
dark Cf. 716.
stumble fall over; get his lines wrong
(*OED v.* 2b); take offence (*OED v.* 2d)
626 **baited** attacked by dogs for sport;
persecuted for fun. Cf. 1.1.6n.
627 **Achilles** Hector's great enemy and
eventually his killer
629 **come . . . me** end up by recoiling
upon me, i.e. I'll pay for this later.

619 is an ass,] is, an Asse, *QF*   622 Jud-as] *F (Iud-as); Judas Q*   624 SD] *Capell*   626.1] *Capell*

KING   Hector was but a Trojan in respect of this.

BOYET   But is this Hector?

KING   I think Hector was not so clean-timbered.

LONGAVILLE   His leg is too big for Hector's.

DUMAINE   More calf, certain.   635

BOYET   No, he is best endued in the small.

BEROWNE   This cannot be Hector.

DUMAINE   He's a god or a painter, for he makes faces.

ARMADO

> *The armipotent Mars, of lances the almighty,*
>   *Gave Hector a gift –*   640

DUMAINE   A gilt nutmeg.

BEROWNE   A lemon.

LONGAVILLE   Stuck with cloves.

DUMAINE   No, cloven.

ARMADO   Peace!   645

> *The armipotent Mars, of lances the almighty,*
>   *Gave Hector a gift, the heir of Ilion;*
> *A man so breathed that certain he would fight, yea,*
>   *From morn till night, out of his pavilion.*

631 **Trojan** an inhabitant of Troy; drinking companion (*OED* B. 2a*). Cf 671.
633 **clean-timbered** well-built (*OED* clean *adj*. and *adv*. in *comb*. 2*, the only citation)
635 **calf** part of the leg (*OED* calf² 1a); stupid fool (*OED* calf¹ 1c), cf. 247n.
636 **endued** endowed (*OED v*. 8a)
     small i.e. the small or thin part of the leg below the calf (*OED* B. 6a *ellipt*.*)
638 The line became proverbial: see Dent, G230.
     makes creates; pulls (*OED* face *sb*. 6b)
639 *armipotent* mighty in arms, in Lat. and later literature a poetical epithet of Mars

641 *gilt nutmeg nutmeg glazed with the yolk of an egg: a common gift of lovers, used for spicing drinks
642–3 A lemon stuck with cloves would be used to flavour drinks.
644 **cloven** split down the middle: Dumaine takes Berowne's *lemon* as 'leman' or lover and by punning on *cloves* refers to her sexual parts and/or to her being *cloven* while having sex.
646–8 The rhyme *almighty/fight, yea* is a particularly poor one and the only time Shakespeare rhymes 'almighty'.
647 *Ilion* Troy
648 *breathed* well exercised, fit
649 *pavilion* See 2.1.249n.

633 SP] *QF; Dumaine Alexander (subst.)*   634 Hector's] *Q (Hectors); Hector F*   639–40] *Pope; prose QF*   640 *gift* –] *Capell (subst.); gift. QF*   641 gilt] *F; gift Q*   644 No,] *Rowe; No QF*   645 Peace!] *Q (Peace.); om. F*   648 *yea*,] yea *F; ye / Alexander*

I am that flower –   650

DUMAINE   That mint!

LONGAVILLE   That columbine!

ARMADO   Sweet Lord Longaville, rein thy tongue.

LONGAVILLE   I must rather give it the rein, for it runs
against Hector.   655

DUMAINE   Ay, and Hector's a greyhound.

ARMADO   The sweet war-man is dead and rotten. Sweet
chucks beat not the bones of the buried. When he
breathed, he was a man. But I will forward with my
device. Sweet royalty, bestow on me the sense of   660
hearing. (*Berowne steps forth.*)

PRINCESS   Speak, brave Hector; we are much delighted.

ARMADO   I do adore thy sweet grace's slipper.

BOYET   Loves her by the foot.

651–2 **mint . . . columbine** Some insult
is implied, but remains obscure unless
it is that Dumaine and Longaville
mean that Armado-Hector is a very
common flower.

653 **rein** restrain, hold back (*OED v.* 3b*)

654 **give . . . rein** give it full scope;
proverbial: see Dent, B671.

656 **greyhound** Hector was famed for his
speed in running.

657 **war-man** warrior, soldier; cf. *Arts-
man*, 5.1.74n.

    dead and rotten proverbial: see
Dent, D126.1.

658 **chucks** See 5.1.103n.

    beat . . . buried Cf. the proverbial
'Speak well of the dead', Dent, D124.

660 **device** masque, dramatic represen-
tation (*OED* 11*)

661 SD The play affords no evidence as
to what Berowne does between this SD
and his next lines at 681. At 4.3.148
Berowne says, 'Now step I forth to

whip hypocrisy'. It is possible that the
problem here is connected with the
setting of 667 as an SD in QF:
'*Berowne*' might have been set in error
for '*Clowne*' and misplaced, so that the
SD 'Clown steps forth' might have followed 667 to prepare for Costard's
intervention at 668. To step forth
means to come out to the front or into
the middle of things, to advance to do
something (*OED* step *v.* 22), and cf.
KJ 3.4.151, *WT* 5.1.221. Similar SDs
occur elsewhere in plays of the period,
e.g. in Dekker's *2 Honest Whore*,
5.2.82.3, the SD specifies that
'Orlando *steps forth*'; see Dekker,
Works, 2.206.

663 Q sets the line in italics, suggesting
the compositor thought it part of
Armado's role as Hector.

664 **by the foot** around her foot; by having sex with her; see 5.2.474n.

650–2] *QF; one verse line Cam*   650] *Theobald; in roman QF*   *flower –*] *Capell (subst.); Flower. QF*
657–9] *Capell; Q lines* rotten. / buried: / man: /. *; F lines* rotten, / buried: /   658–9 When . . . man]
om. F   659–61 But . . . hearing] *F lines* deuice; / hearing. /   661 SD] *QF; Berowne steps forth and
whispers to Costard. / Capell (subst.)*   663] *F; in italic Q*

DUMAINE   He may not by the yard.   665

ARMADO

    This Hector far surmounted Hannibal;
      The party is gone –

COSTARD   Fellow Hector, she is gone! She is two months on her way.

ARMADO   What meanest thou?   670

COSTARD   Faith, unless you play the honest Trojan, the poor wench is cast away: she's quick, the child brags in her belly already. 'Tis yours.

ARMADO   Dost thou infamonize me among potentates? Thou shalt die!   675

COSTARD   Then shall Hector be whipped for Jaquenetta that is quick by him and hanged for Pompey that is dead by him.

DUMAINE   Most rare Pompey!

BOYET   Renowned Pompey!   680

BEROWNE   Greater than 'Great'. Great, great, great Pompey! Pompey the huge!

DUMAINE   Hector trembles.

---

665 **yard** three feet; penis; cf. *ell* at 4.2.58n.

667 *Although set in QF as though it is an SD, this line is presumably a continuation of Armado's speech. T. W. Craik points out (privately) that the line echoes verses on the death in 1588 of the comedian Richard Tarlton in John Scottowe's alphabet book (BL Harl. MS 3885 f. 19r), 'The partie nowe is gone, / and closlie clad in claye': see Foakes, no. 23.
party See 498n.
gone dead (*OED v.* 48c)

668 **gone** pregnant (*OED v.* 7); cf. 2.1.257n.

669 **on her way** i.e. towards giving birth

(*OED* way *sb.*[1] 36)

671 **Trojan** See 631n.

672 **cast away** ruined (*OED v.* 72d)
quick pregnant (*OED* A. 4b*)
brags swaggers, struts, shows off (*OED v.* 2b *fig.**); thus Costard suggests it is Armado the Braggart's. Oxf[1] cites Nashe, *Pierce Penniless* (1.176.12–14), 'properly Pride is the disease of the Spaniard, who is borne a Bragart in his mothers wombe'.

674 **infamonize** defame, a perverted form of 'infamize' (*OED**, the only citation)

676 **whipped** Whipping was the usual punishment for fornication.

677 **quick** pregnant; living

666] *omission marked after this line* Oxf   667] *spoken by Armado* / Pope; *centred and italicized* QF; *given to Costard* / Theobald   *gone* –] Ard[2]; *gone.* QF   674–5] Pope; *verse* QF, *lined* potentates: / die. / 681 'Great'. Great] Kerrigan *(subst.)*; great, great QF

BEROWNE   Pompey is moved. More Ates, more Ates! Stir
   them on, stir them on!   685

DUMAINE   Hector will challenge him.

BEROWNE   Ay, if 'a have no more man's blood in his belly
   than will sup a flea.

ARMADO   By the north pole, I do challenge thee.

COSTARD   I will not fight with a pole like a northern man.   690
   I'll slash, I'll do it by the sword. I bepray you, let me
   borrow my arms again.

DUMAINE   Room for the incensed Worthies.

COSTARD   I'll do it in my shirt.

DUMAINE   Most resolute Pompey!   695

MOTH   Master, let me take you a buttonhole lower. Do
   you not see, Pompey is uncasing for the combat. What
   mean you? You will lose your reputation.

ARMADO   Gentlemen and soldiers, pardon me. I will not
   combat in my shirt.   700

DUMAINE   You may not deny it. Pompey hath made the
   challenge.

ARMADO   Sweet bloods, I both may and will.

684 **Ates** i.e. provocative remarks: the Greek goddess Ate was goddess of strife and discord.
686 **challenge him** summon him to fight (*OED* challenge *v.* 8a*)
687–8 proverbial: see Tilley, B461.1.
688 **sup** provide a supper for (*OED v.*² 3b*)
689 **By . . . pole** Shakespeare is mocking the contemporary vogue for using strange oaths, also ridiculed by Ben Jonson in the character Bobadill in *Every Man in his Humour* (1598); in the sense of 'pole star', the north pole could be taken as a symbol of constancy and determination.
690 **pole . . . man** Poles or staves were often associated with the violent raiders and cattle thieves of the north

and the Scottish borders.
691 **bepray** pray (*OED*'s only citation). F emended the word to 'pray', but perhaps Costard is mixing that word up with 'beseech'.
692 **arms** See 551n.
696 **take . . . lower** unbutton your clothes; humiliate you. Cf. 'I will take you a peg (buttonhole, hole) lower', both of which were proverbial: see Tilley, P181, and *OED* buttonhole *sb.* 1b. See also 717–19n.
697 **uncasing** taking off his clothes (*OED v.* 1c*)
700 **combat** fight (*OED v.* 1a): there is nothing odd about Armado's English here.
703 **bloods** fiery men, hot sparks (*OED sb.* 15a)

684 moved.] *Theobald* (mov'd;)*;* mooued *Q;* moued, *F*   685 them on,] *Rowe;* them, or *QF*   687 in his] in's *F*   691 bepray] pray *F*

BEROWNE   What reason have you for't?

ARMADO   The naked truth of it is, I have no shirt. I go   705
woolward for penance.

MOTH   True, and it was enjoined him in Rome for want of
linen. Since when, I'll be sworn he wore none but a
dishclout of Jaquenetta's, and that 'a wears next his
heart for a favour.   710

Enter a Messenger, Monsieur MARCADÉ.

MARCADÉ
God save you, madam.

PRINCESS   Welcome, Marcadé,
But that thou interruptest our merriment.

MARCADÉ
I am sorry, madam, for the news I bring
Is heavy in my tongue. The King, your father –

PRINCESS
Dead, for my life!

MARCADÉ   Even so; my tale is told.   715

BEROWNE
Worthies, away! The scene begins to cloud.

ARMADO   For mine own part, I breathe free breath. I have

---

705 **The naked truth** Cf. the proverbial 'The truth shows best being naked', Dent, T589.
706 **woolward** wearing wool next to the skin, i.e. without linen; proverbial: see Dent, W757.1.
707 SP* QF assign this speech to '*Boy.*', who could be Boyet or Moth, but Moth would know more about Armado's clothes than the courtier and the speech seems more in the style of the page. **enjoined** imposed on (*OED v.* 2a)
707–8 **it . . . linen** Despite being imposed on him in Rome, Armado's not wear-

ing linen is the result of poverty rather than being a religious penance.
709 **dishclout** dishcloth
710 **favour** See 30n.
714 **tongue** See 1.1.123n.
715 **tale** statement, information (*OED sb.* 3a); story (*OED sb.* 4)
716 **cloud** become gloomy, darken (*OED v.* 8*); cf. 624.
717 **I . . . breath** I can breathe the air freely, i.e. I've had a narrow escape (*OED* breathe *v.* 11*).
717–19 ²**I . . . discretion** i.e. I've been given just enough prudence or circum-

---

705–6] Pope; *verse QF, lined* Shirt. / pennance. /   707 SP] *Capell; Boy. QF;* BOYET *Alexander (subst.)*   709 'a wears] *Q (*a weares*), F (*hee weares*)*   711–12 Welcome . . . merriment] *Capell; prose QF*   713–14] *Rowe²; prose QF*   714 father –] *Rowe;* father *QF*   715 Dead,] *Theobald;* Dead *QF*

seen the day of wrong through the little hole of
discretion and I will right myself like a soldier.

Exeunt Worthies.

KING   How fares your majesty?   720

PRINCESS

Boyet, prepare. I will away tonight.

KING

Madam, not so. I do beseech you, stay.

PRINCESS

Prepare, I say. I thank you, gracious lords,
For all your fair endeavours, and entreat,
Out of a new-sad soul, that you vouchsafe   725
In your rich wisdom to excuse or hide
The liberal opposition of our spirits,
If over-boldly we have borne ourselves
In the converse of breath. Your gentleness
Was guilty of it. Farewell, worthy lord!   730
A heavy heart bears not a nimble tongue.
Excuse me so, coming too short of thanks

spection to know what it is to be ut-
terly humiliated. Cf. the proverbial
'One may see day at a little hole' and
'Discretion is the better part of valour', Tilley, D99 and D354. Armado's
hole may recall Moth's reference to his
buttonhole at 696.

719 **right** revenge (*OED v.* 7a); a homophonic pun on 'write' is possible. The
coupling of *wrong* and *right* is conventional.

720 **your majesty** Although the Princess
is 'A maid of grace and complete
majesty' (1.1.134), the King now
addresses her by her new title as
Queen: see also Appendix 1, pp. 337–8.

726 **hide** overlook, disregard

727 **liberal** unrestrained, licentious

opposition antagonism, hostility
(*OED* 5a*)

729 **converse** intercourse, intimate
exchange (*OED sb.*[1] 3a**); cf. 839n.

gentleness good breeding, courtesy

730 **guilty of** responsible for

731 ***nimble** QF's 'humble' is inappropriate and does not provide the necessary
antithesis to *heavy*; *TxC* points out that
in the nine cases where Shakespeare
uses 'humble' with the indefinite article
it occurs with 'an', not 'a'. Neither
'nimble' nor 'humble' tongue occurs
elsewhere in Shakespeare. Cf. 1.1.123n.

732–3 **coming . . . obtained** The
Princess's suit has evidently been settled to her advantage, but Shakespeare
does not choose to explain when or how.

721+ SP PRINCESS] *F2*; QUEEN *Oxf (after QF)*   724 entreat,] *Q (*intreat:*); entreats: *F*
725 new-sad soul] *Theobald;* new sad-soule *QF*   727–30 spirits . . . it.] *QF (*spirites, / If . . . our
selues, / In . . . breath (your gentlenes / Was . . . it.)); Spirits; / If . . . our selves, / In . . . Breath,
your Gentlenes / Was . . . it. / *Rowe*   731 nimble] *Theobald;* humble *QF*   732 too] so *F*

For my great suit so easily obtained.

KING

The extreme parts of time extremely forms
All causes to the purpose of his speed   735
And often at his very loose decides
That which long process could not arbitrate.
And though the mourning brow of progeny
Forbid the smiling courtesy of love
The holy suit which fain it would convince,   740
Yet, since love's argument was first on foot,
Let not the cloud of sorrow jostle it
From what it purposed; since to wail friends lost
Is not by much so wholesome-profitable
As to rejoice at friends but newly found.   745

PRINCESS

I understand you not. My griefs are double.

BEROWNE

Honest plain words best pierce the ear of grief;
And by these badges understand the King.
For your fair sakes have we neglected time,

734–5 i.e. with very little time left, time forces decisions to be taken quickly
734 **extreme** last, latest (as in 'extreme unction') (*OED* A. 3)
   forms Cf. *runs*, 309n.
735 **causes** matters of concern, affairs (*OED sb.* 10a); the King's language in this part of the speech suggests the law (*causes . . . decides . . . process . . . arbitrate*).
736 **at . . . loose** at the very last moment (*OED sb.* loose 2); the phrase comes from the moment that an arrow is fired.
737 **process** argument, discussion (*OED sb.* 4a)
   arbitrate decide
738 **mourning . . . progeny** i.e. a child's

mourning for a parent
740 **holy suit** i.e. matrimony
   convince demonstrate, give proof of (*OED v.* 8)
741 **on foot** in action (*OED* foot *sb.* 32c*)
742 **jostle** push or force roughly (*OED v.* 5**)
744 ***wholesome-profitable** restoratively beneficial
746 **double** because, in addition to her father's death, she cannot understand what he's saying
748 **badges** See 4.3.250n.; Berowne means the words he is about to speak.
749 **neglected time** paid little attention to time, in whose defiance the play began (1.1.4n.)

739 love] *Hanmer;* Loue, *Q;* Loue: *F*   744 wholesome-profitable] *F (*wholsome profitable*);* holdsome profitable *Q*   746 double] *QF;* dull *Collier MS*   747 ear] *Q (*eare*);* ears *F*   749 time,] *F;* time. *Q*

Played foul play with our oaths. Your beauty, ladies,   750
Hath much deformed us, fashioning our humours
Even to the opposed end of our intents;
And what in us hath seemed ridiculous –
As love is full of unbefitting strains,
All wanton as a child, skipping and vain,   755
Formed by the eye and therefore, like the eye,
Full of strange shapes, of habits and of forms,
Varying in subjects as the eye doth roll
To every varied object in his glance;
Which parti-coated presence of loose love   760
Put on by us, if, in your heavenly eyes,
Have misbecomed our oaths and gravities,
Those heavenly eyes that look into these faults,
Suggested us to make. Therefore, ladies,

750 **foul play** unfairly, treacherously (*OED* foul A. 14b); Berowne's phrase brings out the playfulness of the whole business.

751 **deformed** disfigured, defaced

752 **opposed** opposèd; to the exact opposite of what we intended

754 **unbefitting** unsuitable (*OED ppl. a.* a*)
strains Often glossed to mean 'strong impulse or motion of the mind'; no sense in *OED* quite witnesses this. Given what Berowne goes on to say about love's being like a child, it is possible that *strains* here means 'offspring' (*OED sb.*[1] 4); additionally, the references to *Varying* (758) and *varied* (759) suggest a meaning for *strains* in the sense of varieties of breed. Editors also sometimes detect a hint of 'strains' as in music.

755 **vain** empty-headed, foolish

757 ***strange** QF 'straying' is probably a compositorial misreading of 'strainge' or 'straynge', both variant forms; cf. 'straing formes', *LC* 303.

shapes characteristic appearances
habits usual forms of behaviour; clothes
forms ideal forms; actual forms, of appearance

758–9 **subjects . . . object** The characteristic oppositions suggest logical terms.

758 **eye doth roll** Cf. *MND* 5.1.12, 'The poet's eye, in a fine frenzy rolling'.

760–4 **Which . . . make** i.e. and if in your divine eyes the foolish appearance and behaviour caused by our unrestrained love are not fitting for our oaths and our serious positions, it was those very eyes which observed our faults so clearly that tempted us to behave like this in the first place.

760 **Which** and this; see Abbott, 418.
parti-coated parti-coloured or motley, alluding to the patchwork colours the fool wore (*OED* parti-[1]*, the only citation); cf. 4.2.31n.

762 **misbecomed** suited ill

764 **Suggested** tempted (*OED v.* 2a)

755 vain,] *Rowe;* vaine. *QF*   756 ²eye,] *F4;* eye. *QF*   757 strange] *Capell;* straying *QF*   762 misbecomed] *Q* (misbecombd*), F* (misbecom'd*)   gravities,] *Capell;* grauities. *QF*   764 make.] *F* (make:*); make, *Q;* make them: *Pope*

Our love being yours, the error that love makes   765
Is likewise yours. We to ourselves prove false
By being once false, for ever to be true
To those that make us both – fair ladies, you.
And even that falsehood, in itself a sin,
Thus purifies itself and turns to grace.   770

PRINCESS

We have received your letters full of love,
Your favours, the ambassadors of love,
And in our maiden counsel rated them
At courtship, pleasant jest and courtesy,
As bombast and as lining to the time.   775
But more devout than this in our respects
Have we not been; and therefore met your loves
In their own fashion, like a merriment.

DUMAINE

Our letters, madam, showed much more than jest.

LONGAVILLE

So did our looks.

ROSALINE   We did not quote them so.   780

KING

Now, at the latest minute of the hour,
Grant us your loves.

PRINCESS   A time, methinks, too short

---

765 **Our ... yours** since our love belongs
to you; since you are the cause of our
being in love
766–8 **We ... you** We have been false to
ourselves by breaking our vows once,
so that we can be true for ever to the
fair ladies who make us both – false to
our vows, but true to you.
769 **falsehood** i.e. breaking our vows
770 **grace** virtue (*OED sb.* 13b); the
transformation is neatly enacted by the
end-words of the two lines, *sin/grace.*
773–4 **rated ... At** i.e. valued them as no

more than (*OED* rate *v.*[1] 3b)
774 **courtship** See 363n.
775 i.e. as a way of filling up the time
bombast cotton wool used for stuff-
ing or padding clothes
lining *OED vbl. sb.*[1] 1a *fig.**
776–7 **But ... been** i.e. we haven't taken
the whole business any more seriously
than this
776 **devout** zealous, earnest (Onions)
respects considerations (*OED sb.* 14a)
778 **merriment** See 139n.
780 **quote** look on; see 4.3.84n.

768 both –] *Theobald (subst.);* both *Q;* both, *F*   772 the] *F; not in Q*   776 this in] *Hanmer;* this *Q;*
these are *F*   780 quote] *Q (*cote*), F (*coat*)*

To make a world-without-end bargain in.
No, no, my lord, your grace is perjured much,
Full of dear guiltiness; and therefore this: 785
If for my love – as there is no such cause –
You will do aught, this shall you do for me:
Your oath I will not trust, but go with speed
To some forlorn and naked hermitage,
Remote from all the pleasures of the world,   790
There stay until the twelve celestial signs
Have brought about the annual reckoning.
If this austere insociable life
Change not your offer made in heat of blood;
If frosts and fasts, hard lodging and thin weeds,   795
Nip not the gaudy blossoms of your love,
But that it bear this trial and last love;
Then, at the expiration of the year,
Come challenge me, challenge me by these deserts,
And, by this virgin palm now kissing thine,   800

783 **world-without-end** for ever and ever; the phrase occurs in the Book of Common Prayer at the end of Matins (*OED* world *sb.* 6b); Shakespeare uses the compound phrase again in *Son* 57.5.

785 **dear** grievous, dire (*OED a.*[2] 2), cf. 852; precious, since it has endeared him to her

786 **as . . . cause** i.e. though I don't see why that (if it exists) should make you want to do it

789 **forlorn** abandoned, forsaken (*OED* A. 4a)
naked unfurnished (*OED* A. 10b)
hermitage anticipated by Berowne to the King at 4.3.238 and returned to at 5.2.810. Drawing on medieval imagery, Elizabethan courtiers, like Sir Henry Lee during the Queen's visit to Woodstock in 1575 and to Ditchley in

1592, associated withdrawal from the court with becoming a hermit.

791 **signs** i.e. of the zodiac (*OED sb.* 11a)

792 **annual reckoning** that which mathematically makes up the sum of the year; legally and morally, the yearly account rendered; for *reckoning*, see 1.2.40n.

793 **insociable** See 5.1.18n.

795 **frosts** Cf. 1.1.100–1n.
fasts Cf. 1.1.24n.
weeds clothes

796 **Nip . . . blossoms** Cf. the proverbial 'To nip (blast) in the bud (blossom)', Dent, B702 (*OED* nip *v.*[1] 6b*).

797 **last** continue or endure as

799 **challenge** lay claim to (*OED v.* 5a)
deserts deservings; cf. 'just deserts'.

800–1, 805 **thine . . . thine . . . thou** For the change to the familiar form, see Introduction, p. 52.

792 the] their *F*   794 blood;] *F* (blood:)*;* blood. *Q*   799 challenge . . . me] *QF;* challenge me, challenge *Hanmer;* challenge, challenge me *Malone*

I will be thine. And, till that instance, shut
My woeful self up in a mourning house,
Raining the tears of lamentation
For the remembrance of my father's death.
If this thou do deny, let our hands part,   805
Neither entitled in the other's heart.

KING

If this, or more than this, I would deny,
    To flatter up these powers of mine with rest,
The sudden hand of death close up mine eye!
    Hence, hermit then – my heart is in thy breast.   810
[*They converse apart.*]

DUMAINE

But what to me, my love? But what to me?
A wife?

KATHERINE   A beard, fair health and honesty;
With threefold love, I wish you all these three.

DUMAINE

O, shall I say, 'I thank you, gentle wife'?

KATHERINE

Not so, my lord. A twelvemonth and a day   815
I'll mark no words that smooth-faced wooers say.
Come when the King doth to my lady come;
Then, if I have much love, I'll give you some.

801 **instance** moment, instant (F's reading) (*OED sb.* 4**)
806 **entitled in** having a legal claim to;
written as a title in
808 **flatter up** pamper, coddle (*OED v.*[1]
10a*)
810 ***Hence, hermit then** so, off I go as
a hermit
my . . . breast Cf. the proverbial 'The
lover is not where he lives but where he

loves', Dent, L565. After this line, QF
print six lines of dialogue between
Berowne and Rosaline which are presumably a first draft of 825–59: see
Appendix 2.2.
816 **smooth-faced** plausibly ingratiat-
ing: *OED a.* 1b, citing *KJ* 2.1.573,
'That smooth-fac'd gentleman, tick-
ling commodity'
817–18 **when . . . Then** See 3.1.161n.

801 instance] instant *F*   810 hermit] *Cam*[1] *(Pollard);* herrite *Q;* euer *F*   then – my heart] *F (*then,
my heart*);* then my hart, *Q*   810, 820, 824 SDs] *Cam*[1] *(subst.)*   810+] *at this point QF print the lines
in Appendix 2.2*   812 A wife?] *Dyce; Kath.* A wife? *QF*   SP] *Dyce; not in QF*   816 smooth-faced]
*Q (*smothfast*), F*

DUMAINE

I'll serve thee true and faithfully till then.

KATHERINE

Yet swear not, lest ye be forsworn again.   820

[*They converse apart.*]

LONGAVILLE

What says Maria?

MARIA   At the twelvemonth's end

I'll change my black gown for a faithful friend.

LONGAVILLE

I'll stay with patience, but the time is long.

MARIA

The liker you; few taller are so young. [*They converse apart.*]

BEROWNE

Studies, my lady? Mistress, look on me.   825

Behold the window of my heart, mine eye,

What humble suit attends thy answer there.

Impose some service on me for thy love.

ROSALINE

Oft have I heard of you, my lord Berowne,

Before I saw you, and the world's large tongue   830

Proclaims you for a man replete with mocks,

Full of comparisons and wounding flouts,

---

821 **end** the first of several references (862, 866, 875) suggesting the play is drawing to its close

822 **change** exchange
   friend See 404n.

823 **stay** wait

824 **The liker you** That's more like you.
   taller Maria takes Longaville's *long* to refer to his name or in the sense of tall, or both.

825 **Studies, my lady** i.e. are you deep in melancholy thought? Berowne's question is reminiscent of the concern for study in 1.1.

826 proverbial: see Dent, E231, and esp. *Son* 24.

827–8 **suit . . . service** See 275–6n.

827 **attends** waits for

830 **large tongue** widespread report; free, uninhibited report. The image is that of fame, for which, see 1.1.1n., 123n.

832 **comparisons** satirical or scoffing similes (*OED sb.* 3b*)
   flouts mocking speeches, jeers; Rosaline returns the word that Berowne had spoken to her at 397.

828 thy] my *F*

Which you on all estates will execute
That lie within the mercy of your wit.
To weed this wormwood from your fruitful brain   835
And therewithal to win me, if you please –
Without the which I am not to be won –
You shall this twelvemonth term from day to day
Visit the speechless sick and still converse
With groaning wretches; and your task shall be   840
With all the fierce endeavour of your wit
To enforce the pained impotent to smile.

BEROWNE

To move wild laughter in the throat of death?
It cannot be, it is impossible.
Mirth cannot move a soul in agony.   845

ROSALINE

Why, that's the way to choke a gibing spirit,
Whose influence is begot of that loose grace
Which shallow laughing hearers give to fools.
A jest's prosperity lies in the ear
Of him that hears it, never in the tongue   850
Of him that makes it. Then, if sickly ears,
Deafed with the clamours of their own dear groans,
Will hear your idle scorns, continue then,
And I will have you and that fault withal;

---

833 **estates** people of all ranks and classes
  execute carry out
835 **wormwood** bitterness, from the
  herb
838 **term** See 1.1.16n.
839 **still** continually, always
  converse keep company, be familiar
  with (*OED v.* 2a*); cf. 729n.
840 **groaning** See also 4.3.179.
841 **fierce** ardent, eager (*OED a.* 5a); cf.
  KL 2.1.33–4, 'Some blood drawn on
  me would beget opinion / Of my more
  fierce endeavor'. Cf. 1.1.5n.

842 **the pained impotent** painèd; the
  helpless and feeble who are in pain
845 **agony** throes of death (*OED* 3)
846 **gibing** mocking, sarcastic
847 **influence** i.e. over others (*OED sb.*
  4a*)
  loose grace easy pleasantness or
  charm; but there is an oxymoron present as well, for *loose* could be taken to
  mean licentious or sinful and the grace
  could be divine.
852 **dear** grievous, dire; see 785n.
853 **idle scorns** See 1.1.293n.

835 fruitful] *Q (*fructfull*), F*

But, if they will not, throw away that spirit,   855
And I shall find you empty of that fault,
Right joyful of your reformation.

BEROWNE

A twelvemonth? Well, befall what will befall,
I'll jest a twelvemonth in an hospital.

PRINCESS [*to the King*]

Ay, sweet my lord, and so I take my leave.   860

KING

No, madam, we will bring you on your way.

BEROWNE

Our wooing doth not end like an old play:
Jack hath not Jill. These ladies' courtesy
Might well have made our sport a comedy.

KING

Come, sir, it wants a twelvemonth and a day,   865
And then 'twill end.

BEROWNE   That's too long for a play.

Enter [ARMADO, *the*] *Braggart.*

ARMADO   Sweet majesty, vouchsafe me –
PRINCESS   Was not that Hector?
DUMAINE   The worthy knight of Troy.
ARMADO   I will kiss thy royal finger and take leave. I am a   870

858 **befall . . . befall** proverbial: see
Dent, C529.
861 **bring . . . way** The phrase derives
from Genesis, 18.16.
   bring accompany (*OED v.* 2)
863 **Jack . . . Jill** Cf. the proverbial '(All
shall be well) and Jack shall have Jill',
Tilley, A164, and *MND* 3.2.461–3,
'Jack shall have Jill; / Nought shall go
ill: / The man shall have his mare

again, and all shall be well'.
These ladies' courtesy i.e. courteous
behaviour, courtly politeness, from
these ladies
865 **twelvemonth . . . day** a year and
a day; the phrase is a conventional
one with legal and folk-tale associations. See Introduction, pp. 8–9.
870 **royal finger** See 5.1.96n.

860 SD] *Rowe* 865 and a day] *F;* an'aday *Q* 867 me –] *Theobald;* me. *QF* 870 I . . . leave]
Capell; verse QF 870–2 I am . . . year] *F; verse Q,* lined *Iaquenetta* / yeere. /

votary; I have vowed to Jaquenetta to hold the plough
for her sweet love three year. But, most esteemed
greatness, will you hear the dialogue that the two
learned men have compiled, in praise of the owl and
the cuckoo? It should have followed in the end of our   875
show.

KING   Call them forth quickly; we will do so.

ARMADO   Holla! Approach.

Enter all.

This side is Hiems, winter; this Ver, the spring: the one
maintained by the owl, th'other by the cuckoo. Ver,   880
begin.

THE SONG

VER

When daisies pied and violets blue

871 **votary** one bound by vows; see
2.1.37n.
hold the plough be a farmer; cf. the
proverbial 'Who holds the plough
reaps' no corn', Tilley, P435.1.
Armado's vow has sexual overtones as
in *AC* 2.2.228. Cf. also the *ploughmen's
clocks* of 892n.

872 **three year** At 1.2.35–6 Armado said
he 'promised to study three years with
the Duke'. Traditionally, Omphale
made Hercules spin for her for three
years. Cf. 1.2.64–5n.

873 **dialogue** literary work taking the
form of a conversation between two or
more people (*OED sb.* 2a), for example,
Erasmus's colloquies

873–4 **two learned men** Sir Nathaniel
and Holofernes

874 **compiled** composed; see 4.3.131n.

880 **maintained** defended, asserted
(*OED v.* 14a); *OED v.* 16*, '? To stand
for, represent', the only citation, is
probably unnecessary.

882–917 The singers are presumably *the
two learned men* (873–4) who compiled
the dialogue, in which case they are
Holofernes and Nathaniel, although it
is certainly not in the same style as that
in which they speak in the play. It is
not stated which part each takes but, if
Holofernes is Ver, the song's references to the cuckoo may relate to his
being accused of being a cuckold:
see 5.1.63n. The reference to the *parson's saw* in Hiems's song might be
appropriate to Nathaniel: see 910n.
Onomatopoeic bird songs of this kind
date back at least to 'Sumer is icumen
in'. Ver's song in Nashe's *Summer's*

872 year] *Q (yeere); yeares F*   879–81] *Capell; verse Q, lined* Winter. / Cuckow. / begin. / ; *verse
F, lined* Winter. / Owle, / Cuckow. / begin. /   879 This] *F; Brag.* This *Q*   880 th'other] Th'other
F; The other Rowe   Ver] *F (Ver); B. Ver Q*   882 SP] *Kerrigan; not in QF*

And lady-smocks all silver-white
And cuckoo-buds of yellow hue
   Do paint the meadows with delight,   885
The cuckoo then on every tree
Mocks married men; for thus sings he:
    'Cuckoo!
Cuckoo, cuckoo!' O, word of fear,
Unpleasing to a married ear.   890

When shepherds pipe on oaten straws
   And merry larks are ploughmen's clocks,
When turtles tread and rooks and daws,
   And maidens bleach their summer smocks,
The cuckoo then, on every tree,   895
Mocks married men; for thus sings he:
    'Cuckoo!
Cuckoo, cuckoo!' O, word of fear,
Unpleasing to a married ear.

HIEMS

   When icicles hang by the wall   900

Last Will and Testament (Nashe, 3.238–9) and the song in Lyly's *Mother Bombie* (if it is contemporary with the play) may have supplied a precedent; Autolycus' song at the beginning of *WT* 4.3 shows Shakespeare's later use of the genre.

882–6 **When . . . then** See 3.1.161n.

882 **pied** parti-coloured, produced by art; cf. the discussion in *WT* 4.4.79–108.

883 **lady-smocks** cuckoo-flowers (*OED**); a pun on 'ladies' mocks' is likely: both have sexual connotations. In 894 flowers become women's clothes.
silver-white See *OED* A.* 'As bright (white) as silver' was proverbial: see Tilley, S453.

884 **cuckoo-buds** The plant is not certainly identified (*OED**) and may have

been made up by Shakespeare for its associations with the cuckold's horns.

885 **paint** The natural flowers (even if they are *pied*) colour the landscape artificially.

887 **Mocks married men** because it sounds like 'cuckold' and because the cuckoo, by laying its eggs in the nests of other birds, acts as a usurper; see also 140n.

891 **oaten** belonging to the oat as a plant (*OED a.* 3*)

892 **ploughmen's clocks** because they wake them up or tell them when to get up; the lark is the bird of the dawn.

893 **turtles** turtle-doves
tread mate, copulate (*OED v.* 8b); see also 4.3.275n., 5.2.330n.
daws jackdaws

883–4] *Theobald; in reverse order QF*   900 SP] *Kerrigan; Winter QF and centred*

And Dick the shepherd blows his nail
And Tom bears logs into the hall
    And milk comes frozen home in pail,
    When blood is nipped and ways be foul,
Then nightly sings the staring owl: 905
    'Tu-whit, Tu-whoo!'
A merry note,
While greasy Joan doth keel the pot.

When all aloud the wind doth blow
    And coughing drowns the parson's saw   910
And birds sit brooding in the snow
    And Marian's nose looks red and raw,
When roasted crabs hiss in the bowl,
Then nightly sings the staring owl:
    'Tu-whit, Tu-whoo!'   915

---

901 **Dick** See 5.2.464n.
  blows his nail blows on his finger-
  nails to warm them (*OED* nail *sb.* 3b),
  but the phrase also suggests having
  nothing much to do: under 'Ceincture'
  Cotgrave has '*blow their fingers*' for
  doing something in '*an idle, and lazie
  fashion*'.
902 **Tom** A lower-class name, adopted
  e.g. by Edgar in *KL*. Its association
  with *Dick* (901) suggests a generic formula like 'Tom, Dick and Harry'; cf.
  Tilley, T376.
904 **is . . . be** For the construction, see
  Abbott, 300.
  nipped painfully affected by cold
  (*OED v.*[1] 6a)
  *****foul** muddy (*OED A.* 2); cf. 4.1.136n.
905 **owl** See also 4.1.138n.
906 **Tu-whit, Tu-whoo** *OED**; the owl's
  onomatopoeic cry could be understood
  as 'to it', i.e. to have sex, as in *KL*
  4.6.112, 'to woo' or 'to who'.
908 **greasy** covered with grease; fat,
  sweaty; obscene, filthy (*OED a.* 7); cf.

4.1.136n.
Joan See 3.1.200n., 4.3.179.
keel cool by stirring and so on, to stop
a pot from boiling over (*OED v.*[1] 1b)
909 **all aloud** very loudly
910 **parson's** clergyman's or vicar's.
Rather than the more specific rector
(*OED* 2), *parson* perhaps suggests the
curate Sir Nathaniel; cf. 4.2.80n. and
5.2.882–917n.
saw discourse, sermon
911 **brooding** like hens on eggs (*OED v.*
5*)
912 **Marian's** The name is a diminutive
of Mary (or Maria). Shakespeare uses
it in *CE* 3.1.31, *TS* Ind. 2.21, *Tem*
2.2.48 as a name for lower-class
women. Maid Marian's part in morris
dances and May games, where she
appeared with Robin Hood, led to her
association with loose sexual behaviour; cf. *1H4* 3.3.114, *TN* 2.3.14.
913 **crabs** crab-apples; cf. 4.2.6n. and
note to Costard in the List of Roles.
bowl i.e. bowl of ale

---

904 foul] *F (*fowle*);* full *Q*   906, 915] *QF;* Tu-whoo! / Tu-whit, tu-who *Kittredge (Capell)*

A merry note,
While greasy Joan doth keel the pot.

ARMADO   The words of Mercury are harsh after the songs
of Apollo. You that way, we this way.   [*Exeunt.*]

FINIS

918–19 **The . . . Apollo** In Q this sentence is set in larger type than most of the rest of the play and has no SP. The only comedy which ends with a song is *TN* and of the early comedies only *MW* ends with a prose speech and *TGV* with an unrhymed verse speech. Mercury, the messenger of the gods, associated with eloquence and sophistry, is opposed to Apollo, the god of music who is also the sun god: cf. the play's rich sun imagery which is connected to beauty, e.g. 1.1.84, 4.3.217–24, 308, and particularly *bright Apollo's lute*, 317, 5.2.201–2. Bate, 228, traces the story of the gods' rivalry for Chione in Ovid, *Met.*, 11: she has a twin boy by each god.

Mercury's son is Autolycus, for whom see *WT*, and Apollo's is the famous singer Philammon. The sentiment may be general or may be specifically intended to recall Marcadé's harsh or discordant news in contrast to the lords' love poems in 4.3: cf. also the *harsh indignity* the lords are said to suffer at 5.2.289.

918 **harsh** jarring, discordant; cf. *R2* 3.4.74, *VA* 431.

919 **You . . . ²way** Not in Q, this sentence and the one before it are assigned to Armado in F. The *You* might be the audience or the ladies and *we* the actors or the lords and their associates, or Armado and Jaquenetta together.

918 SP] *F (Brag.); not in Q*   918–19] *Capell; verse F, lined* Mercurie, / Apollo: / way. /   The . . . Apollo.] *set in larger type than the rest of dialogue in Q*   919 You . . . this way.] *F; not in Q*   SD] *F (Exeunt omnes.); not in Q*

APPENDIX 1
THE TEXT

THE TITLE-PAGE

The text of this edition is based on the first surviving quarto (Q1), printed at London by William White for Cuthbert Burby and dated 1598. Q's title-page (Fig. 14) supplies a certain amount of information about the play's production and publishing history.

Burby was a bookseller who is known to have traded from 1592 and by 1598 was well established in a shop by the Royal Exchange. He published a variety of books, but with a fairly strong literary bias, and can be associated with authors like Robert Greene, Thomas Nashe, Angel Day, Francis Meres and so on. By 1598 he also had some experience of publishing plays, including: in 1594 Robert Greene's *Orlando Furioso*, John Lyly's *Mother Bombie* (reprinted 1598), Robert Wilson's *The Cobbler's Prophecy* and the anonymous *The Taming of a Shrew* (reprinted in 1596); in 1596 *Edward III* and *A Knack to Know an Honest Man*, both anonymous. There is no obvious connection between Burby and a specific theatrical company. *Love's Labour's Lost* was the first of Cuthbert Burby's two Shakespeare quartos: in 1599 he published Q2 of *Romeo and Juliet*. Like Q1 of *Love's Labour's Lost*, this proclaimed itself on its title-page as an 'improved' edition, saying it was 'Newly corrected, augmented, and amended'. Both plays were published without entry in the Stationers' Register, but Burby's ownership of the two works was recognized when on 22 January 1607 they, along with *The Taming of a Shrew*, were transferred in the Stationers' Register from him to Nicholas Ling.

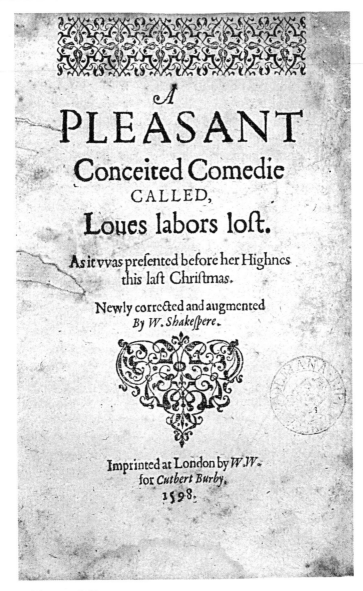

A

PLEASANT

Conceited Comedie

CALLED,

Loues labors loſt.

As it vvas preſented before her Highnes
this laſt Chriſtmas.

Newly correǝcted and augmented
By W. Shakeſpere.

Imprinted at London by *W.W.*
for *Cutbert Burby.*
1598.

14 Title-page of Q1

The presence of Shakespeare's name on the title-page of Q1 *Love's Labour's Lost* is of some interest. Before 1598 no work by Shakespeare had been issued with his name in such a prominent position, although *Venus and Adonis* and *The Rape of Lucrece* both had dedications signed by him ('William Shakespeare'). Earlier dramatic texts name the company which acted the play, not its author, although *2 Henry VI* has neither Shakespeare's name nor his company on its title-page. In 1598 Shakespeare was revealed as the author of *Love's Labour's Lost* ('By W. Shakespere' – quotations from title-pages have all been regularized to roman); in the same year his name also appeared on the title-pages of Q2 and Q3 *Richard II* ('By William Shakespeare'), and on Q2 *Richard III* ('By William Shake-speare'). These three editions of the histories were all published by Andrew Wise. If 1598 marked the public appearance of Shakespeare's name in print, the next year saw its earliest appropriation, on the title-page of *The Passionate Pilgrim*: it was said to be 'By W. Shakespeare' and contained poems from *Love's Labour's Lost*.

The description of *Love's Labour's Lost* as 'A Pleasant Conceited Comedie' yields some indication of what sort of a play it was thought to be. The epithets describing the comedy were not new – they first appeared in *Fedele and Fortunio* (1585), called 'a very pleasaunt and fine conceited Comœdie' – and became popular from the mid-1590s: William Warner's translation of Plautus' *Menaechmi* (1595) was said to be 'A pleasant and fine Conceited Comædie'; Peele's *The Old Wives Tale* (1595) was 'A pleasant conceited Comedie', as was Heywood's(?) *How a Man may Choose a Good Wife from a Bad* (1602). Three plays published by Burby suggest it was a formula he favoured: *A Knack to Know an Honest Man* (1596) and *George a Greene* (1599) were both said on their title-pages to be pleasant conceited comedies, and *The Taming of a Shrew* (1594) was called 'A Pleasant Conceited Historie'. This generic adaptation can be paralleled by Q1 *Romeo and Juliet* (1597), which was headed 'An

Excellent conceited Tragedie' – the description was not retained in Q2 (1599). Shakespeare's only other play with a comparable formula was Q1 of *The Merry Wives of Windsor* (1602), described as 'A Most pleasaunt and excellent conceited Comedie'; it had a similar head title but omitted the word 'Most'.

The two most problematic elements on the title-page of *Love's Labour's Lost* relate to its presentation 'before her Highnes this last Christmas' and to the claim that the quarto was 'Newly corrected and augmented'. These two pieces of information are related and it is best to deal with the second first. It has suggested to most scholars that Q1 was preceded by an earlier quarto and some external evidence may support this theory. In 1656 the publisher Edward Archer drew up a 'An Exact and perfect Catalogue of all the Plaies that were ever printed' in which he included 'Loves labor lost C Will. Sampson';[1] Greg described the attribution to Sampson as 'curious' and posited that if there were an earlier edition than Q1 'it may possibly have borne the initials "W.S." in place of [Shakespeare's] name, and Archer may have seen a copy in which they had been wrongly expanded'. Archer's testimony cannot be considered conclusive, but supports the possibility that the 1598 quarto was not the first printing of *Love's Labour's Lost*. If this were the case, then it becomes necessary to determine the nature of the earlier quarto. Did it contain a text substantially identical to the one preserved in 1598 or was it different in some way? The formula 'Newly corrected and augmented' has suggested to scholars that the lost quarto was in some way corrupt or deficient – that it was what has usually been known as a 'bad' quarto, that is one whose origins are thought to lie in memorial reconstruction. In this way it would be a closely parallel case to Burby's Q2 *Romeo and Juliet* with its title-page claiming it was 'Newly corrected, augmented, and amended', presumably to replace the 'bad' quarto of 1597.

1   W. W. Greg, *A Bibliography of the English Printed Drama to the Restoration*, 4 vols (1939–59), 2.998, θ 142.

In 1598 the claim that a play was 'Newly corrected and augmented' was a relatively unusual and new one. The earliest known instance of such a statement appearing on a title-page was in the first quarto of *The Spanish Tragedy* (1592), which is said to be 'Newly corrected and amended of such grosse faults as passed in the first impression', but as with *Love's Labour's Lost* no earlier quarto survives. The phrase 'Newly set foorth' on the title-page of *Mucedorus* (1598) may suggest it replaced an earlier edition, but this is merely a possibility; the same may be true of *A Knack to Know a Knave* (1594), which also has 'Newlie set foorth' on its title-page. In 1599 a new edition of *Soliman and Perseda* was published which then had a second issue otherwise identical except for the words 'Newly corrected and amended' stamped in by hand after the sheet was printed. The only other plays of the 1590s in which a similar formula appears are Shakespeare's *Love's Labour's Lost* and, from 1599, Q2 of *1 Henry IV* which announced – without justification – that it was 'Newly corrected'. In the new century, again, Shakespeare is particularly associated on title-pages with corrected or revised plays: Q3 of *Richard III* (1602) was unjustifiably said to be 'Newly augmented' and Q2 of *Hamlet* (1604–5) was said, rather more correctly, to be 'enlarged to almost as much againe as it was, according to the true and perfect Coppie'. Other such claims are equally genuine. The 1602 edition of *The Spanish Tragedy* appeared 'Newly corrected, amended, and enlarged with new additions of the Painters part, and others'; Q3 of *The Malcontent* was published in 1604 as 'Augmented' by Marston with 'the Additions' written by Webster; the second edition of *The Fawn* in 1606 was 'corrected of many faults' which the author's absence had permitted in the first edition of the same year; and the 1610 edition of *Mucedorus* rightly said it was 'Amplified with new additions'. When the 1616 'B-text' of *Dr Faustus* was published again in 1619 its title-page stated that it was printed 'With new Additions'.

In this context, however, title-page claims before 1610 for correction and augmentation of Shakespeare's work provide uncertain evidence about the nature of what was supposedly being corrected. Second quartos of *Romeo and Juliet* and *Hamlet* may replace earlier 'bad' quartos, but *Richard III* Q3 and *1 Henry IV* Q2 both wrongly claim improvements on earlier texts. It is also important to note that once a statement of this kind got on the title-page of a book, it tended to stay there whenever it was reprinted. For example, the formula 'Amplified with new additions' which first appeared with the 1610 edition of *Mucedorus* was repeated in 1611, 1613, 1615, 1618, 1619, 1621 and so on. The implications of this may affect an understanding of the other remaining element on the title-page of *Love's Labour's Lost*, that it 'was presented before her Highnes this last Christmas'. From 1570 the title-pages of some eighteen plays assert that they were presented before Queen Elizabeth; of these, five got into second or later editions within thirty years of first publication. In three out of these five, the circumstances of the original performance before the Queen are repeated without significant alteration – *The Shoemakers' Holiday* (1600) went on claiming it was acted before the Queen on New Year's Day at night in 1610, 1618, 1624, 1631 and 1657. There are, however, examples which run counter to this practice. Lyly's *Campaspe* was first published in 1584, stating it was performed on Twelfth Night, and then republished twice more in the same year, advertising a performance on New Year's Day; in the 1591 edition, the title-page reverted to the Twelfth Night performance. As well as being altered, records of royal performances could also be removed. Neither the 1619 nor the 1630 editions of *The Merry Wives of Windsor* repeated Q1's claim that it was performed before the Queen. Nevertheless, the same general repetition of information about royal performances holds for Jacobean plays such as *Mucedorus* (1610), *The Phoenix* (1607) and *King Lear* (1608); the specific New Year's night performance mentioned in Q2 of *A Trick to Catch the Old One* (1608/9) was dropped from Q3 (1616), but the more general royal connection was maintained. The 1610 edition of *Mucedorus*, first published in 1598, supplies a unique example of a revised play ('Amplified with new additions') whose title-page boasts the new information that 'it was acted before the Kings Maiestie at White-hall on Shroue-sunday night'.

Those who supplied the copy for title-pages evidently did not feel that they were writing on oath, and it would be dangerous either to put too much faith in their claims to be providing better and fuller texts than their predecessors or to trust in the accuracy of their apparent statements about performances. The 'last Christmas' referred to on the title-page of *Love's Labour's Lost* in 1598 might correctly refer to the season of 1597–8 but the formula could have been copied from an earlier lost edition referring to a different Christmas season. That earlier lost edition need not have been significantly different from the quarto of 1598, or it may have been as radically different as Q1 of *Romeo and Juliet* is from Q2. Burby published both second quartos (without entering them in the Stationers' Register), but where the tragedy is said to have been 'Newly corrected, augmented, and amended' the comedy is, less radically, 'Newly corrected and augmented': it was not 'amended'. In these circumstances it would be unwise to try to reconstruct the textual history of *Love's Labour's Lost* on the precedent of *Romeo and Juliet* without further corroborative evidence.

The question of revision, which may be raised by the wording of the title-page, has been pursued at length, notably by John Dover Wilson (in Cam[1] 1923 and 1962), whose elaborate arguments centred around new material written for performance before the Queen in the Christmas season of 1597–8. Although the false starts in the text of the quarto appear to show Shakespeare's revising the play as he wrote it, a general scepticism about a later wholesale revision has developed. This was aided by John Kerrigan's conclusive demonstration that Shakespeare need not have taken the lady-smocks in Ver's song from the 1597 edition of John Gerard's *Herbal*, since his fellow Warwickshire countryman Michael Drayton had already used the word in *The Shepherd's Garland* of 1593.[1] In the end, without developing enormously elaborate theories about early and late revision, it is impossible to determine whether the evidence for authorial second thoughts points to immediate or to longer-term alterations.

Q1 (1598)

Much of the earlier career of William White, the printer of Q1, was bound up with the printing and publishing of religious works, especially those of Hugh Broughton. The comedy was the first theatrical text White is known to have printed: in the next year, 1599, he printed and published Q3 of Kyd's *The Spanish Tragedy*, Q2 of Peele's *Edward I* and in 1600 *3 Henry VI* Q2. These might suggest that White was accustomed to reprinting plays and that Q1 of *Love's Labour's Lost* was another such straightforward reprint. There is some internal evidence which supports this view.

Paul Werstine has closely examined seventeen of the twenty books White printed between 1598 and 1600: twelve of these were set from manuscript copy and five, including the three play reprints, from printed copy.[2] In part, Werstine wanted to respond to earlier theories about the copy for Q1 and its printing history put forward by George R. Price and Manfred Draudt. The first had argued that Q1 was set from authorial 'foul papers', the second that Acts 1 to 3 of the play were set from a lost 'bad' quarto and Acts 4 and 5 from authorial 'foul papers', with occasional consultation of the manuscript copy in Acts 1 to 3. In rebutting their work, Werstine examined certain typographic features such as the setting of stage directions and speech prefixes and the indentation of speeches, and touched on

---

1   Mats Rydén, 'Shakespeare's cuckoo-buds', *Studia Neophilologica*, 49 (1977), 25–7; John Kerrigan, '*Love's Labor's Lost* and Shakespearean revision', *SQ*, 33 (1982), 337–9.
2   Werstine's essay reprints and amplifies his earlier article 'Editorial Uses of Compositor Study', *Analytical and Enumerative Bibliography*, 2 (1978), 153–65.

the question of initial capitals and compositorial errors, but devoted particular attention to spelling patterns. With half-a-dozen key discriminators, such as any/anie, eye/eie, fayth/faith, many/manie, very/verie, White's compositors showed an almost exclusive preference for the first form in books set from manuscript copy. However, in works set from printed copy the second form appears in relatively large numbers, sometimes more frequently even than the first form: the distribution of different forms is sufficiently regular throughout these reprints that there is no need to posit an idiosyncratic compositor at work. Werstine's conclusion was that in works set from manuscript White's compositors imposed their own house style on the copy, but that they tended to reproduce underlying features already present in the works they were reprinting. When the same features were examined in *Love's Labour's Lost*, it was clear it belonged to the group of reprints, not to the works set from manuscript copy. Although Werstine's analysis is convincing, it must be remembered that it was largely based on only one kind of evidence. However, it strongly suggested that White's compositors set Shakespeare's play from printed copy: if so, then the printed copy must have been more or less similar to what has come down in Q1. This in turn argues, again, that a putative lost earlier quarto may not have been a 'bad' one.

If that is the case, and Q1 of *Love's Labour's Lost* is in fact a reprint, it follows that White was not the printer of the lost first quarto (Q0), since his compositors would have imposed his characteristic spelling patterns on it. The identities of the printer and the publisher of this putative quarto are unknown and its lack of entry in the Stationers' Register as a 'good' Shakespeare text, not preceded by a bad one, is exceptional. It is therefore impossible to determine by comparison with other work how the unknown printer might have treated his copy-text. With two of the three play texts which White reprinted – *Edward I* and *3 Henry VI* – he did not attempt an exact paginary reprint but with *The Spanish Tragedy* he followed Q2 exactly until the end of sig. I2v so that the remaining eight leaves do not correspond to the same leaves in the earlier quarto. If *Love's Labour's Lost* Q1 is a reprint, it could follow the earlier edition exactly, not at all or only in part. As a result of all this a number of layers of interference complicate the play's textual history.

Editors will always try to determine the nature of the copy which was submitted to the printer. The printer of Q0 would have been given a manuscript of some kind. One or more compositors would have imposed their own habits and preferences on it while at the same time accommodating it to the house's general style and retaining some of the underlying characteristic features of the manuscript. When the play was reprinted by White, his compositor or compositors would have repeated this process, which now, additionally, included the retention of some underlying characteristics from the earlier printer. Although they would have corrected some errors in the earlier print, they would also have introduced new ones of their own. In these circumstances, although it has been generally agreed the copy submitted to the printer of Q0 consisted of some sort of authorial manuscript, attempts to identify the compositors of Q1 and to reconstruct its printing history have been contentious.

In the course of this century bibliographers and editors have argued that the marks of an authorial draft manuscript include irregularity about the naming of the characters, false starts in composition, unclear action, unsatisfactory, permissive and vague stage directions and the appearance of 'ghost' characters. In addition to these, scholars have sought to identify distinctive spellings which can be attributed to the author's own hand and obvious errors caused by difficulties with reading his handwriting (Greg, 106–37, 141–2; *TxC*, 9, 14). Some of these features can be illustrated from a study of Q1 of *Love's Labour's Lost*.

The most prominent of the presumed signs of an authorial manuscript's being behind *Love's Labour's Lost* involves the naming of characters, about which there is much confusion. This mainly affects the King, the Princess, her ladies and the minor comic characters, but not the other lords: in the following discussion I shall regularize speech prefixes and ignore their shortened forms. The King's first speech is delivered as Ferdinand and he appears as such throughout 1.1; but in 2.1 he is Navarre for his first six speeches and thereafter (128) Ferdinand for four speeches until his last one (178) where he reverts to Navarre. He reappears in 4.3 and 5.2 as King throughout. The Princess starts off as Queen in 2.1.13 but for the rest of the scene is Princess. She is Queen throughout 4.1 and 5.2 except for one moment when she appears as Lady (553).

Like the King, Dull also appears in three different guises: in 1.1 he speaks three times as Constable, but once (258) as Anthony; in 1.2 he is again Constable, yet in 4.2 he speaks all seven times and in 5.1 on both occasions as Dull. Costard is Clown in 1.1, 1.2, 4.1, 5.1 and 5.2; but in 3.1 he changes mid-scene to Costard for two speeches (144, 146), reverting to his generic title for his remaining five speeches. Similarly, his first line in 4.2 has him as Clown (83) and his only other one (144) as Costard; in 4.3 there are three Clown speeches to one by Costard (195). Armado appears as himself in 1.2, but in 5.1 and 5.2 he is called Braggart; he begins 3.1 under his generic name, but changes almost midway after Moth and Costard enter (68) to his own name. Moth appears throughout 1.2 as Boy and as the same in 3.1 until his exit (62), when he reappears as Page for five speeches, reverts to Boy once (103) and then back to Page for two last lines (110, 131). Again, in 5.1 his first speech (35) is as Boy, but then he turns back to being Page. In 5.2 when he comes on with the Blackamoors he speaks six times as Page, but in his last two speeches later in the scene (696, 707) he is divided between Page and Boy. Holofernes and Nathaniel have comparable histories. In 4.2 Holofernes appears mainly under his own name, but his first speech (3) is delivered with the prefix Pedant, as is the one assigned to him at 119 and the unnecessary one at 135, followed by his last three in the scene. Nathaniel retains his own name throughout the scene, apart from having one speech as

Curate Nathaniel (8). Thereafter, the two men appear under their generic names in 5.1 and 5.2. Jaquenetta is Maid in 1.2, but speaks her three speeches in 4.3 and three of her four speeches in 4.2 under her own name, but her last (142) as Maid. The large number of these variations have usually been taken to suggest that Shakespeare was not certain about what he wanted to call his characters – or at least some of them. The fluidity of nomenclature, affecting some nine of the play's characters, is exceptional.

The form of the character's name which occurs in stage directions announcing his or her entrance sometimes seems to determine the form used in the following first speech (for example, with Moth as Page in 3.1.67 or as Boy in 5.1.35). However, this is not always the case, as at 2.1.13, where the Princess speaks as Queen, having just entered as Princess, or at 5.2.158, where Moth speaks as Page when he has just entered as '*the Boy*'.

Although the speech headings for the King's male followers, as well as for Boyet, the Forester and Marcadé, are regularly named, there is one notorious problem with assigning speeches – a crux in 2.1 which has come to be known as the Rosaline-Katherine (or Katherine-Rosaline) tangle, despite the fact that it revolves around Berowne. The episode is complicated: some of the solutions which have been put forward to explain it are even more complicated and a simple explanation of it is attractive.[1]

The problem begins in the quarto when each of the Princess's ladies speaks for the first time. At 2.1.40, 56 and 64 they appear respectively as 1 Lady, 2 Lady and 3 Lady and one of them appears in her second speech (53) as Lady. 1 Lady says she has seen Longaville before at a marriage between Lord Perigort and the heir of Jaques Falconbridge, and then as Lady reports

---

1 See John Kerrigan, 'Shakespeare at work: the Katharine-Rosaline tangle in *Love's Labour's Lost*', *RES*, NS, 33 (1982), 129–36; Manfred Draudt, 'The "Rosaline-Katherine tangle" of *Love's Labour's Lost*' and 'Correspondence: the "Rosaline-Katherine tangle"', *The Library*, 6th series, 4 (1982), 381–96 and 5 (1983), 399–404.

further on his humours. 2 Lady talks about Dumaine, whom she once saw at the Duke of Alençon's; and 3 Lady talks about Berowne. Towards the end of a conversation between the King, the Princess and Boyet (80–113) about the men's welcome and their oath the Princess gives the King a paper concerning her demands. While the King reads it in Q Berowne and Katherine have an exchange (114–27) about dancing together at Brabant. The King, the Princess and Boyet then have some talk (128–78) about the letter and its claim for money. At its end an exit is called for, which certainly applies to the King, who does not appear again in the scene; it must cover Dumaine, who enters again fourteen lines later, and probably applies to Longaville. In Q Berowne and Rosaline now have a witty encounter (179–92) and he leaves the stage. Up to this point the audience does not know the names of the ladies. Dumaine enters and asks Boyet, 'What lady is that same?', and before leaving again is told it is Rosaline (194) and that she is 'The heir of Alençon'. Longaville then goes through the same process with Boyet (196–207) but, while learning that she is an heir of Falconbridge (204), is not told his lady's name and exits. The trio is completed when Berowne enters again and is told that his lady is called Katherine (209). He then leaves and the Princess and her ladies chat with Boyet. Here, the ladies appear as Lady Maria (214), as Lady Katherine (218), then in the next three speeches simply as Lady (220–3) and at its end (253-5) as Lady, Lady 2 and Lady 3, then twice again (256–7) simply as Lady.

As it stands the scene is puzzling: besides other difficulties, Berowne flirts first with Katherine, then with Rosaline – in whose name Dumaine is interested – and then is concerned to know Katherine's name. 1 Lady, who has been at a Falconbridge marriage, is associated with Longaville, who is told she is a Falconbridge heir. 2 Lady once saw Dumaine at Alençon's and Rosaline is an heir of his: this does not necessarily make Rosaline identical with 2 Lady, but it is clear we are meant to associate Rosaline with Alençon. This partial information is not quite

enough to identify the three unnamed ladies, but for the rest of
the play, from 3.1.162–4, when Berowne gives Costard a letter
and names its recipient as Rosaline, there is no more serious confusion about which lord is after which lady. As later events
reveal, 1 Lady is Maria, who is courted by Longaville – her name
does not occur in the dialogue until 4.3.53; 2 Lady is Rosaline
but should be Katherine and 3 Lady is Katherine but should be
Rosaline. Taking the names in that corrected order – Maria,
Katherine, Rosaline – it is not hard to assign the remaining
speeches at the end of the scene, especially those which, appearing
as Lady, Lady 2 and Lady 3, follow the same order of names.

  G. R. Hibbard has put forward the simplest explanation for
this tangle: Shakespeare changed his mind about the pairings of
lords and ladies in the scene and altered the name of Berowne's
woman from Katherine (perhaps influenced by the name of the
heroine in *The Taming of the Shrew*) to that of Romeo's dark-
eyed love Rosaline (Oxf[1], 60–3). I accept Hibbard's analysis and
conclusion and have therefore changed 'Katherine' to 'Rosaline'
at 2.1.115–26 and 209 and replaced 'Rosaline' with 'Katherine'
at 194. Other solutions to the crux – involving masks, cancella-
tions, revisions and separate sheets of paper – can and have been
put forward, but Hibbard's theory of authorial indecision
'accounts for more than any other hypothesis and accounts for it
more readily and economically' (Oxf[1], 63).

  This is not the only moment in the quarto where speech prefixes are wrongly or unnecessarily assigned or are simply
missing. Difficulties continue in 5.2 about the naming of the
ladies while they are being courted by the lords, who cannot pen-
etrate their disguises. Rosaline and the King pair off (221–9),
then Berowne and the Princess (230–7) and then Dumaine and
Maria (238–41). The next encounter should therefore be
between Katherine and Longaville (242–55), but instead in Q it
is between Maria and Longaville. Since this is the correct pairing for the play as a whole, it may be that the error is simply
Shakespeare's.

A second set of speech-heading confusions occurs in 4.2 and seems to have seeped into 5.1. It involves the characters Holofernes and Nathaniel, who make their first appearances comparatively late in the play. All goes well until 4.2.65 where a speech in praise of Holofernes' wit, evidently spoken by himself, is assigned to Nathaniel; his next speech is in turn assigned to Holofernes. The confusion of roles continues from 65 to 147, when the correct order is restored. However, there are further difficulties within these lines. Holofernes speaks his first line in the scene as Pedant and Nathaniel his second as Curate Nathaniel; after that the two appear under their own names until about halfway through the wrongly assigned passage. In it Nathaniel is made to ask to 'hear a staff, a stanza, a verse' (103) of Berowne's poem and immediately reads it out. The next speech correctly belongs to Holofernes and the first two sentences of it (119–20) are rightly given to him, but in his role as Pedant. The rest of the speech is assigned to Nathaniel. When they turn their attention to the direction on Berowne's letter, Nathaniel gets to read out its opening and closing formulas (130–4), but then the rest of his speech is (now correctly) given to the Pedant, who starts it by addressing himself, 'Sir *Holofernes*, this *Berowne* is one of the Votaries . . .' (135), when the title ('Sir') correctly belongs to Nathaniel. Once Costard and Jaquenetta have gone, Nathaniel appears incorrectly for the last time (145) as Holofernes; the speeches are correctly assigned to the end of the scene, but Holofernes continues to be called Pedant. When the pair appear again in 5.1 and 5.2 they are regularly called Pedant and Curate. But at 5.1.110 there is one further sign of confusion about which was which. In a complex passage Holofernes proposes the show of the Nine Worthies, but is made to address himself as 'Sir *Holofernes*', when (as at 4.2.135) the title belongs to, and the speech should be aimed at, Nathaniel.

As Stanley Wells has said about these tangles, they are 'more easily solved than explained' (*TxC*, 271). Wells and Taylor detect authorial confusion about personal names which Shakespeare resolved by calling Holofernes and Nathaniel by their generic titles; the important confusion about the superscript of Berowne's letter can be explained by a marginal change from Nathaniel to Pedant – incorrectly carried out by the compositor. Shakespeare's confusion was compounded by thinking Holofernes was the curate, hence his anomalous title. At least this has the advantage of simplicity and credibility: Hibbard proposes (Oxf[1], 64) that Shakespeare began the scene in London and tried to finish it while out of town: he 'jotted the continuation down, caring little whether he had the names right or wrong, since he knew any necessary adjustment could be made in the fair copy'. Nevertheless, the two theories are essentially based on authorial uncertainty.

Hibbard also detected (Oxf[1], 64–5) another sign of authorial confusion in relation to Berowne's letter which Jaquenetta delivered. At first (4.2.89–90) she says it was written by Don Armado and given to her by Costard. She asks 'Good Master Parson' to read it and, although Nathaniel replies to her speech in the quarto, the lines correctly belong to Holofernes. A little later, after Berowne's poem has been read out, Holofernes asks Jaquenetta whether the letter was directed to her. She replies, 'Ay, sir, from one Monsieur Berowne, one of the strange queen's lords' (128–9): not only does Jaquenetta contradict herself about its provenance, but she reveals she knows it comes from Berowne, who she thinks is one of the Princess's lords. Hibbard, following Wells, believed the speech should have been cancelled after 'Ay, sir' and that it was replaced by Holofernes' immediately following description of Berowne as 'one of the votaries with the King' (135–6). In her second speech either Jaquenetta is alarmingly confused or Shakespeare was.

These tangles in 2.1 and 4.2 (and 5.1) are the most serious in the play. Were it not for the evidently incorrect names in the dialogue, it might be possible to attribute the errors in speech prefixes to their being hastily added in the margins after the speeches had been written. Shakespeare may well have begun work with what characters said and turned to their names at a later stage.

There are other possible marginal errors in the assigning of speeches elsewhere. For example, at 1.1.127 Berowne's prefix is missing and has been unnecessarily printed at 131; in 5.2 Rosaline's prefix, which should come before 217, appears before the preceding line, which is the King's; there is a further unnecessarily repeated prefix for the King at 4.3.192. Some prefixes which may be wrongly assigned can be easily explained, as at 1.1.279 where '*Ber.*' in Q is presumably a simple misprint or misreading for '*Fer.*'. On several other occasions it is harder to be certain about the source of the error – if it is one – and to decide between compositorial (or scribal) error and authorial uncertainty. At 1.2.139, just before Dull and Jaquenetta exit, in Q the Clown says, 'Come, Jaquenetta, away': the line could belong to Costard, who remains on stage, as an order to leave, rather than to Dull, to whom it is usually assigned, as an order to accompany him. In Dull's first speech his prefix is '*Constab.*' and so the compositor may have misunderstood a marginal 'C.', or he may have anticipated the string of '*Clo.*' prefixes which follow Dull's exit. Anticipation or repetition may account for Longaville's being given a line, 4.3.46, which clearly belongs to the King. A misunderstood 'B.' may explain Berowne's being given Boyet's line at 5.2.159, but again anticipation may play a part. A similarly ambiguous prefix, '*Boy.*' at 5.2.707, refers to the Boy, that is Moth, not to Boyet. The appearance of Lady for Princess at 5.2.553 is more puzzling and it is possible only to guess why Armado's prefix for the last lines of the play – if they are a speech and they are his – is missing (see further, p. 332).

The evidence of uncertainty about what the characters were to be called in speech prefixes or to whom speeches should be assigned is continued in the stage directions of the quarto, which are unsatisfactory and tend to be rather vague. The King appears in them as 'Ferdinand K. of Nauar' (1.1.0.1), as '*Nauar*' (2.1.88.1) and as the '*King*' (4.3.18.1 and 40 SD, 5.2.309.1);

where his followers are not named they appear as '*Enter the King and the rest*' (5.2.309.1). The Princess and her retinue enter with Boyet as '*the Princesse of Fraunce, with three attending Ladies and three Lordes*' (2.1.0.1–2) and as '*the Princesse . . . her Ladyes, and her Lordes*' (4.1.0.1–2), and without Boyet simply as '*the Ladyes*' or '*the Ladies*' (5.2.0.1, 160 SD, 336.1). Dull is called a '*Constable*' (1.1.178.1) and '*Dull*' (4.2.0.1, 5.1.0.2). Costard is called by his proper name (1.1.178.1), but thereafter '*Clowne*' (1.2.120.1, 3.1.66.1, 4.3.185.1, 5.2.483.1). Jaquenetta appears as '*Wench*' (1.2.120.2) but later as '*Iaquenetta*' (4.3.185.1). Armado and Moth enter first of all as '*Armado and Moth his page*' (1.2.0.1), then as '*Braggart and his Boy*' (3.1.0.1) and '*Bragart, Boy*' (5.1.28.1); on their own they appear as '*Brag[g]art*' (5.2.519.1, 866.1) and '*Page*' (3.1.66.1) or '*the Boy*' (5.2.157.1, 581.1–2). Holofernes and Nathaniel first appear as '*Holofernes, the Pedant and Nathaniel*' (4.2.0.1), as '*the Pedant, the Curat*' (5.1.0.1–2) and separately as '*Pedant*' (5.2.581.1) and '*Curat[e]*' (5.2.557.1 and at his exit). A more general entrance is rather vaguely indicated at the end of the play by '*Enter all*' (5.2.878.1). Apart from entrances and exits, other stage directions are sparse, with the first one, '*Boyet reedes*', not coming until 4.1.61, followed at the end of the scene by 'Shoot within'. At the beginning of 4.3 Berowne is made to enter '*with a paper in his hand, alone*'; '*He standes a side. The King entreth*' (4.3.18 and 18.1); when Longaville enters '*The King steps a side*' (40 SD) and then Longaville '*reades the Sonnet*' (57) as Dumaine later on '*reades his Sonnet*' (98) and Berowne '*reades the letter*' (192). In 5.2, in addition to the slightly unusual '*Berowne steps foorth*' (661), followed soon after by the mistaken direction '*The partie is gone*' (667), there are two slightly longer and more descriptive directions, '*Enter Black-moores with musicke, the Boy with a speach, and the rest of the Lordes disguysed*' (157.1–2) and 'The Ladyes turne their backes to him' (160 SD). There are two further imperative stage directions, '*Draw-out his Table-booke*' (5.1.15 SD) and '*Sound Trom.*' (5.2.156 SD), but these are hardly sufficient to suggest that the quarto's copy-text had been prepared for performance. Two stage directions are missing for entrances by Longaville at 2.1.195.1 and for Costard at 5.1.28.1–2; necessary exits are not indicated at 1.1.291, 1.2.159, 3.1.62, at the end of 3.1 (for Berowne), 4.1.106 and 138, 4.3.209 and 357. All of these descriptions suggest a script which has not yet reached the stage. Yet, although in Greg's words 'One could hardly have more typical author-directions' (221), there are none of the permissive kind of stage directions allowing, for example, two or three attendants to enter, which are usually taken to be indicative of an author's working manuscript.

Similarly, ghost characters, revealing changes in the author's ideas about the play's personnel, are rather thin on the ground: there is no equivalent to *Much Ado About Nothing*'s Innogen. The nearest the play comes to offering named characters who appear but then have no part is at the beginning of 2.1. There the Princess enters with three attending ladies and three lords and it looks as though there is going to be some neat symmetry in the Princess's attendants. However, the lords get only two half-lines and these are assigned in the quarto simply to Lord. Boyet must be one of the three lords, and perhaps Shakespeare found Boyet was sufficiently powerful a character to dispense with speaking parts for the other lords. Even so, the Princess still needed some attendants and her lords are included in the entry direction at the beginning of 4.1. Other signs of authorial uncertainty and confusion in relation to the plot may possibly include Jaquenetta's muddle regarding the origins of her letter in 4.2 and the casting of the Nine Worthies. Critics have also posited a lost or abandoned episode, alluded to by Costard at the end of 4.1, in which Armado walked before his lady, bearing her fan and kissing his hand, but this is not necessary.

There are at least two false starts in composition which survived from the working manuscript and which were transmitted to the quarto: they are reprinted in Appendix 2. As with the Rosaline-Katherine tangle, they both involve Berowne. The first comes after 4.3.291 and consists of some twenty-three lines of which one (22) was meant to be cancelled.[1] The second false start comes after 5.2.810, where six lines exchanged between Berowne and Rosaline anticipate their longer conversation at 825–59. Both reveal something of how Shakespeare's view of Berowne's character changed.[2] In the unrevised first passage Berowne addresses his companions as 'you [who] have vowed to study', but in the revised version he talks about how 'we have made a vow to study'. The original position of the second unrevised passage shows that Shakespeare saw Rosaline's sentence on Berowne as the first of the ones delivered to the three lords and that it was not a witty one. Further false starts have been detected involving Jaquenetta at 4.2.128–9 (p. 313) and the Princess at 5.2.130–1, but these lines modify and amplify rather than repeat the two which follow them. It was not uncommon for revised lines to be reprinted from edition to edition as, for example, in *Romeo and Juliet*, 3.3.40–3 (Q2–4 and, omitting one line, F) and 5.3.108 (Q2–3, F), or in *Titus Andronicus*, 4.3.95–101 (Q1–2, F). A reader of the quarto would certainly be puzzled by these problematic episodes, but there are few other moments in the play where its action or its narrative plot are unclear.

The detection of distinctive authorial spellings and the observation of characteristic typographical errors are usually taken to provide further indication that a text derives at some remove from a manuscript in Shakespeare's hand (Greg, 148). Dover Wilson printed an impressive list of 'archaic and peculiar forms' which led him to describe the quarto as 'a mine for students of Shakespearian spelling' (Cam[1] 1962, 103). Hibbard has removed some of Wilson's forms and added some of his own (Oxf[1], 65–6), with a caution about the difficulty of distinguishing between authorial coinages or idiosyncratic forms and compositorial error. It is possible from these accounts to classify the errors under

1 The incomplete line here is quite different from the verse half-lines elsewhere in the play, 2.1.55, 89, 106, 3.1.66, 4.1.38, 4.3.90.
2 Grace Ioppolo, *Revising Shakespeare* (Cambridge, Mass., and London, 1991), 96–8.

different headings. For example, there are several unusual forms involving vowels such as 'elamentes', 'shoot', 'tuterd' and 'warely' and others involving vowels and the consonants 'b' and 'd', such as 'crambd', 'misbecombd' and 'thume' (5.2.111). In other places a terminal 'e' is missing: 'Charg', 'curat', 'quit', 'smot'; or a medial 'a' is present: 'togeather', 'vearses' or 'weart'. Elsewhere, unusual word divisions cause strange forms, as with 'doote' (do't), 'a leuen' (eleven), 'my none' (mine own), 'neare' (ne'er). None of these is very remarkable or would surprise some-one used to reading texts of the period in manuscript. Equally, some others such as 'holdsome', 'Iermane' or 'frend' are hardly idiosyncratic. More striking are forms such as 'abhortiue' (abortive), 'byes' (buys), 'coffing' (coughing), *'dungil'* (dunghill), 'epythat' (epithet), 'hou' (ho), 'mallicholie' (melancholy), 'mouce' (mouse), 'ortagriphie' (orthography), 'perst' (pierced), 'rescewes' (rescues), 'sedule' (schedule), 'squirilitie' (scurrility), 'sythes' (scythes), 'smothfast' (smooth-faced), 'shue' (sue), 'shooter' (suitor) and 'varrie' (vary). However, when examined against other occurrences of these words in texts usually agreed to be taken from authorial manuscripts, out of all these only 'coff-ing' can be found in similar form (in Q2 *Romeo and Juliet*, 3.1.25) and 'sythes' can be compared to 'Sythe' in Q2 *Henry V*, 5.2.50, although the recurrence of the unusual forms 'sieth' and 'syeth' in the Sonnets (12.13, 60.12, 100.14 and 123.14) is curious. 'Dungell' occurs in Q *King Lear*, 3.7.97; 'how(e)' is fairly com-mon, especially in Q2 *Hamlet*; 'reskew' occurs in Q1 *2 Henry IV*, 2.1.55; 'Cedule' in *The Rape of Lucrece*, 1312. 'Mallicholie' poses other problems since it is related to F *The Merry Wives of Windsor*, 1.4.154, 'Allicholy', and *The Two Gentlemen of Verona*, 4.2.27 'allycholly': both texts are believed to derive from tran-scripts prepared by Ralph Crane.

The evidence, then, that these are distinctive Shakespearean forms is on the whole weak: they may be, but their origins may also lie elsewhere. Two further cases highlight the difficulty of determining which they are. 'Thume' appears to represent an idiosyncratic spelling, one not recorded in the *OED* outside Middle English literature: however, it does not occur in other texts thought to be set from authorial papers and appears as 'thumbe' in an earlier setting of the word in the play at 5.1.123. With 'Necligent', the form is recorded in the *OED* as in use during the sixteenth century, but it (and 'necligence') never occurs in Shakespeare's works thought to have been set from his own manuscripts. Instead of being rich nuggets from Dover Wilson's mine for Shakespearean spellings, these peculiar forms may simply represent scribal or compositorial preferences or errors.

Mistakes which were more certainly made by the compositor(s)[1] can be attributed to the usual problems of simple omission, transposition, turned letters, minim errors, incorrect word division and foul case. The explanation for almost all of these is simple. More puzzling are 'Contempls' (contempts: 1.1.187) and 'Subtit' (Subtle: 4.3.316): it seems unlikely that the first is the result of a misreading of secretary hand, but the second could possibly result from it. In all this, there is very little to suggest widespread problems with reading Shakespeare's hand.

The orthodox view is that these different features point to a text set from authorial 'foul papers' which show Shakespeare still at work on the play: he had not yet settled on final forms for characters' names and was not at this point too concerned about stage directions. Revised and unrevised passages show he was still composing the play. On the other hand, some of the evidence concerning alleged authorial spellings, ghost characters, unclear action, permissive stage directions and so on is distinctly thin. Of course, not all the 'foul-papers' features need necessarily reflect an author at work: some may have been caused by type shortages or by compositors seeking to save or to make space. For example, Armado's speech prefixes suddenly change from his generic name to his proper one in 3.1 at line 68. This occurs

1 There is a convenient list with TLNs in Trevor Howard-Hill's Oxford Shakespeare Concordance to the play (Oxford, 1970), xiii.

on sig. C4v, part of a gathering in which, as Price has noticed (416), there was a distinct shortage of italic *B*s: this may be a coincidence, but it may signal a compositor's intelligent way out of a difficult problem caused by type shortage. These sorts of inconsistencies have also encouraged editors and scholars to believe they can detect different layers of authorial revision in the play and the work of different compositors.

However, there are problems with this analysis of features thought to indicate a text set from authorial 'foul papers'. As Paul Werstine has pointed out (Werstine[2], 67–75), the argument is a circular one: 'foul-paper' texts can be identified by the presence of those features which are characteristic of 'foul-paper' texts. Surviving scribal transcripts of plays show they 'often contain the variety and ambiguity in naming of characters – some of it introduced by the scribes themselves – that McKerrow said was the unique mark of the "author's original MS"' (Werstine[2], 71). Since there are no certain surviving specimens of Shakespeare's manuscripts, it is impossible to know what his practice in writing his plays was – even with the fragment of *Sir Thomas More*, if it is in his hand, there is no certainty as to whether he was composing new material or making a fair copy of material he had already drafted elsewhere. Of the surviving theatrical manuscripts of the period, none exactly conforms to the generally established definition of 'foul papers' (cf. Werstine[2], 81). Furthermore, if compositors were capable of setting in type 'foul-paper' features of the kind I have just outlined, scribes were equally capable of copying and reproducing them by hand. The only way by which scholars could be absolutely certain that a text was set from some kind of an authorial draft or fair copy would be if the printer's copy and the resulting print were both to survive. Unfortunately, no scribal let alone authorial manuscript copy for a printed play survives from this period.

In the case of *Love's Labour's Lost* not only is there no manuscript printer's copy, there is no surviving example of the presumed original quarto. Of course, some of the distinctive features present in Q1 – false starts, problems with the names of characters, bare stage directions – may reflect the manuscript of an author at work, but it would be a mistake to play down the possible layers of interference which might affect the transmission of the manuscript into the printed form in which it now survives. These certainly include at least one if not two sets of compositors and could be extended to a scribe who might have prepared a fair copy of Shakespeare's working papers for the press. The different sorts of wrong, peculiar and unsatisfactory elements which appear in the text of Q1 may allow a glimpse of Shakespeare at work but it is only a brief one seen through several distorting lenses.

The editor's task must therefore be to distinguish between Shakespeare's errors and those of his compositors, between the errors they perpetuated and the ones they created. The certainties that bibliographers bring to these tasks are, I believe, attractive but in the end illusory. The evidence – as is the case with Werstine's account of White's printing practices from 1598 to 1600 – might seem to point in one direction, but unless differing arguments can be proved to be wrong the resulting theory can only be provisional (see Draudt[2]). This principle is particularly worth bearing in mind when it comes to trying to reconstruct Q1's printing history and to identify its compositors.

Without presenting his own case in full, Draudt believed it was possible that only one compositor set the play (Draudt, 121–2). Price, using typographical features, especially the setting of stage directions, and spelling patterns, argued – although he admitted to some doubts – that Compositor I set 17 pages, II set 32 pages and III set 25: A–D were printed on two presses, and E–K on one (Price, 425–6). Werstine rejected Price's evidence concerning indented prose flow-overs, emphasis capitals and typographic errors and instead put forward his theory that the quarto was set by three compositors out of the five who worked for White between 1598 and 1600 (Werstine, 42–54). One of these, whom he called R, set one page in the quarto, sig. B1r (1.1.220–64). The rest of the work was undertaken by S and T:

S probably set sigs A2r–3v and F1r–2r (1.1.0–142 and 4.3.180–286). T was responsible for the remaining sixty-six pages of the text (Werstine, 37–8). It is impossible to reconcile these three accounts in which Draudt, Price and Werstine attribute the same pages to different compositors. Indeed, the question of compositor analysis is far from settled. If Werstine's account looks at first to be the most credible, his spelling tests for the compositors do not look quite so secure (Draudt[2], 150–1). It is unsettling that his attribution of one page to R is based solely on the fact that 'her' is spelled 'hir' twice on the page and that R favoured the latter form (Werstine, 37, 58). S's and T's characteristic spellings are not confined to their presumed stints.

Although some of the play's printing history can be reconstructed in detail, the inferences that can be drawn from this about the numbers of compositors and presses employed have been questioned. The quarto was probably set by formes (Werstine, 38, 48), and two different sets of skeletons were used for A–D, but only one for the rest of the play (Price, 426–9). Werstine convincingly invokes Don McKenzie's article 'Printers of the Mind' along with recurrent type damage to rebut Price's theory that, because two skeletons were used in A–D, they were printed off concurrently on two presses and that, since the setting and machining were more rapid in these gatherings, therefore the copy for the earlier part of the play was easier to deal with than the copy for its later part (Werstine, 54). At the moment it is impossible to say with any certainty how many compositors worked on the quarto and on how many presses it was printed.

In this light, pointing out errors in the quarto and seeking to emend them on the basis of compositorial habits – such as Compositor T's alleged tendency to transposition – is of limited use. The text of the play has its share of errors, but the obloquy heaped on it by Hibbard, for example (Oxf[1], 72–6), is overstated, for, as Werstine pointed out, 'Scores of similar errors are to be found in books set by White's compositors from clear printed copy' (Werstine, 53). Part of the impression of the badness of the quarto is conveyed through its presentation of foreign languages. The argument concerning this revolves around whether the gibberish Holofernes and Nathaniel (principally) speak is meant deliberately to hold them up to ridicule or whether it simply represents a compositorial inability to set Latin and Italian. Evidence from other plays may suggest that part of the fun of such types as the pedant and the braggart lay in their corruption of Latin and other languages (Werstine[3], 43–4), but it does not necessarily follow that this is also the case with *Love's Labour's Lost*. Indeed, if the corruption is authorial rather than compositorial, it is hard in places to see wherein the joke lies. The example of 5.1.26–7 is often cited: in the quarto Nathaniel answers Holofernes' question with '*Laus deo, bene intelligo*' ('Praise God, I understand well'), to which the pedant replies '*Bome boon for boon prescian*'. It is unlikely there is some joke here and most editors have followed Theobald in changing Nathaniel's correct adverb '*bene*' to the incorrect form '*bone*' and then reading '*Bone? "Bone"* for "*bene*"! Priscian', which makes good sense and is graphically credible. On the other hand, when Holofernes mangles the opening of Mantuan's first eclogue (4.2.91–2) J. W. Binns believes the audience would have got some sort of sense from the lines (*TxC*, 273). Furthermore, his translation of them – 'Easily, I pray, since you are getting everything wrong under the cool shade' – seems appropriate to the misquotation and there is something equally fitting in the quarto's reading '*Facile*' for '*Fauste*', since Holofernes has just previously (55) identified the desirability of 'facility' in composition.

Although there is finally no way of knowing for certain who was responsible for the language errors, unless a joke is evidently being made it is probably best not to attribute the corruptions to Shakespeare. At first sight it might seem strange that so many errors survive in a text which was subject to some stop-press proof correction.[1] Werstine has collated the fourteen extant

---

1 See Werstine[3] and his article 'The Hickmott-Dartmouth Copy of *Love's Labour's Lost* Q1 (1598)', *N&Q*, 230 (1985), 473.

copies of the quarto and has discovered corrected and uncorrected states in eight formes out of nineteen. Only the outer forme of A shows two states of correction, outer D has the largest number of corrections (six, with three affecting Armado's letter, 4.1.61–86) and no formes are known to have been corrected after inner E; however, the small number of extant copies makes it unsafe to base any theories on the absence of known corrections to sheets F to K. The corrections that were made mainly affect minor typographical errors or marks of punctuation, and the closest an uncorrected reading comes to affecting the text significantly is in outer E, where one copy reads 'Or grone for Loue?' when the remainder of the corrected copies read 'Or grone for Ione?' (4.3.179). It is probable that at least at this point the proofreader consulted his copy but it would be unsafe to draw inferences about the accuracy of the text here or elsewhere on the basis of this phase of proof correction – earlier phases are, of course, not recoverable.

One final area of possible compositorial error is worth considering (Price, 412–15). Almost all pages in the quarto are thirty-eight lines deep, to which can be added the direction line containing the catchword and, on all rectos (apart from D4 and F4), the signature. There are, however, several exceptions to this. Where a page should have ended with a stage direction at its foot, the compositor preferred to leave it to the next page; if necessary he left a blank line in its place and set the stage direction's first word as a catchword. This happens on E1r, where he set thirty-six lines of text and a blank line, then the catchword and the signature on separate lines, and H1v, where the page is full with thirty-eight lines, but H2r begins with a blank line. But on A4r there are only thirty-six lines of text and no blank line before the direction line, whereas on I2r there is a similarly short page, but also a blank line before the direction line. The short page on A4r may be explained by the compositor's not yet having established a consistent style for the book, especially for stage directions. This may also explain why A4v is too deep at thirty-nine lines with blanks before and after the initial stage direction for Dull's and Costard's entry – this happens nowhere else at the head of a page. At the same time, the compositor may have wished to avoid setting the last two words of Costard's speech ('but so', 1.1.221) as a widow on B1r. He could have avoided this by losing the first blank line on the page and printing the whole of Costard's line at its foot, extending 'but so' into the direction line. This is evidently what happened on D4r, where the end of Nathaniel's speech ('it was a Bucke of the first head', 4.2.10) is set in the direction line so that there was no room for the signature D4. On the other hand there are longer and shorter widows at the head of D1v, I1r and K2r.

The depths of two other pages are less easily explained. F2v and F3r (both outer formes) have only thirty-seven lines to the page and they contain all but four lines of Berowne's women's eyes speech including the unrevised passage (4.3.287–300 with the additional twenty-three lines printed in Appendix 2.1 on F2v and 4.3.301–37 on F3r; Fig. 15). It is curious that these short pages occur at just this point in the play where, it may be assumed, the original manuscript copy must have shown some signs of revision. This may just be a coincidence caused by problems in casting off copy at some stage, but if so it is a remarkable one. The most obvious explanation for the short pages is that material has been omitted – perhaps two lines from the unrevised passage on F2v which were then divided between the two pages to make the opening at least look regular. The discrepancy raises doubts again about the nature of the copy from which White's quarto was set. An exact paginary reprint of an earlier quarto would allow White's compositors to inherit wholesale its difficulties with the text at this point. Although White may have undertaken just such a paginary reprint, on two out of three occasions he does not seem to have favoured this way of working when he was reprinting plays. If he reset the text fully from an earlier quarto, it is remarkable that the short pages occur just here. In these circumstances it seems very slightly more likely

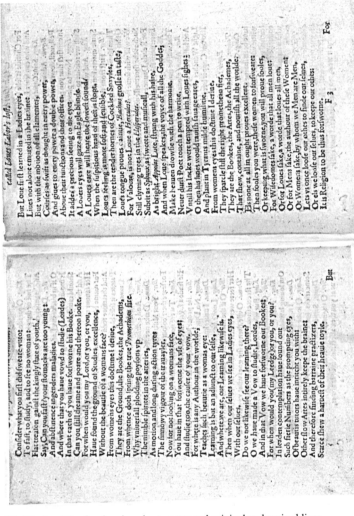

But Loue first learned in a Ladies eyes,
Liues not alone emured in the braine:
But with the motion of all elements,
Courses as swift as thought in euery power,
And giues to euery power a double power,
Aboue their functions and their offices.
It addes a precious seeing to the eye:
A Louers eyes will gaze an Eagle blinde.
A Louers eare will heare the lowest sound,
When the suspitious head of theft is stopt.
Loues feeling is more soft and sensible,
Then are the tender hornes of Cockled Snayles.
Loues tongue proues dainty, *Bacchus* grosse in taste,
For Valour, is not Loue a *Hercules?*
Still clyming trees in the *Hesperides?*
Subtit as *Sphinx*, as sweete and musicall,
As bright *Apollos* Lute, strung with his haire.
And when Loue speakes, the voyce of all the Goddes,
Make heauen drowsie with the harmonie.
Neuer durst Poet touch a pen to write,
Vntill his Incke were tempred with Loues sighes:
O then his lines would rauish sauage eares,
And plant in Tyrants milde humilitie.
From womens eyes this doctrine I deriue.
They sparcle still the right promethean fier,
They are the Bookes, the Artes, the Achademes,
That shew, containe, and nourish all the worlde.
Els none at all in ought proues excellent.
Then fooles you were, these women to forsweare:
Or keeping what is sworne, you will proue fooles,
For Wisedomes sake, a worde that all men loue:
Or for Loues sake, a worde that loues all men:
Or for Mens sake, the authour of these Women:
Or Womens sake, by whom we Men are Men.
Lets vs once loose our othes to finde our selues,
Or els we loose our selues, to keepe our othes:
It is Religion to be thus forsworne.

F 3   For

Consider what you first did sweare vnto:
To fast, to study, and to see no woman:
Flat treason gainst the kingly state of youth.
Say, Can you fast? your stomacks are too young:
And abstinence ingenders maladies.
And where that you haue vow'd to studie (Lordes)
In that each of you haue forsworne his Booke.
Can you still dreame and poore and thereon looke?
For when would you my Lord, or you, or you,
Haue found the ground of Studies excellence,
Without the beautie of a womans face?
From womens eyes this doctrine I deriue,
They are the Ground, the Bookes, the Achadems,
From whence doth spring the true *Promethean* fire.
Why vniuersall plodding poysons vp
The nimble spirits in the arteries,
As motion and long during action tyres
The sinnowy vigour of the trauayler.
Now for not looking on a womans face,
You haue in that forsworne the vse of eyes:
And studie too, the cause of your vow.
For where is any Authour in the worlde,
Teaches such beautie as a womas eye:
Learning is but an adiunct to our selfe,
And where we are, our Learning likewise is.
Then when our selues we see in Ladies eyes,
With our selues.
Do we not likewise see our learning there?
O we haue made a Vow to studie, Lordes,
And in that Vow we haue forsworne our Bookes?
For when would you (my Leedge) or you, or you?
In leaden contemplation haue found out
Such fierie Numbers as the prompting eyes,
Of beauties tutors haue inricht you with?
Other slow Artes intirely keepe the braine:
And therefore finding barraine practizers,
Scarce shew a haruest of their heauie toyle.

But

15   Q1 sigs. F2v–3r, showing short pages and original and revised lines

that White was setting manuscript copy and the short pages reflect immediate difficulties with interpreting his (authorial or scribal) manuscript.

F (1623)

Whether Q1 of *Love's Labour's Lost* was a reprint or not, it did not have a further separate edition until 1631. However, on 22 January 1607 the publishing rights in the play and in *Romeo and Juliet* and *The Taming of the Shrew* were transferred from Cuthbert Burby to Nicholas Ling. On 19 November of the same year the three, with the addition of *Hamlet*, were transferred from Ling to John Smethwick. Smethwick was one of the consortium which published the First Folio of Shakespeare's plays in 1623. It is the seventh of the comedies in the Folio, coming between *Much Ado About Nothing* and *A Midsummer Night's Dream* and occupying sigs L1v to M6v, pages 122 to 144.

The text of the play in F differs in several ways from the text in Q, but there is little doubt that the quarto supplied the copy for the Folio. They share a certain number of misprints and, as Dover Wilson pointed out (Cam[1] 1962, 129), F reproduces Q's 'vene we' for 'venewe' (5.1.55), which resulted from the loosening and movement of type in the forme. F also has a curious error in its uncorrected forme on sig. L5r. In Costard's 'remuneration' speech 3.1.133–9 Q has him say 'Three-farthings remuration . . . Ile giue you a remuneration'; in its corrected form F prints 'remuneration' twice, but in its uncorrected form it prints 'remuneration . . . remuration'. Of course, the compositors of Q and F may have made identical mistakes, but it is hard not to feel that Q's error was inherited and transposed by F.

Modern scholars have identified three compositors, who are designated B, C and D, as working on the Folio text. C set L1v, L2v–4r and M1r–M3v; D set L2r, L4v–L6v and B set M4r–M6v, producing totals of respectively eleven, six and six pages (*TxC*, 149, 152). Setting tended to begin at the centre of the gathering of six leaves with an inner forme, so that the first page of the play set in the Folio was L3v, containing the first hundred or so lines of Act 2, and it then proceeded outwards, ending with the outer forme L1r:L6v in which L1r had the last page of *Much Ado About Nothing*. The process was repeated for gathering M with a slight change in the order of setting the second and third formes.

In addition to inheriting errors from Q, the compositors of F corrected some of the earlier text's mistakes, especially in the speech prefixes, but also introduced new ones of their own and tended to modernize some of the older-fashioned forms in the quarto.[1] For example, at 2.1.167 Compositor C on L4r changed Q's 'I will yeelde' (C2r) to 'would I yeeld' (TLN 665) and modernized 'my none hart' (2.1.179; C2v) to 'my owne heart' (TLN 677). On L6r (TLN 1189–90) Compositor D omitted Q's 'me' in 'Can you tel me by your wit' (4.2.34; D4v), but altered Q's 'neare hit the clout' (4.1.133; D4r) to 'ne're hit the clout' (TLN 1127–8), helping to avoid ambiguity. At the end of the play Compositor B on M6v changed Q's 'three yeere' (5.2.872; K1v) to 'three yeares' (TLN 2847) and modernized Q's 'smothfast' (5.2.816; K1r) to 'smoothfac'd' (TLN 2788). The most substantial of F's errors occurs in D's stint on L4v when he omitted 3.1.81–9, part of the repetitive rhyme about 'The fox, the ape and the humble-bee'. This probably came about as a result of eye-skip: the error was almost certainly not deliberate, since the next page, L5r, is generously leaded around the stage direction for Berowne's entry at 3.1.139.1 and around the act division for '*Actus Quartus.*'; the compositor also made space by setting single lines in Q as double ones (3.1.102, 105–7, 111–12, 131, 169–73; TLN 869–70, 873–6, 880–1, 899–900, 939–44). Other omissions and changes result either from a similar carelessness, such as the omission at 5.2.658–9 ('When he breathed, he was a

1   See MacD. P. Jackson, 'Compositors B, C, and D, and the First Folio text of *Love's Labour's Lost*', *PBSA*, 72 (1978), 61–5.

man') by B, or as D's omission of 'loves thee not' at 4.2.98, or from a desire not to have to turn the line over, as at 3.1.7 where in F (TLN 779) D omits 'Master' at the start of the line.

There are, however, certain QF variants which suggest that, although the Folio text was set from the quarto, a theatrical manuscript of some kind was also consulted (see Wells, 'Copy'). It is possible that some of these differences could represent press variants in copies of the quarto which have not survived or even, if the quarto is a close paginary reprint of a lost original, that the textual differences derive from it and not from 1598. On the whole, though, there are sufficient variants to suggest an independent manuscript was used in conjunction with the quarto. There are several significant changes between Q and F. First of all, F has been divided into five acts. This may have been done, as Greg suggested (223), at the time of printing, but, if Gary Taylor is to be believed, it may possibly reflect theatrical practice some time after about 1607.[1] The printer may have added a centred '*Finis Actus Primus.*' to fill the foot of the second column on L3r (similar formulas, but ranged right, appear at the end of Acts 1, 2 and 4 of *Twelfth Night*), but the remaining act divisions, although they are as Greg called them 'monstrously disproportionate', make some sort of sense and have generally been retained by editors.

A certain number of stage directions have been altered significantly. An exit was supplied for Dull at the end of his first speech at 1.2.125, which did not resolve the problem of which character says 'Come, Jaquenetta, away' at 1.2.139 and thereupon exits (see p. 314). Dumaine lost his exit at 2.1.195 and Armado his at 5.2.529, but the first of these (like others at 2.1.213, 5.1.147, 5.2.156) was probably cut or shortened to save space. One was supplied for the Princess and others at 4.1.106 SD2 and a final '*Exeunt omnes.*' was added at the end of the play. Neither of these

---

1 'The structure of performance', in Gary Taylor and John Jowett, *Shakespeare Reshaped 1606–1623* (Oxford, 1993), 17.

last two needs necessarily reflect theatrical practice, nor does the addition 'Song.' after the opening direction to Act 3: the conversation between Armado and Moth demands one. Nor do the Folio's attempts to sort out the quarto's confusing speech prefixes carry a great deal of conviction that a performance manuscript of some kind has been consulted.

In two cases one can see that some sort of attempt is being made at consistent presentation of characters' prefixes, even if it fails. Except for in his first speech, Armado's prefix in 1.2 was consistently changed from his personal to his generic name, 'Braggart', throughout the scene. Yet other 'Armado' prefixes were allowed to stand in 3.1. At 1.1.284 and 288 F changed two of many such prefixes from Ferdinand to King and did the same to all four Ferdinand prefixes in 2.1 and to the one Navarre prefix (2.1.178). Three reassignments of speeches present different problems. At 1.1.279 the dialogue between Q's '*Fer.*' and '*Clo.*' is interrupted and the line is assigned to '*Ber.*', which F changes to '*Fer.*'. This makes better sense and may simply be the correction of an error, but another change at 2.1.80 where the Lord's words are given to '*Ma.*' is more curious and strictly speaking unnecessary: it may represent an attempt to cut down the already tiny roles of the two lords besides Boyet in the play. A third reassignment occurs at the beginning of 4.1 when F, again without any need to do so, gives the Forester's first speech to Boyet. These last two instances strongly suggest consultation of an independent manuscript.

The nature of that manuscript – if it existed – can be tested by examining F's treatment of speech prefixes in 2.1, which must be found wanting. F starts the scene attempting to sort out the three ladies' prefixes and manages to assign their second speech correctly to 1 Lady and to give the 3 Lady's to Rosaline. She is made to replace Katherine in the initial encounter with Berowne (2.1.114–27), but in their second encounter (179–92) Rosaline becomes, for some reason, Lady Rosaline and Berowne changes to Boyet except for his last line; this is clearly unsatisfactory in more ways than one. Another confusion occurs twenty or so lines later: Boyet is talking to the Princess and her ladies (although Rosaline is silent) when Berowne exits and Maria identifies him by name. In Q Katherine and Boyet make jokes about sheep and ships, but in F (TLN 720–2) Maria makes and muddles the joke:

> *La.Ma.* Two hot Sheepes marie:
> And wherefore not Ships?   (lips.
> *Boy.* No Sheepe (sweet Lamb) vnlesse we feed on your

This conveys no sense and is unnecessary: an M/K misprint is possible, but the subsequent confusion suggests a botched attempt at sorting the exchange out. At the scene's end, with the same group on stage, F again tried to regularize Q's prefixes. Q assigned the last speeches from line 249 to '*Prin.*', '*Bo.*', '*Lad.*', '*Lad.* 2.', '*Lad.* 3.', '*Boy.*', '*Lad.*', '*Boy.*', '*Lad.*', '*Boy.*'. As I have already argued, the three ladies appear in the same order as they should at the beginning of the scene – Maria, Katherine, Rosaline – with Maria taking the last two speeches. F, however, has a completely different solution: the Princess keeps her speech, but Boyet's first one is assigned to '*Bro.*', a half-revealing error perhaps looking back to the earlier confusion between Berowne and Boyet, and then the ladies' speeches are assigned to '*Lad.Ro.*', '*Lad.Ma.*', '*Lad.2.*', '*La.1.*' and '*Lad.2.*'. This is a possible solution to the pre-fixes, for Lady 2 must here be Katherine, as she is at the beginning of the scene, and this final exchange ends plausibly with Maria and Katherine.

If it is evident that an attempt was made to sort out the pre-fixes, it is hard to be certain who was responsible for these changes: they still fail to make the play actable as it stands. It is possible to argue that at one point in it (5.2.316), where Q's 'God' was replaced in F by '*Ioue*', profanity was avoided to conform to the Act of 1606. However, this is the only one out of numerous other occasions in the play where references to God and to Heaven were removed – the sort of highly sporadic censorship which Gary Taylor has found to obtain with other plays in this part of the Folio for whose printing he believes a promptbook was consulted. On the other hand, there is further evidence of expurgation elsewhere in the play: at 5.2.577 'fayth' is changed to 'insooth' in the Folio.[1]

Once again, an editor is faced with the problem of discriminating between compositorial error, revision and reference to an independent source. The principal verbal change F made to the text of the play was to assign Q's final lines, 'The wordes of Mercurie, are harsh after the songes of Apollo.', to Armado, set them in normal-size type but as verse and add a final line, 'You that way; we this way'. The change helps even out the length of the two columns in F, but this could just as easily have been done by transferring material from the foot of the first to the top of the second. The choice of speech prefix and the additional line are sufficiently intelligent and significant to make their being the work of a compositor or editor rather unlikely, so that Greg's statement that they represent a 'desperate attempt to fit the final words of Q into the structure of the play' (223) must be rejected.

The other textual changes made to Q in F are less satisfying. The most puzzling is at 1.1.109, where Q's 'Clymbe ore the house to vnlocke the little gate' became in F (L2r set by D) 'That were to clymbe ore the house to vnlocke the gate', which is, at best, metrically unsatisfactory after a regular iambic pentameter. Some of the other changes in F are simple substitutions which do not seem to have been made to save or to make space: for example, at 1.2.122 Q's 'suffer him to' becomes 'let him' in F. A slightly more complicated substitution occurs at 4.1.14, where Q's 'and againe' became '& then again' in F: here, in the penultimate line of the page, the F compositor (D) introduced the new word and, in order to accommodate it to the line without a

1 ''Swounds revisited', in Taylor and Jowett, *Shakespeare Reshaped*, 53–4, 88–9. For the offensiveness of oaths involving 'faith', see 82, 97 and, for this kind of substitution, 101.

turnover, resorted to an ampersand. Other changes may represent good compositorial or editorial guesses designed to mend an unsatisfactory text. For example, at 5.2.80 Q has Boyet 'stable' with laughter which F emends to the more reasonable 'stab'd'; at first sight Q's 'sleight saine' at 5.2.463 is impenetrable, but F saw through the form to produce 'slight Zanie'; and the emendation of 'herrite' at 5.2.810 to 'euer' (correctly 'hermit') is no more than a reasonable guess. It is harder to explain some other changes without reference to an independent source. For example, the text was mended at 2.1.44 by getting rid of Q's 'peerelsse' and substituting 'parts', which, whatever the correct reading may be, makes better sense. Although the minim error explanation for Q's reading 'nuage' at 5.2.482 may be obvious to modern editors, F's 'manager' (it should be 'manage') is not such an obvious solution to the crux. Similarly, dittography in Q at 5.2.514, 'That sport best pleases, that doth best know how', is an easy reading that F saw through and correctly emended to 'best . . . least'. Even so, there are some F readings which presumably represent compositorial error, such as 2.1.174, where Q's 'faire' lodging became F's 'farther' lodging, or 5.2.149, where Q's 'speakers' was changed to 'keepers', perhaps in an unconscious spoonerism.

If it was 'inconceivable' to Greg (223, n.11) that F was printed from a copy of Q used as promptbook, Stanley Wells – choosing his words with great care – could certainly conceive that F was printed from a quarto which 'had been compared with a manuscript, and that this manuscript was one which presented the play in a form closer to that in which it was performed than the foul papers from which the Quarto was printed' (Wells, 'Copy', 146). Nevertheless, it is striking that the bulk of F's significant changes occur in 2.1 and 5.2, almost as if checking and sorting out were done at the beginning and then towards the end of the play, with its middle left largely undisturbed. The precise origins and date of such a putative manuscript are unknown.

When dealing with the text of *Love's Labour's Lost* an editor is faced with a large number of problems which are hard to resolve. These involve: whether the quarto of 1598 was the play's first appearance in print or not; at what remove it was set from Shakespeare's manuscript; the nature of that manuscript; how many compositors worked on the quarto; the nature of and the reasons for the differences between the Folio and the quarto. In almost all cases the evidence has been closely examined over many years, but scholars have come to different conclusions about it. Although one area of investigation – say the spelling evidence from White's shop or confusions over the characters' names – may yield what has been seen to look like a definitive result, it must be remembered that it is only one area. The more closely the play's texts are scrutinized, the more provisional and partial and the less certain the conclusions that have been reached about them seem to become. *Love's Labour's Lost* appears to be an extreme case because of these unusual circumstances, but it has made editors and bibliographers cautious about how much can be determined even from detailed examination; the same caution ought to obtain for texts which appear, bibliographically, to be more clear-cut cases.

On account of these circumstances the present edition offers a conservatively edited text based on Q with reference in some places to F. It adopts the simplest solutions to the most difficult textual problems, like the Rosaline-Katherine tangle, outlined above. Apart from these, the chief difficulties an editor of *Love's Labour's Lost* faces involve the related issues of the treatment of proper names, of modernization and of foreign languages. It is by no means easy to decide how to punctuate the play's title nor what to call its characters. The page reproduced here (F4r: 5.1.15–54) shows some of these difficulties (Fig. 16). The play's title takes an unfamiliar form, with only one apostrophe (see commentary note). In this part of it the characters are referred to by their generic names (Holofernes appears as '*Peda*.', '*Ped*.' and '*Poda*.'), but the stage direction omits to mention that

called Loues Labor's lost.

Curat. A most singuler and choyce Epithat,
                Draw-out his Table-booke.
Peda. He draweth out the thred of his verbositie, finer
then the staple of his argument. I abhorre such phanatticall
phantasims, such insociable, and poynt deuise companions,
such rackers of ortagriphie, as to speake dout fine, when he
should say doubt; det, when he shold pronounce debt; d e b t,
not det: he clepeth a Calfe, Cause: halfe, haufe: neighbour
vocatur nebour; neigh abreuiated ne: this is abhominable,
which he would call abbominable, it insinuateth me of in-
famie: *ne inteligis domine*, to make frantique lunatique?
   Curat. Laus deo, bene intelligo.
   Peda. Bome boon for boon *prescian*, a litle scratcht, twil serue,
                Enter Bragart, Boy.
   Curat. Vides ne quis venit?
   Peda. Video, et gaudio.
   Brag. Chirra.
   Peda. Quari Chirra, not Sirra?
   Brag. Men of peace well incontred.
   Ped. Most millitarie sir salutation.
   Boy. They haue been at a great feast of Languages, and
   stolne the scraps.
   Clow. O they haue lyud long on the almsbasket of wordes,
I maruaile thy M. hath not eaten thee for a worde, for thou
art not so long by the head as honorificabilitudinitatibus:
Thou art easier swallowed then a flapdragon.
   Page. Peace, the peale begins.
   Brag. Mounsier, are you not lettred?
   Page. Yes yes, he teaches boyes the Horne-booke: What
is Ab spel'd backward with the horne on his head?
   Peda. Ba, *puericia* with a horne added.   (learning.
   Pag. Ba most seely Sheepe, with a horne: you heare his
   Peda. Quis quis thou Consonant?
   Pag. The last of the fiue Vowels if You repeate them,
or the fift if I.
   Peda. I will repeate them: a e I.
   Pag. The Sheepe, the other two concludes it o u.
   Brag. Now by the sault wane of the meditaranium, a
                    sweete

16 Q1 sig. F4r (5.1.15–54)

Costard the Clown enters with Holofernes and Moth. The problem of the form of his name is avoided by calling him '*Boy.*',
although it may lead to confusion with Boyet. Despite his own
name, Holofernes' ranting about the pronunciation of English,
the names of Sir Nathaniel and Costard all suggest the scene is
firmly rooted in England. Yet Holofernes addresses Moth as
'Mounsier' (5.1.43), even though Costard's 'thy M.' (5.1.38)

should presumably be expanded and modernized to 'thy master'. The Latin in the extract poses other problems. I have already discussed the first exchange between Nathaniel and Holofernes which relies on the Curate's making a mistake (*'bone'* for *'bene'*) which here he does not make. The rest of the Latin needs less attention but 'Chirra' (5.1.31–2) does not look English and 'fine' for *'sine'* (5.1.20), 'honorificabilitudinitatibus' (5.1.40) and 'meditaranium' (5.1.54) are certainly not, although both were set in roman, not the italic usually used for Latin.

In a play so much concerned with the nature of words and language this extract shows with what diffidence the Elizabethan printing house could treat typographic niceties. In Holofernes' first speech (5.1.20) the compositor omitted a 'b' after 'fine' and separated different pronunciations with semi-colons and colons; but he deliberately spaced 'd e b t' presumably to mark that it should be spelled out, although he failed to do the same for 'det'. On the same page he did not spell out 'Ab' (5.1.44–5) but did so for 'a e I o u' (5.1.52–3), setting the third vowel in upper case: 'o u' is strictly correct but has to suggest 'Oh, you' and 'Oh, ewe'. An editor has to decide whether Holofernes' version of 'ortagriphie' (5.1.19) is meant to be unusual and whether 'infamie' (5.1.25) is an error for 'insanie' or for Latin *insanire*. Similarly, Armado's 'incontred' (5.1.33) is not recorded in *OED* as a variant spelling form and seems closer to Italian *incontrare* than to anything English: is Armado speaking as a generalized foreigner here? A final modernization problem occurs with Moth's 'most seely Sheepe' (5.1.47). 'Seely' is usually modernized to 'silly', but could also represent 'seely' meaning happy, innocent or helpless: Shakespeare did use 'seely' but elsewhere refers to 'silly' sheep and lambs.

The problems with modernizing this passage are acute in places, but generally the reader needs to bear in mind that all modernization is a form of translation. In some ways the most intractable problems relate to proper names: how French should the evidently French names be? It is inconsistent to print Biron, Longueville and Dumaine, the forms adopted in the Oxford editions, when 'Dumaine' is an anglicized version of 'de Mayenne'. It would be ridiculous and metrically impractical to convert Dumaine to de Mayenne. On the other hand, to retain Q's '*Alansoes*' and '*Alanson*' (2.1.61, 194) would be merely antiquarian. It is also difficult to determine how the names are to be spoken. If they are to be pronounced with a French accent they are going to pose problems with scansion and rhyme; with an English accent Biron will either have to sound like 'birren' or become 'Byron'. 'Beroune' might well represent how the name should be pronounced, but this spelling does not occur in the early texts and resembles neither an English nor a French form: 'Berowne' with its terminal -e could be said to accommodate both languages. Scansion and rhyme usually demand English versions of French names – though Marcadé is an exception – and so do the names of some of the other characters, like Dull, Costard and Nathaniel; Moth or Mote poses problems of his own (see Appendix 3). The kingdom of Navarre, like the forest of Arden (and elsewhere), is both English and other-worldly: to attempt to be wholly consistent about the forms of names is impossible and, finally, unprofitable.

The same argument might be said to apply to the question of whether to change the Princess's speech prefix to 'Queen' after Marcadé has told her that the King, her father, is dead: although the play is much concerned with correct titles for people (and things), an audience will not notice any editorial decision. The Princess is regularly designated a Queen in her speech prefixes throughout the play, but just as regularly referred to as the Princess in its dialogue and stage directions. The Oxford editions change the speech prefixes after Marcadé's announcement on the grounds that Shakespeare thought of her as one – but the evidence is divided as to this – and that the King's question 'How fares your majesty?' (5.2.720) 'suggests that Shakespeare thought of her as succeeding to her father's throne' (*TxC*, 275).

APPENDIX 2
ADDITIONAL LINES

1. After 4.3.291 the following lines are printed in Q and F:

[BEROWNE]
And where that you have vowed to study, lords,
In that each of you have forsworn his book,
Can you still dream and pore and thereon look?
For when would you, my lord, or you, or you,
Have found the ground of study's excellence   5
Without the beauty of a woman's face?
From women's eyes this doctrine I derive:
They are the ground, the books, the academes,
From whence doth spring the true Promethean fire.
Why, universal plodding poisons up   10
The nimble spirits in the arteries,
As motion and long-during action tires
The sinewy vigour of the traveller.

---

1 **where that** whereas: Abbott, 134
you Berowne's choice of pronoun in this unrevised passage draws attention to his sense of not being one of the oath-takers: in the revised version he says that 'we have made a vow'.
2 **have** has: Abbott, 412
3 **pore** Cf. 1.1.74; these are the only occurrences of the word in Shakespeare.
5 **ground** fundamental principle (*OED sb.* 5b)
6 **woman's face** Cf. line 14.
7 **women's eyes** Cf. lines 18, 21.

8 **ground** solid basis, foundation (*OED sb.* 5a)
10 **plodding** dull, uninspired work (*OED vbl. sb.**); cf. 'plodders', 1.1.86.
up completely, finally (*OED adv.*[1] 18a)
11 'It was thought that the *arteries* contained an etherial fluid, called "spiritual blood" or "vital spirits". Quite distinct from the blood in the veins, it was regarded as the source of motion and sensation' (Oxf[1]).
13 **sinewy** having the strength characteristic of sinews (*OED a.* 3b*)

---

2 book,] *Hanmer;* Booke. *QF*   10 poisons] *QF (*poysons*);* prisons *Theobald*   13 sinewy] *QF (*sinnowy*)

Now, for not looking on a woman's face,
You have in that forsworn the use of eyes,   15
And study too, the causer of your vow.
For where is any author in the world
Teaches such beauty as a woman's eye?
Learning is but an adjunct to ourself,
And where we are, our learning likewise is.   20
Then when ourselves we see in ladies' eyes,
With ourselves.
Do we not likewise see our learning there?

2. After 5.2.810 the following lines are printed in Q and F:

BEROWNE
And what to me, my love? And what to me?
ROSALINE
You must be purged too, your sins are rack'd;
You are attaint with faults and perjury.
Therefore, if you my favour mean to get,
A twelvemonth shall you spend and never rest,   5
But seek the weary beds of people sick.

19 **adjunct** something joined to something else in a subordinate position (*OED* B. 1*)
22 Evidently this unfinished line was meant to be cancelled in the first draft.

2 **purged** purgèd
  too The emendation 'till' is attractive,

but it is impossible to tell whether the lack of sense produced by 'purged too, your sins are rack'd' is the result of authorial or compositorial error.
  rack'd tortured on the rack; cf. 5.1.19, 'rackers of orthography'.
3 **attaint** infected (*OED v.* 9); cf. *1H6* 5.5.81 and see 1.1.155n.

18 woman's] *Q (womas), F*

2 too,] *Q (to,); too, F;* till *Oxf¹ (Cam¹)*   rack'd] *Q (rackt), F;* rank *Rowe*

3. In the following version of the first passage, elements which remained unchanged in the revised version are printed in italic. In the process of revision lines 1–6 were reworked into 4.3.292–7; lines 7–9 were reworked as 324–6 and lines 10–13 were rewritten as 298–300; lines 14–23 were replaced by 301–23.

And where that you *have* vowed *to study, lords,*
In that each of you *have forsworn* his book,
Can you still dream and pore and thereon look?
For when would you, my lord, *or you, or you,*
Have found the ground of study's excellence   5
Without the beauty of a woman's face?
From women's eyes this doctrine I derive:
They are the ground, *the books, the academes,*
From whence doth spring *the* true *Promethean fire.*
Why, universal plodding poisons up   10
The nimble spirits in the arteries,
As motion and long-during action tires
The sinewy vigour of the traveller.
Now, for not looking on a woman's face,
You have in that forsworn the use of eyes,   15
And study too, the causer of your vow.
For where is any author in the world
Teaches such beauty as a woman's eye?
Learning is but an adjunct to ourself,
And where we are, our learning likewise is.   20
Then when ourselves we see in *ladies' eyes,*
With ourselves.
Do we not likewise see our learning there?

APPENDIX 3
MOTH'S NAME

The two main arguments about the spelling and the pronunciation of Armado's Page's name can be summarized as follows.

Mote is the spelling adopted by Kerrigan in the Penguin edition (160–1) and by the Oxford editors Wells and Taylor (*Re-Editing*, 23–4, and *TxC*, 272). In Shakespeare's time, they argue, 'moth' and 'mote' were indistinguishable: in the early printings of his works 'moth' in its various forms is used to designate an insect five times and a particle eleven times. The Page in *Love's Labour's Lost* is never referred to as being like an insect, but there are several references to his being tiny (5.1.38–41, 122–4). There is also a joke about his being like a word (5.1.38–40), punning on the French for a word, *mot*, whose final 't' was sounded in this period. 'Modern actors', Kerrigan says (161), 'should pronounce the name as they would "mote", although Shakespeare's players probably said something like "mott"'. Modern editors, they argue, should modernize 'Moth' to the meaning which would have been attached to it in the play, 'Mote'.

Moth is the traditional spelling for the Page's name and has been defended by Hibbard in his Oxford edition (245–6). Moth, he points out, is compared to a small insect at 4.1.147 when Costard calls him 'a most pathetical nit', which can mean (as *OED* says) a 'gnat, or small fly' or can be applied to people 'in contempt or jest'. Costard applies it in jest; Petruchio uses it in contempt for the Tailor in *The Taming of the Shrew*, 4.3.109 ('Thou flea, thou nit, thou winter-cricket thou!'). Moth, Hibbard argues, 'has an insect-like capacity for making a nuisance of himself by pricking and deflating the pretentious . . . What the play insists on most is not his diminutive stature but

342

his youth. And youth is a quality of living, growing things not of inanimate objects such as specks of dust in a sunbeam.' '*Moth*', he believes, is therefore 'a far more appropriate name' for him than '*Mote*'.

These two conflicting arguments, setting insect against dust, raise questions about principles of modernization, but cannot be resolved without reference to points of meaning and interpretation. In the quarto the Page's name is consistently spelled 'Moth' in the stage direction at the beginning of 1.2 and then on four further occasions in the dialogue (1.2.74, 1.2.155, 3.1.111, 3.1.130). Given that 'moth' and 'mote' were indistinguishable spellings, which form should an editor choose? Shakespeare once unequivocally refers to moths in a text thought possibly to have been set from manuscript copy (*The Merchant of Venice*, 2.9.79) and there the word is spelled 'moath' in the quarto; but this may have been determined by its rhyming with 'oath' and 'wroath' in the preceding lines.

One clue for the editor might be that Berowne comes forward to expose his fellow vow-breakers and refers to Christ's remarks on motes and beams. The quarto (4.3.158) has the forms 'Moth . . . Moth'. Perhaps Berowne is making a pun here, but his speech has nothing directly to do with the Page. It may rather pick up the play's imagery of the sun and of light from the eyes. This is especially prominent in the third line of the King's poem, 'As thy eye-beams when their fresh rays have smote' (4.3.25), which contains both 'beams' and a '(s)mote'. Berowne's speech does not therefore rely on the Page's being called 'Mote'.

Elsewhere, as Kerrigan showed, Shakespeare may have thought more often about motes than about moths, and in *A Midsummer Night's Dream* (3.1.162.1) the quarto (and the Folio has substantially the same reading) has an entry for '*Pease-blossome, Cobweb, Moth*, and *Mustard-seede*' accompanied by '*foure Fairyes*'. In his 1994 Oxford edition of the play Peter Holland argued that Shakespeare's certain references to moths tend to be derogatory and that 'Motes and cobwebs are similarly insubstantial; motes and mustardseeds are equivalently minute in the Bible.' In this light he is unconvinced by Hibbard's defence of 'Moth', preferring the insubstantial and minute 'Mote'. Furthermore, Hibbard's argument that motes are inanimate objects could be countered by saying that, far from appearing to be dead, rather they seem to dance about in sunbeams in a lively way. However, this does not transform them into the Page's dominant attribute, his youth, and what is fitting for fairies in one play need not necessarily apply to a page in another.

The choice between the two forms is, therefore, not altogether clear and an editor must determine whether the Page is more to be associated with smallness and the French for a 'word' or with youth and fluttering, insect, energy. Of course, the Page is small, but then both moths and motes are. Hibbard's point, however, that Costard calls him 'a most pathetical nit', is a powerful one for associating him with the insect. Yet it would be a pity to lose the association with the French for 'word', especially when there may be connections between '*mot*' in *Love's Labour's Lost* and '*parolles*' in *All's Well That Ends Well* (see Introduction, p. 16). This neat association can be retrieved, fortunately, through the question of pronunciation. Here it seems that the two forms of the Page's name would have been spoken in more or less the same way, with a short 'o', either as 'mot' or 'mott'. This may allow for the possible pun on Mote/note as in *Much Ado About Nothing*/noting. If pronunciation is unaffected by which of the two forms is adopted, and if it seems that Shakespeare had insects not particles in mind, then it seems that 'Moth' can be retained and 'Mote' rejected.

There may be yet another consideration involved here and that is to do with the play's French setting. Is the audience, which hardly needs to worry about how it is spelled, meant to think that the Page's name – perhaps like Jaquenetta's – is specifically French? The treacherous French governor of Gravelines in 1578 was Valentine Pardieu, variously known in England at the time as la Motte, La Mote and la Mothe (Lamb,

57): the forms seem to have been interchangeable. Similarly, 'Mothe' and 'Motte' in Cotgrave signify more or less the same word.

An editor may wish to modernize 'Moth' to 'Mote', but perhaps the point at issue is not one of interpretation or of modernization, but of the extent to which names in the play should be rendered in French forms. In this edition, I have generally preferred anglicized versions of French names – Berowne not Biron, Longaville not Longueville – on the grounds that Shakespeare was not writing for an international audience (see Appendix 1, pp. 336–7). I therefore, with some hesitation, have adopted a conservative treatment for the Page's name and left it in the form in which it appears in Q, as 'Moth'.

APPENDIX 4
RHYMES IN *LOVE'S LABOUR'S LOST*

This appendix lists rhymes which occur in the play more than once and some rhyme words which occur more than once. The references are always to the first time the first rhyme word appears. See also Helge Kökeritz, *Shakespeare's Pronunciation* (New Haven, 1953), appendix 3.

adieu/you	1.1.110; 2.1.212; 5.2.226; 5.2.234; 5.2.240
advised/disguised	5.2.300; 5.2.433
ask/mask	2.1.122; 5.2.243
away/day	4.1.105 (cf. away/today, 4.3.267)
away/stay	2.1.112; 4.3.208; 5.2.620
book/look	1.1.74; 4.2.23; 4.3.246 (cf. books/looks, 1.1.85)
bowl/owl	4.1.137; 5.2.913
case/face	5.2.387 (cf. cases/faces, 5.2.271)
change/strange	5.2.209 (cf. changed/estranged, 5.2.213)
day/M(m)ay	4.3.99; 5.2.339
day/say	1.1.113; 4.3.86; 5.2.815
days/praise	4.1.22; 5.2.365 (cf. days/dispraise, 4.3.258)
disposed/disclosed	2.1.249; 5.2.466
end/friend	5.2.821 (cf. friends/ends, 5.2.220)
evil/devil	4.3.282; 5.2.105
eye/ay	2.1.187
eye/buy	2.1.241
eye/by	1.1.81
eye/capacity	5.2.375
eye/deny	5.2.807

eye/I	4.3.180
eye/infancy	4.3.239
eye/lie	2.1.251; 4.3.82
eye/majesty	4.3.222
eye/merrily	5.2.475; 5.2.480
eye/perjury	4.3.57
eye/poverty	5.2.379
eye/sky	4.3.76
eyes/cries	4.3.138
eyes/gravities	5.2.761
eyes/lies	1.1.78; 2.1.227; 4.3.274; 5.2.420
eyes/suffice	4.2.109
fool/school	4.2.30; 5.2.71
forsworn/born	1.1.147; 4.3.214 (cf. sworn/born, 5.2.282)
game/shame	5.2.155; 5.2.358
grace/face	3.1.63; 5.2.79; 5.2.128; 5.2.147
grace/space	1.1.51; 1.1.148
half/calf	5.2.246; 5.2.248
here/ear	4.1.58; 4.3.40; 5.2.286; 5.2.435
here/swear	4.1.58; 5.2.357
know/no	1.1.68; 5.2.485
know/show	5.2.319 (cf. known/shown, 1.2.95)
know/so	1.1.59; 2.1.52; 4.3.48; 4.3.126; 5.2.489
lady/may be	2.1.206; 4.1.130
light/bright	4.3.27; 4.3.263
light/night	4.3.227; 4.3.251 (cf. lights/nights, 1.1.88)
lord/word	2.1.214; 4.1.99; 4.3.90; 5.2.238; 5.2.313; 5.2.369; 5.2.448
love/Jove	4.3.116
love/move	4.3.52
love/prove	4.2.105; 4.3.61; 4.3.278
love/reprove	4.3.150
lover/moreover	5.2.49; 5.2.446
lovers/covers	2.1.124
loves/removes	5.2.134

name/fame	1.1.92
name/same	1.1.116; 2.1.193
name/shame	1.1.153; 2.1.198; 4.3.46; 4.3.199
nice/dice	5.2.232; 5.2.325
note/dote	4.3.122; 5.2.75
now/brow	4.1.16; 4.1.116; 4.3.223; 4.3.259
oath/troth	1.1.65; 4.3.140; 5.2.348; 5.2.450
out/doubt	5.2.101; 5.2.151
out/flout	5.2.267; 5.2.395
part/heart	4.1.32; 5.2.55; 5.2.149; 5.2.335; 5.2.805
see/me	2.1.256; 4.3.146
see/three	4.3.158; 5.2.418
shine/mine	4.3.66; 4.3.88
tears/appears	4.3.152; 5.2.117
time/rhyme	1.1.98; 4.3.178 (cf. times/rhymes, 5.2.63)
tongue/belong	5.2.381 (cf. tongues/belongs, 4.3.234)
tongue/wrong	1.1.164; 4.2.117
wit/fit	4.1.49; 4.1.141
wit/it	4.3.144
wit/nit	4.1.146
wit/writ	4.3.96
wit/yet	4.2.34
wits/bits	1.1.26
wits/Muscovites	5.2.264

APPENDIX 5
COMPOUND WORDS IN
LOVE'S LABOUR'S LOST

This appendix lists hyphenated compound words in the play in alphabetical order (see Introduction, pp. 48–9). Words marked with an asterisk do not appear in appendix I, 'Hyphenated Words I', in Marvin Spevack, *The Harvard Concordance to Shakespeare* (Cambridge, Mass., 1973). The forms of the words have been regularized, with upper case and italics eliminated: a few words, like 'newfangled', which do not usually have a hyphen, have been included. Occurrences hyphenated in Q are marked with a dagger (†).

a-breeding	1.1.97
a-coming	5.2.579
a-hooting	4.2.59
a-repairing	3.1.186
all-telling	2.1.21
alms-basket	5.1.37–8
amber-coloured	4.3.85
arts-man	† 5.1.74
best-moving	2.1.29
book-mates	† 4.1.99
breaking-out*	5.1.107
butt-shaft	1.2.168
carry-tale	5.2.463
carved-bone	† 5.2.610
charge-house	† 5.1.76
chimney-sweepers	† 4.3.262
cittern-head	5.2.604
clean-timbered	5.2.633

close-stool	5.2.572
copy-book	5.2.42
corner-cap	4.3.50
cuckoo-buds	† 5.2.884
curious-knotted	1.1.239
daughter-beamed	5.2.172
deep-searched*	1.1.85
demi-god*	4.3.76
deuce-ace	† 1.2.46
dey-woman	1.2.125
dig-you-den	† 4.1.42
dry-beaten	5.2.263
eagle-sighted	† 4.3.222
ebon-coloured	1.1.236
elevenpence-farthing*	† 3.1.166
ever-esteemed	1.1.254
eye-beams	4.3.25
fellow-scholars*	1.1.17
fire-new	1.1.176
first-born	1.1.101
five-score*	4.2.41; 4.3.238
flap-dragon	5.1.41
god-like*	† 1.1.58
half-a-dozen*	5.2.234
half-cheek	5.2.611
halfpenny-farthing*	3.1.144
hard-a-keeping	1.1.65
health-giving	† 1.1.228
hedge-priest	† 5.2.538
high-born	1.1.170
hit-it*	4.1.120
hobby-horse	† 3.1.27, † 28, † 29
honey-tongued	† 5.2.334
humble-bee	† 3.1.82, † 86, † 92
humble-visaged	2.1.34

kingly-poor	5.2.269
lady-smocks	† 5.2.883
love-monger	† 2.1.253
love-rhymes	† 3.1.176
love-suit	† 5.2.123
low-spirited	1.1.240
manor-house	1.1.203
men-at-arms	4.3.286
mirth-moving	† 2.1.71
mumble-news	5.2.464
new-devised*	1.2.61
newfangled	1.1.106
new-sad	5.2.725
night-watch	3.1.171
north-north-east	† 1.1.238 (north north-east)
o'er-eye	4.3.77
over-boldly*	5.2.728
over-view	† 4.3.172
pair-taunt-like	5.2.67
parti-coated	5.2.760
pell-mell	4.3.342
penthouse-like	3.1.16
pick-purses	† 4.3.205
pierce-one*	4.2.81
pigeon-egg	† 5.1.68
pitch-balls	3.1.192
please-man	† 5.2.463
point-device	5.1.18
pole-axe	5.2.571
push-pin	† 4.3.166
sable-coloured	1.1.226
sealed-up	† 3.1.164
seasick	5.2.393
sea-water	† 1.2.80
selfsame	1.2.4

self-sovereignty	† 4.1.36
shame-proof	5.2.510
short-lived	2.1.54; 4.1.15
silver-white	5.2.883
slow-gaited	3.1.52
small-knowing	1.1.242
smooth-faced	5.2.816
snip-snap*	5.1.55
snow-white	1.1.236; † 4.2.131
statute-caps	5.2.281
steep-up	4.1.2
strong-jointed	1.2.71
sun-beamed	5.2.169, 170
tender-smelling	5.2.562
thin-belly	3.1.17
three-farthing-worth*	3.1.145
three-headed	5.2.583
three-piled	5.2.407
thrice-worthy	5.1.135
tooth-drawer	† 5.2.613
town-gates*	† 1.2.69
trencher-knight	5.2.464
tu-whit	† 5.2.906, † 915
tu-whoo	† 5.2.906, † 915
twice-sod*	4.2.22
vapour-vow	† 4.3.67
vow-fellows	2.1.38
war-man	† 5.2.657
weeping-ripe	5.2.274
well-accomplished	2.1.56
well-educated	1.2.90
well-knit	1.2.71
well-liking	† 5.2.268
white-handed	5.2.230
wholesome-profitable	5.2.744

wit–old	[†] 5.1.57–8
world-without-end	[†] 5.2.783

ABBREVIATIONS AND REFERENCES

Quotations and references to plays other than *Love's Labour's Lost* are to *The Riverside Shakespeare*, 2nd edn (Boston, Mass., and New York, 1997), and to Anthony Munday and others, *Sir Thomas More*, ed. Vittorio Gabrieli and Giorgio Melchiori (Manchester, 1990). Biblical quotations are from the 'Bishops' Bible' (1568). In all references, place of publication is London unless otherwise stated.

ABBREVIATIONS

ABBREVIATIONS USED IN THE NOTES

*	precedes commentary notes involving readings that are not found in either Q or F
c.w.	catchword
esp.	especially
Fc	corrected state of F
Fr.	French
Fu	uncorrected state of F
Lat.	Latin
lit.	literally
NS	New Series
OE	Old English
om.	omitted
opp.	opposite
Qc	corrected state of Q
Qu	uncorrected state of Q
SD	stage direction
sig., sigs	signature, signatures
SP	speech prefix
subst.	substantially
this edn	a reading adopted for the first time in this edition
TLN	through line numbering in *The First Folio of Shakespeare*, ed. Charlton Hinman, Norton Facsimile (1968)

WORKS BY AND
PARTLY BY SHAKESPEARE

AC	*Antony and Cleopatra*
AW	*All's Well That Ends Well*
AYL	*As You Like It*
CE	*The Comedy of Errors*
Cor	*Coriolanus*
Cym	*Cymbeline*
E3	*The Reign of King Edward III*
Ham	*Hamlet*
1H4	*King Henry IV, Part 1*
2H4	*King Henry IV, Part 2*
H5	*King Henry V*
1H6	*King Henry VI, Part 1*
2H6	*King Henry VI, Part 2*
3H6	*King Henry VI, Part 3*
H8	*King Henry VIII*
JC	*Julius Caesar*
KJ	*King John*
KL	*King Lear*
LLL	*Love's Labour's Lost*
Luc	*The Rape of Lucrece*
MA	*Much Ado About Nothing*
Mac	*Macbeth*
MM	*Measure for Measure*
MND	*A Midsummer Night's Dream*
MV	*The Merchant of Venice*
MW	*The Merry Wives of Windsor*
Oth	*Othello*
Per	*Pericles*
PP	*The Passionate Pilgrim*
R2	*King Richard II*
R3	*King Richard III*
RJ	*Romeo and Juliet*
Son	*Sonnets*
STM	*The Book of Sir Thomas More*
TC	*Troilus and Cressida*
Tem	*The Tempest*
TGV	*The Two Gentlemen of Verona*
Tim	*Timon of Athens*
Tit	*Titus Andronicus*
TN	*Twelfth Night*
TNK	*The Two Noble Kinsmen*
TS	*The Taming of the Shrew*
VA	*Venus and Adonis*
WT	*The Winter's Tale*

REFERENCES

EDITIONS OF SHAKESPEARE COLLATED

Alexander   *William Shakespeare: The Complete Works*, ed. Peter Alexander (1951)

Ard[1]   *Love's Labour's Lost*, ed. H. C. Hart, Arden Shakespeare (1906)

Ard[2]   *Love's Labour's Lost*, ed. Richard David, Arden Shakespeare (1951; repr. with additions 1968)

Bevington   *Works*, ed. David Bevington (Glenview, Ill., 1980)

Cam   *Works*, ed. William George Clark and William Aldis Wright, 9 vols (Cambridge and London, 1863–6)

Cam[1]   *Love's Labour's Lost*, ed. John Dover Wilson (Cambridge, 1923; 2nd edn 1962)

Capell   *Comedies, Histories, and Tragedies*, ed. Edward Capell, 10 vols (1767–8)

Collier   *Works*, ed. John Payne Collier, 8 vols (1842–4)

Collier MS   *Works*, ed. John Payne Collier, 6 vols (1858)

David   see Ard[2]

Dyce   *Works*, ed. Alexander Dyce, 6 vols (1857)

Dyce[2]   *Works*, ed. Alexander Dyce, 9 vols (1864–7)

F, F1   *Comedies, Histories and Tragedies*, The First Folio (1623)

F2   *Comedies, Histories and Tragedies*, The Second Folio (1632)

F3   *Comedies, Histories and Tragedies*, The Third Folio (1663)

F4   *Comedies, Histories and Tragedies*, The Fourth Folio (1685)

Furness   *Loues Labour's Lost*, ed. Horace Howard Furness, New Variorum Shakespeare (Philadelphia, Penn., 1904)

Halliwell   *Works*, ed. James O. Halliwell, 16 vols (1853–65)

Hanmer   *Works*, ed. Thomas Hanmer, 6 vols (Oxford, 1743–4)

Hart   see Ard[1]

Hertzberg   W. A. B. Hertzberg, *Liebes Leid und Lust* (Berlin, 1869)

Hibbard   see Oxf[1]

Hudson   *Works*, ed. Henry N. Hudson, 20 vols (Boston and Cambridge, Mass., 1886)

Johnson   *Plays*, ed. Samuel Johnson, 8 vols (1765)

Keightley   *Plays*, ed. Thomas Keightley, 6 vols (1864)

Kerrigan   *Love's Labour's Lost*, ed. John Kerrigan, New Penguin Shakespeare (Harmondsworth, 1982)

Kittredge   *Works*, ed. George Lyman Kittredge (Boston, Mass., 1936)

Knight   *Works*, ed. Charles Knight, 8 vols (1838–43)

Malone   *Plays and Poems*, ed. Edmond Malone, 10 vols (1790)

Oxf   *Works*, ed. Stanley Wells, Gary Taylor, John Jowett and William Montgomery (Oxford, 1986)

Oxf[1]	*Love's Labour's Lost*, ed. G. R. Hibbard, Oxford Shakespeare (Oxford, 1990)
Pope	*Works*, ed. Alexander Pope, 6 vols (1723–5)
Pope[2]	*Works*, ed. Alexander Pope, 8 vols (1728)
Q, Q1	*Love's Labour's Lost*, The First Quarto (1598)
Q2	*Love's Labour's Lost*, The Second Quarto (1631)
Ridley	*Love's Labour's Lost*, ed. M. R. Ridley, New Temple Shakespeare (1934)
Riv	*The Riverside Shakespeare*, textual editors G. Blakemore Evans and J. J. M. Tobin, 2nd edn (Boston, Mass., and New York, 1997)
Rowe	*Works*, ed. Nicholas Rowe, 6 vols (1709)
Rowe[2]	*Works*, ed. Nicholas Rowe, 6 vols (1709)
Rowe[3]	*Works*, ed. Nicholas Rowe, 8 vols (1714)
Singer	*Dramatic Works*, ed. Samuel Weller Singer, 10 vols (1856)
Sisson	*Works*, ed. Charles Jasper Sisson (1954)
Steevens	*Plays*, ed. Samuel Johnson and George Steevens, 10 vols (1773)
Steevens[2]	*Plays*, ed. Samuel Johnson and George Steevens, 10 vols (1778)
Theobald	*Works*, ed. Lewis Theobald, 7 vols (1733)
Theobald[2]	*Works*, ed. Lewis Theobald, 8 vols (1740)
Warburton	*Works*, ed. William Warburton, 8 vols (1747)
Wilson	see Cam[1]

OTHER WORKS CITED

Abbott	E. A. Abbott, *A Shakespearian Grammar*, 2nd edn (1870 etc.)
Allusion-Book	*The Shakspere Allusion-Book: A Collection of Allusions to Shakspere from 1591 to 1700*, ed. C. M. Ingleby and others, 2 vols (Oxford, 1932)
AS	*Astrophil and Stella*, in *The Poems of Sir Philip Sidney*, ed. William A. Ringler, Jr (Oxford, 1962)
Auden	W. H. Auden and Chester Kallman, *Libretti and Other Dramatic Writings by W. H. Auden: 1939–1973*, ed. Edward Mendelson (Princeton, NJ, 1993)
Baldwin	T. W. Baldwin, *William Shakspere's 'Small Latine & Lesse Greeke'*, 2 vols (Urbana, Ill., 1944)
Barton	see Roesen
Bate	Jonathan Bate, *Shakespeare and Ovid* (Oxford, 1993)
Booth	Stephen Booth, *'King Lear', 'Macbeth', Indefinition, and Tragedy* (New Haven, Conn., and London, 1983)
Bullough	Geoffrey Bullough (ed.), *Narrative and Dramatic Sources of Shakespeare*, 8 vols (1957–75), vol. 1 (1957)
Carroll	William C. Carroll, *The Great Feast of Language in 'Love's Labour's Lost'* (Princeton, NJ, 1976)

Chambers	E. K. Chambers, *William Shakespeare: A Study of Facts and Problems*, 2 vols (Oxford, 1930)
Chapman	*The Plays of George Chapman: The Comedies: A Critical Edition*, ed. Allan Holaday (Urbana, Ill., Chicago, Ill., and London, 1970)
Chaucer, *Riv*	*The Riverside Chaucer*, ed. F. N. Robinson, revised Larry D. Benson (Oxford, 1988)
Coleridge	*Coleridge's Shakespearean Criticism*, ed. Thomas Middleton Raysor, 2 vols (1930)
Colie	Rosalie L. Colie, *Shakespeare's 'Living Art'* (Princeton, NJ, 1974)
Cotgrave	Randle Cotgrave, *A Dictionarie of the French and English Tongues* (1611)
Daniel, *Delia*	Samuel Daniel, *Delia: with The Complaint of Rosamond* (1592)
Daniel, *Rosamond*	Samuel Daniel, *The Complaint of Rosamond*, in Daniel, *Delia*
Dekker, *Plague*	*The Plague Pamphlets of Thomas Dekker*, ed. F. P. Wilson (Oxford, 1925)
Dekker, *Works*	*The Dramatic Works of Thomas Dekker*, ed. Fredson Bowers, 4 vols (Cambridge, 1953–61)
Dent	R. W. Dent, *Shakespeare's Proverbial Language: An Index* (Berkeley, Calif., and London, 1981)
Draudt	Manfred Draudt, 'Printer's copy for the Quarto of *Love's Labour's Lost* (1598)', *The Library*, 6th series, 3 (1981), 119–31
Draudt[2]	Manfred Draudt, 'The rationale of current bibliographical methods: printing house studies, computer-aided compositor studies, and the use of statistical methods', *SS*, 40 (1988), 145–53
Drayton	*The Works of Michael Drayton*, ed. J. William Hebel and others, 5 vols (Oxford, 1961)
EH	*England's Helicon*, ed. John Bodenham (1600)
Elam	Keir Elam, *Shakespeare's Universe of Discourse: Language-Games in the Comedies* (Cambridge, 1984)
Ellis	Herbert A. Ellis, *Shakespeare's Lusty Punning in 'Love's Labour's Lost'* (The Hague and Paris, 1973)
ES	*English Studies*
J. Evans	Joan Evans, *English Posies and Posy Rings* (1931)
M. Evans	Malcolm Evans, 'Mercury versus Apollo: a reading of *Love's Labor's Lost*', *SQ*, 26 (1975), 113–27
Farmer	Richard Farmer, in Steevens
Florio	John Florio, *Queen Anna's New World of Words* (1611)
Foakes	R. A. Foakes, *Illustrations of the English Stage 1580–1642* (1985)

References

Gesta Grayorum	*Gesta Grayorum 1688*, ed. W. W. Greg, MSR,1914
Gilbert	Miriam Gilbert, *Shakespeare in Performance: Love's Labour's Lost* (Manchester and New York, 1993)
Greene	Robert Greene, *Life and Works*, ed. A. B. Grosart, 15 vols (1881–6)
Greg	W. W. Greg, *The Shakespeare First Folio: Its Bibliographical and Textual History* (Oxford, 1955)
Harington	*Sir John Harington's A New Discourse of a Stale Subject, called the Metamorphosis of Ajax*, ed. Elizabeth Story Donno (1962)
Hazard	Mary E. Hazard, 'Shakespeare's "living art": A live issue from *Love's Labour's Lost*', in *Shakespeare and the Arts*, ed. Cecile Williamson Cary and Henry S. Limouze (Washington, DC, 1982), 181–98
Henslowe	*Henslowe's Diary*, ed. R. A. Foakes and R. T. Rickert (Cambridge, 1961)
Hobbes	Thomas Hobbes, *Leviathan*, ed. A. R. Waller (Cambridge, 1904)
Holdsworth	R. V. Holdsworth, 'Sexual allusions in *Love's Labour's Lost, The Merry Wives of Windsor, Othello, The Winter's Tale*, and *The Two Noble Kinsmen*', *N&Q*, 231 (1986), 351–3
Hutton	James Hutton, 'Honorificabilitudinitatibus', *MLN*, 46 (1931), 392–5
Jackson	MacD. P. Jackson, 'A Shakespearian quibble', *N&Q*, 207 (1962), 331–2
Johnson on Shakespeare	*Samuel Johnson on Shakespeare*, ed. H. R. Woudhuysen (1989)
Jonson	*Ben Jonson*, ed. C. H. Herford and Percy and Evelyn Simpson, 11 vols (Oxford, 1925–63)
Lamb	Mary Ellen Lamb, 'The nature of topicality in "Love's Labour's Lost"', *SS*, 38 (1985), 49–59
Leishman	*The Three Parnassus Plays*, ed. J. B. Leishman (1949)
Lennam	Trevor Lennam, '"The ventricle of memory": wit and wisdom in *Love's Labour's Lost*', *SQ*, 24 (1973), 54–60
Lyly, *Endymion*	John Lyly, *Endymion*, ed. David Bevington (Manchester and New York, 1996)
Lyly, *Sapho and Phao*	John Lyly, *Campaspe*, ed. G. K. Hunter, *Sappho and Phao*, ed. David Bevington (Manchester, 1991)
Marlowe	Christopher Marlowe, *Tamburlaine, Parts I and II, Doctor Faustus, A- and B-Texts, The Jew of Malta, Edward II*, ed. David Bevington and Eric Rasmussen (Oxford and New York, 1995)
Marston, *Malcontent*	John Marston, *The Malcontent*, ed. George K. Hunter (1975)
Mason	John Monck Mason, *Comments on the Last Edition of Shakespeare's Plays* (1785)

Met.	Ovid's *Metamorphoses*; quotations are from *Shakespeare's Ovid: Being Arthur Golding's Translation of the Metamorphoses*, ed. W. H. D. Rouse (1904)
MLN	*Modern Language Notes*
MLQ	*Modern Language Quarterly*
Montrose	Louis A. Montrose, ' "Sport by sport o'erthrown": *Love's Labour's Lost* and the politics of play', *Texas Studies in Language and Literature*, 18 (1976–7), 528–52
MSR	Malone Society Reprints
N&Q	*Notes and Queries*
Nashe	*The Works of Thomas Nashe*, ed. R. B. McKerrow, revised F. P. Wilson, 5 vols (Oxford, 1958)
Nevo	Ruth Nevo, *Comic Transformations in Shakespeare* (London and New York, 1980)
OED	*The Oxford English Dictionary*, ed. James A. H. Murray and others, 13 vols (Oxford, 1933, repr. 1977)
Onions	C. T. Onions, *A Shakespeare Glossary* (1911), revised Robert D. Eagleson (Oxford, 1986)
Parker	Patricia Parker, 'Preposterous reversals: *Love's Labor's Lost*', *MLQ*, 54 (1993), 435–82
PBSA	*Papers of the Bibliographical Society of America*
Pollard	A. W. Pollard, in H. B. Charlton, 'A textual note on "Love's Labour's Lost" ', *The Library*, 3rd series, 8 (1917), 355–70, at 370
PQ	*Philological Quarterly*
Price	George R. Price, 'The printing of *Love's Labour's Lost* (1598)', *PBSA*, 72 (1978), 405–34
Proudfoot	Richard Proudfoot, ' "Love's Labour's Lost": sweet understanding and the Five Worthies', *Essays and Studies*, 34 (1984), 16–30.
Rasmussen	Eric Rasmussen, *A Textual Companion to 'Doctor Faustus'* (Manchester and New York, 1993)
RES	*Review of English Studies*
Roesen	Bobbyann Roesen [Anne Barton], '*Love's Labour's Lost*', *SQ*, 4 (1953), 411–26
Rowse	A. L. Rowse, correspondence in *TLS*, 18 July 1952, p. 469
Rubinstein	Frankie Rubinstein, *A Dictionary of Shakespeare's Sexual Puns and their Significance* (1984), 2nd edn (1989)
Schmidt	Alexander Schmidt, *Shakespeare-Lexicon*, 2 vols (Berlin, 1874–5)
Second Maiden's Tragedy	*The Second Maiden's Tragedy*, ed. Anne Lancashire (Manchester, 1978)
Shakespeare's England	*Shakespeare's England*, 2 vols (Oxford, 1917)

Shakespearian Comedy	*Shakespearian Comedy*, Stratford-upon-Avon Studies, 14 (1972)
Shapiro	I. A. Shapiro, 'Cruxes in "Love's Labour's Lost"', *N&Q*, 200 (1955), 287–8
Sidney, *DP*	*A Defence of Poetry*, in *Miscellaneous Prose of Sir Philip Sidney*, ed. Katherine Duncan-Jones and Jan van Dorsten (Oxford, 1973)
Sidney, *NA*	Sir Philip Sidney, *The Countess of Pembroke's Arcadia (The New Arcadia)*, ed. Victor Skretkowicz (Oxford, 1987)
Sidney, *OA*	Sir Philip Sidney, *The Countess of Pembroke's Arcadia (The Old Arcadia)*, ed. Jean Robertson (Oxford, 1973)
Sidney, OA poem	Old Arcadia poem, in *The Poems of Sir Philip Sidney*, ed. William A. Ringler, Jr (Oxford, 1962)
Simpson	Percy Simpson, *Shakespearian Punctuation* (Oxford, 1911)
Simpson, *TLS*	Percy Simpson, correspondence in *TLS*, 24 February 1945, p. 91
Sisson, *Readings*	C. J. Sisson, *New Readings in Shakespeare*, 2 vols (Cambridge, 1956)
SMC	Bryan N. S. Gooch, David Thatcher, Odean Long and Charles Haywood, *A Shakespeare Music Catalogue*, 5 vols (Oxford, 1991)
Spenser	*The Poetical Works of Edmund Spenser*, ed. J. C. Smith and E. De Selincourt (Oxford, 1912)
Spenser, *FQ*	*The Faerie Queene*, in Spenser
Spenser, *SC*	*The Shepheardes Calender*, in Spenser
SQ	*Shakespeare Quarterly*
SS	*Shakespeare Survey*
SSt	*Shakespeare Studies*
Thirlby	Styan Thirlby, unpublished manuscript conjectures reported by Theobald, Johnson and others
Thompson	Ann Thompson, *Shakespeare's Chaucer: A Study in Literary Origins* (Liverpool, 1978)
Thomson	J. A. K. Thomson, *Shakespeare and the Classics* (1952)
Tilley	Morris P. Tilley, *A Dictionary of the Proverbs in England in the Sixteenth and Seventeenth Centuries* (Ann Arbor, Mich., 1950)
TLS	*The Times Literary Supplement*
TxC	Stanley Wells and Gary Taylor, with John Jowett and William Montgomery, *William Shakespeare: A Textual Companion* (Oxford, 1987)
Tyrwhitt	Thomas Tyrwhitt, *Observations and Conjectures upon some Passages of Shakespeare* (1766)
Vickers, *CH*	*Shakespeare: The Critical Heritage*, ed. Brian Vickers, 6 vols (London and Boston, Mass., 1974–81)
Walker	W. S. Walker, *A Critical Examination of the Text of Shakespeare*, ed. W. N. Lettsom, 3 vols (1860)

References

Wells, 'Copy'	Stanley Wells, 'The copy for the Folio text of *Love's Labour's Lost*', *RES*, NS, 33 (1982), 137–47
Wells, *Re-Editing*	Stanley Wells, *Re-Editing Shakespeare for the Modern Reader* (Oxford, 1984)
Werstine	Paul Werstine, 'The editorial usefulness of printing house and compositor studies', in *Play-Texts in Old Spelling: Papers from the Glendon Conference*, ed. G. B. Shand and Raymond C. Shady (New York, 1984), 35–64
Werstine[2]	Paul Werstine, 'Narratives about printed Shakespeare texts: "foul papers" and "bad" quartos', *SQ*, 41 (1990), 65–86
Werstine[3]	Paul Werstine, 'Variants in the First Quarto of *Love's Labor's Lost*', *SSt*, 12 (1979), 35–47
Wilson, 'Diction'	F. P. Wilson, 'Shakespeare and the diction of common life', in *Shakespearian and Other Studies*, ed. Helen Gardner (Oxford, 1969), 100–29
Wilson, *Plague*	F. P. Wilson, *The Plague in Shakespeare's London*, 2nd edn (Oxford, 1963)
Yates	Frances A. Yates, *A Study of 'Love's Labour's Lost'* (Cambridge, 1936)

INDEX

The index covers the Preface, Introduction, Commentary and Appendices. It omits *OED* references other than to ante-datings, first citations and only citations.

138, 139, 140, 141, 147, 160, 161,
162, 163, 165, 166, 167, 168, 171,
178, 184, 185, 186, 200, 207, 212,
213, 218, 225, 226, 227, 228, 229,
231, 233, 279, 281, 282, 283, 284,
285, 294, 297, 308, 313, 314, 315,
316, 319–20, 324, 329, 330, 332,
336, 342
   homosexuality 63, 129, 134, 135,
     224, 229, 230
   linguistic traits 48, 71, 75, 132
astrology 23, 225, 289
beauty 26, 98, 215, 216, 297
Berowne 5, 7, 10, 12, 13, 17, 19,
20, 23–5, 26, 27, 28, 29, 30, 31,
32, 33, 34–6, 40, 41, 43, 44, 45,
46, 49–50, 51, 52, 53, 54, 56, 57,
58, 59, 63, 73, 74, 75, 82, 83, 85,
87, 88, 92, 96, 98, 102, 104, 105,
109, 112, 114, 115, 116, 118, 119,
121, 122, 123, 127, 146, 150, 154,
169, 170, 171, 172, 173, 180, 194,
196, 198, 199, 200, 201, 204, 205,
208, 209, 210, 213, 214, 215, 216,
218, 219, 220, 222, 223, 238, 240,
246, 248, 251, 259, 262, 263, 264,
265, 268, 273, 274, 275, 280, 281,
286, 287, 289, 290, 291, 309–11,
312, 313, 314, 315, 316–17, 325,
330, 331, 337, 339, 343, 345
Blackamoors 13–14, 63, 64, 88–9,
207, 246, 308, 315
Boyet 4, 7, 15, 18, 20, 24, 31, 32,
34, 35–6, 37, 38, 40, 41, 42, 43,
44, 46, 49, 51, 55, 58, 59, 62, 73,
94, 96, 102, 109, 115, 120, 131,
144, 147, 155, 156, 160, 175, 176,
181, 182, 183, 184, 207, 218, 222,
242, 246, 257, 263, 269, 274, 275,
277, 279, 284, 309, 310, 314, 315,
316, 330, 331, 333, 334
casting 58–9, 87
colloquialisms 138, 176, 231
coins 19, 24, 31–2, 124, 133, 139,
169, 171, 223, 265
compound words xvii, 48–9,
349–53
'Concolinel' 100, 160, 161, 330
Costard 4, 5, 7, 8, 15, 18, 20, 21,
27, 29, 30, 31, 32, 40, 44, 50, 51,
52, 55, 56, 57, 58, 61, 78, 100,
101, 109, 110, 125, 126, 130, 131,
137, 139, 163, 165, 167, 168, 171,

176, 184, 185, 186, 192, 199, 212,
229, 233, 242, 270, 271, 274, 276,
281, 282, 283, 296, 308, 311, 312,
313, 314, 315, 316, 324–5, 327,
330, 334–6, 337, 342, 344
costumes 23–4, 55, 88–90, 244,
245, 254
date xvi, 1, 61
dialect 270
disguise 7, 13, 23, 24, 37, 52, 55,
63, 89, 90, 245, 248, 250, 252,
254, 256, 257, 262
Dull 4, 18, 20, 29, 37, 55, 58, 59,
74, 90, 100, 101, 109, 124, 139,
171, 186, 187, 188, 189, 192, 234,
308, 314, 315, 324–5, 329, 337
Dumaine 7, 12, 13, 17, 27, 29, 56,
57, 58, 62, 81, 88, 92, 109, 119,
138, 146, 194, 199, 201, 204, 213,
238, 255, 280, 281, 310, 311, 315,
329, 336–7
emblems 5, 26, 133, 175, 216, 227
ending 8, 9, 10–11, 15–16, 18, 19,
33, 37–8, 41, 45, 51, 54, 57, 97,
105, 106, 119, 291, 297
exclamations 44, 169, 185, 190,
237, 264
eyes 13, 26, 30, 33, 41, 49, 98, 117,
154, 158, 159, 161, 173, 194, 199,
200, 214, 215, 220, 222, 249, 262,
267, 269, 287, 325, 339, 343
fair 143, 174, 175, 206, 214, 215,
237, 238, 248, 288
Folio, First xvi–xvii, 327–33
   act division 329
   censorship 331–2
   compositors 327–9, 332–3
   copy for 327, 329, 330, 333
   (un)corrected state 327
   dittography 259
   errors 72, 139, 162, 169, 178,
     185, 186, 188, 193, 199, 206,
     224, 225, 226, 230, 240, 243,
     260, 285, 287, 332, 333, 340
   eye-skip 259, 328
   modernizing 328
   punctuation 162, 176, 190, 198,
     230, 233
   speech prefixes 130, 139, 143,
     169, 195, 246, 274, 284, 328,
     330–1, 332
   spellings 111, 113, 124, 171, 178,
     181, 185, 190, 192, 195, 199,

Index